RELIABLE ESSAYS

'When I come across a Clive James essay in a periodical,
I save it for last, knowing it will be a treat . . . [his writing]
adjusts a frequency in the reader's head, and finds thereby
new thoughts, new possibilities of feeling'
Michael Schmidt, *Independent*

'Clive James's brilliance shines on everything from Torvill
and Dean to Seamus Heaney . . . James's critical journalism . . .
extends and honours the tradition established by Johnson, Hazlitt
and Virginia Woolf. And what makes it valuable is the way it testifies
to a passion for literature, and a desire to proselytise for it, that are
nowadays rare, precious, probably anachronistic motives . . . James's
own lucid, witty, metaphorically vivid style is his grateful yet keenly
competitive tribute to all those better makers whose work he
analyses here . . . I finished this book wishing that I knew
as much as James does, and that I wrote as well'
Peter Conrad, *Observer*

'*Reliable Essays* is full of good things . . . The essays are
brilliant . . . James's literary essays, along with the first volume
of *Unreliable Memoirs*, are his best work'
John Lanchester, *Daily Telegraph*

'He is one of the most lively, shrewd and resourceful essayists
currently writing . . . his own writing is impeccably witty, flexible
and urbane . . . Parodies, jokes and slang sit comfortably with moral
and political arguments, lightly-worn erudition and scrupulous
close readings of poetry and prose . . . *Reliable Essays* is an
instructive (and, for a reviewer, fairly intimidating) book,
but it's also immensely enjoyable to read'
Christopher Tayler, *Sunday Telegraph*

CLIVE JAMES is the author of more than twenty books. As well as three volumes of autobiography, *Unreliable Memoirs, Falling Towards England* and *May Week Was in June*, he has published collections of literary criticism, television criticism, verse and travel writing. His most recent novel is *The Silver Castle*. As a television performer he has appeared regularly for both the BBC and ITV, most notably as writer and presenter of the *Postcard* series of travel documentaries. He helped to found the independent television company Watchmaker, and is currently chairman of the Internet enterprise Welcome Stranger: he webcasts in video and audio on www.welcomestranger.com. In 1992 he was made a member of the Order of Australia, and in 1999 an honorary Doctor of Letters of Sydney University.

CLIVE JAMES
RELIABLE ESSAYS

THE BEST OF CLIVE JAMES

PICADOR

First published 2001 by Picador

This edition published 2013 by Picador
an imprint of Pan Macmillan, a division of Macmillan Publishers Limited
Pan Macmillan, 20 New Wharf Road, London N1 9RR
Basingstoke and Oxford
Associated companies throughout the world
www.panmacmillan.com

ISBN 978-1-4472-4104-1

A CIP catalogue record for this book is available from
the British Library.

Typeset by Intype Libra Ltd

To

MARGARET OLLEY and JEFFREY SMART

Sidere mens eadem mutato

'Life is a cemetery of retrospective lucidities'

Jean-François Revel, *La Connaissance Inutile*

Contents

Contents

Author's Note

Every author would like to think that the aggregate of his incidental prose, from the merest book review to that smart written reply to the tax inspector, forms a picture of his complex, subtle, infinitely ramified mentality: hence the tendency to put everything in, and the pain at seeing anything taken out. But if my editor has, as it seems to me, made his selection according to his own interests, at least he has found some of his interests reflected among mine; and a writer can't hope for more from a reader than that. Bewitched by the example of his great precursor Montaigne, the habitual writer of non-fictional pieces goes on filling a long shelf in the belief that he will show the whole of his mind, but the reader he most fears – the one who will see through to his heart – should also be the one he most desires. Eventually he will be remembered only through intelligent appreciation, which is always cruelly selective. Even the aphorist, who tries to do the winnowing in advance, is winnowed in his turn: writing a hundred words to stand for a thousand, he would feel flayed to discover that only ten of them got through.

Peter Straus thinks that this book contains the essence of what I have done in the form. Ambition says that the essence is bigger and more complicated. Common sense should say – when it can get a word in – that an essence is a nice thing for a discursive writer to be thought of as possessing, even if it is only a few pages long. In the long run those few pages will come down to a few sentences, and even then only with luck. Usually they will come down to nothing. The harsh bargain we must accept, if we try to write our prose to last, is that most of it certainly won't, and quite likely none of it will. But if that bargain were foremost in our minds as we sat down at the desk, we would get nothing done that was worth reading. So we write as if we were going to live. After all, we live that way.

To each piece I have added a footnote, meant more as an

afterthought than a second guess. It is always too late to hedge a bet
once the hand is played, but in our heads the game goes on, whether
we won or lost. What we said, when we said it, what we might have
said instead: all these things are part of a writer's story. To think he
has a story might be part of his egomania, but I have never been
convinced that a lust for anonymity is a better guarantee of seeing
the world as it is. A magnificent detachment should be the aim, but
it can't be aimed at except by a man sufficiently interested in himself
to have found out something about his own failings. Julian Barnes
knows my failings very well, so I am doubly grateful that he found
time to write an introduction. He is wrong, though, about those
studio audiences. They do indeed exist, and as with any other kind
of audience their laughter is hard to get, and therefore well worth
getting. But I know what he means, and I am flattered that he
means it.

CLIVE JAMES
London, 2001

Introduction

'I suppose,' said Clive, 'you wouldn't consider writing an introduction to my selected essays?' When he heard a micro-pause from my end of the telephone, he went on, 'Seeing how you've always irritated me by calling them my best work.' And then, as a clincher, 'Because if you don't do it, we'll have to get ----- -------.' He named a famous Professor Dryasdust.

Well, Clive, you asked for it – in both senses. So I'll repeat on the public page what has (for no good reason, it seems to me) wound you up in various restaurants, pubs and domestic quarters down the years. You are, as the *New Yorker* once famously observed, 'a brilliant bunch of guys': literary essayist, TV critic, poet, novelist, autobiographer, rock lyricist, documentary-maker, TV host, famous person. You also draw pretty well and have a natural eye for a tennis ball. I admire you in nearly all of these guises. I frequently quote your incomparable poem of literary revenge, 'The Book of My Enemy Has Been Remaindered'. I bond with strangers over your epic account of childhood karting in *Unreliable Memoirs*. I even remember your flawless impression of Norman Mailer on some long-forgotten TV arts show a quarter of a century ago. I trust there will one day be a blue plaque to you in Tufnell Park where, in your humbler days, you once bunked down inside the discarded brown paper bag from some plutocrat's new mattress. But I still think your literary essays are your best work.

And though we could leave it to Professor Dryasdust, I don't think we should. He'll have his say in one or other of the literary pages. No, this should be an inside job, by one who also lives by pen not stipend. You are, in your own phrase, a metropolitan critic; a Grubstreeter, a passionate amateur, a full-time dilettante. Academe and Grub Street frequently affect to despise one another, and sometimes actually do. You yourself have been spectacularly rude about dons ('There are professors in Cambridge who call the AA to help them park their cars'), but you also revere true, intense, honourable scholarship. You also know – not least because you are married to an Italian scholar – that academe and Grub Street need one another: like teeth, they work best when in nutritious opposition. The republic of letters is no different from any other republic, and thrives best on the separation of powers. The House of Grub Street is currently more under threat than the House of Academe. The pay is poor, the freelance life as precarious as in Gissing's day, and academe contains some grim-eyed abolitionists. A character in a novel some years ago described academics as merely 'reviewers delivering their copy a hundred years late'. This is no longer the case: nowadays they're jostling the freelancers out of the weekly literary pages.

You've always been a key player in our team, not least because your own jostle is pretty muscular. In the late 1970s I worked on the *New Statesman* books pages, to which you were a regular and valued contributor. Normally, the week's lead review would be more or less decided at the point of commissioning: the big book went to the top reviewer with the most generous wordage. One week, the editorial team made a last-minute switch and decided to promote your article to the lead slot. You happened to call by shortly afterwards. On being told the news you did not, as some self-effacing Englishman might, reply, 'Gosh, what a surprise, are you sure?' You said, 'What happened? The other guy didn't make the weight?'

But then you are, as may not need pointing out, Australian. This fact, oddly, seems to cause more problems in your country than in mine. Every eighteen months or so some patriotic, home-based Australian academic takes it upon himself to analyse – i.e. denounce – the careers of successful artistic expatriates. The culprits ritually include yourself, Germaine Greer, Barry Humphries and Robert Hughes; sometimes Peter Porter gets the executioner's nod as well. Such books would normally pass unnoticed in Britain, except for the fact that you and Peter always seem to review them (allowing literary editors to reach brightly for that original headline 'The Wizards of Oz'). According to the Ocker Acker, you stand charged with ambition, lack of a proper insularity or cringefulness, and with displaying certain degenerate or cosmopolitan tendencies. You are accused of not being sufficiently Australian, and at the same time of being a 'professional Australian'. You would be sentenced to transportation back to the Old Country if you had not got in first and done that yourself.

Over here, your presence in the literary community is as uncontested as anyone else's. The Australian counter-invasion is seen as benign and catalytic. We don't think of you as a professional Australian but as a professional writer. An occasional grouch murmurs 'Autodidact', imagining it a slur while failing to understand that what writers teach themselves is the richest part of their entire education. But most of us soap-dodgers associate your Australianness with your literary virtues: energy, appetite, boldness, demotic attack, a revisionist attitude to the canon, a Europhilia which doesn't entail Eurocentricity. It was in an essay of yours that I first came across the word 'panoptic', and it is still the adjective I tacitly apply to you. Panopticism implies generosity, cultural liberalism and a staunchless curiosity. You are, happily, well capable of being both robust and dismissive, of giving the full shoulder-charge to phoney and know-nothing; but you are essentially an enthusiast. Most people enjoy a destructive review (not least because it lets us off reading the book), but few are improved as readers by it. And that is the point of a literary essay: to help us read better – more deeply, more keenly, more widely. To make us, in short, better autodidacts. If you sometimes like putting on the dog (as our friend Terence Kilmartin used to phrase it), then few have more right to such dog than you. If you make us disagree and argue back, so much the better.

At the close of the last millennium, I watched a TV show you presented which had probably taken up several months of your writing time. From a vast stage, you introduced numerous celebrities to an unflaggingly enthusiastic audience. After a while – the case of the dog that barked all the time – a suspicion began to develop into a question. Why weren't there any shots of the audience? Perhaps because its density did not quite match its seemingly thunderous output? Perhaps because in fact it did not exist in the first place? I was told recently of a well-known TV host – let's call him, for the sake of argument, Bob Monkhouse – who can sustain a whole show this way, nudging, teasing and cajoling an increasingly orgasmic audience which is entirely the construct of a back-stage knob-twiddler. With a slide of the thumb and a flick of the switch the technician creates the rippling appreciation, the sudden hysteria, and even that studio standby (and gift to the host) The Guy Who Gets The Joke

After Everybody Else. This seems to me to epitomize the difference between the worlds of television and literature, which over the past twenty years have competed for your attention. In television everyone applauds but there's no one really there. In literature your latest article on that underrated Slovenian satirist may draw only a green-ink letter from Haywards Heath referring to convict ancestry and a polite aerogram from Professor Dryasdustovic addressing the question of folk influence on the satirist's style. But these will be true responses. Oh yes, you'll probably get a third one, from me. 'You know, Clive,' I'll say irritatingly, 'I really do think your literary essays are your best work.'

So the recent news that you are to stop being what the tabloids call 'TV's Clive' has brought joy to the Grub Street team. We need your fully concentrated jostle. A laugh that bursts from a reader nose-down in the *TLS* is worth the acclaim of a hundred warmed-up studio audiences. It was time to give up the day-job. Welcome back, 'Literature's Clive'.

JULIAN BARNES
2001

WRITING ABOUT WRITERS

THE ALL OF ORWELL

Who wrote this? 'Political language – and with variations this is true of all political parties, from Conservatives to Anarchists – is designed to make lies sound truthful and murder respectable, and to give an appearance of solidity to pure wind.' But you guessed straight away: George Orwell. The subject stated up front, the sudden acceleration from the scope-widening parenthesis into the piercing argument that follows, the way the obvious opposition between 'lies' and 'truthful' leads into the shockingly abrupt coupling of 'murder' and 'respectable', the elegant, reverse-written coda clinched with a dirt-common epithet, the whole easy-seeming poise and compact drive of it, a world view compressed to the size of a motto from a fortune cookie, demanding to be read out and sayable in a single breath – it's the Orwell style. But you can't call it Orwellian, because that means Big Brother, Newspeak, The Ministry of Love, Room 101, the Lubyanka, Vorkuta, the NKVD, the MVD, the KGB, KZ Dachau, KZ Buchenwald, the *Reichsschrifftumskammer*, Gestapo HQ in the Prinz-Albrecht-Strasse, *Arbeit macht frei, Giovinezza, Je suis partout,* the compound at Drancy, the Kempei Tai, Let A Hundred Flowers Bloom, *The Red Detachment of Women,* the Stasi, the Securitate, cro-magnon Latino death squad goons decked out in Ray-bans after dark, that Khmer Rouge torture factory whose inmates were forbidden to scream, Idi Amin's Committee of Instant Happiness or whatever his secret police were called, and any other totalitarian obscenity that has ever reared its head or ever will.

The word 'Orwellian' is a daunting example of the fate that a distinguished writer can suffer at the hands of journalists. When, as almost invariably happens, a totalitarian set-up, whether in fact or in fantasy – in Brazil or in *Brazil* – is called Orwellian, it is as if George Orwell had conceived the nightmare instead of analysed it, helped to create it instead of helping to dispel its euphemistic thrall.

(Similarly Kafka, through the word Kafkaesque, gets the dubious credit for having somehow wished into existence the same sort of bureaucratic labyrinth that convulsed him to the heart.) Such distortions would be enough to make us give up on journalism altogether if we happened to forget that Orwell himself was a journalist. Here, to help us remember, are the twenty volumes of the new complete edition, cared for with awe-inspiring industry, dedication and judgement by Peter Davison, a scholar based in Leicester, who has spent the last two decades chasing down every single piece of paper his subject ever wrote on and then battling with publishers to persuade them that the accumulated result would supply a demand. The All of Orwell arrives in a cardboard box the size of a piece of check-in luggage: a man in a suitcase. As I write, the books are stacked on my desk, on a chair, on a side table, on the floor. A full, fat eleven of the twenty volumes consist largely of his collected journalism, reproduced in strict chronology along with his broadcasts, letters, memos, diaries, jottings, *et* exhaustively and fascinatingly *al.* The nine other volumes, over there near the stereo, were issued previously, in 1986–87, and comprise the individual works he published during his lifetime, including at least two books that directly and undeniably affected history. But, lest we run away with the idea that *Animal Farm* and *Nineteen Eighty-Four* are the core of his achievement, here, finally, is all the incidental writing, to remind us that they were only the outer layer, and could not have existed without what lay inside. Those famous, world-changing novels are just the bark. The journalism is the tree.

A four-volume edition of the journalism, essays, and letters, which was published in 1968 (co-edited by Ian Angus and Orwell's widow, Sonia), had already given us a good idea of how the tree grew, but now we get an even better chance to watch its roots suck up the nutrients of contemporary political experience and—But it's time to abandon that metaphor. Orwell never liked it when the writing drove the meaning. One of his precepts for composition was 'Let the meaning choose the word, and not the other way around.' For him, prose style was a matter in which the ethics determined the aesthetics. As a writer, he was his own close reader. Reading others, he was open to persuasion, but he would not be lulled, least of all by mellifluous rhetoric. Anyone's prose style, even his, sets out to seduce. Orwell's, superficially the plainest of the plain, was of a rhythm and a shapeliness to seduce the angels. Even at this distance, he needs watching, and would have been the first to admit it.

*

Orwell was born into the impoverished upper class – traditionally, for its brighter children, a potent incubator of awareness about how the social system works. Either they acquire an acute hunger to climb back up the system – often taking the backstairs route through the arts, à la Sir John Betjeman – or they go the other way, seeking an exit from the whole fandango and wishing it to damnation. Orwell, by his own later accounts, went the other way from his school days onward. In one of his last great essays, 'Such, Such Were the Joys,' he painted his years at prep school (where he nicknamed the head-master's gorgon of a wife Flip) as a set of panels by Hieronymus Bosch:

> 'Here is a little boy,' said Flip, indicating me to the strange lady, 'who wets his bed every night. Do you know what I am going to do if you wet your bed again?' she added, turning to me. 'I am going to get the Sixth Form to beat you.'

Orwell had a better time at Eton – it sounds as if he would have had a better time in Siberia – but twenty years later, after he left it, reviewing his friend Cyril Connolly's partly autobiographical *Enemies of Promise*, he poured scorn on Connolly's fond recollections of the place. When Connolly proclaimed himself fearful that after his climactic years of glory at Eton nothing in the rest of his life could ever be so intense, Orwell reacted as if Flip had just threatened to deliver him to the Sixth Form all over again: ' "Cultured" middle-class life has reached a depth of softness at which a public-school education – five years in a luke-warm bath of snobbery – can actually be looked back upon as an eventful period.'

Orwell often reviewed his friends like that. With his enemies, he got tough. But it should be said at the outset that even with his enemies he rarely took an inhuman tone. Even Hitler and Stalin he treated as men rather than as machines, and his famous characterization of the dogma-driven hack as 'the gramophone mind' would have lost half its force if he had not believed that there was always a human being within the fanatic. His comprehension, though, did not incline him to be forgiving: quite the reverse. Society might have made the powerful what they were as surely as it had made the powerless what they were, but the mere fact that the powerful were free to express whatever individuality they possessed was all the more reason to hold them personally responsible for crushing the freedom of others. When they beat you, you can join them or you can join the fight on behalf of those they beat. It seems a fair guess that Orwell had already made his choice by the time Flip threatened him with a visit from the Sixth Form.

∗

In the early part of his adult life, he was a man of action. He wrote journalism when he could – for him it was more natural than breathing, which, thanks to a lurking tubercular condition, eventually became a strain – but he wanted to be where the action was. Already questioning his own privileged, if penny-pinching, upbringing and education, he went out to Burma at the age of nineteen and for the next five years served as a colonial policeman – an experience from which he reached the conclusion (incorporated later into his novel *Burmese Days* and his essays 'Shooting an Elephant' and 'A Hanging') that the British Empire was a capitalist mechanism to exploit the subjugated poor. Back in Europe, he found out what it was like to be a proletarian by becoming one himself – *Down and Out in Paris and London*, *The Road to Wigan Pier* – and expanded his belief about the exploitative nature of the Empire to embrace the whole of capitalist society, anywhere. He volunteered for service in Spain in the fight against Franco, and the selfless comradeship of ordinary Spaniards risking their lives to get justice – *Homage to Catalonia* – confirmed his belief that an egalitarian socialist society was the only fair and decent alternative to the capitalist boondoggle, of which Franco's Fascism, like Hitler's and Mussolini's, was merely the brute expression.

So here, already formed, were two of his three main political beliefs – about the awfulness of capitalism and the need for an egalitarian alternative. There was nothing uncommon about them except their intensity: plenty of intellectuals from his middle-class background had reached the same conclusions, although few of them as a result of direct experience. The third belief was the original one. It was more than a belief, it was an insight. Again, he was not the only one to have it, or at any rate part of it: though such illustrious invitees to the Soviet Union as Bernard Shaw, H. G. Wells and the Webbs had been fooled into admiration by the standard tricks of Potemkin Village set-dressing, Bertrand Russell, André Gide, E. E. Cummings, Malcolm Muggeridge and several other visiting commentators had already spotted that the vaunted socialist utopia was a put-up job, and in 1938 the Italian-born Croatian ex-Communist Anton Ciliga, in his book *Au pays du grande mensonge* (In the Land of the Big Lie), gave a detailed account of the Gulag system, which he knew from the inside. But nobody ever expressed his revulsion better or more lastingly than Orwell, who got it right without ever having to go there.

He went somewhere else instead. Discovering in Spain, from the behaviour of the Russian representatives and their Communist adherents, that the Soviet Union was as implacable an enemy of his egalitarian aspirations as Nazi Germany or Fascist Italy, he developed the idea that it wasn't enough to be against Mussolini and Hitler: you had to be against Stalin as well, because the enemy was totalitarianism itself. That was as far as he got before his career as a man of action came to an end. Shot in the throat by a sniper, he recuperated, but if he had stayed in Spain any longer he would have almost certainly been murdered. The anarchist group in whose ranks he had fought, the POUM, was being liquidated on Soviet orders, and his name was on the list. (The evidence is all here, in Volume XI, and it is enough to bring on a cold sweat: losing Orwell to the NKVD would have had the same devastating effect on our intellectual patrimony that the loss of the historian Marc Bloch and the literary critic Jean Prévost to the Gestapo had on the French.)

Back in England with his three main beliefs – capitalism was a disease, socialism was the cure, and Communism would kill the patient – the erstwhile man of action carried on his cause as a man of letters. For part of the Second World War, he was a member of the Home Guard, and for a further part he was with the BBC, preparing broadcasts for India, but as far as the main action went he was an onlooker. No onlooker ever looked on more acutely. The journalism he wrote at the close of the thirties and in the forties would have been more than enough by itself to establish him as having fulfilled his life's purpose, which he made explicit in his last years: 'What I have most wanted to do is to make political writing into an art.' The whole heavy atmosphere of the prelude to the war, the exhausting war itself, and its baleful aftermath: it's all there, reported with a vividness that eschews the consciously poetic but never lapses from the truly dramatic, because he had the talent and the humility to assess even a V-1 in terms of its effect on his own character, using his soliloquy to explain the play:

> Every weapon seems unfair until you have adopted it yourself. But I would not deny that the pilotless plane, flying bomb, or whatever its correct name may be, is an exceptionally unpleasant thing, because, unlike most other projectiles, it gives you time to think. What is your first reaction when you hear that droning, zooming noise? Inevitably, it is a hope that the noise *won't stop*. You want to hear the bomb pass safely overhead and die away into the distance before the engine cuts out. In other words, you are hoping that it will fall on somebody else.

Along with the exterior drama, however, an interior drama is now, at long last, fully revealed. Tracking his mind from note to memo, from letter to book review, from article to essay, we can see what happened to those early beliefs – which two of them were modified, and which one of them was elaborated into a social, political, ethical and even philosophical concept whose incorporation into *Animal Farm* and *Nineteen Eighty-Four* would make him into a man of action all over again, a writer whose books helped to bring down an empire, even if it wasn't the same empire he originally had in mind.

First, though, with the Spanish war over and the full European war not yet begun, he had another battle on his hands, bloodless this time but almost as noisy: the battle against Britain's left-wing intellectuals. He realized that they had wilfully declined to get the point about Spain: they still saw Communism as the only bulwark against Fascism. Worse, they thought that the Moscow trials were justified or otherwise to be condoned – a price worth paying to Build Socialism. Orwell's conviction that no socialism worth having could be built that way set him at odds with the progressive illuminati of his generation, and that altercation was made sharper by how much he and they had in common. He, too, had had the generosity to declare his own privileges meaningless if they were bought at the expense of the downtrodden. He, too, believed that the civilization that had given birth to him was a confidence trick. And, although

he had already concluded that free speech was the one liberal institution no putative future society could abolish if it was to remain
just, he still thought that the plutocratic oligarchy allowed liberal
institutions to continue only as part of the charade that favoured the
exploitation of the poor. (In the sixties, the same notion lived again,
as 'repressive tolerance'.) Fascism, he proclaimed, was just bourgeois
democracy without the lip service to liberal values, the iron fist
without the velvet glove. In 1937, he twice ventured the opinion that
democracy and Fascism 'are Tweedledum and Tweedledee'. In the
same year, he warned that 'the moneyed classes' might trick Britain
into 'another imperialist war' with Germany: language hard to
distinguish from Party-line boilerplate.

Orwell could always see the self-serving fallacy of pacifism, but
he had a soft spot for Bertrand Russell's version of it, which should
have been detectable as pure wind even at the time, when Hitler had
already spent more than five years abundantly demonstrating that
the chances of the non-violent to temper his activities by their moral
example were exactly zero. But Orwell gave the philosopher's well-
intended homilies a sympathetic review. Orwell was thus in line
with the Labour Party, which, from the opposition benches, railed
against the threat of Fascism but simultaneously condemned as
warmongering any moves towards rearmament. It was the despised
reactionaries, with Chamberlain at the head of the Conservative
government and Churchill growling encouragment from the back
benches, who actively prepared for war against Hitler. Distancing
himself from the Communists and their fellow travellers in his attitude to the USSR, Orwell was dangerously close to them in supposing
bourgeois democracy to be teetering on the rim of history's dustbin,
into which more realistic forces would combine to shove it beyond
retrieval. In Germany, the same aloof attitude on the part of the social
democrat intellectuals had fatally led them to high-hat the Weimar
Republic while the Communists and the Nazis combined to strangle
it, but Orwell had not yet fully learned the lesson. On the Continent,
or already fleeing from it, there were plenty of veteran political
commentators who had learned it all too well at the hands of one or
the other of the two extremist movements and sometimes both,
but apart from Franz Borkenau, Arthur Koestler and perhaps Boris
Souvarine it is remarkable how few of them influenced Orwell's views.
By international standards he was a late developer.

Pre-war, Orwell was in a false position, and his journalistic output during the war is largely the story of how he came to admit it. But before he started getting round to that, he had one more, even more glaring, false position still to go. When the war began he said that Britain was bound to be defeated unless it had a social revolution, which might even require an armed uprising. Possibly he had been carried away by the rifles issued to the Home Guard, and had visions of an English POUM taking pot shots at the oppressor. (Orwell rose to the rank of sergeant in the Home Guard, but Davison should have found room to say, in a footnote, that his hero was notoriously more enthusiastic than competent: a Court of Inquiry was conducted after he supervised a mortar drill that almost resulted in the decapitation of one of his men.) Even in 1941, well after the Battle of Britain demonstrated that this bourgeois democracy might well hope to withstand Hitler, we can still hear Orwell promising that 'England is on the road to revolution' and that to bring the revolution about a 'real English socialist movement' would be 'perfectly willing to use violence if necessary'.

But if a pious wish helped to sustain him, the facts were simultaneously hard at work on a mind whose salient virtue was its willingness to let them in. He had noticed that Poland, whatever the condition of its liberal institutions under the pre-war regime, was immeasurably worse off now that the Nazis and the Soviets (following the letter of the Molotov-Ribbentrop Pact's secret protocols, although he had no means of knowing that yet beyond guesswork) had combined to expunge all traces of its civilization, including as many of its intelligentsia as they could round up. There were steadily accumulating written indications that he was becoming more and more impressed by the one fact about his country he had never been able to argue away. A state against which he could say out loud that he 'was perfectly willing to use violence if necessary' might have something to be said for it – something central, and not just peripheral – if it was not perfectly willing to use violence against him.

Probably armed more by his ability to interpret news than by solid reading of social theorists, Orwell can be seen elaborating his own theory of society towards the point where he would begin to abandon some of its postulates, which had come from classical Marxism and its dubious historiographic heritage. Reviewing, in that same year, 1941, a book of essays about the English Revolution of 1640 edited by the Marxist historian Christopher Hill, Orwell pinpointed 'the main weakness of Marxism', its inflexible determination to attribute to 'the superstructure' (his inverted commas as well as mine) even the most powerful human motives, such as patriotism. Orwell asked the Marxist contributors an awkward question: 'If no man is ever motivated by anything except class interests, why does every man constantly pretend that he is motivated by something else?'

Orwell had spent a lot of time before the war saying that class interests were indeed predominant – especially the interest of the ruling class in sacrificing the interests of every other class in order to stay on top – but now he had discovered his own patriotism, and typically he followed up on the climb-down. Even before the war, he had been impressed by how the English people in general had managed to preserve and develop civilized values despite the cynicism of their rulers. Now he became less inclined to argue that all those things had happened merely because the sweated labour of colonial coolies had paid for them, and were invalidated as a result. He was even capable, from time to time, of giving some of the cynical rulers a nod of respect: Orwell's praise of Churchill was never better than grudging, but nobody else's was ever more moving, because nobody else would have so much preferred to damn Churchill and all his works. From the early war years until the end of his life, Orwell wrote more and more about British civilization. He wrote less and less about the irredeemable obsolescence of bourgeois democracy. He had come to suspect that the democratic part might depend on the bourgeois part.

Most of the left-wing intellectuals hadn't. After Hitler clamorously repudiated his non-aggression pact with Stalin by launching Operation Barbarossa, they were once again able to laud the virtues of the Soviet Union at the tops of their voices. Even on the right, keeping Uncle Joe sweet was regarded as mandatory. In this matter, Orwell showed what can only be described as intellectual heroism. Though his unpalatable opinions restricted his access to mainstream publications – most of his commentaries were written for *Tribune*, an influential but small-circulation weekly newspaper backed by the Labour Party's star heavyweight, Aneurin Bevan – Orwell went on insisting that the Soviet regime was a tyranny, even as the Red Army battled the Panzers to a standstill on the outskirts of Moscow. At this distance, it is hard to imagine what a lonely line this was to take. But when it came to a principle Orwell was the sort of man who would rather shiver in solitude than hold his tongue.

Solitude fitted his character. Though he was sociable, and even amorous, in his everyday life, he didn't look it: he looked as gauntly ascetic as John Carradine, and in his mental life he was a natural loner. Collectivist theories could appeal to his temperament for only so long, and in this strictly chronological arrangement of his writings we can watch him gradually deconstructing his own ideology in deference to a set of principles. Even with this degree of document- ation, it is not easy to see quite when he shifted aside a neat notion in order to let an awkward fact take over, because for a crucial period of the war he metaphorically went off the air. Literally, he had gone on it. For a two-year slog, from 1941 to late 1943, he expended most of his time and energy broadcasting to India for the BBC. Belated market research on the BBC's part revealed that not many Indians were listening (you guessed it: no radios), but the few who did manage to tune in heard some remarkable stuff from a man who had expended so much ink on insisting that the British would have to quit India. Orwell told them the truth: that they had a better chance with the British than with the Japanese. He also scripted weekly summaries of the war's progress. Writing on the tenth of January, 1942, he remarked on a tonal shift in Germany's official pronouncements:

> Until a week or two ago, the German military spokesmen were explaining that the attack on Moscow would have to be postponed until the spring, but that the German armies could quite easily remain on the line they now occupied. Already, however, they are admitting that a further retreat – or, as they prefer to call it, a rectification of the line – will be necessary . . . Before the end of February, the Germans may well be faced with the alterna- tive of abandoning nearly all their conquests in the northern part of the Russian front, or of seeing hundreds of thousands of soldiers freeze to death.

It was an optimistic forecast for 1942, but it all came true in 1943, and it showed two of Orwell's best attributes operating at once: he had a global grasp, and he was able to guess the truth by the way the other side told lies. The broadcasts make such good reading today that you almost feel sorry he ever stopped. From these indirect sources, you can surmise something of what was going on deep within his mind, and when he started writing journalism again he retroactively filled in some of the gaps. From the realization that the violent socialist revolution would not take place, he was apparently moving towards the conclusion that it should not. Reviewing a collection of Thomas Mann's essays published in English translation in 1943, he praised Mann in terms that would have been impossible for him before the war: 'He never pretends to be other than he is, a middle-class Liberal, a believer in the freedom of the intellect, in human brotherhood; above all, in the existence of objective truth.' While careful to point out that Mann was pro-socialist, and even excessively trustful of the USSR, Orwell went on to note, approvingly, that 'he never budges from his "bourgeois" contention that the individual is important, that freedom is worth having, that European culture is worth preserving, and that truth is not the exclusive possession of one race or class.' For Orwell, who had once preached that bourgeois democracy existed solely in order to bamboozle the proletariat into accepting its ineluctable servitude, this was quite a switch.

At no time did Orwell come quite clean about having rearranged the playing field. Near the end of 1943 he conceded that he had been 'grossly wrong' about the necessity of a revolution in order to stave off defeat. But to concede that he had been grossly wrong about his view of society was beyond even him, and no wonder. It would have been to give away too much. By now he was always careful to say that he wanted a *democratic* socialism, and was even ready to contemplate that reconciling a command economy with individual liberty might be a problem: but he still clung tenaciously to the socialist part of his vision, in his view the only chance of decent treatment for everyone. Piece by piece, however, he was giving up on any notion that his socialist vision could be brought about by coercion, since that would yield liberty for no one. If he had lived long enough, his fundamental honesty might have given us an autobiography which would have described what must have been a mighty conflict in his soul. As things are, we have to infer it.

His socialist beliefs fought a long rearguard action. In that same year, 1943, he gave *The Road to Serfdom* a review tolerant of Hayek's warnings about collectivism, but there was no sign of Orwell's endorsing the desirability of free market economics. Orwell was still for the centralized, planned economy. He never did quite give up on that one, and indeed, at the time, there must have seemed no necessity to. To stave off defeat, Britain had mobilized its industry under state control – had done so, it turned out, rather more thoroughly than the Nazis – and, with the war won and the country broke, even the Royal Family carried ration books without protest. So a measure of justice had been achieved.

In hindsight, the post-war British society that began with the foundation of the National Health Service *was* the socialist revolution – or, to put it less dramatically, the social-democratic reformation which Orwell had gradually come to accept as the only workable formula that would further justice without destroying liberty. The Welfare State began with shortages of almost everything, but at least the deprivations were shared, and for all its faults, British society, ever since World War II, has continuously been one of the more interesting experiments in the attempt to reconcile social justice with personal freedom. (The Scandinavian societies might be more successful experiments, but not even they find themselves interesting.) If Orwell had lived to a full span, he would have been able, if not necessarily delighted, to deal with the increasing likelihood that his dreams were coming true. Even as things were, with only a few years of life left to him, he might have given a far more positive account, in his post-war journalism, of how the British of all classes, including the dreaded ruling class, were at long last combining to bring about, at least in some measure, the more decent society that had haunted his imagination since childhood. But he was distracted by a prior requirement. His own war wasn't over. It had begun all over again. There was still one prominent social group who had learned nothing: the left-wing intellectuals.

The last and most acrimonious phase of Orwell's battle with the left-wing intelligentsia began not long after D-Day. As the Allied forces fought their way out of Normandy, a piece by Orwell landed on a desk in America. *Partisan Review* would publish a London Letter in which Orwell complained about the Western Russophile intellectuals who refused to accept the truth about Stalinist terror. Clearly, what frightened him was that, even if they did accept it, Soviet prestige would lose little of its allure for them. For Orwell, the Cold War was already on, with the progressive intellectuals in the front rank of the foe. Orwell was the first to use the term 'cold war', in an essay published in October 1945 about the atomic bomb – the very device that would ensure, in the long run, that the Cold War never became a hot one. At the time, however, he saw no cause for complacency.

But unreconstructed *gauchiste* pundits who would still like to dismiss Orwell as a 'classic' Cold Warrior can find out here that he didn't fit the frame. For one thing, Orwell remained all too willing to accuse the West of structural deficiencies that were really much more contingent than he made out. When he argued, in the pages of *Tribune,* that the mass-circulation newspapers forced slop on their readership, he preferred to ignore the advice from a correspondent that it was really a case of the readership forcing slop on the newspapers. He should have given far more attention to such criticisms, because they allowed for the possibility – as his own assumptions did not – that if ordinary people were freed from exploitation they would demand more frivolity, not less.

To the end, Orwell's tendency was to overestimate the potential of the people he supposed to be in the grip of the capitalist system, while simultaneously underestimating the individuality they were showing already. In his remarks on the moral turpitude of the scientists who had cravenly not 'refused' to work on the atomic bomb – clearly he thought they should have all turned the job down – there was no mention (perhaps because he didn't yet know, although he might have guessed) of the fact that many of them were European refugees from totalitarianism and had worked on the bomb not just willingly but with anxious fervour, convinced, with excellent reasons, that Hitler might get there first.

On the other hand, he was still inclined to regard Stalin's regime as a perversion of the Bolshevik revolution instead of as its essence: as late as 1946, it took the eminent émigré Russian scholar Gleb Struve (the future editor of Mandelstam and Akhmatova) to tell him that Zamyatin's *We,* written in 1920 but never published in Russia, might well have been, as Orwell thought, a projection of a possible totalitarian future, but had drawn much of its inspiration from the Leninist present. If Orwell took this admonition in, he made little use of it. (He made great use of *We,* however: if the English translation of Zamyatin's little classic had been as good as the French one, a lot more of *Nineteen Eighty-Four*'s reviewers might have spotted that

Orwell's phantasmagoria was a bit less *sui generis* than it seemed.) Already in 1941, reviewing *Russia Under Soviet Rule* by the émigré liberal de Basily, Orwell had taken on board the possibility that Lenin's callous behaviour made Stalin inevitable – after all, Lenin had actually *said* that the Party should rule by terror – but neither then nor later did Orwell push this point very hard. It flickers in the background of his anti-Soviet polemics and can be thought of as the informing assumption of *Animal Farm* and *Nineteen Eighty-Four*, but in his journalism he was always slow to concede that the Bolshevik revolution itself might have been the culprit. Perhaps he thought he had enough trouble on his hands already, just trying to convince his starry-eyed Stalinist contemporaries that they had placed their faith in a cynic who left their own cynicism for dead, and would do the same to them if he got the chance. 'The direct, conscious attack on intellectual decency comes from the intellectuals themselves.'

*

As a journalist, Orwell had laboured long and hard for small financial reward, and overwork had never been good for his delicate health. Life was pinched, not to say deprived, especially after his wife and faithful helpmeet Eileen (he was an unfaithful spouse and she may have been as well, but they depended on each other) died as a result of a medical blunder. The success of *Animal Farm*, in 1945, could have bought him a reprieve. He upped stakes to a small farmhouse on the island of Jura, in the Hebrides, and cultivated his garden. Though he overestimated the strength he still had available for the hard life he lived there – he could grow vegetables to supplement his ration, but it took hard work in tough soil – the place was a welcome break from the treadmill of London. Mentally, however, he found no peace. A heightened anguish can be traced right through his last journalism until he gave it up to work on *Nineteen Eighty-Four*. The left-wing intellectuals, already promoting the revisionism that continues into our own day, not only were giving Stalin the sole credit for having won the war but were contriving not to notice that he had rescinded the few liberties he had been forced to concede in order to fight it; that his rule by terror had resumed; and that in the Eastern European countries supposedly liberated by the Red Army any vestige of liberty left by the Nazis was being stamped flat. Once again, crimes on a colossal scale were being camouflaged with perverted language, and once again the intellectuals, whose professional instinct should have been to sick it up, were happily swallowing the lot. It took a great deal to persuade him that reasoned argument wasn't enough. But it wasn't, so he wrote *Nineteen Eighty-Four.*

There are still diehards who would like to think that *Nineteen Eighty-Four* is not about the Soviet Union at all. Their argument runs: *Animal Farm* is a satire about what happened in Russia once upon a time, but *Nineteen Eighty-Four* is a minatory fantasy about something far bigger – the prospect of a world divided up into a few huge centres of absolute power, of which a Soviet-style hegemony would be only one, and the United States, of course, would be another. It is just possible that Orwell thought the Marshall Plan was meant to have the same imperialist effect in Europe as the Red Army's tanks. He never actually said so, but people as intelligent as Gore Vidal believe much the same thing today. The late Anthony Burgess sincerely believed that *Nineteen Eighty-Four,* because the Ministry of Truth bore such a strong resemblance to the BBC canteen, had been inspired by the condition of post-war Britain under rationing. As Orwell said so resonantly in his essay 'Notes on Nationalism', 'One has to belong to the intelligentsia to believe things like that: no ordinary man could be such a fool.'

He didn't mean that all intellectuals are *ipso facto* fools – he himself was an intellectual if anybody was – but he did mean that verbal cleverness, unless its limitations are clearly and continuously seen by its possessor, is an unbeatable way of blurring reality until nothing can be seen at all. The main drive of all Orwell's writings since Spain had been to point out that the Soviet Union, nominally the hope of mankind, had systematically perverted language in order to cover up the wholesale destruction of human values, and that the Western left-wing intellectuals had gone along with this by perverting their own language in its turn. To go on denying that *Nineteen Eighty-Four* was the culmination of this large part of Orwell's effort is to defy reason. At the time, denying it was still a not wholly unreasonable reaction. After all, the democracies wouldn't have won the war without the Soviet Union, and the book was so black and hopeless. Maybe it was about something else.

If they didn't get it in the West, they got it in the East. From the day of the book's publication until far into the Thaw, it meant big trouble for any Soviet citizen who had a copy in his possession. In the years to come, now that the Soviet archives are opening up, there will be a fruitful area of study in trying to decide which were the Western cultural influences that did most to help the Evil Empire melt down. For all we know, the jokes were always right, and it was the Beatles albums and the bootleg blue jeans that did the trick. But it is a fair guess that of all the imported artefacts it was the books that sapped the repressive will of the people who ran the empire or who were next in line to do so. Robert Conquest's *The Great Terror* might well turn out to be the key factor in the unprecedented turn-around by which those state organizations with a solid track record of pre-emptive slaughter somehow began to spare the very lives they would previously have been careful to snuff out: it is said that even the KGB read it, perhaps as the quickest way of finding out what their predecessors had been up to. (There is no doubt at all, by the way, that they eventually read *Nineteen Eighty-Four*. When head of the KGB, Andropov had a special edition printed and circulated.)

But for all we know they might have been just as much subverted by *samizdat* translations of *The Carpetbaggers* and *Valley of the Dolls*. Nor, of course, can the effect of the dissident literature, whether written in exile or home-grown, be dismissed as merely unsettling, although for the books written at home there will always be the consideration of whether they could have even been conceived of if the set-up were not already crumbling in the first place. What we are talking about is a contrary weather-system of opinion that eventually took over a whole climate, and to trace its course will be like following the dust of Ariadne's crumbled thread back into a ruined labyrinth. But it will be a big surprise if *Nineteen Eighty-Four*, even more than *The Gulag Archipelago*, does not turn out to be the book that did most, weight for weight, to clear thousands of living brains of the miasma sent up through the soil by millions upon millions of dead bodies. It was a portable little slab of spiritual *plastique*, a mind-blower.

But if the part played by Orwell's dystopian novels in the dismantling of the Sovietized monolith will always be hard to assess, there is less difficulty about measuring the effect of his last period of journalism on his own country. Self-immured on Jura, he was a Prospero running on the reserve tank of his magic. Orwell was only forty-two, but he had little physical strength left, and although many friends and colleagues sent him letters and books, and presents of rice and chocolate, and some even made the slow and tricky journey to visit him, he was short of love. A widower of some fame and no longer without means, he offered his affections to a succession of young women and found himself in the humiliating position of being respected and refused. When it emerged recently that he handed a list of fellow-travellers to a government propaganda unit, suggestions that he had conspired in a witch-hunt carried little force. McCarthyism was a nonstarter in Britain, and most of those named on the list were already glad to have it known that they had aligned their prayer mats in the direction of the Kremlin. But if he lapsed from his own standards by tittle-tattling in school the most likely reason was that his Foreign Office contact was a noted beauty. He was sending her a bouquet.

The young woman who finally accepted him, Sonia Brownell (renowned in literary London as the Venus of Euston Road), married him practically on his deathbed: cold comfort. He kept a diary of what was happening in his garden – small things growing as the great man withered. For us, the only consolation is that he could speak so clearly even as the walls of his lungs were giving way against the tide of blood.

'Britain has lost an empire but has not found a role', said Dean Acheson. Raymond Aron said something better: '*L'Angleterre a perdu son empire, sans perdre sa civilization morale.*' In helping Britain to maintain and extend its moral civilization, Orwell's voice was surely crucial. The succession of magnificent essays he wrote as the harsh war wound down into an austere peace add up to a political event in themselves, the culmination of his journalism as a textbook example of how a sufficiently informed commentary on events can feed back into history and help to shape its course.

It takes nothing from Davison's achievement to say that these last essays are probably best encountered in the *Collected Essays*, or even in a single small volume, such as *Inside the Whale*, where they will be found to have the effect of poems, as the paragraphs succeed one another with the inevitability of perfectly wrought stanzas, with every sentence in the right place yet begging to be remembered on its own, like a line from a magisterial elegy. 'Notes on Nationalism', 'The Prevention of Literature', 'Politics and the English Language', 'Why I Write', 'Politics vs. Literature: An Examination of "Gulliver's Travels" ' – read for and by themselves, they tell you all you need to know about Orwell except the one fact so poignantly revealed here: that they were the work of a man who was not only dying but dying young. Very few writers about politics have said much in their forties that is lastingly true; and even Orwell undoubtedly would have continued to deepen, enrich, modulate, and modify his opinions.

But he had come a long way, and, by coming as far as the great last essays, he left a precious heritage to the country that he loved in spite of itself. Though the appeal to a totalitarian model of a just society (and the corresponding contempt for piecemeal solutions) was to remain possible in the academy, it became much more difficult in everyday political journalism, simply because Orwell had discredited the idea in a plain style that nobody could forget and everybody felt obliged to echo. The theoretical work that disenfranchised all total transformations was done by others, such as Karl Popper, Raymond Aron, Leszek Kolokowski and Isaiah Berlin. Orwell never got around to figuring all that out in detail. But he felt it, and the language of his last essays is the language of feeling made as clear and bright as it can ever get.

*

How clear is that? Finally, it comes down to a question of language, which is only appropriate, because, finally, Orwell was a literary man. Politics inspired Orwell the way the arts had always inspired the great critics, which gives us the clue to where he got the plainly passionate style that we are so ready to call unique. It is unique, in its flexibility of speech rhythms and its irresistible force of assertion, but he didn't invent it; he invented its use. George Saintsbury had something of Orwell's schooled knack for speaking right out of the page, and Shaw had almost all of it: Orwell isn't often outright funny, but Shaw, in his six volumes of critical writings about music and theatre, deployed the full range of Orwell's debunking weapons with a generous humour to drive them home. Orwell called Shaw a windbag, but had obviously taken in every word the old man wrote. And there are many other critics who could be named, all the way up to the young F. R. Leavis, whom Orwell read with interest, if not without a certain distaste for his joyless zeal.

Orwell was a superb literary critic himself: he is the first person to read on Swift, on Dickens, and on Gissing, and if he had lived to finish his essay on Evelyn Waugh it would have been the best thing on the subject, the essay that really opens up Waugh's corrosively snobbish view of life without violating his creative achievement. Had Orwell lived to a full term, he might well have gone on to become the greatest modern literary critic in the language. But he lived more than long enough to make writing about politics a branch of the humanities, setting a standard of civilized response to the intractably complex texture of life. No previous political writer had brought so much of life's lesser detail into the frame, and other countries were unlucky not to have him as a model. Sartre, for example, would have been incapable of an essay about the contents of a junk shop, or about how to make the ideal cup of tea – the very reason he was incapable of talking real sense about politics.

In one of the very last, and best, of his essays, 'Lear, Tolstoy, and the Fool', Orwell paid his tribute to Shakespeare. He was too modest to say that he was paying a debt as well, but he was:

> Shakespeare was not a philosopher or a scientist, but he did have curiosity: he loved the surface of the earth and the process of life – which, it should be repeated, is *not* the same thing as wanting to have a good time and stay alive as long as possible. Of course, it is not because of the quality of his thought that Shakespeare has survived, and he might not even be remembered as a dramatist if he had not also been a poet. His main hold on us is through language.

A writer has to know a lot about the rhythms of natural speech before he can stretch them over the distance covered by those first two sentences. Each of them is perfectly balanced in itself, and the second is perfectly balanced against the first – the first turning back on itself with a strict qualification, and the second running away in relaxed enjoyment of its own fluency. They could stand on their own, but it turns out that both of them are there to pile their combined weight behind the third sentence – the short one – and propel it into your memory. It hits home with the force of an axiom.

And it isn't true – or, anyway, it isn't true enough. Elsewhere in the essay, Orwell shows signs of being aware that the relationship of Shakespeare's language to the quality of his thought can never be fully resolved in favour of either term. But not even Orwell could resist a resonant statement that fudged the facts – a clarity that is really an opacity. Yes, Orwell did write like an angel, and that's the very reason we have to watch him like a hawk. Luckily for us, he was pretty good at watching himself. He was blessed with a way of putting things that made anything he said seem so, but that was only a gift. His intellectual honesty was a virtue.

Orwell's standards of plain speaking always were and still are a mile too high for politicians. What finally counts with politicians is what they do, not how they say it. But for journalists how they say it counts for everything. Orwell's style shows us why a style is worth working at: not just because it gets us a byline and makes a splash but because it compresses and refines thought and feeling without ceasing to sound like speech – which is to say, without ceasing to sound human. At a time when ideological politics still exercised such an appeal that hundreds of purportedly civilized voices *had* ceased to sound human, Orwell's style stood out. The remarkable thing is that it still does. Ideologues are thin on the ground nowadays, while any substantial publication has a would-be George Orwell rippling the keys in every second cubicle, but the daddy of modern truthtellers still sounds fresh. So it wasn't just the amount of truth he told but the way he told it, in prose transmuted to poetry by the pressure of his dedication. This great edition, by revealing fully for the first time what that dedication was like, makes his easy-seeming written speech more impressive than ever, and even harder to emulate. To write like him, you need a life like his, but times have changed, and he changed them.

New Yorker, 18 January, 1999: also included in *Even As We Speak*, 2001

Postscript

Even if our intention is the most abject homage, we can't write in praise of heroes without taking their limitations into account, because unless we had noticed their limitations we wouldn't be writing at all: they would have silenced us. While you are reading them, the great stylists make you want to give up, and in the case of Orwell, the stylist with the anti-style, the effect can last a long time after you have finished reading. I was in bed with a convenient nervous breakdown when I read the four volumes of his collected journalism that came out in 1969. I already knew the standard essays quite well, but the accumulated impact of reading them again, along with all the other material which had become generally available for the first time, would have kept me away from the typewriter for years if I hadn't noticed something fundamentally wrong amongst everything that he got right.

He was wrong about the British Empire. He never gave up on the idea that it was a fraud, designed with no other end in view except to stave off rebellion at home by eking out the miseries of capitalism with the exploited fruits of coolie labour in the colonies. Born under the Empire myself, with few coolies in sight, I knew it to be a more equivocal thing. Orwell's procrustean notions on the subject might have served as a useful reservoir of polemical force, but their heritage was all too obvious. In 1902 G. A. Hobson's book *Imperialism* promoted the idea that colonial possessions were critical for advanced, or 'finance', capitalism. In 1916 Lenin took the idea over for his *Imperialism, the Highest State of Capitalism*, and after the Revolution it became a standard item of Comintern dogma, working its worldwide influence even on those Left-inclined intellectuals who refused to swallow the party programme hook, line and sinker. They spat out the line and sinker, but they stayed hooked.

I was thus being as kind as I could to suggest, in my *laudatio*, that Orwell inherited some of his theoretical precepts from classic Marxism. He got at least one of them, and perhaps the most misleading one, from classic Leninism – a still more dubious patrimony. Even in Orwell's own time, it should have been evident that the idea was a misconception. The mere existence of Sweden, for example, was enough to refute it. Sweden had a capitalist system, advanced social welfare, and no imperial dreams that had not died with Gustavus Adolphus. After Orwell's death, when the last of the British Empire was given up and the final accounts came in, it became easy to question whether colonialism had ever yielded a dividend, let alone supported Britain as a capitalist economy. But Orwell, who justly prided himself on his capacity to puncture received notions, should have questioned the assumption when questioning was hard. Had he done so, however, it might have made him a less effective speaker for the independent Left. It might have sapped the confidence that energized his style. Any successful style is a spell whose first victim is the wizard. Unless he is alert to the trickery of his own magic, he will project an air of Delphic infallibility that can do a lot of damage before the inevitable collapse into abracadabra. The obvious example is Shaw, but no master stylist has ever been exempt from the danger. It follows that there is always something useful to say, even about the man who appears to say everything. Orwell said what mattered, and will always matter, about totalitarianism. But he never got far with saying what mattered about democracy. He thought it was a capitalist trick. It's a lot trickier than that.

2001

FOUR ESSAYS ON PHILIP LARKIN

1. Somewhere becoming rain

Collected Poems by Philip Larkin, edited by Anthony Thwaite, Faber

At first glance, the publication in the United States of Philip Larkin's *Collected Poems* looks like a long shot. While he lived, Larkin never crossed the Atlantic. Unlike some other British poets, he was genuinely indifferent to his American reputation. His bailiwick was England. Larkin was so English that he didn't even care much about Britain, and he rarely mentioned it. Even within England, he travelled little. He spent most of his adult life at the University of Hull, as its chief librarian. A trip to London was an event. When he was there, he resolutely declined to promote his reputation. He guarded it but would permit no hype.

Though Larkin's diffidence was partly a pose, his reticence was authentic. At no point did he announce that he had built a better mousetrap. The world had to prove it by beating a path to his door. The process took time, but was inexorable, and by now, only three years after his death, at the age of sixty-three, it has reached a kind of apotheosis. On the British best-seller lists, Larkin's *Collected Poems* was up there for months at a stretch, along with Stephen Hawking's *A Brief History of Time* and Salman Rushdie's *The Satanic Verses*. In Larkin's case, this extraordinary level of attention was reached without either general relativity's having to be reconciled with quantum mechanics or the Ayatollah Khomeini's being required to pronounce anathema. The evidence suggests that Larkin's poetry, from a standing start, gets to everyone capable of being got to. One's tender concern that it should survive the perilous journey across the sea is therefore perhaps misplaced. A mission like this might have no more need of a fighter escort than pollen on the wind.

The size of the volume is misleading. Its meticulous editor, Anthony Thwaite – himself a poet of high reputation – has included poems that Larkin finished but did not publish, and poems that he did not even finish. Though tactfully carried out, this editorial inclusiveness is not beyond cavil. What was elliptically concentrated has become more fully understandable, but whether Larkin benefits from being more fully understood is a poser. Eugenio Montale, in many ways a comparable figure, was, it might be recalled, properly afraid of what he called 'too much light'.

During his lifetime, Larkin published only three mature collections of verse, and they were all as thin as blades. *The Less Deceived* (1955), *The Whitsun Weddings* (1964), and *High Windows* (1974) combined to a thickness barely half that of the *Collected Poems*. Larkin also published, in 1966, a new edition of his early, immature collection, *The North Ship*, which had first come out in 1945. He took care, by supplying the reissue with a deprecatory introduction, to keep it clearly separate from the poems that he regarded as being written in his own voice.

The voice was unmistakable. It made misery beautiful. One of Larkin's few even halfway carefree poems is 'For Sydney Bechet', from *The Whitsun Weddings*. Yet the impact that Larkin said Bechet made on him was exactly the impact that Larkin made on readers coming to him for the first time:

> On me your voice falls as they say love should,
> Like an enormous yes.

What made the paradox delicious was the scrupulousness of its expression. There could be no doubt that Larkin's outlook on life added up to an enormous no, but pessimism had been given a saving grace. Larkin described an England changing in ways he didn't like. He described himself ageing in ways he didn't like. The Empire had shrunk to a few islands, his personal history to a set of missed opportunities. Yet his desperate position, which ought logically to have been a licence for incoherence, was expressed with such linguistic fastidiousness on the one hand, and such lyrical enchantment on the other, that the question arose of whether he had not at least partly cultivated that view in order to get those results. Larkin once told an interviewer, 'Deprivation for me is what daffodils were for Words-worth.'

In the three essential volumes, the balanced triad of Larkin's achievement, all the poems are poised vibrantly in the force field of tension between his profound personal hopelessness and the assured command of their carrying out. Perfectly designed, tightly integrated, making the feeling of falling apart fit together, they release, from their compressed but always strictly parsable syntax, sudden phrases of ravishing beauty, as the river in Dante's Paradise suggests by giving off sparks that light is what it is made of.

These irresistible fragments are everyone's way into Larkin's work. They are the first satisfaction his poetry offers. There are other and deeper satisfactions, but it was his quotability that gave Larkin the biggest cultural impact on the British reading public since Auden – and over a greater social range. Lines by Larkin are the common property of everyone in Britain who reads seriously at all – a state of affairs which has not obtained since the time of Tennyson. Phrases, whole lines, and sometimes whole stanzas can be heard at the dinner-table.

> There is an evening coming in
> Across the fields, one never seen before,
> That lights no lamps . . .
>
> Only one ship is seeking us, a black-
> Sailed unfamiliar, towing at her back
> A huge and birdless silence. In her wake
> No waters breed or break . . .
>
> Now, helpless in the hollow of
> An unarmorial age, a trough
> Of smoke in slow suspended skeins
> Above their scrap of history,
> Only an attitude remains . . .
>
> And as the tightened brakes took hold, there swelled
> A sense of falling, like an arrow-shower
> Sent out of sight, somewhere becoming rain . . .
>
> How distant, the departure of young men
> Down valleys, or watching

> The green shore past the salt-white cordage
> Rising and falling . . .
>
> Steep beach, blue water, towels, red bathing caps,
> The small hushed waves' repeated fresh collapse
> Up the warm yellow sand, and further off
> A white steamer stuck in the afternoon . . .
>
> Later, the square is empty: a big sky
> Drains down the estuary like the bed
> Of a gold river . . .
>
> At death, you break up: the bits that were you
> Start speeding away from each other for ever
> With no one to see . . .
>
> Rather than words comes the thought of high windows:
> The sun-comprehending glass,
> And beyond it, the deep blue air, that shows
> Nothing, and is nowhere, and is endless.

Drawn in by the subtle gravity beam of such bewitchment, the reader becomes involved for the rest of his life in Larkin's doomed but unfailingly dignified struggle to reconcile the golden light in the high windows with the endlessness it comes from. Larkin's sense of inadequacy, his fear of death are in every poem. His poems could not be more personal. But, equally, they could not be more universal. Seeing the world as the hungry and thirsty see food and drink, he describes it for the benefit of those who are at home in it, their senses dulled by satiation. The reader asks: How can a man who feels like this bear to live at all?

> Life is first boredom, then fear.
> Whether or not we use it, it goes,
> And leaves what something hidden from us chose,
> And age, and then the only end of age.

But the reader gets an answer: There are duties that annul nihilism, satisfactions beyond dissatisfaction, and, above all, the miracle of continuity. Larkin's own question about what life is worth if we have to lose it he answers with the contrary question, about what life would amount to if it didn't go on without us. Awkward at the seaside, ordinary people know better in their bones than the poet among his books:

> The white steamer has gone. Like breathed-on glass
> The sunlight has turned milky. If the worst
> Of flawless weather is our falling short,
> It may be that through habit these do best,
> Coming to water clumsily undressed
> Yearly; teaching their children by a sort
> Of clowning; helping the old, too, as they ought.

Just as Larkin's resolutely prosaic organization of a poem is its passport to the poetic, so his insight into himself is his window on the world. He is the least solipsistic of artists. Unfortunately, this fact has now become less clear. Too much light has been shed. Of the poems previously unpublished in book form, a few are among his greatest achievements, many more one would not now want to be without, and all are good to have. But all the poems he didn't publish have been put in chronological order of composition along with those he did publish, instead of being given a separate section of their own. There is plenty of editorial apparatus to tell you how the original slim volumes were made up, but the strategic economy of their initial design has been lost.

All three of the original volumes start and end with the clean, dramatic decisiveness of a curtain going up and coming down again. The cast is not loitering in the auditorium beforehand. Nor is it to be found hanging out in the car park afterwards. *The Less Deceived* starts with 'Lines on a Young Lady's Photograph Album', which laments a lost love but with no confessions of the poet's personal inadequacy. It ends with 'At Grass', which is not about him but about horses: a bugle call at sunset.

> Only the groom, and the groom's boy,
> With bridles in the evening come.

Similarly, *The Whitsun Weddings* starts and ends without a mention of the author. The first poem, 'Here', is an induction into 'the surprise of a large town' that sounds as if it might be Hull. No one who sounds as if he might be Larkin puts in an appearance. Instead, other people do, whose 'removed lives/ Loneliness clarifies'. The last poem in the book, 'An Arundel Tomb', is an elegy written in a church crypt which is as sonorous as Gray's written in a church-yard, and no more petulant: that things pass is a fact made majestic, if not welcome.

As for *High Windows*, the last collection published while he was alive, it may contain, in 'The Building', his single most terror-stricken – and, indeed, terrifying – personal outcry against the intractable fact of death, but it begins and ends with the author well in the background. 'To the Sea', the opening poem, the one in which the white steamer so transfixingly gets stuck in the afternoon, is his most thoroughgoing celebration of the element that he said he would incorporate into his religion if he only had one: water. 'The Explosion' closes the book with a heroic vision of dead coal miners which could be called a hymn to immortality if it did not come from a pen that devoted so much effort to pointing out that mortality really does mean what it says.

These two poems, 'To the Sea' and 'The Explosion', which in *High Windows* are separated by the whole length of a short but weighty book, can be taken together as a case in point, because, as the chronological arrangement of the *Collected Poems* now reveals, they were written together, or almost. The first is dated October, 1969, and the second is dated January 5, 1970. Between them in *High Windows* come poems dated anything from five years earlier to three years later. This is only one instance, unusually striking but typical rather than exceptional, of how Larkin moved poems around through compositional time so that they would make in emotional space the kind of sense he wanted, and not another kind. Though there were poems he left out of *The Less Deceived*, and put into *The Whitsun Weddings*, it would be overbold to assume that any poem, no matter how fully achieved, that he wrote before *High Windows* but did not publish in it would have found a context later – or even earlier if he had been less cautious. Anthony Thwaite goes some way towards assuming exactly that – or, at any rate, suggesting it – when he says that Larkin had been stung by early refusals and had later on repressed excellent poems even when his friends urged him to publish them. Some of these poems, as we now see, were indeed excellent, but if a man is so careful to arrange his works in a certain order it is probably wiser to assume that when he subtracts something he is adding to the arrangement.

Towards the end of his life, in the years after *High Windows*,

Larkin famously dried up. Poems came seldom. Some of those that did come equalled his best, and 'Aubade' was among his greatest. Larkin thought highly enough of it himself to send it out in pamphlet form to his friends and acquaintances, and they were quickly on the telephone to one another quoting phrases and lines from it. Soon it was stanzas, and in London there is at least one illustrious playwright who won't go home from a dinner party before he has found an excuse to recite the whole thing.

> This is a special way of being afraid
> No trick dispels. Religion used to try,
> That vast moth-eaten musical brocade
> Created to pretend we never die,
> And specious stuff that says *No rational being*
> *Can fear a thing it will not feel*, not seeing
> That this is what we fear – no sight, no sound,
> No touch or taste or smell, nothing to think with,
> Nothing to love or link with,
> The anaesthetic from which none come round . . .

Had Larkin lived longer, there would eventually have had to be one more slim volume, even if slimmer than slim. But that any of the earlier suppressed poems would have gone into it seems very unlikely. The better they are, the better must have been his reasons for holding them back. Admittedly, the fact that he did not destroy them is some evidence that he was not averse to their being published after his death. As a seasoned campaigner for the preservation of British holograph manuscripts – he operated on the principle that papers bought by American universities were lost to civilization – he obviously thought that his own archive should be kept safe. But the question of *how* the suppressed poems should be published has now been answered: some other way than this. Arguments for how good they are miss the point, because it is not their weakness that is inimical to his total effect; it is their strength. There are hemistiches as riveting as anything he ever made public.

> Dead leaves desert in thousands . . .

He wrote that in 1953 and sat on it for more than thirty years. What other poet would not have got it into print somehow? The two first lines of a short poem called 'Pigeons', written in 1957, are a paradigm distillation of his characteristic urban pastoralism:

> On shallow slates the pigeons shift together,
> Backing against a thin rain from the west . . .

Even more remarkable, there were whole big poems so close to being fully realized that to call them unfinished sounds like effrontery. Not only would Larkin never let a flawed poem through for the sake of its strong phrasing; he would sideline a strong poem because of a single flaw. But 'Letter to a Friend about Girls', written in 1959, has nothing frail about it except his final indecision about whether Horatio is writing to Hamlet or Hamlet to Horatio. The writer complains that the addressee gets all the best girls without having to think about it, while he, the writer, gets, if any, only the ones he doesn't really want, and that after a long struggle.

> After comparing lives with you for years
> I see how I've been losing: all the while
> I've met a different gauge of girl from yours . . .

A brilliantly witty extended conceit, full of the scatalogical moral observation that Larkin and his friend Kingsley Amis jointly brought back from conversation into the literature from which it had been banished, the poem has already become incorporated into the Larkin canon that people quote to one another. So have parts of 'The Dance', which would probably have been his longest single poem if he had ever finished it. The story of an awkward, put-upon, recognizably Larkin-like lonely man failing to get together with a beautiful woman even though she seems to be welcoming his attentions, the poem could logically have been completed only by becoming a third novel to set beside *Jill* and *A Girl in Winter*. (Actually, the novel had already been written, by Kingsley Amis, and was called *Lucky Jim*.) But there might have been a better reason for abandoning the poem. Like the Horatio poem and many of the other poems that were held back, 'The Dance' is decisive about what Larkin otherwise preferred to leave indeterminate. 'Love Again', written in 1979, at the beginning of the arid last phase in which the poems that came to him seem more like bouts of fever than like showers of rain, states the theme with painful clarity.

> Love again: wanking at ten past three
> (Surely he's taken her home by now?),
> The bedroom hot as a bakery . . .

What hurts, though, isn't the vocabulary. When Larkin speaks of 'Someone else feeling her breasts and cunt', he isn't speaking with untypical bluntness: though unfalteringly well judged, his tonal range always leaves room for foul language – shock effects are among his favourites. The pain at this point comes from the fact that it is so obviously Larkin talking. This time, the voice isn't coming through a persona: it's the man himself, only at his least complex, and therefore least individual. In his *oeuvre*, as selected and arranged by himself, there is a dialogue going on, a balancing of forces between perfection of the life and of the work – a classic conflict for which Larkin offers us a resolution second in its richness only to the later poems of Yeats. In much of the previously suppressed poetry, the dialogue collapses into a monologue. The man who has, at least in part, chosen his despair, or who, at any rate, strives to convince himself that he has, is usurped by the man who has no choice. The second man might well be thought of as the real man, but one of the effects of Larkin's work is to make us realize that beyond the supposed bedrock reality of individual happiness or unhappiness there is a social reality of creative fulfilment, or, failing that, of public duties faithfully carried out.

Larkin, in his unchecked personal despair, is a sacrificial goat with the sexual outlook of a stud bull. He thinks, and sometimes speaks, like a Robert Crumb character who has never recovered from being beaten up by a girl in the third grade. The best guess, and the least patronizing as well, is that Larkin held these poems back because he thought them self-indulgent – too private to be proportionate. One of the consolations that Larkin's work offers us is that we can be unhappy without giving in, without letting our wish to be off the hook ('Beneath it all, desire of oblivion runs') wipe out our lives ('the million-petalled flower/ Of being here'). The ordering of the individual volumes was clearly meant to preserve this balance, which the inclusion of even a few more of the suppressed poems would have tipped.

In the *Collected Poems*, that hard-fought-for poise is quite gone. Larkin now speaks a good deal less for us all, and a good deal more for himself, than was his plain wish. That the self, the sad, dithering personal condition from which all his triumphantly assured work sprang, is now more comprehensively on view is not really a full compensation, except, perhaps, to those who aren't comfortable with an idol unless its head is made from the same clay as its feet.

On the other hand, to be given, in whatever order, all these marvellous poems that were for so long unseen is a bonus for which only a dolt would be ungrateful. Schnabel said that Beethoven's late piano sonatas were music better than could be played. Larkin's best poems are poetry better than can be said, but sayability they sumptuously offer. Larkin demands to be read aloud. His big, intricately formed stanzas, often bridging from one to the next, defeat the single breath but always invite it. As you read, the ideal human voice speaks in your head. It isn't his: as his gramophone records prove, he sounded like someone who expects to be interrupted. It isn't yours, either. It's ours. Larkin had the gift of reuniting poetry at its most artful with ordinary speech at its most unstudied – at its least literary. Though a scholar to the roots, he was not being perverse when he posed as a simple man. He thought that art should be self-sufficient. He was disturbed by the way literary studies had crowded out literature. But none of this means that he was simplistic. Though superficially a reactionary crusader against modernism, a sort of latter-day, one-man Council of Trent, he knew exactly when to leave something unexplained.

The process of explaining him will be hard to stop now that this book is available. It is still, however, a tremendous book, and, finally, despite all the candour it apparently offers, the mystery will be preserved for any reader acute enough to sense the depth under the clarity. Pushkin said that everything was on his agenda, even the disasters. Larkin knew about himself. In private hours of anguish, he commiserated with himself. But he was an artist, and that meant he was everyone; and what made him a genius was the effort and resource he brought to bear in order to meet his superior responsibility.

Larkin went to hell, but not in a handcart. From his desolation he built masterpieces, and he was increasingly disinclined to settle for anything less. About twenty years ago in Britain, it became fashionable to say that all the poetic excitement was in America. Though things look less that way now, there is no need to be just as silly in the opposite direction. The English-speaking world is a unity. Britain and the United States might have difficulty absorbing each other's poetry, but most people have difficulty with poetry anyway. In Britain, Larkin shortened the distance between the people and poetry by doing nothing for his career and everything to compose artefacts that would have an independent, memorable life apart from himself. There is no inherent reason that the American reader, or any other English-speaking reader, should not be able to appreciate the results.

Art, if it knows how to wait, wins out. Larkin had patience. For him, poetry was a life sentence. He set happiness aside to make room for it. And if it turns out that he had no control over where his misery came from, doesn't that mean that he had even more control than we thought over where it went to? Art is no less real for being artifice. The moment of truth must be prepared for. 'Nothing to love or link with,' wrote Larkin when he was fifty-five. 'Nothing to catch or claim,' he wrote when he was twenty-four, in a poem that only now sees the light. It was as if the death he feared to the end he had embraced at the start, just so as to raise the stakes.

New Yorker, 17 July, 1989: previously included in *The Dreaming Swimmer*, 1992

2. On Larkin's Wit

Larkin at Sixty edited by Anthony Thwaite, Faber

There is no phrase in Philip Larkin's poetry which has not been turned, but then any poet tries to avoid flat writing, even at the cost of producing overwrought banality. Larkin's dedication to compressed resonance is best studied, in the first instance, through his prose. The prefaces to the reissues of *Jill* and *The North Ship* are full of sentences that make you smile at their neat richness even when they are not meant to be jokes, and that when they are meant to be jokes – as in the evocation of the young Kingsley Amis at Oxford in the preface to *Jill* – make you wish that the article went on as long as the book. But there is a whole book which does just that: *All What Jazz*, the collection of Larkin's *Daily Telegraph* jazz record review columns which was published in 1970. Having brought the book out, Faber seemed nervous about what to do with it next. I bought two copies marked down to 75p each in a Cardiff newsagent's and wish now that I had bought ten. I thought at the time that *All What Jazz* was the best available expression by the author himself of what he believed art to be. I still think so, and would contend in addition that no wittier book of criticism has ever been written.

To be witty does not necessarily mean to crack wise. In fact it usually means the opposite: wits rarely tell jokes. Larkin's prose flatters the reader by giving him as much as he can take in at one time. The delight caused has to do with collusion. Writer and reader are in cahoots. Larkin has the knack of donning cap and bells while still keeping his dignity. For years he feigned desperation before the task of conveying the real desperation induced in him by the saxophone playing of John Coltrane. The metaphors can be pursued through the book – they constitute by themselves a kind of extended solo, of which the summary sentence in the book's introductory essay should be regarded as the coda. 'With John Coltrane metallic and passionless nullity gave way to exercises in gigantic absurdity, great boring excursions on not-especially-attractive themes during which all possible changes were rung, extended investigations of oriental tedium, long-winded and portentous demonstrations of religiosity.' This final grandiose flourish was uttered in 1968.

But the opening note was blown in 1961, when Larkin, while yet prepared (cravenly, by his own later insistence) to praise Coltrane as a hard-thinking experimenter, referred to 'the vinegary drizzle of his tone'. In 1962 he was still in two minds, but you could already guess which mind was winning. 'Coltrane's records are, paradoxically, nearly always both interesting and boring, and I certainly find myself listening to them in preference to many a less adventurous set.' Notable at this stage is that he did not risk a metaphor, in which the truth would have more saliently protruded. In May 1963 there is only one mind left talking. To the eighth track of a Thelonius Monk album, 'John Coltrane contributes a solo of characteristic dreariness.'

By December of that same year Larkin's line on this topic has not only lost all its qualifications but acquired metaphorical force.

Coltrane is referred to as 'the master of the thinly disagreeable' who 'sounds as if he is playing for an audience of cobras'. This squares up well with the critic's known disgust that the joyous voicing of the old jazz should have so completely given way to 'the cobra-coaxing cacophonies of Calcutta'. In 1965 Larkin was gratified to discover that his opinion of Coltrane's achievement was shared by the great blues-shouter Jimmy Rushing. 'I don't think he can play his instrument' said Rushing. 'This', Larkin observed, 'accords very well with my own opinion that Coltrane sounds like nothing so much as a club bore who has been metamorphosed by a fellow-member of magical powers into a pair of bagpipes.' (Note Larkin's comic timing, incidentally: a less witty writer would have put 'metamorphosed into a pair of bagpipes by a fellow-member of magical powers', and so halved the effect.) Later in the same piece he expanded the attack into one of those generally pertinent critical disquisitions in which *All What Jazz* is so wealthy. 'His solos seem to me to bear the same relation to proper jazz solos as those drawings of running dogs, showing their legs in all positions so that they appear to have about fifty of them, have to real drawings. Once, they are amusing and even instructive. But the whole point of drawing is to choose the right line, not drawing fifty alternatives. Again, Coltrane's choice and treatment of themes is hypnotic, repetitive, monotonous: he will rock backwards and forwards between two chords for five minutes, or pull a tune to pieces like someone subtracting petals from a flower.' Later in the piece there is an atavistic gesture towards giving the Devil his due, but by the vividness of his chosen figures of speech the critic has already shown what he really thinks.

'I can thoroughly endorse', wrote Larkin in July 1966, 'the sleeve of John Coltrane's *Ascension* (HMV), which says "This record cannot be loved or understood in one sitting." ' In November of the same year he greeted Coltrane's religious suite *Meditations* as 'the most astounding piece of ugliness I have ever heard'. After Coltrane's death in 1977 Larkin summed up the departed hero's career. ' . . . I do not remember ever suggesting that his music was anything but a pain between the ears . . . Was I wrong?' In fact, as we have seen, Larkin had once allowed himself to suggest that the noises Coltrane made might at least be interesting, but by now tentativeness had long given way to a kind of fury, as of someone defending a principle against his own past weakness. 'That reedy, catarrhal tone . . . that insolent egotism, leading to 45-minute versions of "My Favourite Things" until, at any rate in Britain, the audience walked out, no doubt wondering why they had ever walked in . . . pretension as a way of life . . . wilful and hideous distortion of tone that offered squeals, squeaks, Bronx cheers and throttled slate-pencil noises for serious consideration . . . dervish-like heights of hysteria.' It should be remembered, if this sounds like a grave being danced on, that Larkin's was virtually the sole dissenting critical voice. Coltrane died in triumph and Larkin had every right to think at the time that to express any doubts about the stature of the deceased genius was to whistle against the wind.

The whole of *All What Jazz* is a losing battle. Larkin is arguing in support of entertainment at a time when entertainment was steadily yielding ground to portentous significance. His raillery against the saxophonists is merely the most strident expression of a general argument which he goes on elaborating as its truth becomes more clear to himself. In a quieter way he became progressively disillusioned with Miles Davis. In January 1962 it was allowed that in an informal atmosphere Davis could produce music 'very far from the egg-walking hushedness' he was given to in the studio. In October of the same year Larkin gave him points for bonhomie. 'According to the sleeve, Davis actually smiled twice at the audience during the evening and there is indeed a warmth about the entire proceedings that makes this a most enjoyable LP.' But by the time of *Seven Steps to Heaven* a year later, Davis has either lost what little attraction he had or else Larkin has acquired the courage of his convictions. ' . . . his lifeless muted tone, at once hollow and unresonant, creeps along only just in tempo, the ends of the notes hanging down like Dali watches . . .' In 1964, Larkin begged to dissent from the enthusiastic applause recorded on the live album *Miles Davis in Europe*. ' . . . the fact that he can spend seven or eight minutes playing "Autumn Leaves" without my recognizing or liking the tune confirms my view of him as a master of rebarbative boredom.' A year later he was reaching for the metaphors. 'I freely confess that there have been times recently, when almost anything – the shape of a patch on the ceiling, a recipe for rhubarb jam read upside down in the paper – has seemed to me more interesting than the passionless creep of a Miles Davis trumpet solo.' But in this case the opening blast was followed by a climb-down. 'Davis is his usual bleak self, his notes

wilting at the edges as if with frost, spiky at up-tempos, and while
he is still not my ideal of comfortable listening his talent is clearly
undiminished.' This has the cracked chime of a compromise. The
notes, though wilting as if with frost instead of like Dali watches, are
nevertheless still wilting, and it is clear from the whole drift of
Larkin's criticism that he places no value on uncomfortable listening
as such. A 1966 review sounds more straightforward. ' . . . for me it
was an experience in pure duration. Some of it must have been quite
hard to do.'

But in Larkin's prose the invective which implies values is always
matched by the encomium which states them plainly. He jokes less
when praising than when attacking but the attention he pays to
evocation is even more concentrated. The poem 'For Sidney Bechet'
('On me your voice falls as they say love should,/ Like an enormous
yes') can be matched for unforced reverence in the critical prose:
' . . . the marvellous "Blue Horizon", six choruses of slow blues in
which Bechet climbs without interruption or hurry from lower to
upper register, his clarinet tone at first thick and throbbing, then
soaring like Melba in an extraordinary blend of lyricism and power
that constituted the unique Bechet voice, commanding attention the
instant it sounded.' He is similarly eloquent about the 'fire and
shimmer' of Bix Beiderbecke and of the similes he attaches to Pee
Wee Russell there is no end – Russell's clarinet seems to function in
Larkin's imagination as a kind of magic flute.

The emphasis, in Larkin's admiration for all these artists, is on
the simplicity at the heart of their creative endeavour. What they do
would not have its infinite implications if it did not spring from
elementary emotion. It can be argued that Larkin is needlessly dismissive of Duke Ellington and Charlie Parker. There is plenty of
evidence to warrant including him in the school of thought known
among modern jazz buffs as 'mouldy fig'. But there is nothing retro-
grade about the aesthetic underlying his irascibility. The same
aesthetic underlies his literary criticism and everything else he writes.
Especially it underlies his poetry. Indeed it is not even an aesthetic:
it is a world view, of the kind which invariably forms the basis of
any great artistic personality. Modernism, according to Larkin, 'helps
us neither to enjoy nor endure'. He defines modernism as intellectualized art. Against intellectualism he proposes, not anti-intellectualism
– which would be just another coldly willed programme – but trust

in the validity of emotion. What the true artist says from instinct, the true critic will hear by the same instinct. There may be more than instinct involved, but nothing real will be involved without it.

> The danger, therefore, of assuming that everything played today in jazz has a seed of solid worth stems from the fact that so much of it is tentative, experimental, private . . . And for this reason one has to fall back on the old dictum that a critic is only as good as his ear. His ear will tell him instantly whether a piece of music is vital, musical, exciting, or cerebral, mock-academic, dead, long before he can read Don DeMichael on the subject, or learn that it is written in inverted nineteenths, or in the Stygian mode, or recorded at the NAACP Festival at Little Rock. He must hold on to the principle that the only reason for praising a work is that it pleases, and the way to develop his critical sense is to be more acutely aware of whether he is being pleased or not.

What Larkin might have said on his own behalf is that critical prose can be subjected to the same test. His own criticism appeals so directly to the ear that he puts himself in danger of being thought trivial, especially by the mock-academic. Like Amis's, Larkin's readability seems so effortless that it tends to be thought of as something separate from his intelligence. But readability *is* intelligence. The vividness of Larkin's critical style is not just a token of his seriousness but the embodiment of it. His wit is there not only in the cutting jokes but in the steady work of registering his interest. It is easy to see that he is being witty when he says that Miles Davis and Ornette Coleman stand in evolutionary relationship to each other 'like green apples and stomach-ache'. But he is being equally witty when he mentions Ruby Braff's 'peach-fed' cornet. A critic's language is not incidental to him: its intensity is a sure measure of his engagement and a persuasive hint at the importance of what he is engaged with.

A critical engagement with music is one of the several happy coincidences which unite Larkin's career with Montale's. If Larkin's *Listen* articles on poetry were to be reprinted the field of comparison would be even more instructive, since there are good reasons for thinking that these two poets come up with remarkably similar conclusions when thinking about the art they practise. On music they often sound like the same man talking. Montale began his artistic career as a trained opera singer and his main area of musical criticism has always been classical music, but he writes about it the same way Larkin writes about jazz, with unfaltering intelligibility, a complete trust in his own ear, and a deep suspicion of any work which draws inspiration from its own technique. In Italy his collected music criticism is an eagerly awaited book, but then in Italy nobody is surprised that a great poet should have written a critical column for so many years of his life. Every educated Italian knows that Montale's music notices are all of a piece with the marvellous body of literary criticism collected in *Auto da fé* and *Sulla poesia*, and that his whole critical corpus is the natural complement to his poetry. In Britain the same connection is harder to make, even though Larkin has deservedly attained a comparable position as a national poet. In Britain the simultaneous pursuit of poetry and regular critical journalism is regarded as versatility at best. The essential unity of Larkin's various activities is not much remarked.

But if we do not remark it we miss half of his secret. While maintaining an exalted idea of the art he practises, Larkin never thinks of it as an inherently separate activity from the affairs of everyday. He has no special poetic voice. What he brings out is the poetry that is already in the world. He has cherished the purity of his own first responses. Like all great artists he has never lost touch with the child in his own nature. The language of even the most intricately wrought Larkin poem is already present in recognizable embryo when he describes the first jazz musicians ever to capture his devotion. 'It was the drummer I concentrated on, sitting as he did on a raised platform behind a battery of cowbells, temple blocks, cymbals, tomtoms and (usually) a Chinese gong, his drums picked out in flashing crimson or ultramarine brilliants.' There are good grounds for calling Larkin a pessimist, but it should never be forgotten that the most depressing details in the poetry are seen with the same eye that loved those drums. The proof is in the unstinting vitality of language.

As in the criticism, so in the poetry, wit can be divided usefully into two kinds, humorous and plain. There is not much need to rehearse the first kind. Most of us have scores of Larkin's lines, hemistiches and phrases in our heads, to make us smile whenever we think of them, which is as often as the day changes. I can remember the day in 1962 when I first opened *The Less Deceived* and was snared by a line in the first poem, 'Lines on a Young Lady's

Photograph Album'. 'Not quite your class, I'd say, dear, on the whole.'
What a perfectly timed pentameter! How subtly and yet how unmistakably it defined the jealousy of the speaker! Who on earth was
Philip Larkin? Dozens of subsequent lines in the same volume made
it clearer: he was a supreme master of language levels, snapping into
and out of a tone of voice as fast as it could be done without losing
the reader. Bringing the reader in on it – the deep secret of popular
seriousness. Larkin brought the reader in on it even at the level of
prosodic technique.

> Flagged, and the figurehead with golden tits
> Arching our way, it never anchors; it's . . .

He got you smiling at a rhyme. 'Church Going' had the ruin-
bibber, randy for antique, 'Toads' had the pun on Shakespeare, 'Stuff
your pension!' being the stuff dreams are made on. You couldn't get
halfway through the book without questioning, and in many cases
revising, your long-nursed notions about poetic language. Here was
a disciplined yet unlimited variety of tone, a scrupulosity that could
contain anything, an all-inclusive decorum.

In *The Whitsun Weddings*, 'Mr Bleaney' has the Bodies and
'Naturally The Foundation Will Bear Your Expenses' has the ineffable Mr Lal. 'Sunny Prestatyn' features Titch Thomas and in 'Wild
Oats' a girl painfully reminiscent of Margaret in *Lucky Jim* is finally
shaken loose 'after about five rehearsals'. In 'Essential Beauty' 'the
trite untransferable/ Truss-advertisement, truth' takes you back to
the cobra-coaxing cacophonies of Calcutta, not to mention forward
to Amis's nitwit not fit to shift shit. Even *High Windows*, the bleakest
of Larkin's slim volumes, has things to make you laugh aloud. In
'The Card-Players' Jan van Hogspeuw and Old Prijck perhaps verge
on the coarse but Jake Balakowsky, the hero of 'Posterity', has already
entered the gallery of timeless academic portraits, along with Professor Welch and the History Man. 'Vers de Société' has the 'bitch/
Who's read nothing but *Which*'. In Larkin's three major volumes of
poetry the jokes on their own would be enough to tell you that wit
is alive and working.

But it is working far more pervasively than that. Larkin's poetry
is *all* witty – which is to say that there is none of his language
which does not confidently rely on the intelligent reader's capacity
to apprehend its play of tone. On top of the scores of fragments that

make us laugh, there are the hundreds which we constantly recall with a welcome sense of communion, as if our own best thoughts had been given their most concise possible expression. If Auden was right about the test of successful writing being how often the reader thinks of it, Larkin passed long ago. To quote even the best examples would be to fill half this book, but perhaps it will bear saying again, this time in the context of his poetry, that between Larkin's humorous wit and his plain wit there is no discontinuity. Only the man who invented the golden tits could evoke the black-sailed unfamiliar. To be able to make fun of the randy ruin-bibber is the necessary qualification for writing the magnificent last stanza of 'Church Going'. You need to have been playfully alliterative with the trite untransferable truss-advertisement before you can be lyrically alliterative with the supine stationary voyage of the dead lovers in 'An Arundel Tomb'. There is a level of seriousness which only those capable of humour can reach.

Similarly there is a level of maturity which only those capable of childishness can reach. The lucent comb of 'The Building' can be seen by us only because it has been so intensely seen by Larkin, and it has been so intensely seen by him only because his eyes, behind those thick glasses, retain the naive curiosity which alone makes the adult gaze truly penetrating. Larkin's poetry draws a bitterly sad picture of modern life but it is full of saving graces, and they are invariably as disarmingly recorded as in a child's diary. The paddling at the seaside, the steamer in the afternoon, the ponies at Show Saturday – they are all done with crayons and coloured pencils. He did not put away childish things and it made him more of a man. It did the same for Montale: those who have ever read about the amulet in 'Dora Markus' or the children with tin swords in *Caffè a Rapallo* are unlikely to forget them when they read Larkin. A third name could be added: Mandelstam. When Mandelstam forecast his own death he willed that his spirit should be resurrected in the form of children's games. All three poets represent, for their respective countrymen, the distilled lyricism of common speech. With all three poets the formal element is highly developed – in the cases of Larkin and Mandelstam to the uppermost limit possible – and yet none of them fails to reassure his readers, even during the most intricately extended flight of verbal music, that the tongue they speak is the essential material of his rhythmic and melodic resource.

In Philip Larkin's non-poetic poetic language, the language of extremely well-written prose, despair is expressed through beauty and becomes beautiful too. His argument is with himself and he is bound to lose. He can call up death more powerfully than almost any other poet ever has, but he does so in the commanding voice of life. His linguistic exuberance is the heart of him. Joseph Brodsky, writing about Mandelstam, called lyricism the ethics of language. Larkin's wit is the ethics of his poetry. It brings his distress under our control. It makes his personal unhappiness our universal exultation. Armed with his wit, he faces the worst on our behalf, and brings it to order. A romantic sensibility classically disciplined, he is, in the only sense of the word likely to last, modern after all. By rebuilding the ruined bridge between poetry and the general reading public he has given his art a future, and you can't get more modern than that.

1981: previously included in *From the Land of Shadows*, 1982

3. Don Juan in Hull

i. WOLVES OF MEMORY

Larkin collections come out at the rate of one per decade: *The North Ship*, 1945; *The Less Deceived*, 1955; *The Whitsun Weddings*, 1964; *High Windows*, 1974. Not exactly a torrent of creativity: just the best. In Italy the reading public is accustomed to cooling its heels for even longer. Their top man, Eugenio Montale, has produced only five main collections, and he got started a good deal earlier. But that, in both countries, is the price one has to pay. For both poets the parsimony is part of the fastidiousness. Neither writes an unconsidered line.

Now that the latest Larkin, *High Windows*, is finally available, it is something of a shock to find in it some poems one doesn't recognize. Clipping the poems out of magazines has failed to fill the bill – there were magazines one hadn't bargained for. As well as that, there is the surprise of finding that it all adds up even better than one had expected: the poems which one had thought of as characteristic turn out to be more than that – or rather the *character* turns out to be more than that. Larkin has never liked the idea of an artist Developing. Nor has he himself done so. But he has managed to go on clarifying what he was sent to say. The total impression of *High Windows* is of despair made beautiful. Real despair and real beauty, with not a trace of posturing in either. The book is the peer of the previous two mature collections, and if they did not exist would be just as astonishing. But they do exist (most of us could recognize any line from either one) and can't help rendering many of the themes in this third book deceptively familiar.

I think that in most of the poems here collected Larkin's ideas are being reinforced or deepened rather than repeated. But from time to time a certain predictability of form indicates that a previous discovery is being unearthed all over again. Such instances aren't difficult to spot, and it would be intemperate to betray delight at doing so. Larkin's 'forgeries' (Auden's term for self-plagiarisms) are very few. He is more original from poem to poem than almost any modern poet one can think of. His limitations, such as they are, lie deeper than that. Here again, it is not wise to be happy about spotting them. Without the limitations there would be no Larkin – the beam cuts *because* it's narrow.

It has always seemed to me a great pity that Larkin's more intelligent critics should content themselves with finding his view of life circumscribed. It is, but it is also bodied forth as art to a remarkable degree. There is a connection between the circumscription and the poetic intensity, and it's no surprise that the critics who can't see the connection can't see the separation either. They seem to think that just because the poet is (self-admittedly) emotionally wounded, the poetry is wounded too. There is always the suggestion that Larkin might handle his talent better if he were a more well-rounded character. That Larkin's gift might be part and parcel of his own peculiar nature isn't a question they have felt called upon to deal with. The whole fumbling dereliction makes you wonder if perhaps the literati in this country haven't had things a bit easy. A crash-course in, say, art criticism could in most cases be recommended. Notions that Michelangelo would have painted more feminine-looking sibyls if he had been less bent, or that Toulouse-Lautrec might have been less obsessive about Jane Avril's dancing if his legs had been longer, would at least possess the merit of being self-evidently absurd. But the brain-wave about Larkin's quirky negativism, and the consequent trivialization of his lyrical knack, is somehow able to go on sounding profound.

It ought to be obvious that Larkin is not a universal poet in the thematic sense – in fact, he is a self-proclaimed stranger to a good half, *the* good half, of life. You wonder what a critic who complains of this imagines he is praising when he allows that Larkin is still pretty good anyway, perhaps even great. What's missing in Larkin doesn't just tend to be missing, it's glaringly, achingly, unarguably *missing*. But the poetry is all there. The consensus about his stature is consequently encouraging, even if accomplished at the cost of a majority of its adherents misunderstanding what is really going on. At least they've got the right man.

*

The first poem in the book, 'To the Sea', induces a fairly heavy effect of *déjà lu*. Aren't we long used to that massive four-stanza form, that conjectural opening ('To step over the low wall . . .') in the infinitive? Actually we aren't: he's never used them before. It's the tone that's reminiscent, and the tactics. The opening takes us back to the child-hood and the lost chance of happiness, the shots that all fell wide –

> The miniature gaiety of seasides.

In the familiar way, sudden brutalities of diction bite back a remembered sweetness –

> A white steamer stuck in the afternoon.

Alienation is declared firmly as the memories build up –

> Strange to it now, I watch the cloudless scene:

Details well up in the mind with Proustian specificity –

> ... and then the cheap cigars,
> The chocolate-papers, tea-leaves, and, between
> The rocks, the rusting soup-tins . . .

The mind, off guard, unmanned by recollection, lets slip the delicately expressed lyrical image –

> The white steamer has gone. Like breathed-on glass
> The sunlight has turned milky.

Whereupon, as in 'Church Going' or 'The Whitsun Weddings', the poem winds up in a sententious coda.

> . . . If the worst
> Of flawless weather is our falling short
> It may be that through habit these do best,
> Coming to water clumsily undressed
> Yearly, teaching their children by a sort
> Of clowning; helping the old, too, as they ought.

The happiness we once thought we could have can't be had, but simple people who stick to time-honoured habits probably get the best approximation of it. Larkin once said that if he were called in to construct a religion he would make use of water. Well, here it is, lapping at the knobbled feet of unquestioning plebs. Such comfort as the poem offers the reader resides in the assurance that this old habit of going to the seaside is 'still going on', even if reader and writer no longer share it. A cold comfort, as always. Larkin tries, he has said, to preserve experience both for himself and for others, but his first responsibility is to the experience.

The next big poem is the famous three-part effort that appeared in the *Observer*, 'Livings'. A galley-proof of it is still folded into the back of my copy of *The Less Deceived*. I think it an uncanny piece of work. The proof is read to shreds, and I can still remember the day I picked it up in the office. Larkin had the idea – preserved, in concentrated form, in one of the poems in this volume, 'Posterity' – that a young American Ph.D. student called Jake Balokowsky is all set to wrap him up in an uncomprehending thesis. The first part of 'Livings' is full of stuff that Balokowsky is bound to get wrong. The minor businessman who annually books himself into 'the —Hotel in ——ton for three days' speaks a vocabulary as well-rubbed and subtly anonymous as an old leather couch. Balokowsky will latch on well enough to the idea that the poem's narrator is a slave to habit,

> . . . wondering why
> I keep on coming. It's not worth it. Father's dead:
> He used to, but the business now is mine.
> It's time for change, in nineteen twenty-nine.

What Jake will probably miss, however, is the value placed on the innocuous local newspaper, the worn décor, the ritual chat, the non-challenging pictures and the ex-Army sheets. It's dependable, it's a living, and 'living' is not a word Larkin tosses around lightly. Judging the narrator is the last thing Larkin is doing. On the contrary, he's looking for his secret. To be used to comfort is an enviable condition. Beer, whisky, cigars and silence – the privileges of the old mercantile civilization which Larkin has been quietly celebrating most of his life, a civilization in which a place like Leeds or Hull (see 'Friday Night in the Royal Station Hotel') counts as a capital city. There *is* another and bigger life, but Larkin doesn't underestimate this one for a minute.

In fact he conjures it up all over again in the third part of the poem. The setting this time is Oxford, probably in the late 17th century. The beverage is port instead of whisky, and the talk, instead of with wages, tariffs and stock, deals with advowsons, resurrections and regicide. Proofs of God's existence lie uncontested on dusty bookshelves. 'The bells discuss the hour's gradations.' Once again the feeling of indoor warmth is womb-like. Constellations sparkle over the roofs, matching the big sky draining down the estuary in Part I.

The central poem of the trio squirms like a cat caught between two cushions. Its narrator is conducting a lone love-affair with the sea.

> Rocks writhe back to sight.
> Mussels, limpets,
> Husband their tenacity
> In the freezing slither—
> Creatures, I cherish you!

The narrator's situation is not made perfectly clear. While wanting to be just the reverse, Larkin can on occasion be a difficult poet, and here, I think, is a case of over-refinement leading to obscurity. (Elsewhere in this volume 'Sympathy in White Major' is another instance, and I have never been able to understand 'Dry Point' in

The Less Deceived.) My guess – and a guess is not as good as an intelligent deduction – is that the speaker is a lighthouse keeper. The way the snow ('O loose moth world') swerves against the black water, and the line 'Guarded by brilliance', seem somehow to suggest that: that, or something similar. Anyway, whoever he is, the narrator is right in among the elements, watching the exploding sea and the freezing slither from seventy feet up on a stormy night. But we see at the end that he, too, is safe indoors. On the radio he hears of elsewhere. He sets out his plate and spoon, cherishing his loneliness. In this central panel of his triptych, it seems to me, Larkin is saying that the civilizations described in the side-panels – one decaying, the other soon to lose its confidence – have an essence, and that this is it. The essence can be preserved in the soul of a man on his own. This is not to suggest that there is anything consolingly positive under Larkin's well-known negativism: the only consoling thing about Larkin is the quality of his art.

*

'High Windows', the next stand-out poem, shows an emotional progression Larkin had already made us used to.

> When I see a couple of kids
> And guess he's fucking her and she's
> Taking pills or wearing a diaphragm,
> I know this is paradise . . .

Larkin is a master of language-levels and eminently qualified to use coarse language for shock effects. He never does, however. Strong language in Larkin is put in not to shock the reader but to define the narrator's personality. When Larkin's narrator in 'A Study of Reading Habits' (in *The Whitsun Weddings*) said 'Books are a load of crap' there were critics – some of them, incredibly, among his more appreciative – who allowed themselves to believe that Larkin was expressing his own opinion. (Kingsley Amis had the same kind of trouble, perhaps from the same kind of people, when he let Jim Dixon cast aspersions on Mozart.) It should be obvious at long last, however, that the diction describes the speaker. When the speaker is close to representing Larkin himself, the diction defines which Larkin it is – what mood he is in. Larkin is no hypocrite and has expressed envy of young lovers too often to go back on it here. The word 'fucking' is a conscious brutalism, a protective way of not conjuring up what's meant. However inevitable it might be that Jake Balokowsky will identify this opening sentiment as a Muggeridgean gesture of contempt, it is incumbent on us to realize that something more interesting is going on.

Everyone young is going down 'the long slide' to happiness. The narrator argues that his own elders must have thought the same about him, who was granted freedom from the fear of Hellfire in the same way that the kids are granted freedom from the fear of pregnancy. But (and here comes the clincher) attaining either freedom means no more than being lifted up to a high window, through which you see

> ... the deep blue air, that shows
> Nothing, and is nowhere, and is endless.

There is no doubt that the narrator is calling these callous sexual activities meaningless. What's open to doubt is whether the narrator believes what he is saying, or, given that he does, whether Larkin (wheels within wheels) believes the narrator. Later in the volume there is a poem called 'Annus Mirabilis' which clearly contradicts the argument of 'High Windows'.

> Sexual intercourse began
> In nineteen sixty-three
> (Which was rather late for me)—
> Between the end of the Chatterley ban
> And the Beatles' first LP.

Evincing an unexpected sensitivity to tone, Jake could well detect an ironic detachment here. To help him out, there is a suggestion, in the third stanza, that the new liberty was merely license.

> And every life became
> A brilliant breaking of the bank,
> A quite unlosable game.

It all links up with the bleak view of 'High Windows'. What Jake might not spot, however, is that it contrasts more than it compares. 'Annus Mirabilis' *is* a jealous poem – the fake-naive rhythms are there for self-protection as much as for ironic detachment. Larkin can't help believing that sex and love ought by rights to have been easier things for his generation, and far easier for him personally. The feeling of having missed out on something is one of his preoccupations. The thing Balokowsky needs to grasp is that Larkin is not criticizing modern society from a position of superiority. Over the range of his poetry, if not always in individual poems, he is very careful to allow that these pleasures might very well be thought meaningful. That he himself finds them meaningless might have something to do with himself as well as the state of the world. To the reader who has Larkin's poetry by heart, no poet seems more open. Small wonder that he finds it simply incomprehensible when critics discuss his lack of emotion. Apart from an outright yell for help, he has sent every distress signal a shy man can.

*

'The Old Fools' – even the ex-editor of the *Listener* blew his cool over that one, billing it as 'marvellous' on the paper's mast-head. And marvellous it is, although very scary. There is a pronounced technical weakness in the first stanza. It is all right to rhyme 'remember' with 'September' if you make it quite clear why September can't be July. Does it mean that the Old Fools were in the Home Guard in September 1939? It's hard to know. Apart from that one point, though, the poem is utterly and distressingly explicit. Once again, the brutalism of the opening diction is a tip-off to the narrator's state of mind, which is, this time, fearful.

> What do they think has happened, the old fools,
> To make them like this? Do they somehow suppose
> It's more grown-up when your mouth hangs open and drools . . .

Ill-suppressed anger. The crack about supposing 'it's more grown-up' is a copybook example of Larkin's ability to compact his intelligibility without becoming ambiguous. Supposing something to be 'more grown-up' is something children do: ergo, the Old Fools are like children – one of the poem's leading themes stated in a single locution.

> Why aren't they screaming?

Leaving the reader to answer: because they don't know what's happening to them. The narrator's real fears – soon he switches to a personal 'you' – are for himself. The second stanza opens with an exultant lyrical burst: stark terror never sounded lovelier.

> At death, you break up: the bits that were you
> Start speeding away from each other for ever
> With no one to see. It's only oblivion, true:
> We had it before, but then it was going to end,
> And was all the time merging with a unique endeavour
> To bring to bloom the million-petalled flower
> Of being here.

The old, he goes on to suggest, probably live not in the here and now but 'where all happened once'. The idea takes some of its force from our awareness that that's largely where Larkin lives already – only his vision could lead to this death. The death is terrifying, but we would have to be like Larkin to share the terror completely. The reader tends to find himself shut out, glad that Larkin can speak so beautifully in his desperation but sorry that he should see the end in terms of his peculiar loneliness. There is always the edifying possibility, however, that Larkin is seeing the whole truth and the reader's defence mechanisms are working full blast.

*

If they are, 'The Building' will quickly break them down. Here, I think, is the volume's masterpiece – an absolute chiller, which I find myself getting by heart despite a pronounced temperamental aversion. The Building is the house of death, a Dantesque hell-hole – one thinks particularly of *Inferno* V – where people 'at that vague age that claims/ The end of choice, the last of hope' are sent to 'their appointed levels'. The ambience is standard modernist hum-drum: paperbacks, tea, rows of steel chairs like an airport lounge. You can look down into the yard and see red brick, lagged pipes, traffic. But the smell is frightening. In time everyone will find a nurse beckoning to him. The dead lie in white rows somewhere above. This, says Larkin with an undeflected power unique even for him, is what it all really adds up to. Life is a dream and we awake to this reality.

> O world.
> Your loves, your chances, are beyond the stretch
> Of any hand from here ! And so, unreal,

> A touching dream to which we all are lulled
> But wake from separately. In it, conceits
> And self-protecting ignorance congeal
> To carry life . . .

There is no point in disagreeing with the man if that's the way he feels, and he wouldn't write a poem like 'The Building' if he didn't feel that way to the point of daemonic possession. He himself is well aware that there are happier ways of viewing life. It's just that he is incapable of sharing them, except for fleeting moments – and the fleeting moments do not accumulate, whereas the times in between them do. The narrator says that 'nothing contravenes/ The coming dark'. It's an inherently less interesting proposition than its opposite, and a poet forced to devote his creative effort to embodying it has only a small amount of space to work in. Nor, within the space, is he free from the paradox that his poems will become part of life, not death. From that paradox, we gain. The desperation of 'The Building' is like the desperation of Leopardi, disconsolate yet doomed to being beautiful. The advantage which accrues is one of purity – a hopeless affirmation is the only kind we really want to hear when we feel, as sooner or later everybody must, that life is a trap.

There is no certain way of separating Larkin's attitude to society from his conception of himself, but to the extent that you can, he seems to be in two minds about what the world has come to. He thinks, on the one hand, that it's probably all up; and on the other hand that youth still has a chance. On the theme of modern life being an unmitigated and steadily intensifying catastrophe he reads like his admired Betjeman in a murderous mood – no banana blush or cheery telly teeth, just a tight-browed disdain and a toxic line of invective. 'Going, Going' is particularly instructive here. In 'How Distant' we hear about

> . . . the departure of young men
> Down valleys, or watching
> The green shore past the salt-white cordage
> Rising and falling

Between the 'fraying cliffs of water' (always a good sign when there's a lot of water about) the young adventurers used to sail, in the time of what we might call *genuine newness*. Larkin's objections to modern innovation are centred on its lack of invention – it's all fatally predictable. Jimmy Porter was nostalgic for the future. Larkin is anticipatory about the past. He longs for the time when youth meant the possibility of a new start.

> This is being young,
> Assumption of the startled century
> Like new store clothes,
> The huge decisions printed out by feet
> Inventing where they tread,
> The random windows conjuring a street.

The implication being that the time of adventure is long over. But in 'Sad Steps', as the poet addresses the Moon, youth is allowed some hope.

> One shivers slightly, looking up there.
> The hardness and the brightness and the plain
> Far-reaching singleness of that wide stare
>
> Is a reminder of the strength and pain
> Of being young; that it can't come again,
> But is for others undiminished somewhere.

An elegantly cadenced admission that his own view of life might be neurotic, and excellent fuel for Jake's chapter on the dialectical element in Larkin in which it is pointed out that his poems are judiciously disposed in order to illuminate one another, Yeats-style. The Sun and Moon, like Water, bring out Larkin's expansiveness, such as it is. It's there, but you couldn't call it a bear-hug. Time is running out, as we hear in the wonderfully funny Vers de Société:

> Only the young can be alone freely.
> The time is shorter now for company,
> And sitting by a lamp more often brings
> Not peace, but other things.

Visions of The Building, for example.

The book ends on an up-beat. Its next to last poem, 'Show Saturday', is an extended, sumptuous evocation of country life ('Let it always be there') which has the effect of making the rural goings-on so enviably cosy that the reader feels almost as left out as the narrator. The final piece is an eerie lyric called 'The Explosion', featuring the ghosts of miners walking from the sun towards their waiting wives. It is a superb thought superbly expressed, and Larkin almost believes in it, just as in 'An Arundel Tomb' (the closing poem of *The Whitsun Weddings*) he almost believed in the survival of love. Almost believing is all right, once you've got believing out of it. But faith itself is extinct. Larkin loves and inhabits tradition as much as Betjeman does, but artistically he had already let go of it when others were only just realizing it was time to cling on. Larkin is the poet of the void. The one affirmation his work offers is the possibility that when we have lost everything the problem of beauty will still remain. It's enough.

ii. SMALLER AND CLEARER

Philip Larkin once told Philip Oakes – in a *Sunday Times* Magazine profile which remains one of the essential articles on its subject – how he was going to be a novelist, until the novels stopped coming. First there was *Jill* in 1946, and then there was *A Girl in Winter* in 1947, and after those there were to be several more. But they never arrived. So Philip Larkin became the leading poet who once wrote a brace of novels, just as his friend Kingsley Amis became the leading novelist who occasionally writes poems: the creative labour was divided with the customary English decorum, providing the kind of simplified career-structures with which literary history prefers to deal.

It verges on the unmannerly to raise the point, in Larkin's case, that the novels were in no sense the work of someone who had still to find his vocation. Chronology insists that they were written at a time when his verse had not yet struck its tone – *The North Ship*, Larkin's mesmerized submission to Yeats, had only recently been published, and of *The Less Deceived*, his first mature collection, barely half the constituent poems had as yet been written. But the novels had struck *their* tone straight away. It is only now, by hindsight, that they seem to point forward to the poetry. Taken in their chronology, they are impressively mature and self-sufficient. If Larkin had never written a line of verse, his place as a writer would still have been secure. It would have been a smaller place than he now occupies, but still more substantial than that of, say, Denton Welch, an equivalently precocious (though nowhere near as perceptive) writer of the same period.

The self-sufficient force of Larkin's two novels is attested to by the fact that they have never quite gone away. People serious in their admiration of Larkin's poetry have usually found themselves searching out at least one of them – most commonly *Jill*, to which Larkin prefixed, in the 1964 edition, an introduction that seductively evoked the austere but ambitious Oxford of his brilliant generation and in particular was creasingly funny about Amis. Unfortunately this preface (retained in the current paperback) implies, by its very retrospection, a status of obsolescence for the book itself. Yet the present reissue sufficiently proves that *Jill* needs no apologizing for. And *A Girl in Winter* is at least as good as *Jill* and in some departments conspicuously better. Either novel is guaranteed to jolt any reader who expects Larkin to look clumsy out of his bailiwick. There are times when Larkin *does* look that, but they usually happen when he tempts himself into offering a professional rule of thumb as an aesthetic principle – a practice which can lay him open to charges of cranky insularity. None of that here. In fact quite the other thing: the novels are at ease with a range of sympathies that the later poems, even the most magnificent ones, deal with only piecemeal, although with incomparably more telling effect.

Considering that Evelyn Waugh began a comic tradition in the modern novel which only lately seems in danger of dying out, and considering Larkin's gift for sardonic comedy – a gift which by all accounts decisively influenced his contemporaries at Oxford – it is remarkable how non-comic his novels are, how completely they do not fit into the family of talents which includes Waugh and Powell and Amis. *Jill* employs many of the same properties as an Oxford novel by the young Waugh – the obscure young hero is casually destroyed by his socially superior contemporaries – but the treatment is unrelievedly sad. Larkin's hero has none of the inner strength which Amis gave Jim Dixon. Nor is there any sign of the Atkinson figures who helped Jim through the tougher parts of the maze. Young John comes up to Oxford lost and stays lost: he is not a symbol of his social condition so much as an example of how his social condition can amplify a handicap – shy ordinariness – into tragedy. All the materials of farce are present and begging to be used, but tragedy is what Larkin aims for and what he largely achieves.

The crux of the matter is John's love for Jill – a thousand dreams and one kiss. Jill is a clear forecast of the Larkin dream-girl in the poems. But if John is Larkin, he is hardly the Larkin we know to have dominated his generation at Oxford. He is someone much closer to the author's central self, the wounded personality whose deprivation has since been so clearly established in the poems. What is remarkable, however (and the same thing is remarkable about the poems, but rarely comes into question), is the way in which the hero's desolation is viewed in its entirety by the author. The author sees the whole character from without. The novel does something which very few novels by 21-year-old writers have ever done. It distances autobiographical material and sets events in the global view of mature personality.

As if to prove the point, *A Girl in Winter* is a similar story of callow love, but seen from the girl's angle. The book perfectly catches the way a young woman's emotional maturity outstrips a young man's. Katherine, a young European grappling with England (an inversion of the Larkin-Amis nightmare in which the Englishman is obliged to grapple with Europe), is morally perceptive – sensitive would be the right word if it did not preclude robustness – to an unusual degree, yet Larkin is able to convince us that she is no freak. While still an adolescent she falls in love with her English pen-pal, Robin, without realizing that it is Robin's sister, Jane, who is really interested in her. Time sorts out the tangle, but just when Katherine has fallen out of love Robin shows up on the off-chance of sleeping with her. Katherine quells his importunity with a few apposite remarks likely to make any male reader sweat from the palms, although finally she sleeps with him because it's less trouble than not to. Yet Katherine is allowed small comfort in her new maturity. The book is as disconsolate as its predecessor, leaving the protagonist once again facing an unsatisfactory prime.

A contributory grace in both novels, but outstanding in *A Girl in Winter*, is the sheer quality of the writing. Larkin told Oakes that he wrote the books like poems, carefully eliminating repeated words. Fastidiousness is everywhere and flamboyance non-existent: the touch is unfaltering. Katherine 'could sense his interest turning towards her, as a blind man might sense the switching on of an electric fire'.

Figures of speech are invariably as quiet and effective as that. The last paragraphs of *A Girl in Winter* have something of the cadenced elegance you find at the close of *The Great Gatsby*.

Why, if Larkin could write novels like these, did he stop? In hindsight the answer is easy: because he was about to become the finest poet of his generation, instead of just one of its best novelists. A more inquiring appraisal suggests that although his aesthetic effect was rich, his stock of events was thin. In a fictional texture featuring a sore tooth and a fleeting kiss as important strands Zen diaphanousness always threatened. (What is the sound of *one* flower being arranged?) The master lyric poet, given time, will eventually reject the idea of writing any line not meant to be remembered. Larkin, while being to no extent a dandy, is nevertheless an exquisite. It is often the way with exquisites that they graduate from full-scale prentice constructions to small-scale works of entirely original intensity, having found a large expanse limiting. Chopin is not too far-fetched a parallel. Larkin's two novels are like Chopin's two concertos: good enough to promise not merely more of the same but a hitherto unheard-of distillation of their own lyrical essence.

iii. YEATS v. HARDY IN DAVIE'S LARKIN

In recent months Philip Larkin, based as always in Hull, and Donald Davie, back in Europe from California, have been conducting a restrained slugging-match concerning Larkin's fidelity to the *locus classicus* in modern times, as defined – or distorted, if you are of Professor Davie's persuasion – in *The Oxford Book of Twentieth-Century English Verse*. Important issues have been raised, and it will be some time before any keeper of the peace will be able to still them. The time is propitious for an assessment of Professor Davie's *Thomas Hardy and British Poetry*, which in a normal climate might be politely – and erroneously – half-praised as a well-bred squib, but for the duration of hostilities demands to be regarded as live, heavy-calibre ammunition.

Professor Davie is a poet of importance – of such importance, indeed, that his academic title can safely be set aside for the remainder of this article – and from poets of importance we want works of criticism that are less safe than strange. There is nothing safe about this volume, and a lot that is strange. *Thomas Hardy and British Poetry* is a surprisingly odd book, but it is also a considerable one. In fact, the forces ranged against each other in the current squabble can now be said to be more evenly matched than might at first appear.

A good part of the secret of what Larkin really thinks about art is distributed through the pages of *All What Jazz*, and if you want to take the weight of Larkin's aesthetic intelligence, it is to that collection (and not so much to his so-far uncollected criticisms of poetry in the magazine *Listen*, although they count) that you must go. On the Davie side, we are given, in this new book, a view of his thought which is at the very least as luminous as the one made available in *Ezra Pound: Poet as Sculptor*. When Davie talks about Hardy he sounds like Larkin talking about jazz. To put it crudely, on their pet subjects they both talk turkey. But this doesn't mean that either man makes himself plain. Larkin worships Bix Beiderbecke and deplores Charlie Parker, believing that Parker destroyed with arid intellectualism the art to which Beiderbecke contributed by lyrical instinct. Conveying this distinction, Larkin apparently makes himself clear; but it would be a suicidally foolish critic who thought that such a distinction could be used unexamined as a light on Larkin's poetry. In poetry, Larkin is Beiderbecke and Parker combined: his criticism chooses sides among elements which are in balance within his complex creative personality. Similarly with Davie: his critical position calls for an even more cautious probing, since he is less aware of self-contradictions by the exact measure that he is more receptive to Literary influence. *Thomas Hardy and British Poetry* raises confusion to the level of criticism: it is a testament to Britain's continuing fertility as an intellectual acreage in which ideas will flourish at rigour's expense, the insights blooming like orchids while the valid syllogisms wither on the vine.

Davie starts by proposing Hardy as a more important influence than Yeats on the poetry of this century. The distinction between *is* and *ought* is not firmly made, with the result that we spend a lot of our time wondering whether Hardy has been the big influence all along, or merely should have been. 'But for any poet who finds himself in the position of choosing between the two masters', Davie says, 'the choice cannot be fudged; there is no room for compromise.' The reason why there is no room for compromise is not made as clear as the ordinary reader might require. 'Hardy', it is said, 'has the effect of locking any poet whom he influences into the world of historical contingency, a world of specific places at specific times.' Yeats, apparently, doesn't have this effect: he transcends the linear unrolling of recorded time and attains, or attempts to attain, the visionary. Davie says that the reader can delight in both these approaches, but that the writer has to choose. It is difficult, at first, to see why the writer can't employ the same combinative capacity as the reader. Difficult at first, and just as difficult later.

The other important thing happening at the beginning of the book concerns Larkin. Davie mentions Larkin's conversion from Yeats to Hardy after *The North Ship* in 1946, thus tacitly proposing from the start that Larkin was doing the kind of severe choosing which Davie asserts is essential. Neither at this initial point, nor later on when Larkin is considered at length, is the possibility allowed that Yeats's influence might have lingered on alongside, or even been compounded with, Hardy's influence. One realizes with unease that Davie has not only enjoyed the preface to the reissue of *The North Ship*, he has been utterly convinced by it: instead of taking Larkin's autobiographical scraps as parables, he is treating them as the realities of intellectual development. Larkin conjures up a young mind in which Hardy drives out Yeats, and Davie believes in it.

But Davie's main comments about Larkin are postponed until some sturdy ground-work has been put in on Hardy. We are told that Hardy's technique is really engineering, and that he is paying a formal tribute to Victorian technology by echoing its precisioned virtuosity. A little later on we find that Davie doesn't wholly approve of this virtuosity, and is pleased when the unwavering succession of intricately formed, brilliantly matched stanzas is allowed to break down – as in 'The Voice', where, we are assured, it breaks down under pressure of feeling.

A crucial general point about technique has bulkily arisen, but Davie miraculously succeeds in failing to notice it. At one stage he is almost leaning against it, when he says that Hardy was usually 'highly skilled indeed but disablingly modest', or even 'very ambitious technically, and unambitious every other way'. For some reason it doesn't occur to Davie that having made these admissions he is bound to qualify his definition of technique in poetry. But not only does he not qualify it – he ups the stakes. Contesting Yeats's insistence that Hardy lacked technical accomplishment, Davie says that 'In sheer *accomplishment*, especially of prosody, Hardy beats Yeats hands down' (his italics). Well, it's a poser. Yeats's critical remark about Hardy doesn't matter much more than any other of Yeats's critical remarks about anybody, but Davie's rebuttal of it matters centrally to his own argument. He is very keen to set Yeats and Hardy off against each other: an opposition which will come in handy when he gets to Larkin. But keenness must have been bordering on fervour when he decided that Hardy had Yeats beaten technically in every department except something called 'craft' – which last attribute, one can be forgiven for thinking, ought logically to take over immediately as the main subject of the book.

Davie argues convincingly that we need to see below the intricate surface form of Hardy's poems to the organic forms beneath. But he is marvellously reluctant to take his mind off the technical aspects of the surface form and get started on the problem of what technical aspects the organic form might reasonably be said to have. 'We must learn to look through apparent symmetry to the real asymmetry beneath.' We certainly must, and with Hardy Davie has. But what Davie has not learnt to see is that with Yeats the symmetry and asymmetry are the same thing – that there is no distance between the surface form and the organic form, the thing being both all art and all virtuosity at the same time. Why, we must wonder, is Davie so reluctant to see Yeats as the formal master beside whom Hardy is simply an unusually interesting craftsman? But really that is a rephrasing of the same question everybody has been asking for years: the one about what Davie actually means when he praises Ezra Pound as a prodigious technician. Is it written in the stars that Donald Davie, clever in so many others matters, will go to his grave being obtuse in this? Why can't he see that the large, argued Yeatsian strophe is a technical achievement thoroughly dwarfing not only Pound's imagism but also Hardy's tricky stanzas?

Davie is continually on the verge of finding Hardy deficient as a working artist, but circumvents the problem by calling him a marvellous workman whose work tended to come out wrong for other reasons. In 'During Wind and Rain' he detects a 'wonderfully fine ear', which turns out to be a better thing than 'expertise in prosody' – the wonderfully fine ear being 'a human skill' and not just a 'technical virtuosity'. It ought to follow that knowing how to get the ear working while keeping the virtuosity suppressed is of decisive importance to poetic technique. It ought to follow further that because Hardy couldn't do this – because he wasn't even aware there was a conflict – he spent a lot of his time being at odds with himself as a poet. What Davie is struggling to say is that Hardy wasn't enough of an artist to make the best of the art that was in him. But the quickness of the pen deceives the brain, and Davie manages to say everything but that.

The strictures Davie *does* put on Hardy are harsh but inscrutable. There is in Hardy a 'crucial selling-short of the poetic vocation'. In the last analysis, we learn, Hardy, unlike Pound and Pasternak (and here Yeats, Hopkins and Eliot also get a mention), doesn't give us a transformed reality – doesn't give us entry 'into a world that is truer and more real than the world we know from statistics or scientific induction or common sense'. This stricture is inscrutable for two main reasons. First, Hardy spent a lot of his time establishing a version of reality in which, for example, lovers could go on being spiritually joined together after death: nothing scientific about that. Second, even if he had not been at pains to establish such a version of reality – even if his themes had been resolutely mundane – his poetry, if successful, would have done it for him. In saying that Hardy's poetry doesn't transform statistical, scientific reality, Davie is saying that Hardy hasn't written poetry at all.

It should be obvious that Davie, while trying to praise Hardy as an artist, is actually diminishing him in that very department. Less obviously, he is also diminishing art. To look for a life-transforming theme, surely, is as self-defeating as to look for a life-enhancing one. Good poetry transforms and enhances life *whatever it says*. That is one of the reasons why we find it so special. In this case, as in so many others, one regrets the absence in English literary history of a thoroughly nihilistic poet. The Italians had Leopardi, who in hating existence could scarcely be said to have been kidding. Faced with his example, they were obliged at an early date to realize that there is poetry which can deny a purpose to life and yet still add to its point.

Larkin, Davie insists, follows Hardy and not Yeats. 'Larkin has testified to that effect repeatedly', he announces, clinching the matter. Yeats's influence was 'a youthful infatuation'. The ground is well laid for a thorough-going misunderstanding of Larkin on every level, and after a few back-handed compliments ('The narrowness of range . . .

might seem to suggest that he cannot hear the weight of significance that I want to put on him, as the central figure in English poetry over the past twenty years' – narrowness of range as compared with whom? With people who write worse?) Davie buckles down to the task.

Hardy, we have already learnt, was neutral about industrialism because his technique mirrored it: his skill as a constructor implicated him. With Larkin it is otherwise. Larkin can feel free to hate industrialism because he has no special sense of himself as a technician: 'The stanzaic and metrical symmetries which he mostly aims at are achieved skilfully enough, but with none of that bristling expertise of Hardy which sets itself, and surmounts, intricate technical challenge.'

By this stage of the book it is no longer surprising, just saddening, that Davie can't draw the appropriate inferences from his own choice of words. Being able to quell the bristle and find challenges other than the kind one sets oneself – isn't that the true skill? The awkward fact is that unless we talk about diction, and get down to the kind of elementary stylistic analysis which would show how Larkin borrowed Hardy's use of, say, hyphenated compounds, then it is pretty nearly impossible to trace Larkin's technical debt to Hardy. Not that Davie really tries. But apart from understandably not trying that, Davie clamorously doesn't try to find out about Larkin's technical debt to Yeats. And the inspiration for the big, matched stanzas of 'The Whitsun Weddings' is not in Hardy's 'intricacy' but in the rhetorical majesty of Yeats. In neglecting to deal with that inspiration, Davie limits his meaning of the word 'technique' to something critically inapplicable. Technically, Larkin's heritage is a combination of Hardy and Yeats – it can't possibly be a substitution of the first by the second. The texture of Larkin's verse is all against any such notion.

Mistaking Larkin's way of working is a mere prelude to mistaking his manner of speaking, and some thunderous misreadings follow as a consequence. In Larkin, we are told, 'there is to be no historical perspective, no measuring of present against past'. Applied to the author of 'An Arundel Tomb', this assertion reminds us of the old Stephen Potter ploy in which a reviewer selected the characteristic for which an author was most famous and then attacked him for not having enough of it.

According to Davie, Larkin is a Hardyesque poet mainly in the sense that he, too, 'may have sold poetry short'. With Larkin established as such a baleful influence, the problem becomes how to 'break out of the greyly constricting world of Larkin'. Davie enlists the poetry of Charles Tomlinson to help us do this, but it might have been more useful to linger awhile and ask if Larkin isn't already doing a good deal by himself to help us get clear of his dreary mire – by going on writing, that is, with the kind of intensity which lit up the gloom and made us notice him in the first place. Here again, and ruinously, Davie is dealing in every reality except the realities of art. He cannot or will not see that Larkin's grimness of spirit is not by itself the issue. The issue concerns the gratitude we feel for such a grimness of spirit producing such a beauty of utterance.

Near the end of the book, Davie draws a useful distinction between poets and prophets. The prophet is above being fair-minded: the poet is not. The poet helps to shape culture, with which the prophet is at war. Prophetic poetry is necessarily an inferior poetry.

To this last point one can think of exceptions, but generally all this is well said, and leaves the reader wondering why Davie did not then go back and find something centrally and vitally praiseworthy in the limitations of the Hardy tradition. Because it is the Hardy tradition which says that you can't be entirely confident of knowing everything that reality contains, let alone of transcending it. The Hardy tradition is one of a mortal scale. It does *not* hail the super-human. As Larkin might put it, it isn't in the exaltation business. That is the real point which Davie has worriedly been half-making all along. In a striking way, *Thomas Hardy and British Poetry* is an eleventh-hour rejection of Davie's early gods. Somewhere in there among the dust and hubbub there is a roar of suction indicating that the air might soon be cleared.

iv. THE NORTH WINDOW

To stay, as Mr Larkin stays, back late
Checking accessions in the Brynmor Jones
Library (the clapped date-stamp, punch-drunk, rattling,
The sea-green tinted windows turning slate,
The so-called Reading Room deserted) seems
A picnic at first blush. No Rolling Stones
Manqués or Pink Floyd simulacra battling

Their way to low-slung pass-marks head in hands:
Instead, unpeopled silence. Which demands

Reverence, and calls nightly like bad dreams
To make sure that that happens. Here he keeps
Elected frith, his thanedom undespited,
Ensconced against the mating-mandrill screams
Of this week's Students' Union Gang-Bang Sit-in,
As wet winds scour the Wolds. The Moon-cold deeps
Are cod-thronged for the trawlers now benighted,
Far North. The inland cousin to the sail-maker
Can still bestride the boundaries of the way-acre,

The barley-ground and furzle-field unwritten
Fee simple failed to guard from Marks and Spencer's
Stock depot some time back. (Ten years, was it?)
Gull, lapwing, redshank, oyster-catcher, bittern
(Yet further out: sheerwater, fulmar, gannet)
Police his mud-and-cloud-ashlared defences.
Intangible revetments! On deposit,
Chalk thick below prevents the Humber seeping
Upward to where he could be sitting sleeping,

So motionless he lowers. Screwed, the planet
Swivels towards its distant, death-dark pocket.
He opens out his notebook at a would-be
Poem, ashamed by now that he began it.
Grave-skinned with grief, such Hardy-hyphened diction,
Tight-crammed as pack ice, grates. What keys unlock it?
It's *all gone wrong*. Fame isn't as it should be—
No, nothing like. 'The town's not been the same,'
He's heard slags whine, 'since Mr Larkin came.'

Sir John arriving with those science-fiction
Broadcasting pricks and bitches didn't help.
And those Jap Ph.D.s, their questionnaires!
(Replying 'Sod off, Slant-Eyes' led to friction.)
He conjures envied livings less like dying:
Sharp cat-house stomp and tart-toned, gate-mouthed yelp
Of Satchmo surge undulled, dispersing cares

Thought reconvenes. In that way She would kiss,
The Wanted One. But other lives than this—

Fantastic. Pages spread their blankness. Sighing,
He knuckles down to force-feed epithets.
Would Love have eased the joints of his iambs?
He can't guess, and by now it's no use trying.
A sweet ache spreads from cramp-gripped pen to limb:
The stanza next to last coheres and sets.
As rhyme and rhythm, tame tonight like lambs,
Entice him to the standard whirlwind finish,
The only cry no distances diminish

Comes hurtling soundless from Creation's rim
Earthward – the harsh *recitativo secco*
Of spaces between stars. He hears it sing,
That voice of utmost emptiness. To him.
Declaring he has always moved too late,
And hinting, its each long-lost blaze's echo
Lack-lustre as a Hell-bent angel's wing,
That what – as if he needed telling twice –
Comes next makes this lot look like Paradise.

'Don Juan in Hull' previously included in *At the Pillars of Hercules*, 1979
'Wolves of Memory' from *Encounter*, June, 1974
'Smaller and Clearer' from *New Statesman*, 21 March, 1975
'Yeats *v.* Hardy in Davie's Larkin' from *TLS*, 13 July, 1973
'The North Window' from *TLS*, 26 July, 1974

4. An Affair of Sanity

Required Writing by Philip Larkin, Faber

Every reviewer will say that *Required Writing* is required reading. To
save the statement from blinding obviousness, it might be pointed

out that whereas 'required writing' is a bit of a pun – Larkin pretends that he wouldn't have written a word of critical prose if he hadn't been asked – there is nothing ambiguous about 'required reading'. No outside agency requires you to read this book. The book requires that all by itself. It's just too good to miss.

Required Writing tacitly makes the claim that it collects all of Larkin's fugitive prose, right down to the speeches he has delivered while wearing his Library Association tie. There is none of this that an admirer of his poems and novels would want to be without, and indeed at least one admirer could have stood a bit more of it. The short critical notices Larkin once wrote for the magazine *Listen* are, except for a single fragment, not here. As I remember them, they were characteristically jam-packed with judgements, observations and laconic wit.

If Larkin meant to avoid repetitiveness, he was being too modest: incapable of a stock response, he never quite repeats himself no matter how often he makes the same point. On the other hand there is at least one worrying presence. The inclusion, well warranted, of the prefaces to *Jill* and *The North Ship* can hardly mean that those books will be dropped from his list of achievements, but the inclusion of the long and marvellous introductory essay to *All What Jazz*, an essay that amounts to his most sustained attack on the modernist aesthetic, carries the depressing implication that the book itself, which never did much business, might be allowed to stay out of print. That would be a shame, because jazz is Larkin's first love and in the short notices collected in *All What Jazz* he gives his most unguarded and exultant endorsement of the kind of art he likes, along with his funniest and most irascible excoriation of the kind he doesn't.

Jazz is Larkin's first love and literature is his first duty. But even at the full stretch of his dignity he is still more likely to talk shop than to talk down, and anyway his conception of duty includes affection while going beyond it, so as well as an ample demonstration of his capacity to speak generally about writing, we are given, on every page of this collection, constant and heartening reminders that for this writer his fellow-writers, alive or dead, are human beings, not abstractions.

Human beings with all their quirks. Larkin proceeds as if he had heard of the biographical fallacy but decided to ignore it. 'Poetry is an affair of sanity, of seeing things as they are.' But he doesn't rule out the possibility that sanity can be hard won, from inner conflict. He has a way of bringing out the foibles of his fellow-artists while leaving their dignity at least intact and usually enhanced. To take his beloved Hardy as an example – and many other examples, from Francis Thompson to Wilfred Owen, would do as well – he convincingly traces the link between moral lassitude and poetic strength. This sympathetic knack must come from deep within Larkin's own nature, where diffidence and self-confidence reinforce each other: the personal diffidence of the stammerer whose childhood was agony, and the artistic self-confidence of the born poet who has always been able to feel his vocation as a living force.

The first principle of his critical attitude, which he applies to his own poetry even more rigorously than to anyone else's, is to trust nothing which does not spring from feeling. Auden, according to Larkin, killed his own poetry by going to America, where, having sacrificed the capacity to make art out of life, he tried to make art out of art instead.

It might be argued that if the Americanized Auden had written nothing else except 'The Fall of Rome' then it would be enough to make this contention sound a trifle sweeping. It is still, however, an interesting contention, and all of a piece with Larkin's general beliefs about sticking close to home, which are only partly grounded in the old anguish of having to ask for a railway ticket by passing a note. He is not really as nervous about Abroad as all that: while forever warning us of the impossibility of mastering foreign languages, he has the right Latin and French tags ready when he needs them, and on his one and only trip to Germany, when he was picking up a prize, he favoured the locals with a suavely chosen quotation in their own tongue.

Lurking in double focus behind those thick specs is a star student who could have been scholarly over any range he chose. But what he chose was to narrow the field of vision: narrow it to deepen it. He isn't exactly telling us to Buy British, but there can be no doubt that he attaches little meaning to the idea of internationalism in the arts. All too vague, too unpindownable, too disrupting of the connections between literature and the life of the nation.

Betjeman was the young Larkin's idea of a modern poet because Betjeman, while thinking nothing of modern art, actually got in all the facts of modern life. Like all good critics Larkin quotes from a writer almost as creatively as the writer writes, and the way he quotes from *Summoned by Bells* traces Betjeman's power of evocation to its source, in memory. The Betjeman/Piper guidebooks, in which past and present were made contemporaneous through being observed by the same selectively loving eye, looked the way Larkin's poetry was later to sound – packed with clear images of a crumbling reality, a coherent framework in which England fell apart. An impulse to preserve which thrived on loss.

In *Required Writing* the Impulse to Preserve is mentioned often. Larkin the critic, like Larkin the librarian, is a keeper of English literature. Perhaps the librarian is obliged to accession more than a few modern books which the critic would be inclined to turf out, but here again duty has triumphed. As for loss, Larkin the loser is here too ('deprivation is for me what daffodils were for Wordsworth') but it becomes clearer all the time that he had the whole event won from the start.

Whether he spotted the daffodil-like properties of deprivation, and so arranged matters that he got more of it, is a complicated question, of the kind which his critical prose, however often it parades a strict simplicity, is equipped to tackle. Subtle, supple, craftily at ease, it is on a par with his poetry – which is just about as high as praise can go. *Required Writing* would be a treasure-house even if every second page were printed upside-down. Lacking the technology to accomplish this, the publishers have issued the book in paperback only, with no index, as if to prove that no matter how self-effacing its author might be, they can be even more so on his behalf.

Observer, 25 November, 1983: previously included in *Snakecharmers in Texas*, 1988

Postscript

To track the closing stages of Larkin's career was among the delights of being a literary critic in the late twentieth century, but the pleasure was not unmixed. Larkin's poetry was, and will always remain, too self-explanatory to require much commentary. Puzzle poems like

'Sympathy in White Major' were few, and on the whole his work made a point of declining in advance all offers of academic assistance. So in praising his accomplishment there was always a risk of drawing attention to the obvious. After I tentatively suggested in print that the source of illumination in the central panel of the 'Leavings' triptych might be a lighthouse, Craig Raine thrust his impatient face very close to mine and hairily hissed: 'Of *course* it's a lighthouse!' And of course it was. It's all there in the poem, if you look hard enough: and no one else's poetry ever so invited you to look hard and look again.

There was edifying fun to be had, however, in pointing out how Larkin's incidental prose was of a piece with his verse. As a device for self-protection, Larkin was fond of proclaiming his loneliness, misery and bristling insularity, but his prose is there to prove his generous and unprejudiced response to the spontaneous joys of life. With T. S. Eliot, the essay on Marie Lloyd is a one-off: clearly he loved the music hall, but he never contemplated allowing the instinctive vigour of popular culture to climb far beyond the upper basement of his hierarchical aesthetic. Larkin never contemplated anything else. His poem about Sidney Bechet saluted the great saxophonist not just as a master, but as *his* master. For Larkin, pre-modern jazz was the measure of all things: he wanted his poetry to be as appreciable as that. His touchstone for the arts lay in what came to be called the Black Experience.

Helping to make this clear turned out to be useful work, because after his death the scolds moved in. They wanted to dismiss him as a racist, and might have carried the day if a body of sane opinion had not already been in existence. He was also execrated as a provincial, a misogynist and a pornophile. He was none of those things except by his own untrustworthy avowal, usually framed in the deliberately shocking language he deployed in his letters for the private entertainment of his unshockable friends. In his everyday behaviour he did the best a naturally diffident man can to be courteous, responsible and civilized at all times, and in his poetry he did even better than that. In no Larkin poem is there an insensitive remark that is not supplied with its necessary nuances by another poem. To believe Larkin really meant that 'Books are a load of crap' you yourself have to believe that books are a load of crap. The arts pages are nowadays stiff with people who do believe that, even if they think they believe otherwise: all they really care about is the movies. There are people reviewing books, even reviewing poetry, who can read only with difficulty, and begrudge the effort. No writer, alive or dead, is any longer safe from the fumbling attentions of the semiliterate literatus. But here again, the exponential proliferation of bad criticism can scarcely deprive the good critic of a role – quite the contrary. There has to be someone to save what ought to be obvious from the mud-slide of obfuscation, if only by asking such childishly elementary questions as: if you can't see that it took Larkin's personality to produce Larkin's poetry, what *can* you see? And if you can't accept Larkin's poetry as a self-sustaining literary achievement, what are you doing putting pen to paper?

2001

EVELYN WAUGH'S LAST STAND

The Letters of Evelyn Waugh **edited by Mark Amory, Weidenfeld & Nicolson**

Unless the telephone is uninvented, this will probably be the last collection of letters by a great writer to be also a great collection of letters. It could be argued that the book should have been either much shorter, so as to be easily assimilable, or else much larger, so as to take in all of the vast number of letters Waugh wrote, but even at this awkward length it is a wonderfully entertaining volume – even more so, in fact, than the *Diaries*. Here is yet one more reason to thank Evelyn Waugh for his hatred of the modern world. If he had not loathed the telephone, he might have talked all this away.

'Would you say I was a very ill-tempered and self-infatuated man?' he asked Nancy Mitford in 1947, and added, answering his own question: 'It hurts.' Waugh was unhappy about himself, and on this evidence he had every right to be. People who want to emphasize his repellent aspects will find plenty to help them here. For one thing, he revelled in his contempt for Jews. In his correspondence he usually spelled the word Jew with a small 'j' unless he was being polite to one of them for some professional reason. In a 1946 letter to Robert Henriques he asks for information about the Wandering Jew to help him in writing *Helena.* 'Please forgive me for pestering you in this way. You are the only religious Jew of my acquaintance.' In the letter to Nancy Mitford printed immediately afterwards, the Jews are back in lower case. 'I have just read an essay by a jew [Arthur Koestler] which explains the Mitford sobriety and other very peculiar manifestations of the family.' If there was ever anything playfully outrageous about this behaviour the charm has long since fled.

But when your stomach has finished turning over it is worth considering that Waugh was equally nasty about any other social, racial, or ethnic group except what he considered to be pure-bred, strait-laced, upper-class Catholic English. In addition to yids, the book is stiff with frogs, dagoes, Huns, coons, chinks, niggers, and buggers. Of necessity Waugh numbered not a few homosexuals among his acquaintances, but it should also be remembered that he knew some Jews too, and that they, like the homosexuals, seem to have been willing enough to put up with his jibes. In other words they drew a line between the essential Evelyn Waugh and the Evelyn Waugh who was a hotbed of prejudice. It wouldn't hurt us to do the same. Waugh was far too conservative to be an anti-Semite of the Nazi stamp. When he carried on as if the Holocaust had never happened, he wasn't ignoring its significance, he was ignoring it altogether. He wasn't about to modify his opinions just because the Huns had wiped out a few yids.

At the end of the *Sword of Honour* trilogy anti-Semitism is specifically identified as a scourge. The whole closing scene of the third book can confidently be recommended for perusal by anyone who doubts Waugh's emotional range. Anti-Semitism is also one of the things that Gilbert Pinfold finds poisonous about his own mind. Waugh was perfectly capable of seeing that to go on indulging himself in anti-Semitism even after World War Two was tantamount to endorsing a ruinously irrational historical force. But Waugh, with a sort of cantankerous heroism, refused to let the modern era define him. He retained his creative right to interpret events in terms of past principles nobody else considered relevant. When the facts refused to sit, they were simply ignored. (It is remarkable, however, how many of them *did* sit. Rereading his work, one is continually struck by how much he got right. He guessed well in advance, for example, that the Jews would not necessarily be much better liked by the Communists than they had been by the Nazis.)

Behaving as if recent history wasn't actually happening was one of Waugh's abiding characteristics. It is the main reason why his books always seem so fresh. Since he never fell for any transient political belief, he never dates. In the 1930s, far from not having been a Communist, he wasn't even a democrat. He believed in a stratified social order and a universal Church, the one nourishing the other. The stratified social order was already crumbling before he was born and the universal Church had disappeared during the reign of Henry VIII. His ideal was largely a fantasy. But it was a rich fantasy, traditionally based. Sustained by it, he could see modern life not just sharply but in perspective. When people say that Waugh was more than just a satirist, they really mean that his satire was coherent. It takes detachment to be so comprehensive.

Waugh seems to have been born with his world view already intact. Even for an English public school boy he sounds unusually mature. The social side of his personality was all set to go. What he had to do was make the facts fit it, since he was neither well off nor particularly well born. In view of these circumstances it is remarkable that he rarely sounds like a parvenu – just like someone waiting to come into his inheritance. If he had not been a writer he might never have made it, but there was no doubt about that side of his personality either. While still at school he was interested in the technicalities of writing and already capable of the first-class practical criticism which he lavished free of charge on his friends' manuscripts throughout his life. At Oxford he was awarded a gentleman's Third but this should not be taken to mean that he was a bad student. He was merely an original one, who absorbed a wide knowledge of history, literature, and the fine arts without appearing to try. As he told Nancy Mitford a long time later, it takes a knowledge of anatomy to draw a clothed figure. Waugh's mind was well stocked.

'I liked the rich people parts less than the poor,' he wrote to Henry Yorke ('Henry Green') about Yorke's early novel *Living*. This was probably a comment about accuracy, or the lack of it. Waugh's preference for the upper classes did not preclude his noting how the lower orders behaved and spoke. Falling for the Plunket Greenes and the Lygon sisters, Waugh was soon able to satisfy his craving for smart company. It would be easy to paint him as an *arriviste*, but really the success he enjoyed at one level of society seems to have sharpened his response to all the other levels. He didn't shut himself off. One of the enduringly daunting things about Waugh's early satirical novels is the completeness with which they reproduce the social setting. Those rural types at the end of *Scoop*, for example, are not caricatures. Waugh took a lot in. His pop eyes missed nothing. He narrowed his mind in order to widen his gaze.

The misery he was plunged into when his first wife left him still comes through. In the pit of despair he finished writing *Vile Bodies*, which remains one of the funniest books in the world. The connection between work and life is not to be glibly analysed in the case of any artist and least of all in Waugh's. 'It has been infinitely difficult,' he told Henry Yorke, 'and is certainly the last time I shall try to make a book about sophisticated people.' This is a salutary reminder that he didn't necessarily *like* the Bright Young Things – he just found them interesting.

Asking whether Evelyn Waugh was a snob is like asking whether Genghis Khan was an authoritarian. The question turns on what kind of snob, and the first answer is – open and dedicated. During the war he was horrified to find himself sharing the mess with officers of plebeian background, 'like young corporals'. (In the *Sword of Honour* trilogy Guy Crouchback puts up stoically with such affronts. In real life Waugh was probably less patient.) He was under the impression that no Australian, however well educated, would be able to tell a real Tudor building from a false one. (Lack of background.) He doubted whether Proust ('Very poor stuff. I think he was mentally defective') ever really penetrated to the inner circles of French society: as a Jew, or jew, all Proust could have met was 'the looser aristocracy'.

In a 1952 letter to Nancy Mitford, Waugh is to be heard complaining about the unsmart company he had been forced to keep at dinner the previous evening. The guests had included Sir Laurence Olivier (as he then was) and Sir Frederick Ashton (as he later became). Apparently Waugh had complained to his hostess that 'the upper classes had all left London'. Ashton was referred to as 'a most unarmigerous dancer called Ashton'. Waugh had started off being pretty unarmigerous himself, but by dint of genealogical research had managed to come up with a few quarterings – a feat which he was untypically bashful enough to dismiss as having been performed 'for the children'. Unlike Ashton's, Waugh's own knighthood was destined never to come through, probably because he turned down the CBE. In Britain, if you want high honours, it is wise to accept the low ones when they are offered.

Such a blunder helps to demonstrate that Waugh, if he calculated, did not calculate very well. In this he differed from the true climber, whose whole ability is never to put a foot wrong. Waugh put a foot wrong every day of the week. Quite often he put the foot in his mouth. He was always offending his high-class acquaintances by being more royalist than the King. The best of them forgave him because they thought he was an important artist and because they liked him better than he liked himself. Most of them belonged to that looser aristocracy which Waugh mistakenly believed Proust had been confined to. In Britain, those aristocrats with genuine artistic interests form a very particular stratum. Waugh idealized the philistine landed gentry but his friends, many of whom came from just such a background, did not make the same mistake. In a 1945 letter quoted here in a footnote, Lady Pansy Lamb told Waugh that *Brideshead Revisited* was a fantasy. 'You see English Society of the 20s as something baroque and magnificent on its last legs . . . I fled from it because it seemed prosperous, bourgeois and practical and I believe it still is . . .'

But for Waugh it was a necessary fantasy. He thought that with no social order there could be no moral order. People had to know their place before they could see their duty. In both life and art he needed a coherent social system. His version of *noblesse oblige* was positively chivalric. Because Sir Cosmo and Lady Duff-Gordon escaped from the *Titanic* in an underloaded boat, Waugh was still jeering at them a quarter of a century later. In *Sword of Honour* the fact that Ivor has behaved badly on Crete is one of the longest and strongest moral threads in the story. Mrs Stitch is brought back from the early novels for the specific purpose of taking pity on him in his shame.

Waugh himself had a disappointing time in the army. The head of the special force in which he hoped to distinguish himself in battle regarded him as unemployable and left him behind. In *Sword of Honour* Waugh presents himself, through Guy Crouchback, as a man misunderstood. Ford Madox Ford performed the same service for himself through Christopher Tietjens in *Parade's End*. In fact Waugh, like Ford, had probably been understood. He was simply too fantastic to have around. But the code of conduct which he so intractably expressed in real life lives on in his books as a permanently illuminating ethical vision. There is something to it, after all.

Snobbery was also Waugh's way of being humble about his art. His paragons were Mrs Stitch and Lady Circumference, both of whom could do the right thing through sheer breeding. Lady Circumference's unswerving philistinism he explicitly regarded as a virtue rather than a vice. He thought more of aristocrats than of artists. This viewpoint had its limitations but at least it saved him from the folly of imagining that behaviour could be much influenced by intellectual fashions and left him free to spot the inevitable gap between people's characters and their political beliefs.

His Catholicism was another thing that kept him humble: saints, he pointed out, attach no importance to art. Not that he ever took a utilitarian view of his faith. Waugh believed that Sir John Betjeman's Anglicanism was essentially self-serving and took frequent opportunities to tell him so, with the result that their friendship was almost ruined. For Waugh, Catholicism's uncompromising theology was an enticement. Just as he was more royalist than the King, he was more Catholic than the Pope. He was a convert who berated born Catholics for their moral lapses. When Clarissa Churchill married Sir Anthony Eden, Waugh abused her for her apostasy – Eden was a divorced man. The Church's eternal strictness was Waugh's comfort. On the Church's behalf he welcomed new converts among his friends with the promise of a bed turned down and a place at the eternal table. Even more than the English social hierarchy, which in his heart of hearts he knew was a shifting structure, the Church was his bulwark against the modern world. Hence his unfeigned despair at the introduction of a vernacular liturgy. 'The Vatican Council', he wrote to Lady Mosley in 1966, a month before his death, 'has knocked the guts out of me.'

In real life Waugh's fight to hold back the present had the same chance as Canute's to hold back the sea. In his books his lone last stand seems more inspired than absurd. The progressive voices are mainly forgotten. Waugh, the arch reactionary, still sounds contemporary. As an artist he was not moulded by his times and hence neither failed to see them clearly nor vanished with them when they were over. As an ordinary man he was no doubt impossibly rude but there were a lot of intelligent people who forgave him for it, as this book proves.

Mark Amory has edited these letters with a fine touch, occasionally calling in an independent witness when Waugh's delightful capacity for wild exaggeration threatens to distort the historical record. It is hard on the late S. J. Simon that the books he wrote in collaboration with Caryl Brahms, which Waugh enjoyed, should be ascribed only to Caryl Brahms, but apart from that I can't see many important slips, although John Kenneth Galbraith, giving this book an appropriately laudatory review in the *Washington Post*, has pointed out that Father Feeny was an unfrocked priest, not 'the Chaplain at Harvard'. What counts is Mr Amory's sensitivity to the nuances of the English class system. For finding his way around in that self-renewing maze he has the same kind of antennae as Waugh had, with the difference that they are attached to a cooler head. The result is an unobtrusively knowledgeable job of editing.

High-handedly rebuking his wife for writing dull letters, Waugh told her that a good correspondence should be like a conversation. He most easily met his own standard when writing to Nancy Mitford but really there was nobody he short-changed. Even the shortest note to the most obscure correspondent is vibrant with both his irascible temperament and his penetrating stare. Above all he was funny – the first thing to say about him. Writing to his wife in May 1942, he described what happened when a company of commandos set out to blow up a tree stump on the estate of Lord Glasgow. The account can be found on page 161 of this book. Anyone who has never read Evelyn Waugh could begin with that page and become immediately enthralled.

But by this time there is no argument about his stature. While academic studies have gone on being preoccupied with the relative and absolute merits of Joyce and Lawrence, Waugh's characters have inexorably established themselves among the enduring fictions to which his countrymen traditionally refer as if they were living beings. In this respect Waugh is in a direct line with Shakespeare and Dickens. Since he was public property from the beginning, a critical consensus, when it arrives, can only endorse popular opinion. The consensus has been delayed because many critics were rightly proud of the Welfare State and regarded Waugh's hatred of it as mean-minded. He was paid out for his rancour by his own unhappiness. For the happiness he can still give us it is difficult to know how to reward him, beyond saying that he has helped make tolerable the modern age he so abominated.

New York Review of Books, 1980: previously included in
From the Land of Shadows, 1982

Postscript

Merely to enjoy the novels of Evelyn Waugh, let alone to praise him as a great writer, it helps to have been born and raised in Australia. As a student at Sydney University in the late fifties I employed his early novels as one of my most effective displacement activities to console me for my neurotic neglect of the set books. I read *Decline and Fall* and *Vile Bodies* over and over, as if they were poems. The class-conscious background of the books was no mystery to me, or to any other Australian of my generation: most of us had been brought up on *Tip-Top*, *Wizard*, *Rover* or their girlish equivalents. We knew what a public school was, even though we had never been to one, except in the sense that our public schools really *were* public. The only misapprehension I laboured under was that Waugh, because he satirized the English social structure to such effect, must have stood outside it. Later on, in England, I read everything else he had written, plus a lot that had been written about him, and realized that he had stood right in it. He turned out to have been more snobbish than any snob in his books, but it was no skin off my nose. It was clear to me that Brideshead, like King's Thursday before it, was a house built in the imagination. In real life he might have dreamed of being the master of Castle Howard, but in his creative life he had better ambitions.

For a visitor like myself it was easy to separate the petty, spiteful and intermittently demented would-be gentleman from the majestically generous artist who had given us his fantastic England. But for the reader born and raised in the actual England this necessary distinction was not so easy to make. Orwell could do it, despite the deep repugnance he felt for everything Waugh stood for both socially and politically. But Orwell had been a long time dead and his indigenous successors in the critical tradition showed few signs of having grasped his point. Forced to explain Orwell's enthusiasm for Waugh, they might well have said that it was no surprise, because both men had the same background. Even today, and to an alarming degree, background remains a factor in any Englishman's perception

of the arts, because it is such a factor in his perception of society –
to the extent that even the most aesthetically sensitive critic finds it
hard to purge himself of the supposition that the arts serve social
ends.

Cleverness is no safeguard against this peculiar obtuseness, of
which F. R. Leavis, still volcanically active during my time at Cambridge, was merely the most flagrant example. There is no cleverer
critic working in Britain today than Professor Carey. (The consideration that I might think this because he gave me the best review I
ever got can perhaps be offset by the fact that he also gave me the
worst.) Professor Carey is an adventurous reader who makes his
judgements according to his enjoyment. He enjoyed *Decline and Fall*
enough to hail it as a comic triumph, but judging from the general
trend of his social commentary he would have liked the book even
better if it had come out of nowhere. He avowedly loathes the whole
ambience of the landed gentry and reserves a special hatred for the
arty social climbers who danced attendance. To find, decades after
the whole *galère* paddled itself out of sight, a sophisticated intelligence
wasting its fine anger in this way would be comic if it were not so
unsettling. What *is* it with the Poms? one asks one's shaving mirror
helplessly. Evelyn Waugh was a snorting prig. He was also a great
writer. Perhaps the ability to hold two such contrary facts in the
mind without their clouding each other and the mind as well is
the bonus for having been born elsewhere and having arrived in
England just in time to see its social coherence fall apart – which no
doubt it deserved to do, but to deny the fruitfulness of its last gasp
looks like perversity. Although here again, where did the perversity
come from, except as a lingering, recriminatory and very understandable reaction to the old iniquities?

After forty years in residence, I think I know something of the
country's social tensions, but it's still a relief to be able to say that
it's not my fight. We who are exempt from the local vendettas should
be slow, however, to erect a relative advantage into an absolute virtue.
It's always possible that we have missed the nub of the matter, and
that an artist like Waugh committed, as a man, sins we have no right
to gloss over. There are bright, well-read people in Argentina who
will tell you that the capacity of Borges to say so little about life
under the military dictatorship irredeemably weakens everything
he had to say about life in general. There are veterans of the old

Czechoslovakia who can't hear the name of Milan Kundera without remarking bitterly on the unbearable lightness of his not being there when it counted. I still think it a privilege of the *Weltbürger,* the man without a country, to be genuinely above such battles. But he should make it his business to know what the battle is about, because some of the people he meets might have been wounded in it, even if they look well.

2001

CHARLES JOHNSTON'S CATACOMB GRAFFITI

Poems and Journeys by Charles Johnston, Bodley Head

Eugene Onegin by Alexander Pushkin, translated by Charles Johnston, Penguin

Appearing unannounced in 1977, Charles Johnston's verse rendering of *Eugene Onegin* established itself immediately as the best English translation of Pushkin's great poem there had yet been. It was an impressive performance even to those who could not read the original. To those who could, it was simply astonishing, not least from the technical angle: Johnston had cast his *Onegin* in the *Onegin* stanza, a form almost impossibly difficult in English, and had got away with it. Only an accomplished poet could think of trying such a feat. Yet as a poet Charles Johnston was scarcely known. Indeed, his profile was not all that high even as Sir Charles Johnston, career diplomat and quondam High Commissioner for Australia. All the signs pointed to gentlemanly dilettantism – all, that is, except the plain fact that anyone who can convey even a fraction of Pushkin's inventive vitality must have a profoundly schooled talent on his own account.

Now a small volume of Johnston's own creations, called *Poems and Journeys*, has quietly materialized, in the unheralded manner which is obviously characteristic of its author. It seems that most of the poems it contains previously appeared in one or other of two even smaller volumes, *Towards Mozambique* (1947) and *Estuary in Scotland* (1974), the second of which was printed privately and the first of which, though published by the Cresset Press, certainly created no lasting impression in the literary world. The poems were written at various times between the late 1930s and now. There are not very many of them. Nor does the Bodley Head seem to be acting in any more forthcoming capacity than that of jobbing printer. 'Published for Charles Johnston by the Bodley Head' sounds only one degree less bashful than issuing a pamphlet under your own imprint.

But this time Johnston will not find it so easy to be ignored. *Poems and Journeys* is unmistakably an important book. Leafing through it, you are struck by its assured displays of formal discipline, but really, from the translator of *Onegin*, that is not so surprising. Hard on the heels of this first impression, however, comes the further realization that through the austerely demanding formal attributes of Johnston's verse a rich interior life is being expressed. Johnston's literary personality is not just old-fashioned: it is determinedly old-fashioned. He has set up the standards of the clubbable English gentry as a bulwark against encroaching chaos. Even those of us whose sympathies are all in the other direction will find it hard not to be swayed by his laconic evocation of the secret garden. It doesn't do, we are led to assume, to go on about one's predicament. Yet somehow a stiff upper lip makes eloquence all the more arresting.

Johnston's diplomatic duties took him to Japan before the war. After Pearl Harbor he was interned for eight months. After being released in an exchange of diplomatic agents, he was sent to the Middle East. After the war there were various other appointments before he took up his post in Australia. Clearly the accent has always been on uncomplaining service. Nor do the poems in any way question the idea of dutiful sacrifice: on the contrary, they underline it. Trying to identify that strangely identifiable voice, you finally recognize it as the voice of someone who has not talked before, but who has been so amply described that you think you know him. Johnston is the sort of man who has been written about under so many names that when he writes something himself he sounds like a legend come to life. He is the faithful servant of Empire, who now emerges, unexpected but entirely familiar, as its last poet.

By an act of imagination, without dramatizing himself, Johnston has made poetry out of his own background. The same background has produced poetry before but most of it has been bad, mainly because of an ineluctable cosiness. Johnston, however, is blessed with a distancing wit. He has the intensity of gift which makes facts emblematic without having to change them. It is the classical vision,

which he seems to have possessed from the start, as the first two
lines of an early poem about Japan clearly show:

> Over the rockbed, over the waterfall,
> Tense as a brushstroke tumbles the cataract.

The visual element is so striking it is bound to seem preponderant,
but there is more at work here than just an unusual capacity to see.
To choose a Greek classical measure, alcaics, is an inspired response
to the inherent discipline of a Japanese landscape subject: the native
poets and painters have already tamed their panorama to the point
that their decorum has become part of it, so to match their formality
with an equivalent procedure from the poet's own cultural stock is
an imaginative coup. Then there is the subtle control of sonic effects,
with the word 'tense' creating stillness and the word 'tumbles'
releasing it into motion. He sees something; he finds the appropriate
form; and then he exploits technical opportunities to elaborate his
perception. The classic artist identifies himself.

But everything he was saying was said from under a plumed
hat. The Lake Chuzéji of his early poems was the playground of the
foreign diplomats. They raced their boats on it, giving way to each
other in such elaborate order of precedence that only a *Chef de
Protocole* knew how to steer a perfect race. They committed genteel
adultery around its edges. A man of Johnston's mentality, no matter
how well he fitted in by breeding, must sometimes have doubted the
validity of his role. He was, after all, a double agent, both loyal
functionary and universal observer. But he had not yet conceived of
his complicated position as his one true subject – hence a tendency,
in these early efforts, towards a Georgian crepuscularity, which even
affects his otherwise scrupulously alert diction. Locutions like 'when
day is gone' crop up with their tone unqualified: something which
would not happen again once his manner was fully developed.

Internment helped develop it. The work commemorating this
experience is called 'Towards Mozambique' and is one of the three
original long poems in the book. Datelined 'Tokyo 1942–London
1946', it should now be seen, I think, as one of the outstanding poems
of the war, even though it is less concerned with fighting than with
just sitting around waiting. Exiles traditionally eat bitter bread, but
the narrator is more concerned to reflect than to rail against fate.
The poem has something of Ovid's sadness in the *Epistulae ex ponto,*

except that Johnston is not being sorry just for himself. He is bent on understanding misunderstanding – the tragedy of incomprehension which has brought Japan to war against the West.

The personal element of the tragedy comes not just from the feeling of his own life being wasted (and anyway, much of the poem seems to have been written after the internment was over) but from regret for the years that were wasted before, when diplomacy was being pursued to no effect. He reflects on what led up to this. A lot did, so he chooses a form which leaves room to lay out an argument – the Spenserian stanza whose clinching alexandrine both Byron and Shelley, in their different ways, found so seductive:

> Wakening, I watched a bundle tightly packed
> That scaled with clockwork jerks a nearby staff.
> Hoist to the top, I saw it twitched and racked
> And shrugged and swigged, until the twists of chaff
> That held it to the halyard broke, and half
> Released the packet, then a sharper tease
> Tore something loose, and with its smacking laugh
> The Jack was thrashing furiously down breeze,
> Mocking the feeble stops that lately cramped its ease.

Ripping, what? (The ambiguity in the third line, incidentally, is less a grammatical error than a mark of class. Osbert Lancaster and Anthony Powell have both always let their participles dangle with abandon, and Evelyn Waugh, in the same chapter of his autobiography which tells us that only those who have studied Latin can write English, perpetrates at least one sentence whose past participle is so firmly attached to the wrong subject that there is no prising it loose. This habit has something to do, I suspect, with a confusion between the English past participle and the Latin ablative absolute.) But some of the young diplomats were not content to shelter behind Britannia's skirts. Greatly daring, they took what opportunities they could to mingle with the locals – to penetrate, as it were, the membranes of inscrutable reserve:

> Climbing with shoeless feet the polished stairs,
> Gay were the evenings in that house I'd known.
> The mats are swept, the cushions that are chairs
> Surround the table like a lacquer throne.
> The geisha have been booked by telephone,

> The whisky brought, the raw fish on the ice,
> The green tea boiled, the saké in its stone
> Warmed to a turn, and seaweed, root and spice
> Await their last repose, the tub of nutcrisp rice.
>
> The scene is set, and soon a wall will slide,
> And in will run, professional as hell,
> Our geisha team, brisk as a soccer side,
> We'll ask the ones we like, if all goes well,
> To luncheon at a suitable hotel . . .

Everything in the diplomatic colony is ordered, decorous and unreal. The unreality becomes most apparent during periods of leave in Shanghai, where a phoney aristocrat rules society:

> 'Le tennis, ce jeu tellement middle-class,'
> Drawls the duchesse, whose European start,
> Whose Deauville background manages to pass
> For all that's feudal in this distant part.
> The locals thought she couldn't be more smart,
> And prized admission to her little fêtes,
> And searched through Gotha with a beating heart,
> But vainly, for the names of her estates,
> And for the strange device emblazoned on her plates.

But only in the enforced idleness of internment is there time to see all this in perspective. Long months of contemplation yield no grand might-have-beens or if-onlys. Nor, on the other hand, do they bring nihilistic resignation. Britain's imperial role is not repudiated. Neither is its inevitable passing particularly regretted. Instead, there is redemption in the moment:

> Time passed. A tramcar screaming in the dark
> Of total blackout down the Kudan hill
> Strikes, out of wire, spark on cascading spark,
> Lights from below the cherry swags that spill,
> In all the thickness of the rich April,
> Their pink festoons of flower above the street,
> Creamy as paint new-slapped. I looked my fill,
> Amazed to find our world was so complete.
> Such moments, in the nick, are strange and sharply sweet.

A stanza MacNeice would have been proud to have written. Even in these few examples you can see how Johnston is beginning to realize the lexical freedom that strict forms offer. Up to the point where restriction cramps style, the more demanding the stanza, the greater the range of tone it can contain. Slang phrases like 'professional as hell' and 'in the nick' sound all the more colloquial for being pieced into a tight scheme.

The second long poem in the book, 'Elegy', is written in memory of Johnston's brother Duncan, 'killed leading a Royal Marine Commando raid on the Burma Coast, on the night of February 22nd 1945'. This, too, ranks high among poems of the war. On its own it would be enough to class Johnston with Henry Reed, Bernard Spencer, F. T. Prince and Norman Cameron. It is a high-quality example of what can by now be seen to be a particular school of Virgilian plangency, the poetry of the broken-hearted fields. But it is probably not one of Johnston's best things.

It loses nothing by its air of doomed gentility. The narrator could be Guy Crouchback talking: there was a seductive glamour about the squires going off to war, and a potent sorrow when they did not come home. But though Johnston can be impersonal about himself, he cannot be that way about his brother. The poem tries to find outlets for grief in several different formal schemes, including blank verse. The stiff upper lip relaxes, leaving eloquence unchastened. There is no gush, but there is too much vague suggestion towards feeling, made all the more unsatisfactory by your sense that the feeling aimed at is real, harsh, and unblunted even by time. A first-hand experience has aroused a second-hand artistic response. The air is of an Owenesque regret, of the dark barge passing unto Avalon in agony, of a drawing-down of blinds. The few details given of the lost, shared childhood leave you wanting more, but the author is caught between his forte and an ambition foreign to it: he is a poet of controlled emotion who can give way to anguish only at the cost of sapping his own energy:

> Only through the hard
> Shaft-face of self-esteem parsimonious tears
> Are oozing, sour distillate from the core
> Of iron shame, the shame of private failure
> Shown up by the completeness of the dead.
> I wrote in the fierce hope of bursting loose

> From this regime, cracking its discipline . . .
> I wrote, but my intense assertion found
> No substance and no echo, and all I did
> Was raise an empty monument to grief.

'Elegy' is something better than an empty monument, but it is tentative beside its predecessor 'Towards Mozambique', and scarcely begins to suggest the abundant assurance of its successor, the third long poem in the book, 'In Praise of Gusto'. This contains some of Johnston's best work and instantly takes its place as one of the most variously impressive long poems since Auden and MacNeice were at their peak. It is not as long as either 'Letter to Lord Byron' or *Autumn Journal* but it has much of their verve and genial bravura. It embodies the quality to which it is dedicated.

'In Praise of Gusto' returns to some of the same subject-matter dealt with in earlier works, but this time it is all brought fully within the purview of what can now be seen to be his natural tone, a tone which taps its power from the vivacity of experience. His dead brother is again mentioned. This time all the emphasis is on the life they enjoyed together when young. Nevertheless the effect of loss is more striking than it is in 'Elegy', where death is the direct subject. One concludes, aided by hindsight, that Johnston loses nothing, and gains everything, by giving his high spirits free rein. It might have taken him a long time completely to realize the best way of being at ease with his gift, but with consciously formal artists that is often the case. The last thing they learn to do is relax.

The poem is written in two different measures, the *Onegin* stanza and the stanza which Johnston insists on referring to as *Childe Harold*, although really Spenser has the prior title. Johnston's mastery of the latter form was already proven. But by this time he could read fluent Russian and had obviously become fascinated with the breakneck measure in which *Eugene Onegin* unfolds its story. The *Onegin* stanzas of 'In Praise of Gusto' give every indication that their author will one day be Pushkin's ideal translator. As well as that, they serve the author's present purpose. The *Onegin* stanza is a born entertainer. As Johnston points out in his Author's Note, 'it has an inner momentum, a sort of infectious vitality of its own'. It packs itself tight and then springs loose like a self-loading jack-in-the-box. Comic timing is crucial to it:

Beauties who manage the conjunction
Of glamour and fireside repose
Pack what I call without compunction
The deadliest of knockout blows.
Japan bewitched me. Half forgotten
Were home and faith. The really rotten
Part of it all, which, when it came
Back later, made me sweat with shame,
Was that our worlds were fast dividing
And that my fondness must ignore
The headlong chute direct to war
Down which Japan was quickly gliding
With all its ravishingly queer
Compound of sensual and austere.

The rapacious hostesses of pre-war Shanghai and wartime Alexandria now find their perfectly appropriate rhythmic setting. One of the many things that attracted Johnston to his Russian exemplar must have been the way Pushkin gives full value to the glamour of imperial court life without romanticizing its meretriciousness. Nobody who admires both will ever tire of counting the ways in which Pushkin and Mozart are like each other. Each could see all the world as it was yet neither could reshape it in any way except by making masterpieces. Even their own disasters lifted their hearts. (Pushkin said that trials and tribulations were included in his family budget.) Everything that happened belonged. Johnston has something of the same defiant exuberance:

How Egypt's hostesses detested
The victories in our campaign:
'Assez de progrès,' they protested,
'Vous étiez bien à Alamein';
And then they'd stress in full italics
The point of being close to Alex,
The races and the gay weekends
Of bathing parties with one's friends.
They saw no merit in advancing
Far from the nightclub and the beach
Out beyond invitation's reach
To worlds remote from cards and dancing

> With absolutely not a face
> They'd ever seen in the whole place.

But the *Onegin* stanza enforces epigrammatic terseness. As a countervailing force, Johnston employs the Spenserian stanza to luxuriate in his visual memories. Without sinning against cogency, they amply exploit this traditionally expansive form's magically self-renewing supply of pentameter – a copiousness of rhetorical space which is symbolized, as well as sealed, by the long sweep of the alexandrine at the end:

> Mersa Matruh. A fathom down, the sun
> Lights on the faintest ripple of the sand
> And, underseas, decyphers one by one
> The cursive words imprinted on the strand
> In the Mediterranean's fluent hand;
> For eastern waters have the graceful trick,
> By way of compliment from sea to land,
> Of signing their imprint, with curl and flick
> Of the vernacular, in floweriest Arabic.

An extended metaphysical conceit has been matched up to a rigorous physical form: two kinds of intellectual strictness, yet the effect is of a single, uncalculated sensory celebration.

The essence of classical composition is that no department of it gets out of hand. After aberrations in artistic history the classic principle reasserts itself as a balancing of forces. In 'In Praise of Gusto' Johnston uses his Spenserian stanzas to specify his remembered visions, but he uses them also to unfold an argument. The same contrast and balance of perception and rhetoric was demonstrated by Shelley – a romantic with irrepressible classic tendencies – when he used the same stanza in 'Adonais'. Shelley obtains some of his most gravid poetic effects by deploying what sounds like, at first hearing, a prose argument. The same applies, *mutatis mutandis*, to Johnston, when he remembers what the Western Desert looked like after the battles:

> Such scenes have potency, a strange effect,
> Contagion with an undefined disease.
> They throw a chill on all whom they infect,
> Touch them with sadness, set them ill at ease.

> The sense that friends now dead, or overseas,
> Fought here and suffered, hoped here and despaired,
> Transports us outside time and its degrees.
> Here is a new antique, already paired
> With the most classic sites that scholar's trowel has bared.

The poem begins in the *Onegin* stanza, takes a long excursion in the Spenserian, and returns to the *Onegin*. Though tipping its plumed hat to a younger version of the author – a satirical youth who 'shot down other people's fun' – it conveys a whole-hearted acceptance of the good life, which apparently includes plenty of foie gras, champagne and personally slain partridges. If Dr Leavis were still with us it would be hard to imagine him appreciating any of this, especially when he noted the book's dedication to Sacheverell Sitwell, familiarly addressed as Sachie. Yet the spine of the poem's argument is that prepared pleasures, though it is churlish to eschew them, are not what inspires gusto, which is

> Immediately sustained delight,
> Short-lived, unhoped for, yet conclusive,
> A sovereign power in its own right.
> It lends itself to recognition
> More aptly than to definition . . .

The reason it can't easily be defined is that it is something more all-pervading even than a view of life. It is a way of being alive. Those gifted with it, if they have artistic gifts as well, can tell the rest of us what it is like. Reviewing his own life in search of its traces, Johnston now becomes one of those who have done so. The poem ends in a clear-eyed exultation.

The fourth long poem in the book is a translation of 'Onegin's Journey' which was originally designed to go between the present chapters seven and eight of *Eugene Onegin*. Pushkin eventually decided to leave it out, but it remains a logical subject for the translator of *Eugene Onegin* to tackle. He makes the accomplished job of it that you would expect, revelling in the inspiration engendered by the physical obstacles of the tetrameter and the rhyme that continually looms too soon. They help contain his prolific knack – so appropriate in a translator of Pushkin – for sonic effects.

Throughout his work Johnston is to be found exploiting prosodic conventions (such as eliding 'the' into the initial vowel of the next word) for all they are worth. Sometimes he overcooks it, so that you have to read a line twice to pick out the rhythm. Sometimes the conversational stress and the metrical stress separate to the point where the reader must strain to put them back in touch with each other. Usually, though, Johnston maintains the old rules only in order to increase the number of ways he can speak freely. All those ways are on view in his rendition of 'Onegin's Journey'. But anyone wanting to acquaint himself with Pushkin would be advised to turn in the first instance to the *Eugene Onegin* translation itself, which Penguin has now brought out.

The appearance of this great translation in a popular format is made even more significant by the fact that it carries a twenty-page introduction specially written by John Bayley. The author of the most distinguished book on Pushkin in any language, Bayley here gives the essence of his thoughts on Pushkin in general and *Eugene Onegin* in particular. Bayley's book has always been the best full-length introduction to Pushkin, but until now Edmund Wilson's essay in *The Triple Thinkers* (backed up by two further pieces in *A Window on Russia*) has been the best short one. Now Bayley has captured the second title as well as the first. I recommend this essay without hesitation as the first thing to read on Pushkin.

As for the translation itself, it is what it was hailed as when it came out, and what it will go on being for the foreseeable future. Johnston knows better than I do what it lacks of the original. When, in Chapter Eight, he makes Tatyana tell Onegin, 'Today it's turn and turn about,' he is well aware that there is an element of artificiality. In the original, Tatyana says just, 'Today it is my turn,' and it is one of the mightiest lines in all poetry. There is endless artifice in Pushkin but no artificiality. Yet by patient craft Johnston has kept to a minimum those necessarily frequent occasions when the painfully demanding form of the stanza forces an awkward phrase. Much more often he hits off the correct blend of intricate contrivance and easily colloquial expression. He catches the spirit of the thing, and a large part of the spirit of the thing is the *formal* spirit of the thing.

To a remarkable extent, Johnston possesses, not just the same sort of temperament as his model, but the same sort of talent. We had no right to expect that any English poet who combined these attributes would make translating Pushkin the object of his life.

But as *Poems and Journeys* shows, Johnston has done a few things of his own. He has recently finished a translation of Lermontov's *The Demon*. There are other Russian poems one can think of that he would be ideally fitted to give us, among them the last and most intensely organized of Pushkin's tetrametric creations, *The Bronze Horseman*. But on the strength of this volume it might also be wished that Johnston would go on to compose a long original work which would go even further than 'In Praise of Gusto' towards transforming the age he has lived through into art.

One of the things art does is to civilize the recent past. In *Poems and Journeys* there are poems, both long and short, which add significantly to the small stock of works that have helped make sense of the British Empire's passing and of Britain's part in the Second World War. Johnston's voice might have been more often heard in this respect, but he chose perfection of the life rather than of the work. As Auden noted, some artists have everything required for high distinction except the desire to come forward.

If Johnston had come forward earlier and more assertively, there can be no doubt that he would have received a hearing. In some of his short pieces he makes fun of the 'Trend Police' and describes the poems turned out by himself and his fellow gifted amateurs as 'catacomb graffiti'. In fact, the Trend Police would not have stood much chance of shouting down work done to this standard. The *locus classicus* is in no more danger of being obscured than the privileged orders are in danger of losing their privileges, although Johnston would have you think, in his more predictable moments, that the contrary was true in each case.

The best reason for Johnston to think of himself as a part-time poet was that as a full-time diplomat he was well placed to write the kind of poetry which is necessarily always in short supply – the poetry of the man who spends most of his day being fully professional at something else, the poetry for which the young Johnston so admired Marvell.

> Yours to restore the wasted field
>   And in distress to health
>   To serve the Commonwealth;
>
> Yet with a wider-sweeping eye
>   To range above the land, and spy

The virtue and defect
Of empires, to detect

In vanquished causes, and in kings
Dethroned, the tragedy of things,
And know what joys reside
Where the Bermudas ride.

In recent times we have grown used to the externally formless epic – Berryman's *Dream Songs*, Lowell's *History* – and striven to convince ourselves that it possesses an internal form which makes up for its lack of shape. But this pious belief has become harder and harder to sustain. The virtues of the informal epic are prose virtues, not poetic ones. Only discipline can give rise to the full freedom of mature art. Charles Johnston has given us a better idea than we had any right to hope for of what Pushkin's epic sounds like. But his long poems suggest that he has it in him to write an epic of his own. Even if he does not, his small but weighty output of original work, now that we have at last come to know it, enriches the poetic legacy of his generation and helps clarify that nebulous, nearby area of literary history where uninspired innovation creates its permanent disturbance.

London Review of Books, 1980: previously included in
From the Land of Shadows, 1982

Postscript

To meet, Sir Charles Johnston was something out of the past, and the past wasn't even mine. He was an empire builder, and I came out of the empire he built. Somebody like him probably stepped ashore in Botany Bay with Captain Cook and explained to the Aboriginal reception committee, in a very clear voice, that he could recommend a good tailor. Upon his retirement from the diplomatic service he set about publishing, in small volumes under his own imprint, all the poetry he had written, and writing a lot more. But he never overproduced. Every poem was the finished product, four-square and deeply polished, like a rosewood military chest neatly packed with an administrator's kit. The total effect was formal, confidently traditional, expensively turned out and unapologetically direct, and as such was duly ignored by most of the regular reviewers. But one of his little books was dedicated to his translation of *Eugene Onegin*. Much occupied with Pushkin at the time, I was able to recognize the Johnston version as a success, and am still proud of having been among the first to say so. Having tried to write in the Onegin stanza myself, I was in a position to salute Johnston's astonishingly high level of sustained technical accomplishment, and having used the original as one of my text books for learning Russian, I knew Pushkin's meaning well enough to spot that his translator had worked the miracle of transferring it almost intact. So it was not entirely out of naivety that I hailed Johnston's translation without reserve. Making it clear that unstinting praise was the kind he liked – he was direct in that way too – he invited me round to his flat. We were four for lunch. Johnston's wife, a Russian princess descended by not too many generations from one of the military heroes in *War and Peace*, had had a stroke by that stage which rendered her silent, but she was a keen observer. She observed me as if she had last seen someone like me on the wrong side of a barricade. The Johnstons made a majestic couple: an appropriate adjective, because their other guest, and therefore my opposite number across the tiny table, was the Queen Mother.

Conversation, except of course from the princess, was free and often funny, but there was no denying that the scene harked back to a vanished era. I wouldn't have been surprised if the lady in the hat had picked up a bottle of champagne by the neck, walked out on to the balcony and launched a battleship. I wouldn't even have wondered how the battleship had got there. I was too busy wondering how I had got there. It was an eloquent demonstration of what art can do to join worlds. Johnston's world was on its way out, my world was on its way in, and my suspicion of his must have been nothing beside his of mine. But classically ordered verse provided a common ground. Perhaps because of the phenomenon that Freud calls *Doppelgängerscheu*, our personal acquaintance didn't develop much beyond that date. Like any writer, of whatever background, he was concerned with himself above all things, and I soon felt bound to make it clear to him how in that respect, if in no other, he had met his match.

In the daunting energy of his Indian summer he went on turning out his little volumes, and forthrightly indicated his belief that a further instalment of publicity from my pen would not come amiss. (He wasn't rude, he just had no notion of how the literary world is supposed to work, lacking as he did even the slightest connection with it.) Cravenly I never found the words to convey that I thought this might be a bad plan. I just made myself scarce. But his work stayed with me as an extreme example of what I have always held – presumably by instinct, considering that the contrary evidence begins with Shakespeare – to be a truth about poetry: that it can release its full force only within a framework. Frameworks don't come more framed or fully worked than they do in the verse of Charles Johnston. At first reading, his meticulous carpentry looks like his main concern. But then you notice, singing inside it, phrases that would never have been there otherwise. Build the cage well enough and it will fill itself with rare birds. It takes a rare bird to do it, but he was certainly one of those.

2001

NABOKOV'S GRAND FOLLY

Eugene Onegin: A Novel in Verse **by Aleksandr Pushkin, translated with a commentary by Vladimir Nabokov, Routledge & Kegan Paul**

Nabokov Translated: A Comparison of Nabokov's Russian and English Prose **by Jane Grayson, Oxford University Press**

In the week of his death, it is instructive to remember that Nabokov's translation of *Eugene Onegin* was a project dear to his heart. Expert opinions of the recent second edition were not much more favourable than they were for the first, mainly because the translator had not done enough to eliminate what were earlier judged to be eccentricities of diction, while the commentary obstinately remained unmodified in all its idiosyncrasies. There is undoubtedly a sense in which the whole enterprise is a great folly. But even those Russianists who have been most inclined to question Nabokov's success in transmitting the essence of Pushkin are usually willing to concede that this cranky monument of scholarship might at least come in useful to the beginner.

As it happens, I am in a position to test this idea, being very much a beginner with Pushkin, and therefore in dire need of a good crib. Pushkin is never wilfully complicated, but his simplicities can be highly compressed. There are times when even an advanced student of the language is certain to need help, while the stumbler is likely to bog down completely. I should say at the outset that in several respects Nabokov's Folly serves the turn. It is a work to be valued, although even the tyro is bound to find it silly as well as brilliant.

The ideal crib, of course, should merely be the servant of the original. But Nabokov was incapable of being anybody's servant, even his admired Pushkin's: in paying homage to his giant predecessor he did his best to keep his own ego in the background, but ever and anon it shouldered its way forward. Nabokov's theory of translation was based on 'humble fidelity' to the original, yet try as he might to give us nothing more pretentious than a word-for-word equivalent, he still managed to make Pushkin sound like Nabokov.

Nor is the commentary free from quirks. In fact it is largely made up of them. He has set out to be more scholarly than the scholars; it is doubtful whether anybody else inside or outside Russia knows as much about Pushkin; but you don't have to know a thousandth as much to realize that Nabokov is no more *reasonable* on this subject than on any other. I switch to the present tense because it would be unfitting to talk about the author of so cantankerous a commentary as if he were not alive – he is at you all the time, continually asserting himself against those hordes of translators and academics who have either misunderstood Pushkin or, worse, understood him too quickly. But there are limits to how far insight can go without common sense to back it up.

Following Gautier, Nabokov thought the ideal translation should be an interlinear lexicon. The theory is ably expounded by Jane Grayson in her painstaking *Nabokov Translated*, a book which has the additional merit of showing that in the case of his own writings the master is tactfully flexible about putting it into practice. But where *Eugene Onegin* is concerned there can apparently be no departure from dogma. Throughout the commentary, Nabokov is forever telling you the words he *might* have used in the translation if he had set out to do anything so misguided as convey the spirit of the original. But no, he has resisted against overwhelming odds: awkwardness is not only not to be avoided, it is positively to be sought, if that happens to be the price of exactitude.

There is something in this view, although not as much as Nabokov thinks. It is true that a translator who sets out to render the 'spirit' is likely to traduce the original author. But Nabokov's paroxysms of accuracy traduce Pushkin's spirit as thoroughly as any academic poetaster has ever done. He makes Pushkin sound like a Scrabble buff. Certainly there are words in Pushkin that don't now mean what they once did, and even words that would have seemed odd at the time. Hence the modern foreign reader's need for more help than an ordinary dictionary can provide. But none of this means that Pushkin wants to be puzzling. On the contrary, what impresses you about him is his unforced naturalness of tone. The sad thing about Nabokov's translation is that he is not really capable of echoing such a quality. Instead, he dithers pedantically in the very area of verbal sophistication which for Pushkin was never more than a playground.

It is well known that Nabokov keeps saying 'mollitude' where either 'bliss' or 'languor' would have done. Sometimes you can make a better case for 'bliss' than for 'languor' and sometimes vice versa, but what nobody normal can doubt is that there is no case to be made for 'mollitude'. Yet after all the uproar which greeted his use of 'mollitude' in the first edition, here it still is in the second, having the effect, every time it appears, of wrinkling the reader's brow. The idea behind using 'mollitude' is evidently to convey something of the Russian word's Frenchified feeling. But 'mollitude' does nothing to make the English reader think of French influence. It just makes him think about the weight of the OED.

At least he can find 'morgue' in the *Concise*, defined in roughly the same way Nabokov uses it, to mean 'arrogance'. But arrogance is scarcely the first thing an English reader thinks of when he sees the word 'morgue'. He thinks of dead bodies on zinc tables. Why not just use 'arrogance'? The answer, I'm afraid, is that Nabokov wants to indulge himself in the Euphuism of 'I marvelled at their modeish morgue'. (In the introduction we learn of Onegin and Lensky that 'both are blasé, bizarre beaux'. Always the virtuoso of his adopted tongue, Nabokov never quite grasped that half the trick of composing in English is *not* to write alliteratively.)

Why use 'trinkleter' where 'haberdasher' would have done? Why 'larmoyant' for 'lachrymose'? What does 'debile' give you that 'feeble' doesn't? Why 'cornuto' for 'cuckold'? Certainly the Russian word has horns which the Italian word reproduces. Unfortunately the Italian word is not in English. Nor is Nabokov correct in supposing that there is any word in *Inferno* III, 9, which might mean 'forever'. He quibbles so relentlessly himself that you would have to be a saint not to quibble back.

On this showing, Nabokov has no call to despise those less informed translators who have had the temerity to cast their versions in rhyme. His unrhyming version sounds at least as weird as the very worst of theirs. But as a crib it is the best available, especially in this second edition, where each line matches a line in the original – even, in many cases, to the extent of reproducing the word order. Worse than useless for the reader without Russian, for the learner Nabokov's translation would be just the ticket, if only the commentary were better balanced. But Nabokov's ambitions as a scholar are thwarted by his creativity. He starts shaping the facts before he has fully submitted himself to them. He is immensely knowing, but knowingness is not the same as knowledge.

Expending too much of his energy on being bitchy about other writers, scholars and critics, Nabokov the commentator sounds at best like A. E. Housman waspishly editing an obscure classic. At worst he sounds like A. L. Rowse trying to carry a daft point by sheer lung-power. Calling Dostoevsky 'a much over-rated, sentimental and Gothic novelist' is dull if it is meant to be funny and funny if it is meant to be serious. We are told that Balzac and Sainte-Beuve are 'popular but essentially mediocre writers'. I can't pretend to know much about Balzac, but I am reasonably familiar with Sainte-Beuve, and if he is mediocre then I am a monkey's uncle. Madame de Staël is thoroughly patronized ('a poor observer') without any mention being made of the fact that Pushkin himself thought highly of her. As for Tchaikovsky's version of *Eugene Onegin*, it is not a 'silly opera'. It is a great opera.

But most of this is casual snidery. Distortions of Pushkin's meaning are less forgivable. Commenting on the exchange of dialogue between Tatiana and her nurse, Nabokov, forgetting even to mention *Romeo and Juliet*, concentrates on discrediting the official Soviet view of the nurse as a Woman of the People. Yet that view is part of the truth. When the nurse talks about being given in marriage without regard to her own wishes, she is illuminating the condition of slavery. Tatiana might not be really listening to her, but Pushkin is listening, and so should the reader be. This acute social awareness runs right through Pushkin, building up all the time, until in the later prose he provides the model for the social consciousness of all the Russian literature to come. There is nothing naive about taking cognizance of this elementary fact. Nabokov is naive in trying to avoid it. Pushkin really *is* the Russian national poet, even if the Soviet regime says so. Above all, he is the national poet of all the people who have been persecuted by that regime in the name of an ideal of justice which Pushkin's very existence proves was once generous and merciful.

Nabokov seems determined to miss the point of what is going on even among the main characters. He tells us all about the books Tatiana has read but fails to notice her gifts of psychological penetration. He can't seem to accept that Tatiana ends by slamming the door in Onegin's face. He claims to detect in Tatiana's final speech 'a confession of love that must have made Eugene's experienced heart leap with joy'. Incredibly, the moral force of Tatiana's personality seems to have escaped him. Nor can he see that Onegin is arid and Lensky fruitful; that the difference between them is the same difference Pushkin saw between Salieri and Mozart; and that the outcome is the same – envy and revenge. Presuming to avoid sentimentality, Nabokov's homage diminishes its object, limiting the reader's view of the range of emotion which Pushkin embraced. Pushkin's artistic personality was the opposite of Nabokov's. Pushkin had negative capability. Not that Pushkin can be equated with Keats, even if you think of Keats's sensibility combined with Byron's airy manner. *Eugene Onegin*'s stature is Shakespearean: you have to imagine a Shakespeare play written with the formal compactness of a poem.

On technique Nabokov gives us what we had a right to expect from the man who invented John Shade. (If only Shade, instead of Charles Kinbote, had written this translation!) There is a long disquisition on prosody which is ruined by pseudo-science. (The spondee is proved mathematically not to exist.) But when Nabokov calls Pushkin's tetrameter 'an acoustical paradise', and takes time to examine the miracle of simple words producing great sonorities, he is writing criticism of the first order. He is also good on trees, houses, carriages, visitors' books, methods of travel, manners – although even here he can't resist going over the top. He finds himself saying that Pushkin was not especially sympathetic with the Russian landscape. There is a certain pathos about that, as if Nabokov were trying to insert himself into the physical reality of the old, lost Russia that will never now return. A doomed attempt and a superfluous one, since by pointing to the source of its literary tradition Nabokov has helped remind us of the Russia that really *is* undying, and in which his place is now secure.

New Statesman, 1977: previously included in
From the Land of Shadows, 1982

Postscript

Edmund Wilson was no fool, but his magisterial self-confidence could make him do foolish things, and one of the most foolish was to lay himself open to Nabokov's genius for aggressive pedantry by suggesting that Nabokov might have lost his grip on the Russian language. Wilson was merely a gifted amateur student of languages. Nabokov was a Russian, and thus well qualified to make Wilson's pontifications on the subject look ridiculous. In the subsequent outburst of hilarity, it was forgotten that Wilson had generously helped Nabokov to secure his position in the United States. It was also forgotten that Nabokov himself was capable of the misplaced self-confidence of the autodidactic crank. For an appreciation of the resources Nabokov could bring to his prose when writing fiction, there is nothing better than Martin Amis's introduction to the Everyman reissue of *Lolita*. But I still think Kingsley Amis had a point when he took a passage of that novel apart and detected as much self-admiration as evocation. Nabokov would have to be rated as a writer of sublime talent if he had composed nothing else except *Speak, Memory*. But there is such a thing as getting so close to language that you can no longer keep your distance from what you are writing about with it, and that awkward propensity really shows up in Nabokov's version of *Eugene Onegin*.

I was careful, when reviewing it, not to claim too much knowledge of the original and thus fall into the same trap in which Wilson's corpse already lay impaled, with plenty of bamboo stakes left unoccupied for further victims. But I wouldn't have needed a word of Russian – except perhaps *nyet* – to know that something weird was going on. Nabokov had scrupulously registered the minor meanings from moment to moment but the grand meaning (or moral: there is no other word for it) he had either missed or misinterpreted. Why he should have done so remains a puzzle, but the clue might lie somewhere in the absurdity of his remarks about Tchaikovsky's opera. Among Russians familiar with both opera and poem, there are not many who would say that either makes the other trivial: in the light of historical events, they would rather count their blessings, and leave the two masterpieces in fruitful, complementary contention. Nabokov admitted that he had a tin ear for music, so why did he not disqualify himself in this instance? The answer might be elementary: he couldn't bear the competition. If he thought an area was his, he would turn his full firepower on anyone else who strayed into it. He was solipsistically proprietorial about Russia, the novel, and art itself. Perhaps forced exile encourages that condition. But we can't expect every great artist to have a great soul. If more of them were like Verdi, we could read artists' biographies for uplift; but we would be so repelled by Wagner that we would forget to listen, or by Picasso that we would forget to look.

2001

HOW MONTALE EARNED HIS LIVING

The Second Life of Art: Selected Essays of Eugenio Montale edited and translated
by Jonathan Galassi, Ecco Press

Prime alla Scala by Eugenio Montale, Mondadori

If Eugenio Montale had never written a line of verse he would still
have deserved his high honours merely on the basis of his critical
prose. The product of a long life spent clearing the way for his
poetry, it is critical prose of the best type: highly intelligent without
making mysteries, wide-ranging without lapses into eclecticism or
displays of pointless erudition, hard-bitten yet receptive, colloquial
yet compressed. The only drawback is that it constitutes a difficult
body of work to epitomize without falsifying.

For a long time Montale's English translators added to the difficulty by not being able to read much Italian or, sometimes and, not
being able to write much English. Then a few competent, if restricted,
selections emerged. But the problem remained of transmitting
Montale's critical achievement in its full, rich and all too easily
misrepresented subtlety. Now Jonathan Galassi has arrived to save
the day. His style does not always catch Montale's easy rhythm,
but much of the time he comes close, and the explanatory notes on
their own would be enough to tell you that he has mastered all
the necessary background information. One of the most active of
Montale's previous translators was under the impression that Dante
employed the word *libello* to mean 'libel' instead of 'little book'.
A dedicated and knowledgeable student of the tradition from which
he emerged, Montale was a stickler for detail, so Mr Galassi's wide
competence comes as a particular refreshment. In all his phases as a
poet, from the early, almost Imagist toughness to the later anecdotal

relaxation, Montale started with the specific detail and let the general significance emerge. His prose kept to the same order of priority, so it is important that the details be got right. Galassi had several volumes of prose to consider, all published late in the poet's life. *Sulla Poesia* of 1976 is the principal collection of literary criticism as such, and indeed one of the most interesting single collections of literary essays in modern times, but the earlier *Auto da Fé* of 1966 (Montale must have been unaware that Elias Canetti had given the English version of *Die Blendung* that same title) is its necessary complement, being concerned with the question of mass culture – a question made more vexing for Montale by the fact that, although he didn't like mass culture, he did like popular culture and thought that élite culture would kill itself by losing touch with it.

There are also some important discursive writings on literature in *Fuori di Casa* (1969), the book about being away from home, and the *Carteggio Svevo/Montale* (1976), which chronicles Montale's early involvement with the novelist whose merits he was among the first to recognize, and whose concern with the artistic registration of the inner life helped encourage Montale in the belief – crucial to his subsequent development – that what mattered about modern art was not its Modernism but the way it allowed private communication between individuals, the sharing of deep secrets in a time of shallow rhetoric. In addition, there is the abundant music criticism, but most of that, at the time this book was being prepared, was not yet available in book form, so Mr Galassi largely confined himself to the general articles on music scattered through the volumes mentioned above.

Even with so considerable a restriction, however, there was a lot to choose from. The *richesse* must have been made doubly embarrassing by Montale's habit of returning to the same point in essay after essay in order to elaborate it further, so that there is a real danger, if you settle on a single essay in order to demonstrate how he has aired a given topic, of getting the idea that he glosses over difficulties in passing, whereas in fact one of his salient virtues was to stay on the case, sometimes for decades on end, until he had it cracked. To sample him is thus almost always to belittle him: it is misleading, for example, to have him speaking as an anti-academic unless you also have him speaking as an appreciator of solid scholarship, and no representation of Montale as the hermeticist young poet can be anything but a travesty unless he is also allowed to speak as the reasonable man who didn't just end up as the advocate of appreciability, but who actually started out that way. One of the big compliments Mr Galassi should be paid is that, given this very real problem, he has selected well. All the books are fairly represented, most of the main different emphases in Montale's stable but manifold critical position are touched upon if not covered, and the quiet giant comes alive before us, as a personality and a mind.

To an extraordinary extent the two things were co-extensive. Like one of those periods in Chinese history when Confucian self-discipline and Taoist impulsiveness nourished each other, Montale's inner life was both naively fruitful and sophisticatedly self-aware. It makes him great fun to read, as if the smartest man in the world were a friend of the family, one of those good uncles who aren't avuncular. In Italian the title essay of the book was called 'Tornare nella Strada' ('Back into the Street'), but the term 'second life' recurs throughout the piece and comes right from the centre of Montale's essentially generous artistic nature. No poet could be more learned about the cultural heritage of his own country and his learning about the cultural heritage of other countries is impressive too, but he says, and obviously believes, that it is not the appeal of art to adepts that interests him most. It is not the first life that matters, but the second life, when a theme from an opera gets whistled in the street, or a phrase from a poet is quoted in conversation. This view might sound crudely populist or even philistine when excerpted, but as argued in a long essay, and fully considered during a long career, it proves to be a highly developed exposition of the elementary precept that art must be appreciable, even if only by the happy few. It doesn't have to be immediately appreciable, and indeed in modern times any attempt to make it so is likely to be just a coldly intellectualized programme of a different kind, but if it rejects the possibility of being appreciated then it disqualifies itself as art. 'The piece goes on and on,' he says regretfully of Schoenberg's *Ode to Napoleon*, 'but it does not live during the performance, nor can it hope to do so afterward, for it does not affect anything that is truly alive in us.'

Montale realized quite early that to propose such a line would involve a perpetual obligation to dissociate himself from unwanted allies who would mock any kind of difficulty, even when it was legitimate. That there could be such a thing as legitimate difficulty Montale did not doubt, since he himself embodied it as a poet. But he also didn't doubt that Modernist enthusiasms would open the way for illegitimate difficulty in large quantities, and that the enemies of art would therefore have a lot at which to point the finger while they made their strident calls for a responsible culture. Mussolini liked quotable quotes, and Palmiro Togliatti's idea of art was of something which people could sing or recite while they were lining up to join the Communist Party. If you don't much like Expressionism, the way you say so is bound to be modified by the fact that Hitler didn't like it either. Montale's lifelong apoliticism was very political in this sense – that he spoke for the autonomy of culture at a time when political forces were trying to co-opt it. Art should be responsible only to itself. But responsible it should be. 'Mastery,' he said in twenty different ways, 'consists of knowing how to limit yourself.' It was the necessary corollary of his other famous proposition, the one about how it isn't the man who wants to who continues the tradition, but the man who can.

The man who can is the man with inspiration. But the inspiration has to come from life. This was where Montale parted company from the Modern movement as a whole. For Montale, art which had nothing except its own technique for subject matter could only be a monster. 'An art which destroys form while claiming to refine it denies itself its second and longer life: the life of memory and everyday circulation.' It would be a conventional enough conclusion for any artist to reach in old age but all the evidence suggests that Montale started out with it. Even back in the 1920s, when he was the unfathomable, linguistically revolutionary young poet of *Ossi di Seppia*, he had that social humility to go with his fierce artistic pride. Maturity was part of his gift.

'Style,' he wrote in 1925, the year of the first publication of *Ossi di Seppia*, 'perhaps will come to us from the sensible and shrewd disenchanted, who are conscious of the limits of their art and prefer loving it in humility to reforming humanity.' The idea had been made very relevant by the events of the 1920s. The international avant-garde had already projected, and was bringing into being, an art without limits. Fascism was bringing into being a reformed humanity, or supposed it was. To this latter end, the mobilization of art was alleged to be essential. In the event, Italian artists and intellectuals were slow to provide Mussolini with the accreditation he would have liked. He gave them medals but, as Montale points out, even when they accepted the medals they did not give much in return.

Montale accepted no medals and gave nothing – not to the state, anyway. What he gave, he gave to his country. As a poet he continued and deepened his original course of writing a new, compressed poetry which, from the puffy and sugared *cappuccino* that the Italian lyric had become, was a direct and vertiginous return to the Dantesque *espresso basso.* Later on, when his early manner relaxed into the luminous transparency of the love poetry and the slippered reminiscence of the verse diaries, that initial rigour was still there underneath, keeping everything in terse proportion. In the most rhetorical age of Italian history, his poetry was always as unrhetorical as could be. His prose kept the same rule, to the end of his long life – a *serietà scherzevole*, a joking seriousness, a humane ease whose steady claim on your attention reminds you that he is the opposite of dispassionate. He is a passionate man in control of himself, having seen, or guessed in advance, what self-indulgence leads to.

Montale's defence of art against utilitarian pretensions, whether from the state or on behalf of the mass audience, has general relevance for the modern world, but the specific conditions of recent Italian history brought it into being. Faced with the stentorian claims of bogus novelty, it was inevitable that he would appeal to tradition. Yet it was a tradition from which he personally was trying to fight free. Certainly his unusual capacity to speak generally about the arts without declining into abstraction springs partly from a detailed engagement with his European literary predecessors. But that much he had been born to. Eliot, with whose name Montale's was often linked, got into the European tradition from outside. Montale, born inside, had to get out from under its crushing weight. He talked his way out. Mr Galassi's selection from Montale's many essays on Italian writers shows the poet humanizing the past, pointing out what is permanently current. The great figures rise from their tombs of scholarship and speak as contemporaries, even the grandiose and torrentially eloquent D'Annunzio, the poet who was everything Montale strove not to be. In fact, the essay on D'Annunzio leaves you thirsty for more. If it were as long as the one on Svevo, you would feel that D'Annunzio was at arm's reach, instead of still soaring around above you with goggles preposterously flashing, pursuing those 'flights of omnivorous fancy which does not always turn what it touches into gold, but which will never cease to amaze us'.

Montale's admiration for D'Annunzio was real, but a long way within bounds. For Svevo it was a profound sympathy. D'Annunzio wanted to conquer the world – an uninteresting prospect. Svevo's universe was in his own soul, and that interested Montale very much. Montale's young enthusiasm helped the diffident Triestine businessman to the recognition he deserved as Italy's most important modern novelist. But here again it is necessary to emphasize that Montale was much less concerned with Svevo's technical advance into Modernism than with his thematic return to a solid, communicable, everyday subject – which just happened to be the one subject everybody could recognize: namely, the failed adventures in the soul. At a time of heated bombast, Svevo offered concreteness and the slow maturity of considered awareness. 'Removed from contact with the world of letters, Svevo developed in solitude.' Montale was also talking about himself. He was not removed from the world of letters, which was never likely to leave him alone, but he always cultivated his solitude in a way which Svevo had helped show him was the key to being a modern artist. The life had to be private before it could be public. The other way round was just publicity.

The essay on Svevo would be enough by itself to demonstrate that Montale, if he was ever anti-academic, was not so for lack of scholarly instinct. He had respect for scholarship but was early aware that it would tend to put the past beyond reach, if only by providing 'too much light'. He had a knack for making then seem as close as now – the obverse of another knack, equally valuable, for sensing what was eternal about the present. The section on foreign artists has essays about Valéry, Auden and Stravinsky which bring out their full dignity. A keen student of English, he enjoyed Auden's verbal playfulness in a way which would have horrified F. R. Leavis, who admired Montale and therefore assumed that he took a stern line against frivolity. But Montale was always willing to forgive intellectual sleight-of-hand if something unexpectedly lyrical should come out of it. His admiration for Stravinsky was withdrawn only when Neo-Classicism, which at least allowed the possibility of spontaneous feeling, gave way to serialism, which didn't. Apart from a few sour words about Brancusi, who was a bad host, Montale never belittles a real artist, no matter how variable his work or questionable his personal odyssey, believing that 'true poetry is in the nature of a gift, and therefore presupposes the dignity of the recipient'. But he isn't dewy-eyed either: the false positions that creative people can get themselves into, especially politically, fascinate and appal him.

Foreign students who own the monumental, fully annotated Contini/Bettarini *L'Opera in Versi* of 1980 are likely to remain deprived for a long time yet of an equivalent edition of the prose. They will find Galassi's book a useful tool even if they don't need the translation. Experts might sniff at being told who Svevo was, but it doesn't hurt to be told that Federico Frezzi was a poet of Foligno who wrote a long poem in imitation of Dante, thus, apparently, earning himself immediate and lasting oblivion. Montale would have approved of a footnote that gave Federico Frezzi of Foligno the dignity he had coming. Even a very minor artist was a good thing to be.

I can't see that Mr Galassi has fudged much in the way of information. Where Montale speaks of genius as a long patience, I think he expects us to know that Flaubert said it to Maupassant, although lately I have seen the remark attributed to Balzac. Here it is attributed to no one but Montale, who was good enough at aphorisms of his own not to need other people's wished on him. Also when the humiliated and offended are mentioned at one point, and the humiliated and afflicted at another, these are indeed accurate translations from two different essays, but Montale is almost certainly referring to the title of the same novel by Dostoevsky in both cases.

But this is nit-picking. Montale's range of literary reference is so wide that even the most alert editor is bound to let a few allusions get through unannotated. More serious is Mr Galassi's seeming determination, despite his evident familiarity with Benedetto Croce's basic works, to remain unaware that you must be very careful not to translate the word *fantasia* as 'fantasy', when it should be 'imagination'. In English, thanks to Coleridge, 'imagination' is the categorically superior term. In Italian, after Croce, *fantasia* is categorically superior to *immaginazione*. Imprecision on this point is made galling by the fact that for Montale, as for every other Italian writing in the twentieth century, it was Croce who made precise discussion of the subject possible.

More serious still, the translation is often glutinous. Montale's enviably colloquial flow can't be reproduced unless you are sometimes content to write several sentences where he wrote one. The arbitrary genders of Italian enable a *prosatore* of Montale's gifts to construct long sentences in which you don't lose track. It's impossible to transpose them intact, as Mr Galassi proves on several occasions by producing a construction so labyrinthine that Ariadne's thread would run out halfway.

This prevalent fault of lumpishness – so unfaithful to Montale's conversational urbanity – is exacerbated by a light peppering of strange English usages, or misusages. On page fifty-seven, to take one example, 'the game is up' should be 'the game's afoot' or possibly 'the game is on', but as it stands it means the exact opposite of what Montale wrote. 'Poetry is the art that is technically available to everyone: all it takes is a piece of paper and a pencil and the game is up.' On page 134, 'gild the pill' literally translates the Italian expression (*indorare la pillola*) but in English sounds like an unhappy conflation of 'gild the lily' and 'sugar the pill', which mean something separately but not a lot together.

The Second Life of Art, of the books in English by or concerned with Montale, is easily the most important to date. Of the books in Italian, *Prime alla Scala* has been long awaited. From 1954 to 1967 Montale wrote regular opera notices for the *Corriere d'Informazione*. It was always clear that when the pieces were collected the resulting volume would be one of the strongest on his short shelf. But the complete work, which he did not live to see published, is beyond expectation. It shows him at his best: in love with the subject and full of things to say.

Montale attended most of the La Scala first nights in the great period when much of the conducting was being done by his ideal maestro, Gianandrea Gavazzeni. The *bel canto* operas were being rediscovered, mainly because of Callas. Early and middle Verdi was being honoured for the first time as the full equivalent of the later operas and not just as the preparation for them. Meanwhile it was becoming ever clearer that the tradition could be added to only by reassessing the past. The new composers, with the qualified exceptions of Stravinsky and Britten, lacked the secret.

Montale's criticism, underpinned by his early training as a singer, was part of all this. The book abounds with solid detail. ('Her diction was clear and precisely articulated,' he says of Callas, 'even if her almost Venetian Italian rendered difficult the doubling of consonants.') Beyond that, in his usual way, he draws conclusions about art in general. The crisis in music is traced as it happens, by someone who was there, in 1916, at the first performance of one of Leoncavallo's last operas and lived to hear the endlessly repeated notes of a new work by Nono bore the audience starry-eyed in the name of social awareness. Yet Montale's own repeated note is one of endurance, a refusal to be crushed under the weight of justifiable pessimism: the new composers might have lost touch with any possible public except themselves, but Bellini lives again, Verdi is reborn in full glory, the past enthralls the present and reminds it of what art is. In the modern era there is no way for music *not* to be self-conscious. Being that, it has small chance of being spontaneous. But Montale, remembering how he himself found a way of being both, always talks as if other people might somehow manage it too.

These are necessary books about the arts, in a troubled period when one of the threats facing the arts is that there are too many books about them. Montale said he thought of journalism as his *secondo mestiere*, the day-job whose demands relegated his real calling, poetry, to evenings and spare time. But the fact that he was obliged to spend so much time thus earning a living is a good reason for liking the age we live in – a liking that he shared, despite everything. He was the kind of pessimist who makes you feel optimistic, even when he can't do the same for himself.

London Review of Books, February–March, 1983: previously included in
Snakecharmers in Texas, 1988

Postscript

Sadly, the first thing I feel bound to say about this essay on Montale is that I still believe he was a great artist. It shouldn't need saying. But all too soon after his death his copybook was retroactively blotted in a big way. It emerged that a good few, and perhaps most, of his reviews of books in the English language had been written by someone else. Montale had made a practice of handing the book to a subaltern, specifying the word length, publishing the results under his own name, and splitting the payment. If it had been discovered that Vermeer had known van Meegeren personally, and actually supplied him with paint, the scandal could not have been more rancid. It could be said in Montale's defence that in Italy there has long been a tradition by which prominent painters whistle in the apprentices of their *bottega* to help fill the less challenging stretches of a canvas. It could also be said that in Italy there is a long tradition of outright corruption in all walks of life. At the time when Montale was posthumously rumbled, about half of Italy's politicians were facing a stretch in gaol, and nobody was surprised except them, because when *everyone* is on the take the moral outrage is confined to those who get pinched. But Montale should have been above all that.

Most of the time he was. Take away the stuff he farmed out and there is still a large amount of steady, responsible, thoughtful and generous reviewing – criticism in its most nourishing form. Take all *that* away, and there is still the poetry, which remains near the apex of European achievement in modern times. It should subtract nothing from a quiet triumph to find out that its author was a bit more complicated than we thought. I wouldn't go as far as to say that I was pleased when the man I revered as the epitome of selfless literary endeavour turned out to share a few characteristics with the man who fixed the World Series. But I wasn't displeased either; just even more fascinated. The way to avoid that kind of fascination is to concern yourself entirely with art and learn nothing about artists: an impossible ideal and probably a hollow one. There are still a few major compositions by Stravinsky that I haven't sat down to listen to properly. I could have devoted some of the time to them that I spent reading the first volume of Stephen Walsh's biography. It reveals Stravinsky to have been a nasty piece of work in several respects. But I don't, on that account, love the music I already know any the less, and might even feel inspired to search through the rest of it with reinvigorated concentration, having found out that the demigod really was a human being all along. There was something perfect about Montale, and now there isn't, but somehow the bones of the cuttlefish are picked cleaner than ever, now that the soul which chose them for an emblem of purity turns out to have dealt the occasional card from the bottom of the deck.

2001

ON SEAMUS HEANEY

Door into the Dark by Seamus Heaney, Faber

Of all the newer tight-lipped poets Mr Heaney is the hardest case, and the tight-lipped critics whose praise is not usually easy to get have been sending quite a lot of approbation his way. His technique is hard-edged: a punchy line travels about two inches. The subject matter is loud with the slap of the spade and sour with the stink of turned earth. Close to the vest, close to the bone and close to the soil. We have learnt already not to look to him for the expansive gesture: there are bitter essences to compensate for the lack of that. *Door into the Dark* confirms him in his course, its very title telling you in which direction that course lies. I will show you fear in a tinful of bait. It should be said at the outset that poetry as good as Mr Heaney's best is hard to come by. But it is all pretty desperate stuff, and in those poems where we don't feel the brooding vision to be justified by the customary dense beauty of his technique we are probably in the right to come down hard and send our criticism as close as we can to the man within. The man within is at least in some degree a chooser. If he chose to be slick, to let his finely worked clinching stanzas fall pat, there would be a new kind of damaging poetry on the way – squat, ugly and unstoppable.

But first let us demonstrate the quality of the poetic intelligence with which we have to deal. This is the first stanza of his two-stanza poem 'Dream': it should be quickly apparent that his virtuoso kinetic gift can find interior equivalents in language for almost any movement in the exterior world, so that the mere act of sub-vocalizing the poem brings one out in a sweat.

> With a billhook
> Whose head was hand-forged and heavy

> I was hacking a stalk
> Thick as a telegraph pole.
> My sleeves were rolled
> And the air fanned cool past my arms
> As I swung and buried the blade,
> Then laboured to work it unstuck.

All the correct chunks and squeaks are caught without being said. But where does it get us? It gets us to the second stanza.

> The next stroke
> Found a man's head under the hook.
> Before I woke
> I heard the steel stop
> In the bone of the brow.

He had a dream, you see, and his skill brings you close to believing it – but not quite. This deadfall finish is really a conventional echo of the professional toughies, 'realistic' about violence, who have been giving us the jitters for some time. Most of the other symptoms in the syndrome are manifest somewhere or other in the book. Human characteristics tend to be referred back to animals and objects. As with Ted Hughes, it takes a visit to the zoo, the game reserve, or an imaginary dive below the sod before the idea of *personality* gets any showing at all. The people themselves are mostly clichés disguised in heroic trappings. A stable vacated by a horse ('Gone') offers more character than the smithy still occupied by the smith ('The Forge'). This latter poem, surely fated to be an anthology piece for the generations to come, can usefully be quoted in full:

> All I know is a door into the dark.
> Outside, old axles and iron hoops rusting;
> Inside, the hammered anvil's short-pitched ring,
> The unpredictable fantail of sparks
> Or hiss when a new shoe toughens in water.
> The anvil must be somewhere in the centre,
> Horned as a unicorn, at one end square,
> Set there immoveable: an altar
> Where he expends himself in shape and music.
> Sometimes, leather-aproned, hairs in his nose,
> He leans out on the jamb, recalls a clatter

Of hoofs where traffic is flashing in rows;
Then grunts and goes in, with a slam and flick
To beat real iron out, to work the bellows.

The numbered questions in the back of the school anthology are
obvious. What is the attitude of the smith to modern civilization? Is
it the same as the poet's attitude? And (for advanced students) would
you consider the Leavisite views on the organic relationship of work
to life relevant? But it should also be obvious that the interest of the
poem drops considerably when the human being replaces the object
at stage centre. Those hairs in his nose don't do much to establish
him, except as a character actor sent down at an hour's notice
from Central Casting. If he were more real, his attitudes towards
mechanized culture might not fall so pat. Get through that doorway
in the dark and you might find him beating out hubcaps or balancing
the wire wheels on a DB6 – both jobs which can be done with as
much love as bending your millionth horseshoe. There is no conflict
here: there is just a received opinion expressed in hints and cleverly
overblown in unexpected places – that altar, and the unicorn's horn,
which ought to be a rhino's only that's too easy. On the page the
refined poem has its attractive spareness: it's the implication, the area
of suggestion, that worries the reader through the ordinariness of its
assumptions about culture. Self-employed artisans are usually tough
enough to see reality straight: given the chance, the leather-aproned
subject might well remind Mr Heaney that there ain't no pity in the
city.

Things live; animals almost live; humans live scarcely at all. The
inverse progression holds disturbingly true in well-known efforts like
the poem about the frozen pump, 'Rite of Spring'.

That sent the pump up in flame.
It cooled, we lifted her latch,
Her entrance was wet, and she came.

It's a roundabout way for passion to get into print. The obverse
poems to this are 'Mother', in which the lady ends up wanting to be
like the pump, and 'The Wife's Tale', a brilliantly tactile poem in
which you touch everything – cloth, stubble, grass, bread, seed and
china cups – except flesh.

Mr Heaney's 'A Lough Neagh Sequence' forms an important section of the book and could well be pointed to if one were asked to isolate a thematic area absolutely his.

> They're busy in a high boat
> That stalks towards Antrim, the power cut.
> The line's a filament of smut
>
> Drawn hand over fist
> Where every three yards a hook's missed
> Or taken (and the smut thickens, wrist-
>
> Thick, a flail
> Lashed into the barrel
> With one swing). Each eel
>
> Comes aboard to this welcome:
> The hook left in gill or gum,
> It's slapped into the barrel numb
>
> But knits itself, four-ply,
> With the furling, slippy
> Haul, a knot of back and pewter belly
>
> That stays continuously one
> For each catch they fling in
> Is sucked home like lubrication.

Evocation could go no further: the eels ('hatched fears') are practically in your lap. Similarly in poems like 'Bann Clay' and 'Bogland' his grating line, shudderingly switched back and forth like teeth ground in a nightmare, finds endless technical equivalents for the subject described: he really is astonishingly capable. And in 'Bogland' there is an indication that he can do something even more difficult – state the open statement, make the gesture that enlivens life.

> They've taken the skeleton
> Of the Great Irish Elk
> Out of the peat, set it up
> An astounding crate full of air.

The spirits lift to the flash of wit. There ought to be more of it. Nobody in his right mind would deny that Mr Heaney's is one of

the outstanding talents on the scene, or want that talent to settle in
its ways too early.

TLS, 1969

Postscript (i)

One of my earliest notorieties was obtained by mentioning Seamus
Heaney in the same breath as Yeats. I was right not to regret it,
because sooner rather than later everyone was doing it. More com-
mendably, this piece paid Heaney the compliment of careful writing
on the reviewer's part. By using 'symptom' and 'syndrome' in the
same sentence to show that they did not mean the same thing (strictly,
a syndrome is a group of symptoms) I pioneered a technique which
I have been using ever since in the attempt to do my share of saving
useful distinctions threatened with decay through misuse. As a TV
critic, writing every week, I would frequently form a sentence around
such paired words as 'disinterested' and 'uninterested', or 'mitigate'
and 'militate', in order to prove that the precision conferred by using
them correctly was worth preserving. If the campaign had succeeded
I could be more modest about it. It failed completely. As Kingsley
Amis has pointed out, there is an iron law operating which dictates
that anyone working in the media who makes such errors somehow
never gets to read articles deploring them.

The Metropolitan Critic, 1994

Postscript (ii)

To hitch a ride on the coat-tails of a comet is a bad ambition, but
can be gratifying if it happens accidentally. I was lucky enough to be
the first critic into print with the nerve, or the naivety, to suggest
that Heaney might have a Yeatsian gift. For some time afterwards

the comparison was cited by my detractors as clear evidence of hysteria. Later on it was called a boldly premature tip that turned out to be right, and still later everyone forgot that I had ever said it. But it was fun while it lasted. With another flight of fancy I was less lucky. In my mock epic poem *Peregrine Prykke's Pilgrimage* I fielded a Guinness-voiced character called Seamus Feamus. The nickname caught on, but I never got the credit for it. In profiles about Heaney, its coinage (but with the second name spelt 'famous', which loses half the point, one would have thought) is usually ascribed to his old literary chums in Ireland. This might very well have been so: it was an idea begging to be had, so anything less than multiple authorship would have been surprising. Fortunately it is not possible to copyright a coinage, or else professional jealousy would spawn a million lawsuits. If you invent a word or a phrase, you should be ready to see other people lift it without acknowledgement; why else did you invent it, except to get it into the language? In the best critics of any medium there is always a poetic urge, and in the critic of poetry it can lead to a professional deformation. Almost always he is, or has been, a poet himself, and when faced with a brilliant new arrival he needs to guard himself against his own envy. The best way is to admit it. From his first book, it was obvious that Heaney commanded, as a natural dispensation, a vocal register well fitted for grandeur – rather more grandeur, in fact, than the emergent Yeats, who spent a long time trilling lightly near the top of the stave before his voice finally broke. The comparison was elementary. Yet one poet of my acquaintance – famous himself later on, although not quite *Seamus* famous – spent years telling me that it was the silliest thing he had ever heard.

2001

THE POETRY OF EDMUND WILSON

Apart from *Poets, Farewell,* which was published in 1929 and has been unobtainable for most of the time since, the two main collections of Edmund Wilson's verse are *Note-Books of Night* and *Night Thoughts.* Of these, *Note-Books of Night* was published in America in 1942, took three years to cross the Atlantic (Secker & Warburg brought it out in May 1945) and has since become fairly unobtainable itself, although it is sometimes to be found going cheap in the kind of second-hand book shop that doesn't know much about the modern side. *Night Thoughts,* published in America in 1961 and in Britain a year later, is still the current collection. It regroups most of the work in *Note-Books of Night* into new sections, interspersing a good deal of extra matter, ranging from lyrics written in youth to technical feats performed in age. The final effect is to leave you convinced that although *Night Thoughts* is good to have, *Note-Books of Night* remains the definitive collection of Wilson's verse. Less inclusive, it is more complete.

Being that, it would be an interesting book even if Wilson's verse were negligible – interesting for the sidelight it threw on the mind of a great critic. But in fact Wilson's verse is far from negligible. Just because Wilson's critical work is so creative doesn't mean that his nominally creative work is a waste of time. Even without *Memoirs of Hecate County* and *I Thought of Daisy,* the mere existence of *Note-Books of Night* would be sufficient evidence that Wilson had original things to say as a writer. It is a deceptively substantial little book which looks like a slim volume only by accident. There are more than seventy pages of solid text, with something memorable on nearly every page. Thirty pages are given to prose fragments and the rest to poetry. It isn't major poetry, but some of it is very good minor poetry – and in an age of bad major poetry there is very little good minor poetry about.

Wilson was no shrinking violet, but he knew his limitations. He knew that his touch with language wasn't particularly suggestive so he went for precision instead. He possessed a lot of information to be precise with. Where his verse is excessive, it is the excess of the seed catalogue – a superfluity of facts. He never usurps the lyrical genius's prerogative of saying more than he knows. Nor did he ever consider himself talented enough to be formless – his formal decorum always reminds us that he stems from the early 20th-century America which in retrospect seems more confident than Europe itself about transmitting the European tradition. The work is all very schooled, neat, strict and assured. And finally there is his gift for parody, which sometimes led him beyond mere accomplishment and into the realm of inspiration. In 'The Omelet of A. MacLeish', for example, the talent of his verse is reinforced by the genius of his criticism, with results more devastating critically than his essays on the same subject, and more vivid poetically than his usual poems.

In *Note-Books of Night* the poems are arranged in no chronological scheme. From the rearrangement in *Night Thoughts* it is easier to puzzle out when he wrote what, but even then it is sometimes hard to be sure. Eventually there will be scholarly research to settle the matter, but I doubt if much of interest will be revealed touching Wilson's development as a writer of verse. After an early period devoted to plangent lyricism of the kind which can be called sophomoric as long as we remember that he was a Princeton sophomore and an exceptionally able one into the bargain, Wilson quickly entered into his characteristic ways of seeing the world. Like other minor artists he matured early and never really changed. Indeed he was writing verse in the Thirties which forecast the mood of the prose he published in the early Seventies, at the end of his life. The desolate yearning for the irretrievably lost America which makes *Upstate* so sad a book is already there in *Note-books of Night*, providing the authentic force behind the somewhat contrived Arnoldian tone of poems like 'A House of the Eighties'.

> —The ugly stained-glass window on the stair,
> Dark-panelled dining-room, the guinea fowl's fierce clack,
> The great gray cat that on the oven slept—
> My father's study with its books and birds,
> His scornful tone, his eighteenth-century words,

> His green door sealed with baize
> —Today I travel back
> To find again that one fixed point he kept
> And left me for the day
> In which this other world of theirs grows dank, decays,
> And founders and goes down.

Wilson's poetry of the Thirties frequently deals with houses going to rack and ruin. The houses are in the same condition that we find them in forty years later, in *Upstate*. They are in the same places: Talcottville, Provincetown, Wilson's ancestral lands. Houses pointing to the solid old New England civilization which once found its space between the sea and the Adirondacks and was already being overtaken by progress when the poet was young. In his essays of the Thirties (notably 'The Old Stone House' collected in *The American Earthquake*) Wilson wrote optimistically about an America 'forever on the move'. But if his essays were true to his then-radical intellect, his poetry was true to his conservative feelings. His dead houses are metaphors for a disappearing way of life.

> And when they found the house was bare
> The windows shuttered to the sun
> They woke the panthers with a stare
> To finish what they had begun

The poem is called 'Nightmare'. As we know from his great essay of 1937, 'In Honour of Pushkin' (collected in *The Triple Thinkers* and rightly called by John Bayley the best short introduction to Pushkin – a generous tribute, considering that Bayley has written the best long one), Wilson was particularly struck by the supreme poetic moment in *Evgeny Onegin* when Lensky is killed in a duel and his soulless body is compared to an empty house, with whitewashed windows. The image is one of the climactic points in all poetry – it is like Hector's address to Andromache, or Eurydice holding out her useless hands, or Paolo kissing Francesca's trembling mouth – so it is no wonder that Wilson should have been impressed by it. But you also can't help feeling that the image was congenial to his personal psychology. Although in books like *Europe Without Baedeker* Wilson did his best to secede from the weight of the European heritage, the fact always remained that by his education – by his magnificent education – and by his temperament he was inextricably committed to an American past which owed much of its civilized force to the European memory. This was the America which was dying all the time as he grew older. One of the several continuous mental struggles in Wilson is between his industrious loyalty to the creative impulse of the new America and his despairing sense – which made itself manifest in his poetry much earlier than in his prose – that chaos could in no wise be staved off. The decaying houses of his last books, with their cherished windows broken and highways built close by, are all presaged in the poetry of his early maturity.

But in some respects maturity came too early. Coleridge, perhaps because he had trouble growing up, favoured a slow ripening of the faculties. There was always something unsettling about the precocity of Wilson's mimetic technique: his gift as a parodist was irrepressibly at work even when he wanted it not to be, with the result that his formally precise early lyrics tend towards pastiche – they are throwbacks to the end of the century and beyond. The tinge of Arnold in 'A House of the Eighties' – the pale echo of his melancholy, long withdrawing roar – is compounded even there, it seems to me, by memories of Browning. At other times you can hear Kipling in the background. Wilson's attempts at plangent threnody call up the voices of other men.

Wilson's elegiac lyrics are never less than technically adroit: their high finish reminds us forcibly not only of the standards which were imposed by Christian Gauss's Princeton (standards which we can see otherwise in the poetry of John Peale Bishop) but of a whole generation of American poets, now not much thought about, who had complete command of their expressive means, even if they did not always have that much to express. Edna St Vincent Millay and Elinor Wylie have by now retreated into the limbo of the semi-read – Eleanor Farjeon and Ruth Pitter might be two comparable examples from this side of the water – but when you look at the work of Elinor Wylie, in particular, it is astonishing how accomplished she was. Wilson's criticism helped American writing grow out of its self-satisfaction at mere accomplishment, but he knew about the certain losses as well as the possible gains. In his poetry he committed himself to the past by synthesizing its cherishable tones, but he paid the penalty of mimetic homage in not sounding enough like himself. In 'Disloyal Lines to an Alumnus' he satirized the poetry of Beauty –

> And Beauty, Beauty, oozing everywhere
> Like maple-sap from maples! Dreaming there,
> I have sometimes stepped in Beauty on the street
> And slipped, sustaining bruises blue but sweet . . .

But his own lyric beauty was not different enough from the Beauty he was satirizing. These lines from 'Riverton' take some swallowing now and would have needed excuses even then.

> —O elms! O river! aid me at this turn—
> Their passing makes my late imperative:
> They flicker now who frightfully did burn,
> And I must tell their beauty while I live.
> Changing their grade as water in its flight,
> And gone like water; give me then the art,
> Firm as night-frozen ice found silver-bright,
> That holds the splendour though the days depart.

Give me then the art, indeed. He had the artifice, but the art was mainly that of a pasticheur. When consumed by Yeats's business of articulating sweet sounds together, Wilson was the master of every poetic aspect except originality. Listen to the judiciously balanced vowel-modulations in 'Poured full of thin gold sun':

> But now all this—
> Peace, brightness, the browned page, the crickets in the grass—
> Is but a crust that stretches thin and taut by which I pass
> Above the loud abyss.

A virtuoso is only ever fully serious when he forgets himself. Wilson is in no danger of forgetting himself here. In his later stages, which produced the technical games collected in *Night Thoughts*, his urge to jump through hoops clearly detached itself from the impulse to register feeling; but it should also be noted that even early on the division existed. His penchant for sound effects, like his ear for imitation, usually led him away from pure expression. On occasions, however, when consciously schooled euphuistic bravura was lavished on a sufficiently concrete subject, Wilson got away from tricksy pastoralism and achieved a personal tone – urban, sardonic, tongue-in-cheek, astringent. The consonant-packed lines of 'Night in May'

> Pineapple-pronged four-poster of a Utica great-great

were a portent of what Wilson was able to do best. Such a line is the
harbinger of an entire, superb poem: 'On Editing Scott Fitzgerald's
Papers', which first appeared in the preliminary pages of *The Crack-
Up* and stands out in *Note-Books of Night* as a full, if regrettably
isolated, realization of the qualities Wilson had to offer as a poet.

Speaking personally for a moment, I can only say that it was this
poem, along with certain passages in Roy Campbell's bloody-minded
satires, which first convinced me that the rhyming couplet of
iambic pentameter was still alive as a form – that in certain respects
it was *the* form for an extended poem. Wilson, like Campbell, by
accepting the couplet's heritage of grandeur was able somehow to
overcome its obsolescence: once the effect of archaic pastiche was
accepted, there was room for any amount of modern freedom. In
fact it was the fierce rigour of the discipline which made the freedom
possible. And Wilson was more magnanimous than Campbell: his
grandeur really *was* grandeur, not grandiloquence.

> Scott, your last fragments I arrange tonight . . .

The heroic tone is there from the first line. (It is instructive, by
the way, that only the tone is heroic: the couplets themselves are not
heroic but Romance – i.e. open rather than closed.) It would have
been a noble theme whatever form Wilson had chosen, because
Wilson's lifelong paternal guardianship of Fitzgerald's talent is a noble
story. Fitzgerald was the Princeton alumnus who *didn't* benefit from
the education on offer. From Wilson's and Fitzgerald's letters to
Christian Gauss we can easily see who was the star student and who
the ineducable enthusiast. But Wilson, like Gauss, knew that Fitzgerald was destined to make his own way according to a different
and more creative law. Wilson called *This Side of Paradise* a compen-
dium of malapropisms but knew that it had not failed to live. When
the masterpieces arrived he saw them clearly for what they were.
Much of his rage against Hollywood was on Fitzgerald's behalf: he
could see how the film world's sinister strength was diabolically
attuned to Fitzgerald's fatal weakness. He understood and sympathized with Fitzgerald even in his most abject decline and guarded
his memory beyond the grave.

Such a story would be thrilling however it was told. But the
couplets are ideal for it: the elegaic and narrative strains match
perfectly, while the meretricious, Condé Nast glamour of the imagery

is entirely appropriate to Fitzgerald's debilitating regard for the high life – the well-heeled goings-on to which, as Wilson well knew, Fitzgerald sacrificed his soul but which he superseded with his talent. Hence Wilson evokes the memory of Fitzgerald's eyes in terms of a *Vogue* advertisement. Passing their image on to what they mint, they

> . . . leave us, to turn over, iris-fired,
> Not the great Ritz-sized diamond you desired
> But jewels in a handful, lying loose:
> Flawed amethysts; the moonstone's milky blues;
> Chill blues of pale transparent tourmaline;
> Opals of shifty yellow, chartreuse green,
> Wherein a vein vermilion flees and flickers—
> Tight phials of the spirit's light mixed liquors;
> Some tinsel zircons, common turquoise; but
> Two emeralds, green and lucid, one half-cut,
> One cut consummately—both take their place
> In Letters' most expensive Cartier case.

The consummately cut emerald is obviously *The Great Gatsby*; the half-cut emerald is probably *Tender Is The Night*; and we suppose that the tinsel zircons are the hack stories Fitzgerald turned out in order to pay his bills. But apart from the admittedly preponderant biographical element, what strikes you is the assured compression of the technique. In lines like 'Tight phials of the spirit's light mixed liquors' Wilson was forging a clear, vital utterance: that he was to take it no further is a matter for regret. In this poem his complicated games with language are confined within the deceptively simple form and serve the purpose. Here is the public voice which Wilson so admired (and by implication adumbrated for our own time) in the artistry of Pushkin. In 'On Editing Scott Fitzgerald's Papers' his playfulness, his seriousness, his severe humour and his sympathetic *gravitas* are all in balance. The proof of Wilson's mainly fragmentary achievement as a poet is the conspicuous force he attained on the few occasions when his gifts were unified. The artist who is all artist – the artist who, even when he is also a good critic, is nevertheless an artist first of all – can recognize this moment of unity within himself and lives for nothing else but to repeat it. Wilson had too many other interests: which, of course, it would be quixotic to begrudge him.

There are other narrative poems by Wilson but they lack the transforming discipline of the couplet. Similarly he has other strong subjects – especially sex – but as with most revelations their interest has become with time more historical than aesthetic. Yet other poems are full of named things, but the names deafen the vision. Three different kinds of deficiency, all of them interesting.

The first deficiency is mainly one of form. Wilson's narrative poems are an attempt at public verse which certainly comes off better than comparable efforts by more recognized American poets. Nobody now could wade through Robinson Jeffers' *Roan Stallion*, for example. Wilson's 'The Good Neighbour' is the story of Mr and Mrs Pritchard, who become obsessed with defending their house against invaders. Wilson guards against portentousness by casting the tale in hudibrastics, but the results, though very readable, are less popular than cute. The technique is too intrusive. Another narrative, 'The Woman, the War Veteran and the Bear', is an outrageous tale of a legless trapeze artist and a girl who married beneath her. It is full of interesting social detail but goes on too long: a glorified burlesque number that should have been a burlesque number. The stanzas are really ballad stanzas, but the poem wants to be more than a ballad. 'Lesbia in Hell' is better, but again the hudibrastics are the wrong form: they hurry you on too fast for thought and leave you feeling that the action has been skimped. Doubly a pity, because the theme of Satan falling in love with Lesbia involves Wilson in one of his most deeply felt subjects – sexual passion.

It still strikes the historically minded reader that *Note-Books of Night* is a remarkably sexy little book for its time. Wilson, we should remember, had a share in pioneering the sexual frankness of our epoch. *Memoirs of Hecate County* was a banned book in Australia when I was young. Wilson lived long enough to deplore pornographic licence but never went back on his liberal determination to speak of things as they were. Poems like 'Home to Town: Two Highballs' convey something of the same clinical realism about sex which made Wilson's prose fiction extraordinary and which still gives it better than documentary importance. In *Memoirs of Hecate County* Wilson drew a lasting distinction between the high society lady, who appealed to the narrator's imagination but left his body cold, and the low-born taxi-dancer who got on his nerves but fulfilled him sexually. The chippie seems to be there again in 'Two Highballs'.

And all the city love, intense and faint like you—
The little drooping breasts, the cigarettes,
The little cunning shadow between the narrow thighs. . . .

Paul Dehn, mentioning this passage when the poem was reprinted in *Night Thoughts*, found it ridiculous, but I don't see why we should agree. Wilson's attempts at a bitter urban poetry—

And the El that accelerates, grates, shrieks, diminishes,
            swishing, with such pain—
To talk the city tongue!

are at least as memorable, and certainly as frank about experience, as the contorted flights of Hart Crane. Of Crane, when I search my memory, I remember the seal's wide spindrift gaze towards Paradise and the bottles wearing him in crescents on their bellies. There were things Crane could do that Wilson couldn't – the wine talons, the sublime notion of travelling in a tear – but on the whole Wilson did at least as good a job of reporting the city. And in matters of sex he was more adventurous than anybody – ahead of his time, in fact.

But if you are ahead of your time only in your subject, then eventually you will fall behind the times, overtaken by the very changes in taste you helped engender. So it is with Wilson's sexual poetry: all the creativity goes into the act of bringing the subject up, with no powers of invention left over for the task of transforming it into the permanence of something imagined. Ideally, Wilson's sexual themes should have been a natural part of a larger poetic fiction. But as we see in 'Copper and White' (not present in *Note-Books of Night*, but *Night Thoughts* usefully adds it to the canon) what they tended to blend with was greenery-yallery *fin de siècle* lyricism.

I knew that passionate mouth in that pale skin
Would spread with such a moisture, let me in
To such a bareness of possessive flesh!—
I knew that fairest skin with city pallor faded,
With cigarettes and late electric light,
Would shield the fire to lash
The tired unblushing cheeks to burn as they did—
That mouth that musing seemed so thin,
Those cheeks that tired seemed so white!

It is as if Ernest Dowson and Lionel Johnson had been asked to versify Edith Wharton's discovery of passion as revealed in her secret manuscript *Beatrice Palmato*. The very tones of out-of-dateness. But the informing idea – of loneliness in love – is still alive. It should have been the poem's field of exploration, but Wilson was content to arrive at the point where his much admired Proust began. Wilson was protective about his selfhood, as major artists never can be.

As to the naming of names – well, he overdid it. Great poetry is always full of things, but finally the complexity of detail is subordinated to a controlling simplicity. Wilson wrote some excellent nature poetry but nature poetry it remains: all the flowers are named but the point is seldom reached when it ceases to matter so much what kind of flowers they are. In 'At Laurelwood', one of the prose pieces in *Note-Books of Night*, he talks of how his grandfather and grandmother helped teach him the names of everyday objects. His range of knowledge is one of the many marvellous things about Wilson. In poems like 'Provincetown, 1936' he piled on the detail to good effect:

> Mussels with broken hinges, sea crabs lopped
> Of legs, black razor-clams split double, dried
> Sea-dollars, limpets chivied loose and dropped
> Like stranded dories rolling on their side:

But in the long run not even concrete facts were a sufficient antidote to the poetry of Beauty. Humour was a better safeguard. On the whole, it is the satirical verse which holds up best among Wilson's work. Quite apart from the classic 'The Omelet of A. MacLeish', there are 'The Extrovert of Walden Pond' with its *trouvé* catchphrase 'Thoreau was a neuro' and 'The Playwright in Paradise', a minatory ode to the writers of his generation which borrows lines from 'Adonais' to remind them that in Beverly Hills their talents will die young. In these poems Wilson's critical intelligence was at work. If he had possessed comic invention to match his scornful parodic ear, he might have equalled even E. E. Cummings. But 'American Masterpieces' (which makes its only appearance in *Night Thoughts*) shows what Cummings had that Wilson hadn't: in mocking the clichés of Madison Avenue, Wilson can win your allegiance, but Cummings can make you laugh. At the last, Wilson's jokes are not quite funny enough in themselves – they don't take off into the self-sustaining Empyrean of things you can't help reciting. His humour, like his frankness, ought ideally to have been part of a larger fiction.

Useless to carp. A minor artist Wilson remains. But it ought to be more generally realized that he was a very good minor artist, especially in his poetry. Of course, *Night Thoughts* didn't help. Inflated with juvenilia and senescent academic graffiti even duller than Auden's, the book blurred the outlines of Wilson's achievement – although even here it should be noted that its closing poem, 'The White Sand', is one of Wilson's most affecting things, a despairing celebration of late love so deeply felt that it almost overcomes the sense of strain generated by the internally-rhymed elegiacs in which it is cast.

What has worked most damagingly against Wilson's reputation as a poet, however, is his reputation as a critic. It is hard to see how things could be otherwise. As a critical mind, Wilson is so great that we have not yet taken his full measure. He is still so prominent as to be invisible: people think they can know what he said without having to read him. When he is read again, it will soon be found that he saw both sides of most of the arguments which continue to rage about what literature is or ought to be. Among these arguments is the one about modern poetry and its audience. Nobody was more sympathetic than Wilson to the emergence of a difficult, hermetic poetry or better-equipped to understand its origins. But equally he was able to keep the issue in perspective. First of all, his standards were traditional in the deepest sense: knowing why Homer, Virgil, Dante, Shakespeare and Pushkin were permanently modern, he knew why most of modern poetry was without the value it claimed for itself. Secondly, he had an unconquerable impulse towards community. All his writings are an expression of it, including his verse. He would have liked to read fully intelligible works while living in an ordered society. As things turned out, the works he admired were not always fully intelligible and the society he lived in was not ordered. But at least in his own creative writings, such as they were, he could try to be clear. So his poems are as they are, and the best of them last well.

1977: previously included in *At the Pillars of Hercules*, 1979

Postscript

Edmund Wilson is a city, of which his poetry is only an outer suburb, but with a direct subway line to the downtown district. When I was young he filled a lot of my sky. Later on – and partly through following up the trails of reading he had opened to me – I found that not even so voracious a mind as his could take in the whole world. Politically he was an isolationist by temperament, with Marxist overtones: two different ways of getting things wrong both working at once to undermine his social commentary. (*Europe Without Baedeker* was enough to prove that he had barely understood even World War II.) After his death, the diary volumes kept on coming out: reminiscence packaged by the decade, their unsympathetic streak made him look steadily less monumental. Perhaps that was his original plan in writing them at all: a kind of edifying self-sabotage. If so, it was too successful. Wilson began to disappear, buried under his own books. I hated to see it happen. When his name was minimized at a literary lunch table, I always made a point of recommending *The Shores of Light* and *Classics and Commercials* as the books that gave you the essential man, who was essentially a critic. The way he would learn a new language, forge on into a new literature – the fearless gusto of his approach still seems to me the finest example in modern times of what a critic should have by nature, the quality that the mighty philologist Menendez Pidal called a spontaneous yearning after the totality of knowledge. The totality can't be had, of course: but the yearning can.

Even in that department, however, Wilson had his blind spots, and at least one of them was disabling. It was all very well for him to say that he had never 'got around' to reading *Middlemarch*: George Eliot had enough admirers not to need the endorsement. But he was shamefully feckless in not bothering to learn Spanish. He could hardly plead that he didn't have the time: though learning Hebrew – a hard nut to crack – might have brought results, did Hungarian really repay the effort? He could have mastered Spanish with a tenth of the sweat, but he thought there was nothing to read. (Mercifully Cervantes was no longer around to hear him say so.) Thus the whole story of what was going on in Latin America in his lifetime – a story whose political aspects alone, by the target they offered, would have suited his isolationist convictions down to the ground – escaped him, and we lost the clarifying intelligence he might have brought to it. There was also the story of how the writers in the Spanish homeland reacted to the bountifully accumulating literary achievement in the Americas. He would have found Unamuno a man after his own heart, and would have been able to contend with Ortega's critical writings on the level at which they were composed, with a poet's judgement of weight and balance. For Wilson, Spanish was the road not taken. But the roads he took are enough to be going on with, and poetry was one of them. Not many full-time poets write even one poem that will live. Wilson's verse tribute to Scott Fitzgerald still brings at least one reader to the point of tears with its opening line: 'Scott, your last fragments I arrange tonight . . .' Prosaic perhaps; forgettable never.

2001

WORLD-BESOTTED TRAVELLER

POSTCARD FROM ROME

British Airways were justifiably proud of getting your correspondent to Rome only three hours behind schedule. After all, Heathrow had been in the grip of those freak snow conditions which traditionally leave Britain stunned with surprise.

In England, British Rail loudspeakers had been smugly announcing prolonged delays due to locomotives coming into contact with inexplicable meteorological phenomena, such as heaps of water lying around in frozen form. Airport officials were equally flabbergasted to discover more of the same stuff falling out of the sky. But now my staunch Trident was leaving all that behind. In a dark but clear midnight, Rome lay below. Those strings of lights were roads all leading to the same place.

All my previous visits to the Eternal City had been done on the cheap. In those days I was still travelling on the weird escape routes frequented by students. Some of the students turned out to be eighty-year-old Calabrian peasant ladies carrying string bags full of onions. The charter aircraft belonged to semi-scheduled airlines whose pilots wore black eyepatches and First World War medals. Their point of arrival was Ciampino, Rome's no. 2 airport – an inglorious military establishment ringed with flat-tyred DC-4s and Convair 240s too obsolete for anything except fire drill.

I used to live in the kind of cold-water *pensione* on the Via del Corso where the original rooms had been partitioned not only vertically but horizontally as well, so that the spiral staircase beside your bed led up to a bare ceiling. You had to apply in writing to take a bath. Lunch was half a plate of pasta on the other side of the Tiber. Dinner was the other half.

A lot of water has gone over the viaduct since then, and this time I was a *bona fide* traveller. Even at one o'clock in the morning Leonardo da Vinci airport, tastefully done out in fluted chromium, was a treat for the eyes. My hotel was in Piazza Trinità dei Monti at the very top of the Spanish Steps. The décor was strictly veneers and cut glass, but it was heavily tricked out with the Medici coat of arms and the bath came ready equipped not just with a plug, but a dinky sachet of foam-producing green goo. My waiting readers were subsidizing this luxury. Could I justify their confidence? What can you say about so old a city in so short a space? I sank cravenly into the foam.

Sleep allayed my fears, but they came back in the morning. I appeared on the Spanish Steps just in time to be greeted by the cold weather, which had been racing down Europe during the night. Rome suddenly froze up solid. The Triton, forever blowing his conch in the Piazza Barberini, abruptly became festooned with icicles. As unashamedly ostentatious as ever, the wealthier Roman women shopping in the Via Condotti instantly adopted a uniform – mink and boots. In a bar a little fat lady who looked like a bale of furs reached up to spoon the cream from a glass of hot chocolate higher than her head. For once nobody was in any danger of being kidnapped. Cold weather meant plenty of snow in the mountain resorts. The terrorists were all away skiing.

With only a few days at my disposal I decided to leave most of my usual haunts unvisited, apart from a quick trip to St Peter's to see how well the Michelangelo *pietà* had been repaired. Since I had last seen this masterpiece it had been attacked by a hammer-wielding Australian of Hungarian origins. Perhaps he was trying to effect improvements. Anyway, he had given the Madonna a nose-job. The nose was now back on and the whole statue, I was glad to see, had been separated from its adoring public by a glass wall. Taking it for granted that none of my compatriots had been flicking ink darts at the Sistine ceiling, I headed out by car to the Catacombs.

Out on the old Appian Way it was as cold as Caligula's heart. Sleet drenched the roadside ruins. Like a leftover from *La Strada*, a lone whore solicited business from passing cars. A couple of millennia ago the cars would have been chariots but she would have looked roughly the same. Hilarius Fuscus has a tomb out there somewhere. Apart from his name he is of no historical interest, but with a name like Hilarius Fuscus how interesting do you have to be? The Catacombs, however, were mainly for the nameless. In the Catacombs of Domitilla, for example, more than 100,000 people were buried, but only seventy of them came down to modern times with any identity beyond that conferred by the heap of powder their bones turned into when touched by air.

A German monk took me down into the ground. 'Zer soil is called tufa. Volcanig. Easy for tunnels. Mind zer head.' In this one set of catacombs there are eleven miles of tunnels, one network under another. The two top levels have electric light throughout. 'Mine apologies for zer electric light. Mit candles is more eerie. Zis way.' People had been filed away down here by the generation. Some of the frescos remain intelligible. You can see the style changing through time: suddenly a Byzantine Christ tells you that the Empire of the West is in decline. The sign of the fish is everywhere. 'You also see zer sign of zer turdle dove. Symbol of luff und piss.'

When we arrived back at the surface the good friar's next party was alighting from its coach – a couple of hundred Japanese, all of them with cameras round their necks. Some of the cameras had tripods attached. I had been lucky to get what amounted to a private view. Nor were there many tourists at the newest of the Catacombs, the Fosse Ardeatine. The people buried here all died at once, on March 24, 1944. For the whole story you have to go to Anzio, about thirty-five miles down the coast.

Anzio is a small town built around a port. A few hundred yards from the port there are some ruined foundations on a low cliff. Standing in the ruins, you can look along the beaches. The Allied forces came ashore here in January 1944. The landing was unopposed but it took a long time to develop a beachhead. Italy was already out of the war but the Germans were not: far from it. Kesselring counterattacked with horrific violence. The whole area became an enormous battlefield. The flat littoral terrain was ideal for the German armour. Right over your head, the Ju88s came bombing and strafing. The Allied forces were stymied for months.

In Rome, the Italian resistance fighters grew tired of waiting. They ambushed an SS detachment in the Via Rasella, just down from the gates of the Palazzo Barberini, killing thirty-two men. Hitler ordered reprisals at the rate of ten to one. The SS, enthusiastically exceeding requirements, trucked 335 people out to the Fosse Ardeatine and shot them all.

But back to those ruins at Anzio. I am still standing in them, a bedraggled figure washed by the rain. They are the ruins of Nero's seaside villa. And back in time beyond Nero, on that low hill behind the town, Cicero had the country house of whose amenities he boasted in his letters to Atticus. In those days Anzio was called Antium. Further back than that, Coriolanus went into exile here. And even further back, at about the time the city of Rome was being founded – the year zero *ab urbe condita* – Antium was one of the main hangouts of the dreaded Volsci.

The Volsci feature on almost every page in the early books of Livy. The Romans were still confined to an area about the size of Hampstead and whenever they ventured outside their seven hills they had the Volsci breathing garlic down their necks. Eventually, through discipline, the Romans prevailed. That was Livy's message to his contemporary readers: remember your origins.

Everything and everywhere in and around Rome is saturated with time. If you look too long, you will be hypnotized. I went out to Lago Albano in the Alban Hills. The lake is in a giant crater. High on the rim is a town called Marino, where Sophia Loren owns a house. The Pope's summer residence is somewhere up there too. But take a close look at that sheltered lake. Imagine it in tumult. In Imperial times it was called Lacus Albanus and mock naval battles were held on it. That would have been my job in those days: writing reviews of mock naval battles. 'Once again Hilarius Fuscus made mincemeat of the opposition . . .'

Until recently, Sophia Loren faced serious charges with regard to the national currency. She was accused of trying to export some of her money. Almost everybody who owns any has been doing the same, but Sophia is supposed to be a woman of the people. Even the Press has turned against her. Her latest film has been greeted with massed raspberries. I went to see it. The critics were right.

The movie is directed by Lina Wertmueller and is crisply entitled *Fatto di sangue tra due uomini per causa di una vedova: si sospettano moventi politici.* This may be loosely rendered as 'A matter of honour between two men because of a widow: political motives are suspected.' My translation loses something of the original's flaccidity. Ms Wertmueller has an international reputation but her idea of a joke reveals her to be a humourless scold. The movie is all about hard times in Sicily. Apart from Sophia, it is a disaster. Sophia, playing a passionate charcoal-burner, looks better than ever and acts a storm. It is ridiculous that so life-giving an individual should be made a scapegoat.

The same thought occurred to me when I attended a Rome Opera production of Bellini's *I Capuletti ed i Montecchi*. Romeo and Juliet both sang magnificently. The settings were a reminder of how a lot can be made out of little – Covent Garden please copy. The audience in the stalls consisted mainly of the Roman bourgeoisie. They behaved like pigs. A man near me recited the whole plot to his deaf wife while she ate chocolate which had apparently been wrapped in dead leaves. The stalls were empty before the curtain calls were half over. But the gallery went crazy with gratitude.

Here was an opera company for any city to be proud of. Yet half of its members are in trouble with the police because of alleged corruption. While terrorists maim and murder at will, the cops are chasing contraltos. It's a clear case of fiddling while Rome burns.

In the Via Michelangelo Caetani a shrine of wreaths and photographs marks the spot where ex-Prime Minister Moro's body was dumped midway between the respective headquarters of the Communists and the Christian Democrats. To the terrorists, Moro stood for compromise. It followed logically that his life was forfeit. Most of the terrorists are *figli di papà* – sons of daddy. If daddy spends most of his time making money, shooting him is a good way of getting his attention. Under the absolutism there is petulance.

There have been bodies in that street before. As the Middle Ages gave way to the Renaissance, the Caetani fought the Colonna who fought the Orsini who fought the Caetani. Rienzo called himself tribune and reunited Rome for a few days. The great families used the Papacy to further their earthly ambitions. But ever since the fall of the old Empire the very idea of a renewed temporal hegemony had been an empty dream.

As Machiavelli bitterly noted, the Church, while not powerful enough to unite the country, was certainly powerful enough to make sure nobody else did. Machiavelli's remarks on the topic remain pertinent today, when even the Christian Democrats are appalled at the prospect of a Pope who seems intent on discrediting the legislature over the matter of abortion. The last thing the country needs is any more dividing. Italy's besetting weakness is government without authority. The result is not sweet anarchy but gun law.

You don't have to go all the way out to the Alban Hills in order to look down on Rome and discover it to be a small place. All you have to do is climb the Aventine. What you can see from there is just about all there is. When Rome ceased to be the capital city of an international empire, it reverted to being a provincial town. Though it has been officially called so since 1870, it has never really become the capital of Italy – not in the way London is the capital of England or Paris of France. Rome produces little. For a long time it has been a consumers' town. Even the Renaissance was produced in Florence and consumed in Rome. Bringing Michelangelo to Rome was like bringing Tolstoy to Hollywood.

Rome is a good place for madmen to dream of building empires. It is a bad place from which to govern Italy. Mussolini chose the first option, with the inevitable consequences. The most recent of Rome's overlords, he left the fewest traces. Apart from the embarrassingly fine architecture of the EUR district out on the periphery, the city gives almost no indication that he ever lived. The Palazzo di Venezia is, of course, still there. You can pick out the balcony from which he shouted to the crowds and the window behind which he left a light burning at night to encourage the notion that he never slept. Wealthy ladies used to visit him there, but by all accounts his technique as a lover was long on preliminary chest-beating and short on follow-through. It seems that he just hurled them to the floor and passed over them in a shallow dive.

The reason that the Empire could never be restored was that the world grew out of it. The Roman Empire died of success. It was already dying when Scipio Africanus became the first Roman to take a bath as often as once a week. It was already dying when the legions in Sicily met their first Greeks and began learning the ways of cultivated leisure. Livy's history is one long lament for the old Republic – a warning to Augustus that the tribe's disciplined impulse was on the wane.

But Livy never saw that he himself was part of the problem. Nor did Tacitus at a later time. The city which had once been little more than a base camp had become a civilization. It was changing at the centre. The decline was really a transformation. The Empire became the Church, which became other churches, which became the Enlightenment, which became the modern age. The centurions became the priests who became us. With the eyes history has given us, we can now see that to unite the world is no longer a sane aim. It has already become united, within the individual soul.

Meanwhile the city of Rome is left with nothing but its heritage.

There is a lot to look after. Things get stolen, or just fall apart. In the Piazza Navona I found the Bernini fountains plump with ice, like overfilled tubs of lemon *gelato*. In a dark alley behind the piazza stands the little church of Santa Maria della Pace. On the outside walls are the usual political graffiti. Inside there are some sibyls by Raphael. The doors are open only between 7 and 8.30 in the morning, for Mass. Outside the portico when I arrived, the body of a man was being hauled out of an abandoned car and loaded into a grey plastic bag. He was a tramp who had frozen to death in the night. A policeman signed for the corpse. Dirt, litter and decay. Raffaello Sanzio of Urbino was here once.

But it's unfair on Rome to let the weather get you down. In spring and summer the fountains ionize the air to the point that even the third-rate expatriate American writers who infest the city feel themselves brimming over with creative energy. Yet even then you can detect the weariness beneath the fervour. No less afraid of dying than anybody else, I still like the idea of what Lucretius describes as the reef of destruction to which all things must tend, *spatio aetatis defessa vetusto* – worn out by the ancient lapse of years. But I don't want to see the reef every day.

The Spanish Steps were a cataract. Climbing them like an exhausted salmon, I passed the window of the room in which Keats coughed out the last hours of his short life with nothing to look at except a cemetery of time. No wonder he forgot his own vitality and declared that his name was writ in water. As he should have realized, the thing to do when you feel like that is to pack up and catch a plane to London. Which I did.

1979: previously included in *Flying Visits*, 1984

Postscript

Though never a staff member of the *Observer*, I always received from it the best benefits of a welcoming home. As a freelance journalist working on a rolling contract, I had to do without the security of participation in the paper's pension scheme, but that was only a money matter, and the liberty was worth the price. Far more important was the editorial respect for careful writing. As always, the respect existed because the editors themselves knew how to compose a sentence. Donald Trelford, the successor to David Astor's chair, could write a succinct, correct and yet easily speakable prose, and Terence Kilmartin was outstanding even among the literary editors of the time for his knowledge of how the language worked and his enjoyment of that same knowledge in others – he wielded a fierce blue pencil but it would never hurt your rhythm. At the *Observer* I felt free to try things out. I got too much credit, then and later, for inventing the post-modern television column. Maurice Richardson (otherwise the author of that unjustly forgotten comic classic *The Exploits of Engelbrecht*) had been there already, and the most I ever did was transfer to a new subject the same wide tonal range with which Penelope Gilliatt and John Coleman had been writing about cinema – and they themselves were writing in a tradition that had been brought to a high point by C. A. Lejeune and Paul Dehn.

The genre I really did do something to invent was the Postcard travel piece. There were precedents for it – A. J. Liebling could arrive on a wartime airstrip and generate a whole treatise on the state of the campaign in North Africa while being strafed by an Me 109 – but nobody had yet developed a workable matrix for reconciling general knowledge with the necessarily superficial experience of a flying visit in the jet age. Donald Trelford supported me in my conviction that first impressions were worth something: after all, there must be a mind to back them up, or they wouldn't even have been received. The thing to do was to forget about writing the nuanced letter of a long-term resident or a slow traveller by camel, and send back the postcard of someone who was flying in and out in a few days, just like everybody else. On that basis, any background information I could get in – and especially the background information I took there with me – would count as a plus. Thus a format was born, which, I like to think, never became a formula, because every city gave a new impetus to the delicious task of squaring what had happened to it over centuries with what happened to me in the course of a week. Ten years later, when I transferred the idea to television, the week became two weeks or even three, and the combined periods of pre- and post-production stretched to months, but the principle was the same: dump your bags in the hotel room, get out there and let things happen.

Postcard from Rome is a typical example of the Postcard written for the page, unusual only in the depth of background information that demanded to be got in. Much of that I already had, which left me free to wander, rub up against the locals, and generally indulge in the benefits of spontaneous friction. The importance of this last point can't be over-stressed. If a piece is nothing but a potted history lesson, it might as well be written at home. And even if you go there and put in the footwork like some latterday *flâneur*, you have to decide which kind of *flâneur* you want to be, Baudelaire or Borges. Baudelaire, when he roamed the suburbs of Paris, bumped into people. Borges roamed the suburbs of Buenos Aires in the deep night, with the specific intention of meeting as few people as possible: his city of moonlit ruined villas is as empty of human beings as a photograph by Atget. You also have to decide whether you want to be a Guide to Kulchur or something less specialized. Stefan Zweig, in his late, long but too-soon-over essay about Montaigne, said that Montaigne, on his visit to Rome, was a Goethe who had the great advantage of never having met Winckelmann. Zweig meant that Montaigne had not felt obliged to treat his visit as a roundup of the historic buildings and works of art. He felt free to meet people. One of them was the Pope, and several of them were prostitutes. The latter, in particular, taught him a great deal about Rome. Apparently they charged him a lot more for conversation than for their regular services, but if he had been working for the *Observer* he could have claimed that on expenses.

2001

MRS T IN CHINA

The Dragon Lady Flies East

It was Wednesday in Peking. Out of a pale sky as delicately transparent as the finest *ch'ing-pai* ware of the Sung dynasty came the wolf-grey and sharktooth-white RAF VC-10 bearing the great British War Leader Margaret Thatcher and her subservient retinue.

The British Media, who were along for the ride, tumbled down the rear gangway and took up their positions in a tearing hurry, because the War Leader would be among the first of the official party to deplane. Hands in China have to be shaken in order of precedence. Alphabetical order is out of the question, especially when you consider that the Chinese version is calculated by counting the number of brushstrokes in the surname.

The British Ambassador introduced his illustrious visitor to the Chinese official greeters and to the British military attaché, whose particular job, it was rumoured, was to make sure that the War Leader's Husband didn't run into difficulties with the *mao tai*. A clear white local fluid in which toasts are drunk, *mao tai* has the same effect as inserting your head in a cupboard and asking a large male friend to slam the door.

Every world power, down to and including the Fiji islands, likes to think that its indigenous liquor can rob visiting dignitaries of the ability to reason, but let there be no doubt about *mao tai*. China runs on it. Without it, the Chinese hierarchs would be forced to listen to one another. It was therefore plainly advisable that the War Leader's Husband should be limited to a single crucible of the stuff per banquet, if necessary by military force. The Media, needless to add, were under no such compulsion.

Moving a discreet step behind his all-powerful wife, the Husband was looking ravishing in a silk tie of Ming underglaze blue and a smile of inlaid ivory, but it was the War Leader herself who captured all eyes. Her champagne and rhubarb jersey suit recalled painted silk of the Western Han period, her shoes were dawn carnations plucked at dusk, but it was her facial aspect that must have struck the first thrill of awe into her prospective hosts.

Nothing like that skin had been seen since the Ting potters of Hopei produced the last of their palace-quality high-fired white porcelain with the creamy glaze; her hair had the frozen flow of a Fukien figurine from the early Ch'ing; and her eyes were two turquoise bolts from the Forbidden City's Gate of Divine Prowess, an edifice which, it was clear from her manner, was just a hole in a wall compared to the front door of 10 Downing Street.

The official greeters having been dealt with, the War Leader's party climbed into the waiting limousines and howled off towards town, followed closely by the British Media in a variety of specially arranged transport. The basic Chinese written character for any wheeled vehicle looks like a truck axle viewed from above. I was thinking this while standing there alone. The only Media man to watch the plane land instead of being on it, I was now the only Media man left behind at the airport: a bad augury for my first stint as a foreign correspondent.

By the time I reached town in the back of a Mitsubishi minibus laden with ITN camera boxes, the War Leader had lunched privately and was already due to arrive at the Great Hall of the People in the Square of Heavenly Peace, there to press the flesh with the inscrutable notables of the regime's top rank.

The War Leader's transit through China was competing with a simultaneous visitation by Kim Il Sung of North Korea. Despite respectful articles about Mrs Thatcher in the daily papers (both the English-language *China Daily* and the Chinese-language *Renmin Ribao* carried the official No. 10 handout glossy that makes a Shouchou bronze mirror look relatively unpolished) there was a general feeling that Kim was being given the more effusive welcome, possibly as a tribute to his prose style, by which he has already, single-handed, outdone those Chinese encyclopaedists who codified the classic writings into 36,000 volumes nobody ever read.

But if Kim was hogging the local television time, it could only be said that he was, after all, the leader of a fraternal Socialist country attuned to the way of Lenin and Mao, who have the same embalming fluid flowing through their veins even though they now lie in separate mausoleums. The War Leader was something else, something alien. And yet, somehow, something familiar. Where had the Chinese seen that icy strictness before?

There were only a few thousand people in the Square of Heavenly Peace, which meant that it was effectively deserted, because it can hold half a million spontaneously cheering enthusiasts on a big day. The armies of eight different Western countries paraded there in 1900 without even touching the sides. But they did leave a lasting feeling of humiliation, and when you take into account the fact that it was the British who actually burned down the Summer Palace in 1860 it will be understood that the Chinese were under no obligation to go berserk with joy. They hung out a few Red flags and laid on a Combined Services honour guard of troops all exactly the same size, like one of those terracotta armies buried by Qin Shi Huangdi in Shaanxi Province, a district which was even at that moment being toured by the heavily publicized Kim.

While the War Leader checked the honour guard for any deviation in altitude, Peking's only remaining large portrait of Mao looked down from the Gate of Heavenly Peace across the thinly populated square. Some Young Pioneers suddenly slapped their tambourines but the War Leader didn't flinch. She didn't smile at them either. She was a mask, no doubt practising her inscrutability for the encounter with Premier Zhao Ziyang, whom she accompanied inside, there to begin the opening dialogue which instantly became famous as the Great Fog Conversation.

Among the gilt friezes and cream plaster columns of the Great Hall, far below a ceiling full of late-Odeon period light fittings with frosted globes, Zhao Ziyang, the man whose name sounds like a ricochet in a canyon, asked the War Leader whether the cause of fog in London had anything to do with the climate. His guest said that it was due to the burning of coal but now there was no coal burned, so there was no fog. But people in Peking, her host countered, burn much coal, yet there is no fog. Clearly he had no intention of letting the point go, but her tenacity equalled his, and as the Media were ushered from the hall the War Leader was to be heard giving Zowie a chemistry lesson. Apparently the coal smoke had been more concentrated in London than it ever could be in Peking.

The Welcoming Banquet that night was in the Banqueting Hall of the Great Hall of the People: different room, same light fittings. The War Leader was in a long dress the colour of potassium permanganate, thus to drive home her superiority in chemistry. Zowie's speech was tough on the Hegemonists, meaning the Soviet Union and Israel. Of China's hegemonial activities in Tibet, not a mention. He sat down and she stood up, to deliver a speech ten times as Chinese as his, both in its subtlety and range of cultural reference. She quoted 'one of your T'ang poets' to the effect that distance need be no division. The T'ang poet in question was, I am able to reveal, Wang Wei, but for her to name him would have sounded like showing off.

She was far enough ahead already, since Zowie had neglected to quote even a single Lake poet. There was also the possibility that she was making an arcane reference to Mao, who was, in his own poetry, much drawn to the T'ang style. Out there hovering above his mausoleum, his immortal spirit was no doubt wondering whether his successors would be up to handling a woman of this calibre. Inside the mausoleum, his wax-filled corporeal manifestation lost one of its ears some time ago but it was rapidly sewn back on, thus restoring the physical integrity which had been denied to his fellow artist Vincent van Gogh. Mao was out of it, but Zowie was in the land of the living, where the real decisions are made.

There were two main toasts, both taken in *mao tai*. The Media watched the War Leader's Husband, and pooled their observations afterwards. The consensus of their data was that he had scored a hole-in-one on the first but had settled for a par four on the second. Behind the flower-and-frond, yellow-dove-decorated centrepiece of the main table, the War Leader and the Premier kept talking. Nobody knew what they had said during the afternoon, but it seemed possible that the War Leader had now shifted the subject of casual conversation from fog to the light fittings. She spent a lot of time looking at them, when not eating. The military orchestra played a rhythmically questionable cha-cha, but the food was sensational, especially a crispy noodle pancake which the Westerners attacked futilely with chopsticks until they noticed the Chinese sensibly picking it up with their fingers.

Next morning, before more talks with the War Leader, Zowie told the assembled Media that there was no prospect of the Chinese yielding on the very point at issue, namely Hong Kong. Since the assembled Media included the Hong Kong Media, there was some consternation at this show of inflexibility, but as far as I know only one foreign correspondent, myself, formed the opinion that it might have been prompted by fear. Even without the Falklands Factor, Mrs Thatcher would have been perceived by the Chinese as a strong woman. Indeed they call her the Strong Woman. But in addition to her already renowned strictness she had fought and won a war. That rings a bell with the Chinese – a large bronze *chung* bell of the Western Chou period, decorated with projecting knobs and interlaced dragons.

The Chinese think historically at all times, and in their long history there have been at least three notoriously tough women: the Empress Wu of the T'ang dynasty, the Empress Dowager Ci Xi of the Chi'ing dynasty, and Jiang Qing of the Mao dynasty, otherwise known as Madame Mao. Though none of these women, especially the last, could be considered precisely sound from the modern Socialist viewpoint, they had undoubtedly shared the virtue of decisiveness.

The Empress Wu, for example, had ascended from the status of Grade Four concubine (massage and hot towels) all the way to the throne, partly through having a child by the Emperor, smothering it, and pointing the finger at his favourite. Having attained unchallenged rule, she dealt with any potential criticism by depriving its perpetrator of all four limbs and keeping what was left alive in a jar of pickle, or hanging it up on a hook.

Mrs Thatcher had not been quite so firm with Norman St John-Stevas, but there could be little doubt that she belonged to a great tradition. She was the Fourth Strong Woman in Chinese history, an invader from the strange kingdom of the Two Queens, in which one Queen stayed at home minding the palace while the other came marching towards you carrying a severely cut handbag like an Anyang Shang dagger-axe with a jade blade. Give her an inch and she would take the whole of Chang'an Avenue, from the Dongdan intersection to the Babaoshan Cemetery for Revolutionaries (number 10 bus).

After further secret conversations with Zowie about fog and light fittings, the Strong Woman arrived at the British Embassy to meet the British and Chinese communities. This was the second big party of the year for the diplomats of the China station. The first had been the QBP (Queen's Birthday Party), but that was an annual event, well understood. This one was for the other Queen, the one that gets out there and wins wars.

For many of the minor diplomatic faces it was a big moment in a hard life. The Strong Woman gratified them by looking her best, in a plum-blossom and quince-juice silk dress finely calculated to remind Chinese guests of a *mo ku* painting of the Late Northern Sung, although the Chinese might equally have reminded her that William the Conqueror successfully invaded England during that period.

But the garden party was not an occasion for confrontation. Instead she socialized, meeting, *inter alios*, the delightful Katherine Flower, presenter of BBC TV's 'Follow Me', which teaches English to the Chinese. Francis Matthews, the star actor in the programme, is the most famous British face in China. Katherine comes second and Mrs Thatcher third, but by this time she was catching up fast, although getting barely half as much air time as Kim Il Sung, who was still checking out that terracotta army. Perhaps he had at last found the ideal audience for his brand of oratory: statues don't shuffle. Also present at the garden party was the Hong Kong shipping magnate Sir Y. K. Pao. Destined to crop up everywhere in the itinerary, Powie is a name you should note. He and the War Leader go back a long way together, to the time, one gathers, when he was before the mast and she was being called to the bar.

Thursday afternoon was culture gulch, meaning that the Strong Woman could plan her upcoming talks with Deputy Prime Minister Deng Xiaoping while her face and feet were on automatic pilot. At the Conservatory of Music there was much emphasis on Beethoven, of whom there is a plaster bust in even the most humble homes, but the star act was undoubtedly the girl Wu Man. Later on she will be the woman Wu Man, but punning on Chinese names is a low form of humour. Meanwhile she is the best young player of the *pipa* in China. On the *pipa*, which is less unlike a zither than it is unlike anything else, Wu Man played some dance music of the Yi tribe. The Yi tribe sounded like a fun outfit, and for a moment the War Leader relaxed.

Relaxing at the British Book Exhibition was less easy, because the joint was packed with a chosen spontaneous crowd of nervous intellectuals. One of my own books was among the carefully selected thousand and I had visions of helping to make a three-pronged impact on China's spiritual future, along with Margaret Drabble and Iris Murdoch, but there is the problem of distribution. The War Leader's Husband found it hard to see why all the rest of the Chinese couldn't just walk into the library like this lot and sit down to read. A very impressive British Council lady, who speaks effortless Mandarin and is also able to communicate with the Strong Woman's Man, explained that there was a considerable number of Chinese out there, many of them living quite a long way away.

After the standard plum-blossom beauty of a Peking sunset the War Leader dined privately with the British business community while the Media formed groups to eat Peking Duck, a large beast which needs a team of people sitting around its perimeter and all eating inwards for several hours before it disappears. Apart from duck demolition there is practically nothing to do in Peking after 10 p.m. except dance to old Fats Domino 45 rpm EPs, usually on your own. The Chinese opera on television is OK if you like acrobats. Then comes a blank hissing screen followed by a fitful sleep and one million bicycle bells at dawn. It is Friday, and the population is on the move again.

So was the War Leader, entering the increasingly familiar Great Hall of the People for the first meeting with Deputy Prime Minister Deng Xiaoping, hero of the biggest comeback story since de Gaulle. Mrs Mao had him down and almost out, but he hung in. Deng knows a Strong Woman when he sees one. He was seeing one now, with the strawberry-blotched blue taffeta suavely off-setting the *cloisonné* enamel of her *maquillage,* so reminiscent of a Ming dynasty incense-burner. He had heard how Zhao had been bested in the Great Fog Conversation, but Zhao was a youngster. He, Deng, was an old hand.

Deng initiated the Great Food Conversation, using the Governor of Hong Kong, invited for that very purpose, as an unwitting foil. Deng said it had been great fun welcoming Kim Il Sung. Having thrown his right, he crossed with his left, saying the food had been very good in Sichuan. The Governor of Hong Kong agreed that the food was good in Sichuan. But the War Leader refused to be drawn. She said that on her earlier visit to China – managing to imply that she would visit China more often if there were not so many wars to win – she had found the food best in Suzhou. 'Well,' said Deng,

'I don't think so.' He had been forced into a hollow protestation, an uncomfortable position for beginning secret talks. The widow of Chou En-lai, holding a bouquet of roses specially flown out by British Airways, complimented the War Leader on her wisdom and tact. 'At your age,' she added, 'it can be said it is the Golden Age.' The Strong Woman took the compliment as her due, forgetting to return it. What was she, a devil? For in the great Sung painting 'The Picture of the Search in the Mountain', are not the women of angelic appearance more ferocious than the dragons?

The War Leader stumbled on the way down the steps but the Media's excitement soon subsided – she was merely preoccupied, not fatigued. Off she went with the Chinese for a visit to the Summer Palace, the replacement, on a different site, for the one the British burned down. Actually the interloping forces burned down the replacement too, but it had been replaced again. If the Chinese should bring this awkward subject up, she could always remind them that they, in turn, burned down the British Embassy in the days of the Cultural Revolution.

Later on Friday afternoon the Media were granted access to the War Leader so that she could announce what sounded like a stand-off in negotiations. Confucians among the Media might have said her voice was choked with emotion. T'ang positivists might have said she had Negotiator's Throat. She herself could hardly speak, but this fact meant nothing unless you could see what shape Deng was in, and he wasn't available.

It was a pity that, whether for protocol reasons or because of strained vocal cords, Deng didn't show up at the Return Banquet thrown by the visiting team in the Great Hall of the People, because the War Leader had saved her most stunning outfit until last. A magenta silk gown that recalled Chi'en-lung *flambeau* ware at its most exquisitely uninhibited, it clashed with the pink tasselled chairs, but that wasn't her problem. Let them change the chairs. Her throat was still in tatters but she delivered a Chinese proverb in both languages. 'It is better to come and see for yourself than to read a hundred reports.' The Chinese version sounded a bit short. The Party functionary sitting beside me described it as 'understandable'. His name was Fang so I did not argue.

Zowie's return speech was the usual railway station announcement read at high speed, but when the eating started he indicated bilateral flexibility by employing a fork. The toasting fluid was a pale British equivalent of *mao tai*, and some of the British dishes bore a close resemblance to shark's fin soup and fish lips, but the imported thin mints were a hit. The rapidly improving military band played a very good arrangement of 'Greensleeves'. There are some instrumentalists in that combo who would make von Karajan drop his whip.

As they dined on relentlessly, it was dusk outside, with the curved yellow-tiled roofs of the Forbidden City glowing softly like honeycomb through a sea of grey powder. The War Leader had chosen the right time for Peking – a time of transition, when the Lotus Lake in the Winter Palace Park is thick with green leaves, after the blossoms have fallen and before the roots have been collected to be eaten. Out on the lake rises the Jade Island, coming to a point, like a lovely pimple, in the dome of the White Dagoba. When Mrs Mao was at the height of her power, she closed the Winter Palace Park to the people and reserved the Jade Island for her own use, so that she could ride her horse in private.

In China's history, a few women are tyrants and millions of them are chattels. The problem is to make them something in between. You can still see thousands of women in Peking whose feet were bound when they were young. You can't miss that awkward splay-footed walk: they must forever struggle to keep their balance. Feet are no longer bound but that does not mean that minds are free. Despite everything the Revolution can do, the women still serve the men, the girls are still snobs who marry boys who get ahead, and you still can't get ahead without connections. The Revolution, like any other Chinese dynasty, is behind the times. Margaret Thatcher is a democratic product to an extent of which even the most radical Chinese theorist can hardly dream. She doesn't even have to think about it, and often forgets to.

On Saturday morning the Strong Woman rose into the air, heading for Shanghai with the Media clinging to her wings. After that would come Canton, with Hong Kong soothingly employed as the gate of departure. For does not Wang Wei's poem say that a chip off the dragon's tooth is a spear in its side? No, it does not. I made that one up.

September, 1982: previously included in *Flying Visits*, 1984

The Great Leap Homeward

Her negotiations in Peking for the nonce complete, the Dragon Lady flew south towards Shanghai, altering her image in mid-air, as dragons are wont to do. For the purpose of hard bargaining with the Chinese political leaders she had been the Woman of Jade, a material so tough that it was not until the period of the Warring States that the tools were discovered which could make it fully workable into such treasurable artefacts as the *pi* disc. But now her purpose was to spread enlightenment, so she took on the aspect of the Woman of Science, Yin Sage of the Book of Changes, Adept of the sixty-four Symbolic Hexagrams, and regular reader of the *New Scientist*. Corralled into the back end of her winged conveyance, the British Media, showing distinct signs of wear, resigned themselves to yet another punishing schedule.

The Yin Sage arrived in Shanghai to find herself lunching with the omnipresent Hong Kong shipping magnate Sir Y. K. Pao, a sort of soy-sauce Onassis. The Chinese need Powie to build ships, but unfortunately for them Powie's expertise comes accompanied by his personality. Powie puts on a show of dynamism that makes Jimmy Goldsmith seem like a Taoist contemplative. As an old pal of the British Prime Minister, Powie was well placed to make her visit look like an occasion for which he had helped grease the wheels.

The PM's advisers must have realized that it was enough for her to be representing democracy without also representing capitalism in one of its more unpalatably flagrant forms, because the bleary-eyed British Media were eventually allowed to get the impression that Powie's knighthood did not, in HMG's view, necessarily entitle him to behave as if he were carrying ambassadorial credentials to the Far East. But for the moment Powie was at the controls and hustling full blast. He had a new ship all set to be launched and there were no prizes for guessing who would swing the bottle.

After the big lunch, the big launch. Shanghai's Jiangnan shipyards look pretty backward beside the Japanese equivalent, in which half a dozen engineers in snow-white designer overalls converse with one another by wrist-video while a team of Kawasaki Unimate robots transforms a heap of raw materials into a fully computerized bulk carrier with a jacuzzi in the captain's bathroom. Here there were about a thousand Chinese queueing up to borrow the spanner. But the atmosphere was festive. An air of spontaneity – real spontaneity, as opposed to the mechanical variety laid on by Party directives – was generated by a band truck tricked out with balloons and dispensing the Shanghai equivalent of Chicago jazz. A very big drum and several different sizes of gong combined to produce the typical Chinese orchestral texture of many obsolete fire-alarms going off at once.

Next to the completed ship, which Powie had cunningly named *World Goodwill*, there was a sign in English saying BE CAREFUL NOT TO DROP INTO THE RIVER. The Yin Sage was dressed in navy blue with a white hat, thereby establishing a nautical nuance, an impression furthered by her consort's azure tie. Actually it was the same tie he had worn when arriving in Peking, but this was a different city, and in China every city is a whole new nation. It is not just that there are a thousand million Chinese who have never seen the world. There are a thousand million Chinese who have never seen China. So if you wear the same tie at different ends of the country it is unlikely that you will cause the locals to whisper behind their hands. No stranger to the Far East, the Yin Sage's Yang Companion has got such considerations well taped.

Powie rose to his Gucci-shod feet in order to convince anybody who still needed convincing that he bears a truly remarkable resemblance to the late Edward G. Robinson. He thanked his distinguished sponsor for being there. He thanked everybody else for being there as well. He thanked the Chinese Government for its breadth of vision. He was on the point of thanking the population of China individually, but the Woman of Science had a schedule to meet. Referring, in her Falklandish capacity as a connoisseur of naval architecture, to 'this splendid ship', she spoke of how it epitomized the ability of Socialist China and the freely enterprising West to work in harmony. 'This ship . . . is a symbol of the close relationship.' It was a relationship ship.

She launched the relationship ship by swinging an axe to cut the line that released the bottle. The bottle declined to break, but according to Chinese tradition it is the blow of the axe which matters,

not the result. In the *I Ching*, according to the great naturalist philosopher Chu Hsi's justly celebrated interpretation, *Li*, the cosmic
principle of organization at all levels, is coterminous with and ulti-
mately inseparable from *chhi*, or matter-energy. To put it another
way, it's the thought that counts.

The relationship ship was already in the water and thus destined
to remain immobile after being launched, but the band truck, or
Truck of Good Luck, erupted into a rousing rendition of its signature
tune, 'Seven Ancient Fire-Engines Failing to Discover the Location
of Chow Fong's Burning House'. The Yin Sage, charmingly referred
to by a nervous young female interpreter as 'the Rather Honourable
Margaret Thatcher', took leave of Powie with the air of one who
knows that the separation will be all too short.

She was headed for the Shanghai Institute of Biochemistry of
the Academica Sinica, whither all the British Media, except one,
decided not to accompany her. My colleagues, wise in the trade,
had knowledgeably concluded that now was the time to file their
copy, take a well-earned nap, or check out the attractions of what
had once been China's most westernized big city, the first one to
import every occidental fad up to and including Communism. In
Shanghai it is even possible to buy an alcoholic drink if you turn the
right corners. The girls are just as unattainable as in Peking but
they dress more provocatively, with a cut to their comradely trousers
which suggests that they are not above withholding some of their
labour from the commune in order to sit up at night resewing the
odd seam.

It would have been good to spend more than just a few minutes
following Sidney Greenstreet's ghost past the old Western Concession
compounds of the Bund, and on top of that there was the Shanghai
National Museum, containing pictures which I had been waiting to
see half my life, and of which I can only say that if I could write the
way those guys painted I would use up a lot less Tipp-Ex. But like a
fool I went to the Biochemistry Institute, and like a fool I got lucky.
The Woman of Science put on her best public performance of the
tour so far, and I was the only scribe there to cover it.

The performance was good because for once she wasn't performing. Biochemistry is her field and the assembled scientists were
among the top boys in it, so when they spoke she was for a moment
distracted from her usual self-imposed task of proving her superiority

to everyone else. The head of the Institute apologized, in beautifully eloquent English, for his English, which he had not spoken for forty years. 'Today we are very honoured to have you with us. First of all, may I introduce Professor . . .' He introduced a dozen professors, respectively in charge of such departments as insulin synthesis, nucleic acids, biomemory, molecular radiation and a lot of other things I couldn't catch. Most of it was Chinese to me but clearly it was grist to the mill of the Woman of Science, especially the stuff about insulin, which she was concerned with when studying under her famous mentor, the Nobel Prizewinner Dorothy Hodgkin – a name revered by the Shanghai scientists, who had a picture of her in their visitors' book.

That the Yin Sage was Dorothy Hodgkin's Pupil plainly went down a storm with the Chinese, in whom the dynastic principle is well ingrained. The Pupil's pupils sharpened, I noticed, when one of the scientists announced that the laboratory was working on leukaemia and liver cancer. Since the same laboratory had already developed, among other things, such eminently applicable ideas as the reprogramming of fish to breed in still water, there was no need to think they would not crack the case, always provided that their government gave curing old humans the same priority as feeding new ones. Of these latter, needless to say, there is no shortage, and in fact the Shanghai laboratory is working on a fertility drug (derived from the same LH–H analysis that fixed the fish) which could produce irreversible infertility at high dosages – a possibility which the Woman of Science immediately saw might be open to abuse, and said so.

Touring the individual laboratories, she interviewed the scientists working in each. They all spoke dazzling scientific English, with words like 'cucumber' falsely emphasized and phrases like 'polypeptide macromolecular electrokinesis' fluently delivered. After she left each room I backtracked to ask the interviewees, relaxing after their ordeal, whether she still knew her stuff. Without exception they said she did. She missed a trick, though, in the room where they analyse proteins by counting dots. Reminiscing, the Woman of Science said: 'We had no computers in those days to analyse the dots.' Her hosts were too polite to tell her the truth, which was that as far as they were concerned those days were still here. Even to the inexpert eye, the laboratory is painfully underequipped. The rubber tubes are perished, glass is hoarded like gold, and there is obviously no more computer time in a year than there are rainy days in the Gobi. They're counting those dots with an abacus. When the Woman of Science handed a Sinclair desk computer to the Japanese it was coals to Newcastle, or at any rate bamboo shoots to Tokyo. The same computer given to the Shanghai Biochemistry Institute would have made some long friends.

The banquet that night was hosted by the Mayor of Shanghai, who generously announced in his speech of welcome that 'British people have always had a great feeling for the Chinese'. He could have put this another way, saying that British people were instrumental in poisoning half the country with opium and showed an enthusiasm unusual even among the European nations when it came to humiliating the Chinese by such practices as shutting them out of their own cities. The park which was denied to 'dogs and Chinese' is still there on the river side of the Bund. Nowadays it is enjoyed by the indigenous population but they allow us to share it, which is a lot more than we ever did for them. One only hoped that the Yin Sage knew how tactful the Mayor was being in not mentioning any of that.

The possibility that the Woman of Science might be a bit thin in the area of Chinese history was a constant worry to those of us in her entourage who wished her well on her delicate mission. But she caught all eyes in her dress of vivid *K'ang-hsi* cobalt blue, a veiled reminder that in the eighteenth century (our time) the European demand for Chinese porcelain was matched by an equally eager supply. The Mayor, perhaps forewarned, had countered in advance by gracing every table with a full kit of Yi Sing stoneware specially procured for the occasion. It looked like bitter chocolate and provided an ideal container for the dreaded *mao tai*, the liquid land-mine, the anti-personnel potion employed by Chinese functionaries to render one another's official speeches inaudible. Since first encountering the stuff a week before, the British Media had settled on two ways of coping with it. You could down it in one and get drunk straight away or you could sip at it and get drunk almost straight away.

In Shanghai, however, one was likely to forget about drinking in favour of eating, because the food was astonishing – compared with Peking, there was a playful savour to its presentation which suggested that we were already getting closer to the West. The same thing was suggested by the attire and general demeanour of the waitresses, who wore skirts instead of trousers and in an alarming number of cases were unmanningly pretty. British scriveners and cameramen fought one another for a smile. If you are the kind of man who falls in love through the eyes, you will fall in love a hundred times a day in China. No wonder that in the Chinese artistic heritage the pictures outweigh the words and even the words are pictures. The whole place soaks the optic nerve like a long shot of morphine into a fresh vein. I smiled like a goof from daylight to dusk.

Among those prominent behind the top table's array of carved pumpkins was the inevitable Powie. The Mayor referred to him as 'Mr' Y. K. Pao, thereby depriving him of his knighthood, which he must have received for services to athletics, because when the Woman of Science went up to congratulate the orchestra Powie was out of his starting blocks and congratulating them right along with her. The great Australian sprinter Hector Hogan used to move that fast but he needed spiked shoes to do it.

Onward to Canton, where there was another banquet, this time for lunch instead of dinner. The venue was the Dong-fang hotel, a Disneyland Chinese emporium all dolled up in funfair gilt filigree. By now you could feel the West close by, just outside the Pearl River delta, a jetfoil ride across a short stretch of the South China Sea. People from Hong Kong come here to visit their relatives and give them that greatest of all gifts, a television set. The girls at the cashier's desk have pocket calculators which the scientists in Shanghai would covet and which the clerks in the Minzu hotel in Peking would probably fail to recognize. China is a big place. Here, at the edge, it is a bit like the West, but the edge, we had learned, is a long way from the middle.

We were all Old China Hands now. Even the Woman of Science, clad today in a green dress recalling the *famille verte* teapots of the Ch'ing, was looking blasé. The locals kept bringing forth food fit to change the mind of anyone who had been harbouring the notion that Cantonese cuisine means offal rolled in red ochre and glazed like a brick. It was wonderful, but after a week of banqueting we had had enough. The Yin Sage's impeccable chopstick technique did not falter. She could still pick up a greased peanut without lifting either elbow. But her usually transparent azure eyes had grown slightly occluded, like the milky-violet glaze which the Chinese collectors of ceramics call *kuei-mien-ch'ing*, or ghost's-face blue. Perhaps she had seen too much of Powie.

She escaped him on the short flight to Hong Kong. When her plane took off he was not on it. I was not on it either, having failed to fill out the right forms some weeks before. After several hours spent anxiously facing the prospect of staying in China for ever – imagine how long it will be before they get breakfast television – I secured the last seat on a packed Trident and scrambled aboard. As I came stooping through the door I recognized a certain pair of Gucci shoes. It was Powie. He assured me that Mrs Thatcher's trip was 'very successful' and that she had done a grand job. Powie has a lot in common with David Frost – permanent jet-lag, an unusual way with the English language, and an infallible nose for the main action.

The approach to Kai Tak, Hong Kong's notorious airport, starts between mountains and continues between buildings. As the joke says, Hong Kong is the only city where street-vendors sell you things before you land. The place struck me, even at the very moment when I thought I was about to strike it, as a kind of slant-eyed Las Vegas. No sooner had the plane stopped rolling than Powie was outside and into a black Toyota, while your reporter was making his solitary and sweat-soaked way to the Hilton, where the rest of the British Media were already up to their necks in pine-scented suds while they filed copy on the bathroom telephone. The wealth of Hong Kong would seem ridiculous anyway, but after the Chinese People's Republic you feel like a nun dropped into Babylon. To dial room service is to experience disgust, and for half an hour I hesitated. All right, half a minute.

The Dragon Lady, guarded by police SWAT squads up on the roofs, had by now transformed herself into the Keeper of Secrets. The fate of Hong Kong, known to her faithful consort as Honkers, was locked in her mind and safe from divination, even by the methods of geomancy or *feng-shui* (the winds and the waters). While the Hong Kong Media went crazy with speculation, she did her chores, starting with a visit to the Scots Guards at Stanley Fort. After Northern Ireland, Honkers is a cushy posting. The wives swim in the clear water of Repulse Bay and have babies while the going is good. The Keeper of Secrets dropped out of the sky by helicopter and moved among them in a midnight-blue dress sprinkled with almond blossoms. The heat was breathtaking. 'Are you *all* pregnant?' she asked. The teeth of a pretty child called Joanna were duly inspected. The British Media rushed to interview Joanna. I interviewed the wives, who all said, without being prompted, that their visitor looked too tired to last out the day.

As she climbed back into the thwacking helicopter, one could only agree. Her stamina is impressive but she is overly proud of it, and this trip she had pushed herself too far. Along with the punch-drunk British Media I strapped myself into the back-up helicopter and found myself hanging into space over an open door with Kowloon lying sideways underneath. If she felt half as bad as I did then the upcoming, all-important press conference was going to be a disaster.

In fact, it was her best yet. On the last day in Peking she had made a bad press conference worse by showing obvious impatience with the halting English of some of the Hong Kong Media. This propensity probably springs less from intolerance than from her urge to get cracking, but to possess it is a handicap and to indulge it is a grievous fault. Now, however, on the day that mattered, she kept her irascibility bottled up. She said all she could say, which was that an agreement had been reached that there should be an agreement, and that from here on in it was all down to the diplomats. When a Hong Kong girl reporter said that the question of renewing the lease could have simply been ignored, the Stateswoman turned a potential minus into a plus by insisting that a contract is a contract and the means of meeting it should be found early, 'in good time'. Clearly she spoke with conviction, from the deep core of her nature, where the Good Housekeeping Seal of Approval has the force of law. In Peking she had got away for a few minutes on her own in search of a bolt of fabric. The one she liked was too pricey at £39 a yard, so she had not bought it. Her passion for managing the household along sound lines was what got her elected in the first place, and was what now reassured the people of Hong Kong that things might just conceivably, in the long run, be going to be all right. On Hong Kong television the assembled pundits, posing in front of blown-up Thatcher glossies that looked like publicity stills of Eleanor Parker in *Return to Peyton Place*, began a long analysis of what little she had said, as if there could have been more. Next day the stock market dipped but there was no crash. When the rabbits had finished pulling out, the smart money would probably buy back in.

The smart money was there in force at the Government House reception. Chinese businessmen whose personal wealth made Powie look like a pauper were jostling to breathe the Dragon Lady's perfume. If her mission had been a flop then they would already have been in Acapulco, so the signs were favourable. I met such mighty Hong Kong *tai pan*s as Mr Lee of real estate, Mr Fong of many boats, and the ineffable Sir Run Run Shaw, who had made a hill of money out of those terrible films in which bad actors kick each other. (In the days when he was plain Mister, Run Run invented a cinematic process called Shawscope, a version of the widescreen ratio which allowed more actors to kick each other at the same time.) One after the other I asked all these characters whether they had been in Peking lately. It turned out that all of them had been spending a lot of time there. Mr Lee told me how much the Chinese leaders respected his honesty.

So the boys are smoothing the road to the inevitable. Only Sir Run Run had the cheek to say that if a new regime asked him to make a Socialist movie he would run-run for cover. Actually it is hard to see why he should be worried: his movies would be readily adaptable to Marxist–Leninist ideological content. Just make the bad guys the capitalists and the good guys could start kicking again straight away.

The Dragon Lady's VC-10 screamed out of Kai Tak like a fighter and banked steeply towards India. All RAF transport aircraft have the passenger seats facing backwards, so the British Media, once again confined to the rear of the aircraft, could see where they had been. Laden down with electronic devices and paper kites for the children, they were too tired to sleep. So was the Dragon Lady, but she had no choice. Soon it would be the Conservative Party Conference. It was time for another transformation. The cabin lights went out to denote that she had retired. Her mind stirred in the darkness, putting away China and putting on Britain, forgetting Zhao Ziang and remembering Francis Pym. She was turning herself back into a Party Leader. While she dreamed and the Media drank, I looked back through the window along the Road of Silk, the ancient trade route which brought Marco Polo to Cathay and the Land of Prester John, and which was already old when Chinese lacquer boxes were on sale in the markets of Imperial Rome.

As you might have gathered, I loved China. But Westerners have always loved China. In the last century they drugged her, stripped her naked, tied her hands above her head, and loved her as they pleased. We were lucky that a revolution was all that happened. If we are luckier still, the current bunch of Chinese gerontocrats will be smoothly replaced by a generation of intellectuals who were so appalled at the Cultural Revolution that they are now less frightened by democracy than by despotism. If that happens, the Chinese revolution might manage what the Soviet version so obviously can't – to civilize itself. Here, as in every other aspect of Chinese life, tradition is a comfort. China knew totalitarianism two hundred years before Christ, when the mad First Emperor of the Ch'in obliterated all memory of the ancient glory of Chou, burned the classical texts and put to death anybody caught reading the *Book of Songs*. But he unified the tribes, and on that strong base rose the majestic dynasty of Han, on whose era the Chinese of today still pride themselves, as will the Chinese of tomorrow.

In Delhi Mrs Thatcher had breakfast with Mrs Gandhi: a hen session. In Bahrain she shook hands with a sheik. At 34,000 feet over Europe she invited the Media forward for a drink. God knows what she thought of us: prominent in the front row of the scrum were at least two journalists who had been blotto since Peking. As for what we thought of her, the answer is not easy. Some had their prejudices confirmed. None thought less of her. I still wouldn't vote for her, because I favour the Third Way, the Way of Tao, in which the universal principle is made manifest through the interlocking forms of David Steel and Roy Jenkins.

But I had grown to admire her. She is what she is, and not another thing, and on such issues it is better to be crassly straight than subtly devious. Perhaps being haunted by the Falklands, where for want of a nail she was obliged to send many young men to their deaths, in the matter of Hong Kong she seemed determined to be well prepared. The business touches me personally, because on Hong Kong Island, in the war cemetery at Sai Wan Bay, my father has lain since 1945, cut down at the age of thirty-three because the British did not know how to avoid a war in the Pacific. If firm talk and a steely glance can stop that happening again, Mrs Thatcher is ideal casting. She deserves credit for her iron guts, even if you think her brains are made of the same stuff.

While thinking all this I was searching the cabin. He wasn't there. Finally I wangled an invitation to the flight deck. He wasn't there either. Powie was not at the controls. She had got away from him at last. As the VC-10 dived towards Heathrow the wings suddenly shone like water gardens. After ten days and a dozen countries it was raining for the first time. The Han dragons could control the rain but ours must have been too tired. She had just enough energy for the last transformation, into the mother of her children. Mr and Mrs Thatcher stepped down to embrace their son Mark, who had driven all the way from town without getting lost once.

October, 1982: previously included in *Flying Visits*, 1984

Postscript

The first part of this two-part Postcard was the biggest single technical trick I ever pulled off as a journalist, not so much in the manner of its writing as in the way I filed the copy. To get it home in time I had to phone it in. There were no mobiles in 1982, and the hotel phones in Beijing went not much further than the front desk. International calls had to be made at the post office, for cash on the nail. From my fellow journalists, in return for sterling, IOUs and hasty promises, I raised a small mountain of Chinese money and spent the lot on a call to London that would have been at least an hour and a half long even if it had been uninterrupted. It was interrupted every fifteen minutes by something going wrong with the system, probably a diesel generator in the basement. To get the connection restored I had repeatedly to rejoin the queue and threaten the nice girl behind the desk. The gleam of her incipient tears is with me still. But the pony express got through, mainly because of the *Observer*'s copy taker at the other end. In those days the copy takers were fine-point grammarians: they all knew how to sort out solecisms, maintain the integrity of your subordinate clauses, and punctuate accurately just from the inflection of your voice, although my copy taker might have been unique in knowing something about Chinese porcelain as well.

The whole piece got into the paper without a single misprint. The second part I was able to write at leisure in Hong Kong and on the plane back to London – by hand, in an exercise book, the only item of advanced technology I ever carried. If the modem had existed, and I had known how to work it, the whole job would have been a lot easier, but I don't think it would have turned out any better. Making those little marks on paper was the heart of the thrill, and still is. The rattle of plastic keys reminds me of a squadron of butterflies failing to fight their way out of a paper bag.

2001

THE AURA OF CELEBRITY

MAILER'S *MARILYN*

'She was a fruitcake,' Tony Curtis once told an interviewer on BBC
television, and there can't be much doubt that she was. Apart from
conceding that the camera was desperately in love with her, professional judgements of Marilyn Monroe's attributes rarely go much
further. It would be strange if they did: there's work to be done, and
a girl blessed with equivalent magic might happen along any time –
might even not be a fruitcake. Amateur judgements, on the other
hand, are free to flourish. Norman Mailer's new book, *Marilyn*, is
just such a one.

Even if its narrative were not so blatantly, and self-admittedly,
cobbled together from facts already available in other biographies,
the Mailer *Marilyn* would still be an amateur piece of work. Its
considerable strength lies in that limitation. As far as talent goes,
Marilyn Monroe was so minimally gifted as to be almost unemployable, and anyone who holds to the opinion that she was a great
natural comic identifies himself immediately as a dunce. For purposes
best known to his creative demon, Mailer planes forward on the
myth of her enormous talent like a drunken surfer. Not for the first
time, he gets further by going with the flow than he ever could have
done by cavilling. Thinking of her as a genius, he can call her
drawbacks virtues, and so deal – unimpeded by scepticism – with
the vital mystery of her presence.

Mailer's adoration is as amateurish as an autograph hunter's. But
because of it we are once again, and this time ideally, reminded of
his extraordinary receptivity. That the book should be an embarrassing and embarrassed rush-job is somehow suitable. The author
being who he is, the book might as well be conceived in the most
chaotic possible circumstances. The subject is, after all, one of the
best possible focal points for his chaotic view of life. There is nothing
detached or calculating about that view. It is hot-eyed, errant,

unhinged. Writhing along past a gallery of yummy photographs, the text reads as the loopiest message yet from the Mailer who scared Sonny Listen with thought waves, made the medical breakthrough which identified cancer as the thwarted psyche's revenge, and first rumbled birth control as the hidden cause of pregnancy. And yet *Marilyn* is one of Mailer's most interesting things. Easy to punish, it is hard to admire – like its subject. But admire it we must – like its subject. The childishness of the whole project succeeds in emitting a power that temporarily calls adulthood into question: The Big Book of the Mad Girl. Consuming it at a long gulp, the reader ponders over and over again Mailer's copiously fruitful aptitude for sub-mission. Mailer is right to trust his own foolishness, wherever it leads: even if the resulting analysis of contemporary America impresses us as less diagnostic than symptomatic.

Not solely for the purpose of disarming criticism, Mailer calls his *Marilyn* a biography in novel form. The parent novel, we quickly guess, is *The Deer Park*, and we aren't 75 pages into this new book before we find Charles Francis Eitel and Elena Esposito being referred to as if they were people living in our minds – which, of course, they are. The permanent party of *The Deer Park* ('if desires were deeds, the history of the night would end in history') is still running, and the atom bomb that lit the desert's rim for Sergius O'Shaugnessy and Lulu Meyers flames just as bright. But by now Sergius is out from under cover: he's Norman Mailer. And his beloved film star has been given a real name too: Marilyn Monroe. Which doesn't necessarily make her any the less fictional. By claiming the right to launch vigorous imaginative patrols from a factual base, Mailer gives himself an easy out from the strictures of verisimilitude, especially when the facts are discovered to be contradictory. But Mailer's fantasizing goes beyond expediency. Maurice Zolotow, poor pained scrivener, can sue Mailer all he likes, but neither he nor the quiescent Fred Lawrence Guiles will ever get his Marilyn back. Mailer's Marilyn soars above the known data, an apocalyptic love-object no mundane pen-pusher could dream of reaching. Dante and Petrarch barely knew Beatrice and Laura. It didn't slow them down. Mailer never met Marilyn at all. It gives him the inside track.

Critical fashion would have it that since *The Deer Park* reality has been busy turning itself into a novel. As Philip Roth said it must, the extremism of real events has ended up by leaving the creative imagination looking like an also-ran. A heroine in a 50s novel, Lulu was really a girl of the 40s – she had some measure of control over her life. Mailer now sees that the young Marilyn was the true 50s heroine – she had no control over her life whatsoever. In the declension from Lulu as Mailer then saw her to Marilyn as he sees her now, we can clearly observe what is involved in dispensing with the classical, shaping imagination and submitting one's talent (well, Mailer's talent) to the erratic forces of events. Marilyn, says Mailer, was every man's love affair with America. He chooses to forget now that Sergius was in love with something altogether sharper, just as he chooses to forget that for many men Marilyn in fact represented most of the things that were to be feared about America. Worshipping a doll was an activity that often came into question at the time. Later on, it became a clever critical point to insist that the doll was gifted: she walks, she talks, she plays Anna Christie at the Actors' Studio. Later still, the doll was canonized. By the time we get to this book, it is as though there had never been any doubt: the sickness of the 50s lay, not in overvaluing Marilyn Monroe, but in undervaluing her.

*

Marilyn, says Mailer, suggested sex might be as easy as ice cream. He chooses to forget that for many men at the time she suggested sex might have about the same nutritional value. The early photographs by André de Dienes – taken before her teeth were fixed but compensating by showing an invigorating flash of panty above the waistline of her denims – enshrine the essence of her snuggle-pie sexuality, which in the ensuing years was regularized, but never intensified, by successive applications of oomph and class. Adorable, dumb tomato, she was the best of the worst. As the imitators, and imitators of the imitators, were put into the field behind her, she attained the uniqueness of the paradigm, but that was the sum total of her originality as a sex-bomb. Any man in his right mind would have loved to have her. Mailer spends a good deal of the book trying to drum up what mystical significance he can out of that fact, without even once facing the possibility of that fact representing the *limitation* of her sexuality – the criticism of it, and the true centre of her tragedy. Her screen presence, the Factor X she possessed in the same quantity as Garbo, served mainly to potentiate the sweetness. The sweetness of the girl bride, the unwomanly woman, the *femme* absolutely not *fatale.*

> In her ambition, so Faustian, and in her ignorance of culture's dimensions, in her liberation and her tyrannical desires, her noble democratic longings intimately contradicted by the widening pool of her narcissism (where every friend and slave must bathe), we can see the magnified mirror of ourselves, our exaggerated and now all but defeated generation, yes, she ran a reconnaissance through the 50s. . . .

Apart from increasing one's suspicions that the English sentence is being executed in America, such a passage of rhetorical foolery raises the question of whether the person Mailer is trying to fool with it might not conceivably be himself. If 'magnified mirror of ourselves' means anything, it must include Mailer. Is Mailer ignorant of culture's dimensions? The answer, one fears, being not that he is, but that he would like to be – so that he could write more books like *Marilyn.* As Mailer nuzzles up beside the shade of this poor kitten to whom so much happened but who could cause so little to happen, you can hear the purr of sheer abandon. He himself would like very much to be the man without values, expending his interpretative powers on whatever the world declared to be important. Exceptional people, Mailer says (these words are almost exactly his, only the grammar having been altered, to unveil the epigram), have a way of living with opposites in themselves that can be called schizophrenia only when it fails. The opposite in Mailer is the hick who actually falls for all that guff about screen queens, voodoo prize fighters, and wonder-boy presidents. But his way of living with it hasn't yet quite failed. And somehow, it must be admitted, he seems to get further, see deeper, than those writers who haven't got it to live with.

In tracing Marilyn's narcissism back to her fatherless childhood, our author is at his strongest. His propensity for scaling the mystical ramparts notwithstanding, Mailer in his Aquarius/Prisoner role is a lay psychologist of formidable prowess. The self-love and the un-assuageable need to have it confirmed – any fatherless child is bound to recognize the pattern, and be astonished at how the writing generates the authentic air of continuous panic. But good as this analysis is, it still doesn't make Marilyn's narcissism ours. There is narcissism and there is narcissism, and to a depressing degree Marilyn's was the sadly recognizable version of the actress who could read a part but could never be bothered reading a complete script. Mailer knows what it took Marilyn to get to the top: everything from betraying friends to lying down under geriatric strangers. Given the system, Marilyn was the kind of monster equipped to climb through it. What's debilitating is that Mailer seems to have given up imagining other systems. He is right to involve himself in the dynamics of Hollywood; he does better by enthusiastically replaying its vanished games than by standing aloof; but for a man of his brains he doesn't *despise* the place enough. His early gift for submitting himself to the grotesqueness of reality is softening with the years into a disinclination to argue with it. In politics he still fights on, although with what effect on his allies one hesitates to think. But in questions of culture – including, damagingly, the cultural aspects of politics – he has by now come within an ace of accepting whatever is as right. His determination to place on Marilyn the same valuation conferred by any sentimentalist is a sure token.

*

On the point of Marilyn's putative talents, Mailer wants it both ways. He wants her to be an important natural screen presence, which she certainly was; and he wants her to be an important natural actress, which she certainly wasn't. So long as he wants it the first way, he gets it: *Marilyn* is an outstandingly sympathetic analysis of what makes somebody look special on screen, and reads all the better for its periodic eruptions into incoherent lyricism. But so long as he wants it the second way, he gets nowhere. He is quite right to talk of *Some Like It Hot* as her best film, but drastically overestimates her strength in it. Mailer knows all about the hundreds of takes and the thousands of fluffs, and faithfully records the paroxysms of anguish she caused Billy Wilder and Tony Curtis. But he seems to assume that once a given scene was in the can it became established as a miracle of assurance. And the plain fact is that her salient weakness – the inability to read a line – was ineradicable. Every phrase came out as if it had just been memorized. *Just* been memorized. And that film was the high point of the short-winded, monotonous attack she had developed for getting lines across. In earlier films, all the way back to the beginning, we are assailed with varying degrees of the irrepressible panic which infected a voice that couldn't tell where to place emphasis. As a natural silent comedian Marilyn might possibly have qualified, with the proviso that she was not to be depended upon to invent anything. But as a natural comedian in sound she had the conclusive disadvantage of not being able to speak. She was limited ineluctably to characters who rented language but could never possess it, and all her best roles fell into that category. She was good at being inarticulately abstracted for the same reason that midgets are good at being short.

To hear Mailer overpraising Marilyn's performance in *Gentlemen Prefer Blondes* is to wonder if he has any sense of humour at all. Leaving out of account an aberration like *Man's Favourite Sport* (in which Paula Prentiss, a comedienne who actually knows something about being funny, was entirely wasted), *Gentlemen Prefer Blondes* is the least entertaining comedy Howard Hawks ever made. With its manic exaggeration of Hawks's already heavy emphasis on male aggressiveness transplanted to the female, the film later became a touchstone for the Hawksian cinéastes (who also lacked a sense of humour, and tended to talk ponderously about the role-reversals in *Bringing Up Baby* before passing with relief to the supposed wonders of *Hatari*), but the awkward truth is that with this project Hawks landed himself with the kind of challenge he was least likely to find liberating – dealing with dumb sex instead of the bright kind. Hawks supplied a robust professional framework for Marilyn's accomplishments, such as they were. Where I lived, at any rate, her performance in the film was generally regarded as mildly winning in spite of her obvious, fundamental inadequacies – the *in spite of* being regarded as the secret of any uniqueness her appeal might have. Mailer tells it differently:

> In the best years with DiMaggio, her physical coordination is never more vigorous and athletically quick; she dances with all the grace she is ever going to need when doing *Gentlemen Prefer Blondes*, all the grace and all the bazazz – she is a musical comedy star with panache! Diamonds Are a Girl's Best Friend! What a surprise! And sings so well Zanuck will first believe her voice was dubbed . . .

This is the language of critical self-deception, fine judgement suppressed in the name of a broader cause. What does it mean to dance with all the grace you are ever going to need? It doesn't sound the same as being good at dancing. The fact was that she could handle a number like the 'Running Wild' routine in the train corridor in *Some Like It Hot* (Wilder covered it with the marvellous cutaways of Lemmon slapping the back of the bull-fiddle and Curtis making ping-pong-ball eyes while blowing sax), but anything harder than that was pure pack-drill. And if Zanuck really believed that her voice was dubbed, then for once in his life he must have made an intuitive leap, because to say that her singing voice didn't sound as if it belonged to her was to characterize it with perfect accuracy. Like her speaking voice, it was full of panic.

It took more than sympathy for her horrible death and nostalgia for her atavistic cuddlesomeness to blur these judgements, which at one time all intelligent people shared. The thing that tipped the balance towards adulation was Camp — Camp's yen for the vulnerable in women, which is just as inexorable as its hunger for the strident. When Mailer talks about Marilyn's vulnerability, he means the inadequacy of her sense of self. Camp, however, knew that the vulnerability which mattered was centred in the inadequacy of her talent. She just wasn't very good, and was thus eligible for membership in the ever-increasing squad of Camp heroines who make their gender seem less threatening by being so patently unaware of how they're going over. On the strident wing of the team, Judy Garland is a perennial favourite for the same reason. If common sense weren't enough to do it, the Camp enthusiasm for Monroe should have told Mailer — Mailer of all people — that the sexuality he was getting set to rave about was the kind that leaves the viewer uncommitted.

Mailer longs to talk of Monroe as a symbolic figure, node of a death wish and foretaste of the fog. Embroiled in such higher criticism, he doesn't much concern himself with the twin questions of what shape Hollywood took in the 50s and of how resonantly apposite a representative Marilyn turned out to be of the old studio system's last gasp. As the third-string blonde at Fox (behind Betty Grable and June Haver) Marilyn was not — as Mailer would have it — in all that unpromising a spot. She was in luck, like Kim Novak at Columbia, who was groomed by Harry Cohn to follow Rita Hayworth in the characteristic 50s transposition which substituted apprehensiveness for ability. For girls like them, the roles would eventually be there — mainly crummy roles in mainly crummy movies, but they were the movies the studios were banking on. For the real actresses, times were tougher, and didn't ease for more than a decade. Anne Bancroft, for example, also started out at Fox, but couldn't get the ghost of a break. Mailer isn't careful enough about pointing out that Fox's record as a starmaker was hopeless in all departments: Marilyn was by no means a unique case of neglect, and in comparison with Bancroft got a smooth ride. Marilyn was just another item in the endless catalogue of Zanuck's imperviousness to box-office potential. James Robert Parish, in his useful history, *The Fox Girls*, sums up the vicissitudes of Marilyn's career at Fox with admirable brevity and good sense, and if the reader would like to make up his own mind about the facts, it's to that book he should turn.

Right across Hollywood, as the films got worse, the dummies and the sex-bombs came into their own, while the actresses dropped deeper into limbo. Considering the magnitude of the luminary he is celebrating, it might seem funny to Mailer if one were to mention the names of people like, say, Patricia Neal, or (even more obscure) Lola Albright. Soon only the most fanatic of students will be aware that such actresses were available but could not be used. It's not that history has been rewritten. Just that the studio-handout version of history has been unexpectedly confirmed – by Norman Mailer, the very stamp of writer who ought to know better. The studios created a climate for new talent that went on stifling the best of it until recent times. How, for example, does Mailer think Marilyn stacks up against an artist like Tuesday Weld? By the criteria of approval manifested in *Marilyn*, it would be impossible for Mailer to find Weld even mildly interesting. To that extent, the senescent dream-factories succeeded in imposing their view: first of all on the masses, which was no surprise, but now on the elite, which is.

*

Mailer is ready to detect all manner of bad vibes in the 50s, but unaccountably fails to include in his read-out of portents the one omen pertinent to his immediate subject. The way that Hollywood divested itself of *intelligence* in that decade frightened the civilized world. And far into the 60s this potato-blight of the intellect went on. The screen was crawling with cosmeticized androids. Not content with gnawing her knuckles through the long days of being married to a test pilot or the long nights of being married to a band leader, June Allyson sang and danced. Betty Hutton, the ultimate in projected

insecurity, handed over to Doris Day, a yelping freckle. The last
Tracy-Hepburn comedies gurgled nostalgically in the straw like the
lees of a soda. The new Hepburn, Audrey, was a Givenchy clothes-
horse who piped her lines in a style composed entirely of mannerisms.
And *she* was supposed to be class. Comedy of the 30s and 40s, the
chief glory of the American sound cinema, was gone as if it had
never been. For those who had seen and heard the great Hollywood
high-speed talkers (Carole Lombard, Irene Dunne, Rosalind Russell,
Katharine Hepburn, Jean Arthur) strut their brainy stuff, the let-
down was unbelievable. Comic writing was pretty nearly wiped out,
and indeed has never fully recovered as a genre. In a context of
unprecedented mindlessness, Marilyn Monroe rose indefatigably to
success. She just wasn't clever enough to fail.

Marilyn came in on the 50s tide of vulgarity, and stayed to take
an exemplary part in the Kennedy era's uproar of cultural pretension.
Mailer follows her commitment to the Actors' Studio with a credu-
lousness that is pure New Frontier. The cruelty with which he satirizes
Arthur Miller's ponderous aspirations to greatness is transmuted
instantly to mush when he deals with Mrs Miller's efforts to explore
the possibilities hitherto dormant within her gift. That such possibilities existed was by no means taken as gospel at the time of her
first forays into New York, but with the advent of the Kennedy era
the quality of scepticism seemed to drain out of American cultural
life. *Marilyn* is a latter-day Kennedy-era text, whose prose, acrid with
the tang of free-floating charisma, could have been written a few
weeks after Robert Kennedy's death rounded out the period of the
family's power. Mailer's facility for confusing the intention with
the deed fits that epoch's trust in façades to perfection. He is delicately
tender when evoking the pathos of Marilyn's anxious quest for self-
fulfilment, but never doubts that the treasure of buried ability was
there to be uncovered, if only she could have found the way. The
true pathos – that she was simply not fitted for the kind of art she
had been led to admire – eludes him. Just as he gets over the problem
of Marilyn's intellectual limitations by suggesting that a mind can be
occupied with more interesting things than thoughts, so he gets over
the problem of her circumscribed accomplishments by suggesting
that true talent is founded not on ability but on a state of being.
Nobody denies that the snorts of derision which first greeted the
glamour queen's strivings towards seriousness were inhuman, vision-

less. In rebuttal, it was correctly insisted that her self-exploration was the exercise of an undeniable right. But the next, fatal step was to assume that her self-exploration was an artistic activity in itself, and had a right to results.

*

Scattered throughout the book are hints that Mailer is aware that his loved one had limited abilities. But he doesn't let it matter, preferring to insist that her talent – a different thing – was boundless. Having overcome so much deprivation in order to see that certain kinds of achievement were desirable, she had an automatic entitlement to them. That, at any rate, seems to be his line of reasoning. A line of reasoning which is really an act of faith. The profundity of his belief in the significance of what went on during those secret sessions at the Actors' Studio is unplumbable. She possessed, he vows, the talent to play Cordelia. One examines this statement from front-on, from both sides, through a mirror, and with rubber gloves. Is there a hint of a put-on? There is not. Doesn't he really mean something like: she possessed enough nerve and critical awareness to see the point of trying to extend her range by playing a few fragments of a Shake-spearean role out of the public eye? He does not. He means what he says, that Marilyn Monroe possessed the talent to play Cordelia. Who, let it be remembered, is required, in the first scene of the play, to deliver a speech like this:

> Good my lord,
> You have begot me, bred me, lov'd me: I
> Return those duties back as are right fit,
> Obey you, love you, and most honour you.
> Why have my sisters husbands, if they say
> They love you all? Haply, when I shall wed,
> That lord whose hand must take my plight shall carry
> Half my love with him, half my care and duty:
> Sure I shall never marry like my sisters,
> To love my father all.

Leave aside the matter of how she would have managed such stuff on stage; it is doubtful she could have handled a single minute of it even on film: not with all the dialogue coaches in the world, not even if they had shot and edited in the way Joshua Logan is reputed to have put together her performance in some of the key scenes of *Bus Stop* – word by word, frame by frame. The capacity to apprehend and reproduce the rhythm of written language just wasn't there. And even if we were to suppose that such an indispensable capacity could be dispensed with, there would still be the further question of whether the much-touted complexity of her character actually contained a material resembling Cordelia's moral steel: it is not just sweetness that raises Cordelia above her sisters. We are bound to conclude (if only to preserve from reactionary scorn the qualities Marilyn really *did* have) that she was debarred from the wider range of classical acting not only by a paucity of ability but by a narrowness of those emotional resources Mailer would have us believe were somehow a substitute for it. Devoid of invention, she could only draw on her stock of feeling. The stock was thin. Claiming for her a fruitful complexity, Mailer has trouble conjuring it up: punctuated by occasional outbreaks of adoration for animals and men, her usual state of mind seems to have been an acute but generalized fear, unreliably counterbalanced by sedation.

Mailer finds it temptingly easy to insinuate that Marilyn's madness knew things sanity wots not of, and he tries to make capital out of the tussle she had with Laurence Olivier in *The Prince and the Showgirl*. Olivier, we are asked to believe, was the icy technician working from the outside in, who through lack of sympathy muffed the chance to elicit from his leading lady miracles of warm intuition. It's a virtuoso passage from Mailer, almost convincing us that an actor like Olivier is a prisoner of rationality forever barred from the inner mysteries of his profession. You have to be nuts, whispers Mailer from the depths of his sub-text, to be a *real* actor. The derivation from Laing's psychology is obvious.

The author does a noble, loyal, zealous job of tracing his heroine's career as an artist, but we end by suspecting that he is less interested in her professional achievement than in her fame. The story of Norma Jean becoming Somebody is the true spine of the book, and the book is Mailer's most concise statement to date of what he thinks being Somebody has come to mean in present-day America. On this theme, *Marilyn* goes beyond being merely wrong-headed and becomes quite frightening.

As evidence of the leverage Marilyn's fame could exert, Mailer recounts a story of her impressing some friends by taking them without a reservation to the Copacabana, where Sinatra was packing the joint to the rafters every night. Marilyn being Monroe, Sinatra ordered a special table put in at his feet, and while lesser mortals were presumably being asphyxiated at the back, he sang for his unexpected guest and her friends, personally. Only for the lonely. Mailer tells such stories without adornment, but his excitement in them is ungovernable: it infects the style, giving it the tone we have come to recognize from all his previous excursions into status, charisma, psychic victory, and the whole witchcraft of personal ascendancy. *Marilyn* seems to bring this theme in his work to a crisis.

In many ways *The Naked and the Dead* was the last classic novel to be written in America. The separately-treated levels of the military hierarchy mirrored the American class structure, such as it was, and paralleled the class structure of the classic European novel, such as it had always been. With *The Deer Park* the American classes were already in a state of flux, but the society of Hollywood maintained cohesion by being aware of what conditions dictated the mutability of its hierarchy: Sergius the warrior slept with Lulu the love queen, both of them qualifying, while fortune allowed, as members of the only class, below which was the ruck – the unlovely, the unknown, the out. *The Deer Park* was Mailer's last attempt to embody American society in fictional form: *An American Dream* could find room only for its hero. Increasingly with the years, the broad sweep of Mailer's creativity has gone into the interpretation of reality as it stands, or rather flows, and he has by now become adept at raising fact to the level of fiction. Meanwhile society has become even more fluid, to the extent that the upper class – the class of celebrities – has become as unstable in its composition as the hubbub below. Transformation and displacement now operate endlessly, and the observer (heady prospect) changes the thing observed. Mailer's tendency to enrol himself in even the most exalted action is based on the perception, not entirely crazed, that the relative positions in the star-cluster of status are his to define: reality is a novel that he is writing.

On her way to being divorced from Arthur Miller, Marilyn stopped off in Dallas. In Dallas! Mailer can hardly contain himself. 'The most electric of the nations,' he writes, 'must naturally provide the boldest circuits of coincidence.' Full play is made with the rumours that Marilyn might have had affairs with either or both of the two doomed Kennedy brothers, and there is beetle-browed speculation about the possibility of her death having placed a curse on the family – and hence, of course, on the whole era. Mailer himself calls this last brainwave 'endlessly facile', thereby once again demonstrating his unfaltering dexterity at having his cake and eating it. But this wearying attempt to establish Marilyn as the muse of the artist-politicians is at one with the book's whole tendency to weight her down with a load of meaning she is too frail to bear. Pepys could be floored by Lady Castlemaine's beauty without ascribing to her qualities she did not possess. The Paris intellectuals quickly learned that Pompadour's passion for china flowers and polite theatre was no indication that artistic genius was in favour at Versailles – quite the reverse. Where hierarchies were unquestioned, realism meant the ability to see what was really what. Where the hierarchy is created from day to day in the mind of one man interpreting it, realism is likely to be found a hindrance.

Mailer doesn't want famous people to mean as little as the sceptical tongue says they do. To some extent he is right. There *is* an excitement in someone like Marilyn Monroe coming out of nowhere to find herself conquering America, and there is a benediction in the happiness she could sometimes project from the middle of her anguish. Without Mailer's receptivity we would not have been given the full impact of these things; just as if he had listened to the liberal line on the space programme we would not have been given those enthralling moments in *A Fire on the Moon* when the launch vehicle pulls free of its bolts, or when the mission passes from the grip of the earth into the embrace of its target – moments as absorbing as our first toys. Mailer's shamelessness says that there are people and events which mean more than we in our dignity are ready to allow. He has nearly always been right. But when he starts saying that in that case they might as well mean what he wants them to mean, the fictionalist has overstepped the mark, since the patterning that strengthens fiction weakens fact.

*

Mailer's Marilyn is a usurper, a democratic monarch reigning by dint of the allegiance of an intellectual aristocrat, the power of whose regency has gone to his head. Mailer has forgotten that Marilyn was the people's choice before she was his, and that in echoing the people he is sacrificing his individuality on the altar of perversity. Sergius already had the sickness:

> Then I could feel her as something I had conquered, could listen to her wounded breathing, and believe that no matter how she acted other times, these moments were Lulu, as if her flesh murmured words more real than her lips. To the pride of having so beautiful a girl was added the bigger pride of knowing that I took her with the cheers of millions behind me. Poor millions with their low roar!

At the end of *The Deer Park* the dying Eitel tells Sergius by telepathy that the world we may create is more real to us than the mummery of what happens, passes, and is gone. Whichever way Sergius decided, Mailer seems finally to have concluded that the two are the same thing. More than any of his essays so far, *Marilyn* tries to give the mummery of what happens the majestic gravity of a created world. And as he has so often done before, he makes even the most self-assured of us wonder if we have felt deeply enough, looked long enough, lived hard enough. He comes close to making us doubt our conviction that in a morass of pettiness no great issues are being decided. We benefit from the doubt. But the price he pays for being able to induce it is savage, and Nietzche's admonition is begining to apply. He has gazed too long into the abyss, and now the abyss is gazing into him. Bereft of judgement, detachment, or even a tinge of irony, *Marilyn* is an opulent but slavish expression of an empty consensus. The low roar of the poor millions is in every page.

Commentary October, 1973: previously included in
At the Pillars of Hercules, 1979

Postscript

Years later, when I finally met Norman Mailer in the back of a limousine in New York, he generously neglected to punch me out for a review he must have thought unfair. He certainly could have decked me had he wished, and in the limo I would not have had far to fall. I never saw a more threatening neck on a writer: his ears sat on top of it like book-ends on a mantelpiece. But on this occasion he was civility itself. Perhaps he remembered that I had studded my diatribe with tributes to his gift. In retrospect I only wish that there had been more of them. Opportunities to register gratitude should never be neglected, and gratitude is what I have always felt for Mailer, over and above – or should it be under and below? – the inevitable exasperation. *A Fire on the Moon* (called *Of a Fire on the Moon* in the United States: a striding title crippled by an extra word) was to remain one of my models for how prose can reflect the adventure of high technology without lapsing into a hi-fi buff's nerdish fervour, and later he restored himself triumphantly as a writer of fiction with the remarkable *Harlot's Ghost*. But I still think he got it all wrong about Marilyn Monroe. He was right to think that film stardom hasn't got much to do with acting talent. He was just wrong about the talent. In conversation it might have been edifying, if dangerous, to pursue the point, but as I remember it he raised the subject of Iris Murdoch. Since there were about half a dozen other people in the car better qualified to pursue that topic than I, my colloquy with the patriarch was soon suspended, along with any chance of a fist fight.

It was a pity Mailer ever saddled himself with a reputation as a brawler, because in the New York literary context fisticuffs rate as a hopelessly anachronistic weapons system. At the kind invitation of Norman Podhoretz of *Commentary*, my review of Mailer's *Marilyn* was the first big piece I published in the United States. Not long afterwards, Robert Silvers asked me to write for the *New York Review of Books*, whose personnel felt about the *Commentary* crowd the way Iraq later felt about Iran. It was an ideological battlefield, and the free-floating contributor was very likely to get zapped in the contending force-fields of influence. Later on I moved to the *New Yorker* and fancied that I had got above the battle, but I never moved to New York. Fed-Ex, fax and then e-mail made it steadily more easy to maintain a safely detached participation in a literary scene that resembled a John Carpenter movie with better dialogue. (Exercise: armed with a video of *Escape from New York* and a list of prominent Manhattan *culturati*, re-cast the roles of the Duke, Brains, Cabbie and that babe with the big maracas. Keep the Kurt Russell part for yourself.) It helps to know one's weaknesses, and the hypertrophied celebrity culture in New York appeals too much to my sweet tooth. In London I find it hard enough to preserve my rule not to be quoted on anything that I am not prepared to write about. In New York, where not to be quoted is to be considered dead, pressure from publishers would soon make it compulsory to succumb. Mailer himself is a case in point. After the criminal Jack Abbott, for whose release Mailer had campaigned, celebrated his freedom by murdering a waiter who looked at him sideways, Mailer was caught saying that Abbott's action might have had some redeeming use as a 'challenge to the suburbs'. But he would never have been caught *writing* something so callously foolish. Writers should stay off the air unless they can keep their equilibrium, and the media in the United States devote a lot of money and effort to making sure you can't keep that.

2001

APPROXIMATELY IN THE VICINITY OF BARRY HUMPHRIES

Snails in the letterbox. It is a surrealist image which might have been cooked up by Dali in the presence of Buñuel, by André Breton in the presence of Eluard. But the words were said by Barry Humphries in the persona of the ruminating convalescent Sandy Stone, and in the Australian context they are not surreal. They are real. Every Australian, even if he lives in Sydney's Point Piper or Melbourne's Toorak, has at some time or other found snails in the letterbox. When you step outside on a dark and dewy night, the snails crunch under your slippered feet like liqueur chocolates. Snails in Australia are thick on the ground. Nothing could be less remarkable than a cluster of them in your letterbox.

But Humphries, through Sandy's comatose vision, remarked them, and his countrymen shouted with recognition. In Australia the familiar is seen to be bizarre as soon as it is said. Or else the English language, fatigued by 12,000 miles of travel, cracks up under the strain of what it is forced to connote. There is a discrepancy between fact and phrase, a discrepancy which Humphries, linguistically more sensitive than any Australian poet before him, was the first to spot.

Laughter at his discovery was immediate, but honour came slowly. The man who makes people laugh is rarely given quick credit, even in those fully developed countries which realize that serious writing can take a comic form. In Australia, whose literary journalism has sometimes attained vigour but rarely subtlety, the possibility that Humphries might be some kind of poet has been raised more often than analysed, and most often it has been laughed out of court. Even as a man of the theatre, he has usually been put in that category where freakish spontaneity is held to outweigh craft, and where the word 'effortless', if not pejorative, is not laudatory either. His popular success has served only to reinforce this early interpretation. Australia was the country in which the swimming performances of Dawn Fraser, who went faster than anybody else and with less training, were belittled on the grounds that she was a natural athlete.

Yet a detailed appreciation of Humphries's poetic gift is a pre-requisite for criticism of his work. Otherwise approval becomes indiscriminate gush, and disapproval, which it is sometimes hard not to feel, degenerates quickly into the cutting down to size of someone who, beyond a certain point, can't *be* cut down to size: as a pioneer in Australia's sense of its own vernacular he must be allowed his stature even if his theatrical creations are found unsatisfactory either individually or all together. Humphries, for reasons of his own, seems determined to present at least one *alter ego* during the evening who will offend you whoever you are. As it happens, I can just stand Les Patterson even when he belches while dribbling on his loud tie, but to sit there with your eyes closed is sometimes to wonder at the price of the ticket. Other people find the trade-union con-man Lance Boyle hard to take – offended in their radical beliefs or having decided (correctly, by his creator's own confession) that Lance has set out to bore them rigid.

No matter how rebarbative the preliminary acts, Aunt Edna saves the night in the second half, but not even she has escaped worried objections or been guiltless of deliberately provoking them. There is a self-mortifying element in Humphries's theatre which is all the more striking because the selves are multiple, and which goes all the way back to the beginning of his career. But so does his extra-ordinary sense of language, best studied in the monologues of Sandy Stone, a character so enduring that he has proved unkillable. Like Conan Doyle precipitating Sherlock Holmes over the Reichenbach Falls, Humphries at one stage compelled Sandy to drop off the twig, but he came back from the dead more talkative than ever.

Talkative but torpid. You have to have seen the shows, or at least listened to the records, to realize that the Sandy transcripts collected in *A Nice Night's Entertainment* (London, 1982) falsify the character by moving as fast as you can read, whereas the sentences should produce themselves the way Sandy speaks, glacially. A valetudinarian Returned Serviceman – not even Humphries is sure which of the two world wars Sandy returned from – he has always been laid up. Twenty-five years ago he was tottering around the house: the famous

Kia Ora, 36 Gallipoli Crescent, Glen Iris. Later on he graduated to a repatriation hospital and eventually to the beyond, back from which he rolled in the same hospital bed. On stage, he has always been mainly a face in soft limelight, thus betokening the acknowledged influence of Samuel Beckett on his creator. Combine the Beckettian talking head with the pebble-collecting word-play of Gertrude Stein's *Three Lives*, cross the result with *The Diary of a Nobody* and you've got the beginning of Sandy, but you have to slow it all down even further, not just from 45 rpm down to 33⅓, but all the way down to the rarely used 16⅔. Sandy in his own mind is a dynamo. 'I got home in time for a bit of lunch and then I had to whiz out again to the football.' But on record you can hear the effort it takes him to say the word 'whiz' and on stage you can actually see it − a little heave of the shapeless body as he evokes the memory of his dizzy speed.

On the page, it is impossible to savour Sandy's eloquent silence. 'So, Beryl and I went to bed.' On stage, his eyeballs slowly pop and then roll slightly upwards after that line, telling you all you need to know about the hectic love-life of Sandy and Beryl. (Not that a torrid romance is any longer on the cards, what with Beryl rarely feeling 100 per cent, although, as Sandy is always as quick as he can be to point out, there is nothing *organically* wrong.) But there is plenty to cherish in just reading the words, even if you have to fill in the timing and the facial movements as best you can. Sandy's slowness of speech could be the fastidiousness of the connoisseur. He fondles words like a philologist. A polysyllable is a joy to him, and with luxuriating gradualness he bursts its grape against his palate fine. His circumlocutions − 'the occasional odd glass', 'approximately in the vicinity', 'altogether it was a really nice night's entertainment for us all' − are a way of getting more to gustate into each sentence. The repetitions are not so much echolalia as a kind of epic verbal land-marking, in the same way that prepared phrases keep on coming back in Virgil and Homer. Sandy had 'a bit of strife parking the vehicle' on his first record, *Wild Life in Suburbia*, back in 1959. He has had a bit of strife parking the vehicle ever since, often several times in the same monologue, when the announcement that there was a bit of strife involved in parking the vehicle usually opens a new phase in his interminable account of a more or less recent nice night's entertainment or at any rate indicates that the previous phase is over. A recurring figure of speech is thus more a punctuation mark than a sign of impoverished vocabulary. All the evidence suggests that Sandy is lexically acquisitive. The events in his life don't leave him at a loss for words. The words are at a loss for events.

> Clive Nettleton hadn't had a real break from work since the marriage and *she* was a bundle of nerves and as thin as a rake, so seeing as they were tantamount to being friends of ours, through the Clissold girls, Beryl and I had a bit of a confab in the kitchen and we intimated to them that we were desirous to mind the youngsters for them over the Easter period while they had a bit of a breather down at her people's home.

On stage, the word 'home' would, in Sandy's mouth, die the sad death of an overparted substitute for 'house', and the duly hysterical audience might forget that the word 'tantamount' had made its struggling appearance, incongruous but naturally so, because Sandy's higher brain centre collects incongruities. Even more than Aunt Edna, Sandy is linguistically a magpie. But he is a magpie in slow motion. Edna attacks, Sandy retreats. He is consequently better qualified than she as an emblem and paradigm of Australian English, which is less fascinating for its newly created slang – Humphries, *per media* Barry McKenzie, has created a lot of that himself – than for the way old formal utterances have been strangely preserved and may be used in all innocence.

By his original sure instinct, fine ear, and the formidable scholarship with which he later reinforced them, Humphries identified the pristine quality of everyday Australian English, a language which the self-consciousness of a literary culture had not yet dulled. Not having read Shakespeare is no guarantee that you will talk like him, but vividness of expression comes most easily to those who aren't always mentally testing the way they speak against how someone else wrote. Sandy doesn't just treasure words, he treasures detail. For him, the dissociation of sensibility has not set in. He is a neo-Elizabethan whose world picture, although restricted to the radius which can be attained without strife by the slowly cruising vehicle, is dazzling in its clarity. Everything is picked out as if seen with peeled eyes.

> Beryl had cut some delicious sandwiches. Egg and lettuce. Peanut butter. Marmite and walnut. Cheese and apricot jam. And lots of bread and butter and hundreds and thousands – and one of

her own specialties – a chocolate and banana log. She'd only
baked it that morning and the kiddies were most intrigued. Beryl
said if they promised to behave themselves at Wattle Park they
could lick the beaters. We packed some of Beryl's home-made
ginger beer and a Thermos for ourselves but unfortunately Beryl
forgot to put the greaseproof paper round the cork appertaining
to the calamine lotion bottle we used for the milk with the
resultant consequence that by the time we got off the bus the milk
had soaked right through the sandwiches and half-way up the
log.

The appertaining cork and the resultant consequence are verbose
but superficial: deeper down, there is an imagist precision that can
come only out of a full submission to the phenomenal world. Sandy
is Ezra Pound with the power off. You feel that Humphries himself
remembers what it was like to be allowed to lick the egg-beater and
bowl. To the extent that Sandy exists on the intellectual plane at all,
he is the kind of dimwit who takes anti-Semitism for an impressively
complicated political theory. 'Personally speaking, I wouldn't have
any objection if they started up their own golf club.' But Sandy would
never risk the strife of translating his distaste into action, and has
probably never heard about the same ideas creating a certain amount
of disturbance elsewhere in the world. Hence the child-like vision,
which on occasions can express itself with a purity that silences the
theatre, as the audience is propelled helplessly backwards into time.

There's a tennis club right next to the Repat outside my window
and I can hear them playing right up until the light goes and the
couples laughing when there's nothing particularly funny and
the sprinkler on the spare court and the couples saying thank
you to the kiddies when a ball lobs over the fence and I can hear
them shut the cyclone gate and the cicadas and the different cars
going off into the distance.

The accepted wisdom is that Sandy Stone is Humphries's most
rounded character. If he is, it is partly because of his physical immo-
bility: Humphries is a hypomanically physical actor who with his
other characters gets a lot of effects from stage business, so with the
catatonic Sandy he is obliged to put more into the writing. But
the main reason for Sandy's satisfying density of texture is that
Humphries is not taking revenge on him. Humphries, for once feeling

more complicity than contempt, is at his most poetic with Sandy because he is at his least satirical. To Sandy, and to Sandy alone, he is fair – and as Kurt Tucholsky once memorably insisted (in his 1919 essay 'Was darf die Satire?'), satire is unfair in its deepest being: in satire the just shall suffer along with the unjust, as the Bible says.

Driven to death by the Nazis, Tucholsky perhaps had occasion during his last days to wonder whether satirizing bourgeois democracy, as opposed to merely criticizing it, had ever been a particularly good idea. Golo Mann, writing after the Second World War, usefully dared to suggest that post-First World War society in Germany and Austria got far more satire than it needed. This suspicion is not necessarily dispelled by an extended study of Karl Kraus, who in my experience becomes more disheartening as you read on through *Die Fackel* and its attendant works. His aggressive sensitivity to journalistic and political clichés – a critical propensity of which Humphries is a latterday incarnation – remains a thing for wonder, but we can legitimately doubt whether he had a proper estimation of the forces which held the society he castigated together. Other products of the Viennese cabaret world, most notably the polymath Egon Friedell and the essayist Alfred Polgar, seem in retrospect to have the deeper insight which comes from a greater range of sympathy. Their *Kleinkunst*, the little art of cabaret and intimate revue, gave rise to a thorough understanding of the modern world, but in the process they left satire behind them, having embraced fairness as a principle. Polgar, indeed, however toughened by the bitterness of exile, is the most heartening example imaginable of just how sweet reason can be. He wrote the prose that tells us what we lost.

The rich, doomed Vienna of these brilliant men might seem to constitute an over-mighty standard of comparison, but there can be no doubt that Humphries, by world standards already a master of *Kleinkunst*, also has a conscious mission to correct taste and criticize morals in the society of his birth. He would be the first to point out that Moonee Ponds is not Vienna. To disabuse the allegedly burgeoning Australia of its notions about a New Renaissance is one of his aims in life. But equally one of his aims in life is to mount a full-scale satirical critique of a whole culture, even if, especially if, it is a culture in which Beryl's chocolate log counts as a work of art.

He has the required range of talents. As a writer-performer of one-man cabaret the natural figure to compare him with would have to be adduced not from Vienna but from Munich – Karl Valentin. Humphries's own choice of an informing background would no doubt be Paris. In real life he dresses expensively as an English gentleman, but that broad-brimmed trilby, tending towards a sombrero, is worn at an angle reminiscent of Aristide Bruant. One night during the filming of the Paris location scenes for the second Barry McKenzie film – directed, like the first, by Bruce Beresford – Humphries led a party to see the cabaret at the Alcazar, which was then still in its full glory. As a bit player in the film, I was along for the ride. The Alcazar cabaret had visual effects which I had never known were even possible. There was a Zizi Jeanmaire impersonation in which Zizi's head appeared from the top of an enormous feather boa while her feet pounded out a frantic flamenco underneath. Halfway through the number the boa underwent a sudden meiosis and there were two Zizis half the original size. One midget girl had been riding on the other's shoulders.

Humphries drank the spectacle in as if he were lapping fresh water from the source. He is a dandy who has studied Europe's history of style more intensely than any of its own dandies. But his hunger for this kind of knowledge has never been slavish. Grub Street literary reviewers who find something risible about how the Australian expatriates gulp at Europe often neglect the possibility that there is such a thing as an unjaded appetite. Humphries is among the most adventurously well-read people I have ever met. He has also spent a quarter of a century assiduously collecting Symbolist paintings. He was a pioneer in re-establishing the reputation of Charles Conder and at one time, before a divorce intervened, he had the most important collection of Conder's paintings in private hands. He is so learned in the more arcane regions of late nineteenth- and early twentieth-century culture that there is scarcely anyone he can talk to about more than a part of what he has in his head. Most of us know of Marmaduke Pickthall, for example, only as someone who collaborated with Christopher Isherwood in the translation of the Upanishads. But Humphries has read all the works of Marmaduke Pickthall. And the name Marmaduke Pickthall – I thought Humphries was making it up when I first heard him mention it – is a blazing light compared with the names of some of the composers whose complete recorded works probably exist nowhere else except on his shelves.

As so often happens with the Australian expatriates, however, Humphries discovered his Europe before he got there. When an undergraduate in Melbourne in the early 1950s, he was already a Dadaist – the first Dadaist Australia had ever had, and the last thing it knew how to handle. The story has often been told of how in his first revue, *Call Me Madman,* the curtain went up only so that the cast could pelt the audience with fruit and vegetables, after which it went down again. Humphries also staged the first-ever Australian exhibition of Dadaist art works, all of them confected by himself. They included a pair of wellingtons full of custard ('Pus in Boots') and a large canvas empty except for three tiny newspaper clippings of the word 'big' centrally arranged ('The Three Little Bigs'). If this came a long way after Tristan Tzara, it came a long way before Yoko Ono and was much funnier than either, but more prophetic was his knack for street theatre. Still a schoolboy in Sydney, I heard about these daring adventures only later, but everybody in Australia got to hear about them eventually. Apparently there was a progressive breakfast, in which Humphries, riding towards Melbourne University on a train, was handed a new course through the carriage window at each station by an accomplice. He particularly favoured public transport because of the captive audience. Having had his right leg specially immobilized in a large white plaster cast (the immense trouble he will take to get an effect has been a trademark throughout his career), he would sit in a crowded railway carriage with the glaringly encased leg sticking out into the aisle until everyone on board was aware of nothing else. Then an accomplice would come along and jump on it. Women accomplices were known as hoydens and doxies. He would dress them up as schoolgirls and passionately kiss them in the street until the police arrived, whereupon birth certificates would be produced.

The theatrical gift inspiring all this was unmistakable from an early date. So was the desire to shock. Humphries sprang from the bourgeoisie himself but never seems to have doubted the validity of his mission to shock it. Those of us who think that everyday life in the modern world can be relied upon to be unsettling enough on its own account sometimes find it hard to see why the bourgeoisie needs to be shocked in the theatre as well, but no doubt this attitude is complacent, not to say squeamish. Humphries has always had a strong stomach. One of his tricks as a junior Dadaist was to plant a chicken dinner in a public garbage bin during the night so that he could come along dressed as a tramp in the morning, search the bin and dine gluttonously off what he found. At a later stage, when he started commuting between Australia and Britain on the jet airliners, he would stuff the sick-bag with potoato salad early in the flight so that he could conspicuously eat from it with a spoon later. Even today he is likely to fall with glee upon any medical textbook featuring deformities, abortions and disfiguring maladies. His first book, *Bizarre*, was a freak show that you had to be a pathologist to find funny.

Although this Ubu-esque taste for the manufactured atrocity gradually faded as he uncovered more of the truly grotesque in everyday Australian life, nevertheless his scope of apprehension has remained either bravely comprehensive or morbid, perhaps both. Perhaps he thinks we are not really revolted, just pretending to be. But there can be no question that in the theatre one of his ambitions is to put you off. Les Patterson is hard to watch even from a distance and in the front row you need a mackintosh. He is so excessive a reaction that you wonder at the provocation. Surely the worst thing about Australian official spokesmen for the Yartz since the Whitlam era has been not that they are totally ignorant, but that they do know all the right names yet push them like commodities. I once heard Humphries fondly reminiscing about a mayor of Armidale, NSW, who shook hands, called him Brian and apologized for not having met him at the railway station 'owing to the pressure of affairs of state'. Probably Les began from moments like that, but in the course of time he has grown into an ogre so colossal as to have lost his outline. Lance Boyle the careerist shop steward is perhaps closer to identifiable reality. One looks in vain for a redeeming feature, but no doubt one would have done the same with the original. Seeing, however, that Lance establishes himself as an unmitigated horror in the first five minutes on stage, when he goes on being horrible for twenty-five minutes more you can be excused for wondering about a point so obsessively made, even if his self-revealing speech patterns are never less than well caught. The same applies to Neil Singleton, the pretentious and vindictive grant-subsidized intellectual. He is accurately observed in detail, but he is a perfect monster rather than that more edifying occurrence, a human being gone wrong.

Humphries impersonates these incubi in solo playlets which are astonishing for their stagecraft. As a combination of writer, actor, singer and self-producer he is more plausibly compared with Noël Coward than with any of the cabaret stars. But Humphries, along with the right to shock, claims the right to bore. The originals of his satirized characters bore him, and he takes his revenge by making their simulacra boring in turn. They go on until the audience squirms. On the first night of one of his London shows I saw him nearly lose the audience by giving Les, Neil and a record-breakingly long-winded Lance one after the other in the first half. The second half belonged entirely to Edna but by the time she got on stage to save the night there wasn't much of the night left – it was almost dawn. The remarkable thing was that Humphries, with his radar antennae for audience reaction, must have been well aware of the risk he was running. The Devil gets into him, and he seems to welcome the invasion.

Certainly Edna welcomes the invasion. She would, being a witch. Edna incarnates everything Humphries finds frightening about his homeland – which includes its raw energy. At her most philistine when she is interested in art, she breaks the balls of the whole world. She knackers Kerry Packer and she bollocks Jackson Pollock. She has a Balzacian *gourmandise*. She is a tiger shark wearing Opera House glasses. She is also the active principle in her author's creative personality, just as Sandy is the passive principle. While Sandy Stone lies contemplatively stationary, Dame Edna Everage, Housewife Superstar, indulges that part of her creator's nature which craves world fame. Once Humphries searched Australia for a town called Carnegie so that he could stand in front of its town hall with his body obliterating the word TOWN and be photographed for the cover of his album BARRY HUMPHRIES AT CARNEGIE HALL. Nowadays Edna satisfies that urge on his behalf. She punishes Australia for its vulgarity by personifying it for a startled world, and especially a startled Britain, where she is a bigger star than her inventor. But she could never have been so terrifying if the docile Sandy had not first gathered the banal information she purveys, and Sandy would not have had such a finely calibrated ear if the young Humphries had not first embraced the culture of far-off Europe in its most refined, preferably decadent, forms. When Humphries writes *in propria persona* his prose can scarcely contain its freight of cultivated allusions. He writes the most nutritiously rococo English in Australia today, but nobody will be able to inherit it. To know him would not be enough. You would have to know what he knows.

In London during the early 1960s, he stayed alive as an actor. Visiting Australians who knew his legend would go to see him improvising his way through Christmas pantomimes. (Bruce Beresford, who saw him as Captain Hook, once told me that his catchphrase was 'I'm going to take a peep around the poop' and there were children saying it in the foyer during the interval.) His memory sharpened by absence and new experience, he became more conscious than ever of the all-pervading oddness into which he had been born. On every voyage home his ears were tuned more keenly, his eyes skinned another layer. If he had not had his Europe, he would never have completed his rediscovery of Australia. That is the saving grace to remember when his less sympathetic characters punish their birthplace by representing its pretensions and ignorance to the world, or when Edna shows an unlikely knowledge of minor Belgian pointilliste painters. By bringing his country more understanding than it understands, he is acting out a conflict, living a problem. A thoroughly introspective artist, he is well aware of the anomaly.

The anomaly is resolved nowhere else but in language. Audiences will always leave the theatre wondering where Humphries stands, because to raise such questions and leave them unanswered is part of his purpose, which is in its turn a complex mixture of the worthy desire to raise consciousness and the incurably Mephistophelean urge to raise Hell. At school, so they say, when forced to attend a rugby match he sat facing away from the field, knitting; and as an army cadet he turned up on parade in immaculately blancoed webbing and polished brass, except that it was all put on over his pyjamas. He would have been a handful in any society. He is a misfit and fully conscious of it. The punctilio of his old-world manners, the dandified scrupulosity of his Savile Row suits, are compelled by an unsleeping awareness that he has no more business among ordinary human beings than a Venusian. But his language, at its best, is the language of unfeigned delight. As all his characters, but especially as Sandy, he makes long nominative lists in the way of those writers who are in on the historic moment of discovering the verbal tradition of their young country. Sandy's diction, if not his aphasic voice, was heard before in the glossaries and prose poems which H. L. Mencken composed after the First World War. 'Pale druggists in remote towns of the hog and Christian Endeavour belts, endlessly wrapping up bottles of Peruna . . .'

The rest of it is in Mencken's little *Book of Burlesques*, published by Knopf in 1924. It is a chrestomathy of essays, sketches and wise-cracks rather along the lines of the Peter Altenberg scrapbooks popular in the German-speaking countries right through the First World War. *A Nice Night's Entertainment* would have been more digestible if it had been compiled in the same way, with a few more of Humphries's adroit lyrics and some of the captions, usually signed by Aunt Edna, which he throws away in soft-covered photo books – a bad genre because nobody reads them twice, whoever writes them. The tradition of the catch-all cabaret book sorely needs to be revived. But the mention of Mencken is a reminder to get things in proportion. He brought a cutting wit, hard sense and tireless word-collecting diligence to the business of educating a world power. Australia is, and is likely to remain, a less important place.

One of the most successful representatives of the new energy conferred by an immature country, Humphries has never lost sight of its immaturity. Instead of empty boosting, he has given it a sharp tongue. Australia has allegedly progressed from an inferiority complex to a sense of its own worth. Humphries is inclined by nature to question complacency of any kind but in this instance he has had special reason to be scathing, since so much of the new confidence has proved simple-minded. As a notable contributor to the resurgent Australian film industry he has a right to be sceptical about some aspects of the strong sense of story which is supposed to be its peculiar virtue. Some of the strong stories are simplifications: *Gallipoli*, for example, contributes seductively to the euphoria of the Australian present but denigrates Britain in a way that disowns the past. Sandy Stone lived and died at Gallipoli Crescent without ever being so cocksure on the subject either way. Humphries has the right idea about that sort of unearned assertiveness.

Beyond that, he has the right idea about popular culture. His instinct led him away from a respectable literary career and towards the people. Earlier, in the 1930s, Kenneth Slessor had felt and responded to the same compulsion, having realized that high art was a watched pot. Slessor's popular lyrics for *Smith's Weekly*, later collected in *Darlinghurst Nights* and *Backless Betty from Bondi*, were an important step in his own work, and in the brief history of Australian poetry should be regarded as one of those moments when an individual talent breaks through to a new set of possibilities that lie so close at hand they are hard to see. Humphries is another such talent, but with him the effort looks set to last a lifetime.

A difficult lifetime. For someone so clever there are no days off. Being him is obviously not easy. Like many people who know them both, I have always got on better with Edna. I suspect she is happier than he is. But peace of mind could never have produced such a quality of perception. Barry Humphries is original, not just for what he has created, but for how he has attuned himself to what created him. Hence the feeling of community which he arouses in his countrymen even when the night's entertainment turns out to be not so nice. Bringing out the familiar in its full strangeness, he helps make them proud of their country in the only way that counts – by joining it to the world.

London Review of Books, 6–19 October, 1983: previously included in
Snakecharmers in Texas, 1988

Postscript

Underneath the appropriately awe-stricken innocence of this homage there was a cunning purpose. Knowing that the *London Review of Books*, like the *Times Literary Supplement*, was read religiously in Australia by those very intellectuals who most loudly deplored the excessive respect given to opinions of colonial literature expressed in the old country, I planned to give the home-grown discussion of Humphries's achievement a nudge towards a higher plane than the one on which it was currently stuck. Cunning confounded itself and my plan failed. Today, even as then, Humphries is assessed in the proliferating cultural columns of his homeland according to how his creations are seen to square with nationalist pretensions. In the long run it won't matter: the Australian literati will become as proud of their prodigal son's creative stature as the common people have always been delighted by his comic inventions. But in the short run it is a piquant farce. Luckily its subject is well qualified to turn the attendant ironies to effect. He doesn't need help to fight his battles. Any artist, however, can only benefit from being understood. Egon Friedell, who like Humphries laid a direct path to the public stage from his private library, once summed the matter up: even the strongest character needs a magnetic field in which he can work. Humphries has had to conquer the world in order to find his way home, and what that says about home is for him to say.

To avoid misunderstanding, I should make explicit here what I left implicit at the time: that the Australian 'immaturity' I had in mind was cultural immaturity, not political. Australia has come on a lot since I wrote the piece, but even in 1983 I already believed that as a stable, functioning democracy it was in an enviable position, and that its success had a lot to do with its Constitution. The Republican movement was already up and running, and it was predictable that republicanism would become a consensus among the intelligentsia as a whole, but by a process of cultural fashion rather than political enlightenment. Politically, Australian cultural fashions tend to be obscurantist: a truth which Humphries has done much to illuminate, earning himself many vocal enemies along the way. He has always been able to turn their attacks to material, but even he is hard put to give back as good as he gets. Speaking as one who has always found it more comfortable below the parapet, I can only salute the insane bravery of a man who dances on top of it in full drag.

2001

GERMAINE GREER: GETTING MARRIED LATER

Germaine Greer's first and very considerable book *The Female Eunuch* drops into the intelligentsia's radar accompanied by scores of off-putting decoy noise-sources: a panicky response is virtually guaranteed. Granada Publishing (the command group for MacGibbon and Kee) have done an impressive job with the highbrow press, and weeks before publication date Dr Greer was already well known.

If this makes it seem that the reviewer is too concerned with media reactions and media values, let it be made clear that there is little chance of any other kind of reactions and values operating in the present instance. Germaine Greer is a storm of images; has already been promoted variously as Germaine de Staël, Fleur Fenton Cowles, Rosa Luxemburg and Beatrice Lillie; and at the time of writing needs only a few more weeks' exposure in order to reoccupy the corporeally vacant outlines of Lou Andreas-Salomé, George Sand, Marie von Thurn und Taxis-Hohenlohe and Marjorie Jackson (the Lithgow Flash). Media-hype is never sadder than when something decent is at the centre of the fuss. These forebodings might be wrong, and there could just be a slim chance that *The Female Eunuch* will be appreciated on its merits. But I wouldn't count on it.

The book's merits are of a high order. It possesses a fine, continuous flow of angry power which both engenders and does much to govern the speed-wobble of its logical progression; it sets out an adventurous analysis of social detail which does much to offset the triteness of its theoretical assumptions; and all in all it survives its flaws of style, falsities of assessment and excesses of sentimentality to present an argument of terrific polemical force. 'Now as before, women must refuse to be meek and guileful, for truth cannot be served by dissimulation. Women who fancy that they manipulate the world by pussy power and gentle cajolery are fools. It is time for the demolition to begin.' It's a revolutionary position from first to last, and a lot of people, many of them ladies, are going to be interested in taking the sting out of it, principally by institutionalizing the authoress. A six-foot knock-out freak don with three degrees and half a dozen languages who can sing, dance, act, write and turn men to stone with an epigram – what a target for the full media treatment!

Meanwhile the book's content demands summary and analysis, neither of which is easy to give. *The Female Eunuch* begins with a lushly overwritten dedication to various female companions in the struggle and ends with twenty pages of dauntingly erudite notes. In between are four main sections of argument and one minor section: 'Body', 'Soul', 'Love', 'Hate' and (the minor one) 'Revolution', which last I found to be mainly rhetoric. Of the main sections, the first one, 'Body', is the most ill-considered, so it's rather a pity that it sets the terms of the book as well as the tone. She argues very well in the 'Soul' section that the supposedly ineluctable differences of emotional and intellectual make-up between the sexes are imposed by stereotype and are consequently alterable, if not eliminable and indeed reversible. There was not the slightest need to peg this argument back to the 'Body' section and there pronounce that the differences of physical shape between men and women are likewise metaphysically determined. It makes for a poor start and surely a false one. The anthropological, ethnological, biological and chromosomal evidence adduced is scarcely convincing, and the notes given for this section are relatively thin – relative, that is, to the mass of reading which has been drawn upon to substantiate the arguments of the subsequent sections. The import of this opening section really amounts to the notion that women and men are more similar than they are different, which is unarguable, like its converse: like its converse it is merely a chosen emphasis, providing a preliminary to argument. It is one thing to say that 'the "normal" sex roles that we learn to play from our infancy are no more natural than the antics of a transvestite', since that deals with the psychology of the business. It is another thing to say that in order 'to approximate those shapes and attitudes which are considered normal and desirable, both sexes deform themselves, justifying the process by referring to the primary, genetic difference between the sexes.' (Shapes? The *whole* shape? Everybody?

All the time?) And it is a hell of a thing to say both those things in two succeeding sentences.

'But of 48 chromosomes only one is different: on this difference we base a complete separation of male and female, pretending as it were that all 48 are different.' Only if we are clowns. What we actually do is something far more insidious: realizing that differences based on physique are not seriously worth considering, we keep everything on a mental plane, and attribute to women intellectual virtues we do not possess, in order to palm off a mass of responsibilities we don't propose to handle. The same trick works in reverse: women flatter men in much the same way. The result, until recently, has been a workable (I don't say just) division of labour. A good deal of the woman's share (I don't say a fair share) of the labour centres on the fact that she has the babies – which is where the physical difference really does come in, or did. After Miss Greer has cleaned up the question of subsidiary physical differences (it appears that women wouldn't have so much subcutaneous fat if they didn't leave so much skin exposed on things like, for example, legs) and gets on to the social forms and structures which are governed by this one remaining, glaring physical difference, the book picks up. Because she instantly realizes that if women are to be free, the reproduction of the race is the rap they have to beat.

All the ensuing major sections of *The Female Eunuch* really amount to a brilliant attack on marriage and the psychological preparation for it, and on the nuclear family which is the result of it. This attack traces all the correct connections, from Barbara Cartland's powdered cleavage to the aspirin industry that thrives on frustration, from the doomed cosmetic ritual to the furtive adultery, and from the mother who sacrifices everything to the son who is grateful for nothing. The case has seldom been so well argued. One misses the wit that Dr Greer wields in conversation, but the headlong rush of mordant disenchantment is all there. The book would be worth the price merely to read her anatomizing of the advice columns in the women's magazines – an effort comparable in approach (and, one hopes, in effect) to Gabriella Parca's masterly *Le Italiane si confessano*.

Passages of sympathetic fury like this constitute the book's solid worth: there are enough of them to establish Dr Greer as an individual voice in popular social debate for some time to come. But suppose we take her condemnation of the received relationship between the sexes for granted – what alternatives does she offer? On this point, the book runs into trouble.

On a practical level – the level of *likelihoods*, of what might conceivably be brought about – Dr Greer recommends little that you will not find equally well put (and put equally passionately) in the prefaces to *Man and Superman* and *Getting Married*. If the ideas of female freedom, liberation from the 'feminine' stereotype, and the economic key to sexual equality strike the new semi-intelligentsia as revolutionary, it will only be because of the thoroughness with which touch has been lost with the old radical tradition. Here as elsewhere in the wide spectrum of the currently fashionable revolutionary spirit, it's the theoretical atavism of the practical recommendations which strikes the concerned reader as extraordinary. One gets the sense, after a while, that living philosophical insights curve away from history to re-enter it later on as psychodrama, posturings and myth. Perhaps Pareto's diagrams on this subject were correct after all, and something like this has to happen before ideas take the form of action: but it is very eerie to be an onlooker. When Dr Greer conjures up a loose-knit, 'organic' family, with several footloose fathers for the organic kids, and sets the imagined scene in Italy, we smile for two reasons. Not just because of the ill-judged setting (the courtyard would be stiff with the khaki Alfas of the *carabinieri di pronto intervento* before you could get the toys unpacked), but because the idea itself has already been and gone – the grass grew over it long ago in some abandoned Owenite phalanx, the kids grew up, moved out and went square.

But just because ideas like this have been and gone, it doesn't mean that the wished-for condition couldn't come again, and this time to stay. The question is: for how many? So far, only for a few. And for how long? Up to now, usually not long. The problem of substituting individual initiative for received social forms can be solved, but only at the cost of an extraordinary application of energy, and usually only in conditions of privilege.

The coming generations are obviously going to get many of the privileges that the old socialists fought for, prepared the ground for, but saw distorted, half-realized, and even abandoned. This is one of the reasons why the old radical hands are intolerant of the new bloods: the new bloods lack the intellectual preparation, the realization of continuous difficulty. The main message of the preface to

Getting Married was that no matter how much she needed to be free, a woman needed to marry in order to protect herself socio-economically. Shaw had no illusions about what most marriages were. But equally he had no illusions about the currently feasible alternatives. The main message of *The Female Eunuch* is that the nuclear family is a menace, that the feminine role is a poisonous sham and that the farce ought to be wound up. If this position now looks tenable, it's not because Dr Greer has a capacity for analysis superior to Shaw's, but because the socio-economics of the matter have changed. The opportunities for making a claim to individuality have vastly increased. But one can recognize this fact without being seduced by it – without forgetting that the benefits of living a liberated life are probably not to be measured on the scale of happiness. To do Dr Greer credit in this regard, it is not an easier life she is asking for, but a more difficult, more honourable one.

She does not gloss over the fact that the alternatives will take a lot of guts. In my view, though, she seriously overrates the reserves of creative initiative that people have to draw upon. There is a sound assessment of their personal likelihoods behind the instinct of most people to settle for a quiet, unadventurous life. It's unusual for even highly gifted people to be original, to express a 'unique' self, in more than just a few areas. Dr Greer argues that the female state of mind is enforced by the stereotype. She doesn't consider that the stereotype might have grown out of the state of mind – doesn't consider, that is, that the state of mind might be logically prior, historically evolved out of a steadily reinforced realization that most women, like most men, are not heroic.

Like most of the recent revolutionary ideologists, Dr Greer glibly assumes that it is desirable for everybody to be not only fully aware of their condition, but fully politicized. This is to overrate the amount of originality a civilization can sustain, while simultaneously underrating the mass of people in it, whose ordinary affairs should rightly be regarded as consumingly complex and self-justifying, rather than as a poor substitute for the life of adventure which the genuine originals supposedly enjoy. Dr Greer brilliantly uncovers the hoaxes governing ordinary feminine subservience, but always with the air that the millennium will arrive once these poor dumb ladies realize they are being conned. What just might happen, though, if the polemic message of her book gets through to a wide range of women, is something better: a further measure of equality. Getting a square shake is not as exciting to look at as blazing your way to immortality, but it counts.

The Female Eunuch states the case for altering all the conditions that leave women less free than men. In doing this, it creates several kinds of confusion about the amount and nature of the freedom conceivably available to either. But perhaps the case needs to be wrongly stated in order to take effect, to convince the next lot of guileless women seemingly predestined for a life of frustration and cheap dreams that there's no need to go through with it – you can just walk away from it, and hang loose. Getting married later, rather than sooner, would be a good start.

Observer, 1970

Postscript (i)

Considering the provocation, which included the unsettling spectacle of a contemporary becoming world famous overnight, this piece could have been worse. I still think it encapsulates the only possible balanced view both of what Germaine Greer was pronouncing to be necessary and of what she could reasonably hope to play a part in bringing about – two things that needed to be seen in strict relationship to each other. The reference to the Italian feminist Gabriella Parca was no mere window-dressing: in Italy, women's rights were a serious and sometimes deadly matter to those wives who could not hope to divorce even the most violent husbands. I would still write the last sentence the same way but nowadays would be careful to add that nature doesn't agree, and that feminism's reluctance to admit its absolute dependence on advanced technology was, and remains, its single greatest weakness. There is no natural order worth going back to. A just society is well worth working for, but any suggestion that it won't be a version of the modern industrial society we already have can only be moonshine.

The Metropolitan Critic, 1994

Postscript (ii)

In June 1946, the distinguished Argentinian woman of letters Victoria Ocampo visited the Nuremberg tribunal and took meticulous notes of what she saw in the auditorium. What she didn't see was any women. The absence of women among the accused Nazi hierarchs, she concluded, was all the more reason why there should have been some among the judges. It is a measure of the symbolic status deservedly attained by Germaine Greer that you can't read such a pregnant statement without thinking of her. Outside Latin America, few among even the most literate people have heard of Victoria Ocampo. In the whole world, few among even the least literate have not heard of Germaine Greer. At this distance it is hard to imagine what she must have been like before she was famous. I was there before it happened, and can only say that it was no surprise when it did. Her powers of expression were always bound to require the biggest stage on offer. In full flight of conversation she commanded a spontaneity of outrageous image that left any listening male writer ready to give up his pen – the Freudian implications are fully appropriate – so it was a foregone conclusion that if she ever wrote the same way she spoke she would stun the world. That was the key to her: her fearless, vaulting fluency was the embodiment of the energetic originality that she generously believed was ready to break out in all women, if only they could storm the walls society had put up to keep it in. Other women's liberationists merely had views, which they expressed more or less well. Germaine Greer expressed a capacity for life. As a consequence, time spent on analysing her equally startling capacity to contradict herself was time wasted. Another false trail was to look for the source of her inspiration in the rock culture of the Sixties. It might seem fustian to say so now, but the truth about the rock culture was that it was male chauvinist to the core: if anything, she reacted against it, a Janis Joplin without the heroin habit and with every talent except for being a victim.

Australia's very own Queen Christina had precursors among males who despised bourgeois conformity from the haughty viewpoint of the aristocratic aesthete. There was a whole tradition of them: men like de Tocqueville and Ortega were merely the most illustrious. But the man who counted was Byron, with whom she had a love affair that defied death. When you consider the position, ambition and achievement of gifted women in the Romantic era, you are getting close. The emergent Germaine Greer was neither of her time nor ahead of it: she was a hundred and fifty years too late. She was, and is, a Romantic visionary whose dream of universal female liberation can never come true, because the dream of universal male liberation can never come true either. For most people, conformity is a blessing, conferred by a society which has been centuries in the making, and to which the alternative is a slaughterhouse. Most people are not artists, and to imagine that they might be is the only consistent failure of her remarkable imagination.

2001

LITTLE MALCOLM AND HIS STRUGGLE AGAINST THE MASSES

Malcolm Muggeridge: A Life by Ian Hunter, Collins

Even those of us who don't know Malcolm Muggeridge personally can be certain that the charm to which his friends attest would quickly enslave us too, should we be exposed to it. One would probably soon give up quarrelling with him. But his public persona invites quarrel and not much else. He is not really very illuminating even when he is right. As a writer and television performer he has always had the virtue of embodying the questioning spirit, but he has been even more valuable as an example of what happens to the questioning spirit when it is too easily satisfied with its own answers. Self-regard makes him untrustworthy even in the pursuit of truth. Life has been brighter for his having been around, but for a long time his explanations have not done much more than add to the general confusion. From one who makes so much noise about being hard to fool it is hard to take being fooled further. There he is waiting for you up the garden path, all set to lead you on instead of back.

Ian Hunter, billed as Professor of Law at Western University in London, Canada, was born in 1945, which makes him about half the age of his hero. Blemishes can thus partly be put down to exuberance. Professor Hunter still has time to learn that when you discomfit somebody you do rather more than make him uncomfortable. On page 109 a passage of French has gone wrong and on page 138 'exultation' should be 'exaltation', although it is hard to be sure. Referring to 'the historian David Irving' is like referring to the metallurgist Uri Geller. There were, I think, few ball-point pens in 1940. On page 160 the idea that the USA passed straight from barbarism to decadence is praised as if it had been conceived by Muggeridge, instead of Oscar Wilde. When Professor Hunter finds time to read other philosophers he might discover that such an example of an epigram being borrowed, and muffed in the borrowing, is characteristic of Muggeridge's essentially second-hand intelligence. But on the whole Professor Hunter does not fail to be readable.

What he fails to be is critical. Instead he has allowed himself to be infected by Muggeridge's later manner, so that for much of the time we have to put up with an old fogey's opinions being endorsed by a young fogey. This callow enthusiasm sometimes has the advantage of revealing the fatuity underlying the master's show of rigour, but the reader must work hard to stay patient. When Muggeridge goes on about the futility of liberalism or the gullibility of the masses, you can just about see why he should think such things, but when Professor Hunter does the same, you know it is only because he has been influenced by Muggeridge. Professor Hunter is a born disciple.

Not that Muggeridge, on the face of it anyway, was a born prophet. He made a quiet start, enjoying a sheltered upbringing among Fabians. Early insecurity might have been a better training for life, whose disappointments can easily seem to outweigh its attractions unless one learns in childhood that the dice are rolling all the time. As a young adult, Muggeridge lost one of his brothers in bitterly casual circumstances. Later on he lost a son in a similarly capricious way. These events perhaps changed a tendency to bless fate for being kind into an opposite tendency to curse it for being cruel, but you can never tell. For all I know, solipsism is genetically determined. What is certain is that Professor Hunter drastically underestimates Muggeridge's capacity for being fascinated with his own personality and its requirements. Our infatuated author honestly thinks he is dealing with a case of self-denial.

But Muggeridge is a clear case of self-indulgence. On his own evidence, he indulged himself in fleshly pleasures while he still could. At the same time, he indulged himself in heated warnings against the frivolity of all earthly passion. These warnings waxed more strident as he became less capable. Finally he was warning the whole world. Professor Hunter has not been at sufficient pains to distinguish this behaviour from ordinary hypocrisy. If he had been, he might have helped Muggeridge to sound less like a Pharisee and more like what he is – a victim of rampant conceit, whose search for humility is doomed to remain as fruitless as Lord Longford's. Like his friends and mentors Hugh Kingsmill and Hesketh Pearson, Muggeridge mocked the world's follies but never learned to be sufficiently humbled by the turmoil within himself. He could detect it, but he blamed the world for that too. Self-indulgence and severity towards others are the same vice. The epigram is La Bruyère's. It could just conceivably have been Kingsmill's. It could never have been Muggeridge's.

Later on, in his memoirs, Muggeridge pretended that Cambridge had been a waste of time. At the time, as Professor Hunter reveals, he thought being up at Selwyn frightfully jolly. All memoirists simplify the past to some extent but Muggeridge tarts it up at the same time. He turns changes of heart into revelations, probably because he has always seen himself as being on the road to Damascus, if not Calvary. It became clear to him that the socialists at whose feet he had once sat had got everything wrong. The world could never be as they wished it, since suffering was inevitable. Professor Hunter gaily sings a descant to these opinions, as if Muggeridge had actually provided a serious commentary on intellectual history, instead of just a cartoon. Celebrating the young Muggeridge's failure to carry out his planned study of economics, Professor Hunter sums up a century of economic debate. 'Fortunately, like so many of his schemes at this time, nothing came of it, and the dismal science was left to Keynes and his contemporaries to wreak their particular brand of havoc through recessions, deficits and inflated, worthless currency on an unsuspecting world.' Students of law at Western University in London, Canada, will be familiar with Professor Hunter's wide sweep, but for those of us in the provinces it is all a bit daunting.

Working for the *Manchester Guardian* in the early 1930s Muggeridge learned to distrust, not just socialism in particular, but liberal thought in general. No doubt there were good reasons at the time to be contemptuous of a newspaper whose leader columns were always assuring 'moderate men of all shades of opinion' that 'wiser counsels' would 'prevail'. But it was typical of Muggeridge, and went on being typical, to extend his loathing from the cliché to the idea behind it. Professor Hunter enthusiastically backs him up, without pausing to consider the likelihood that without an appropriate supply of moderate men and wiser counsels there would be no stage for Muggeridge to strut his stuff on.

But Muggeridge, before passing on once and for all to the higher realms of spiritual insight, made at least one contribution to moderation and wisdom. He was right about the Soviet Union. Professor Hunter takes it for granted that nobody else was, but once again this can be put down to the demands that the study of law must make on his time. In his memoirs Muggeridge makes himself out to have been, before his visit, completely sold on the Soviet Union's picture of itself. Professor Hunter shows that Muggeridge was in fact less gullible than that, but typically neglects to raise any questions about Muggeridge's habit of reorganizing his past into an apocalyptic drama. Muggeridge saw forced collectivization at first hand, wrote accurate reports of it, and aroused, in the brief time he could get them published, the hatred of fellow-travelling propagandists. Muggeridge fought the good fight and deserves admiration. But he was not alone in it, and would not have been alone even if he had been the only writer to raise his voice on that side of the argument. The liberal reaction against Marxism had already become so deep-seated that the Left intelligentsia was unable to take the centre with it. Muggeridge disdains and disclaims the title of intellectual, but he shares the intellectual's tendency to overestimate the importance of formal intellect in politics. At the time, Muggeridge performed a valuable service in helping to reveal how the majority of the Left intelligentsia worshipped power in one form or another. But in the long run he undid his share of the good work by expanding his contempt for the Soviet Union into an indiscriminate attack on any form of social betterment whatever. The Soviet Union, according to the early Muggeridge, had claimed to be paradise but had turned out to be Hell. Yet the Welfare State, according to the later Muggeridge, was a kind of Hell too. Do-gooding attempts to make the masses happier were misguided at best and at worst were the machinations of those driven crazy by the will to power. In a way, the Welfare State and the New Deal were even worse than the Soviet Union and Nazi Germany, which at least disciplined their citizens. Eleanor Roosevelt was a bigger threat than Hitler. Suffering was man's fate. To pretend otherwise was to defy the natural order. Eventually Muggeridge roped God in, so that the natural order could be backed up by a heavenly dispensation.

There are good arguments to be made against welfare ideology but Muggeridge has always gone out of his way to make bad ones. He succeeded in convincing himself, for example, that if the masses are mollycoddled they become bored. He has always been able to read the collective mind of entire populations. Stalin's example was not enough to teach him that there is no such thing as the masses. Nor was Hitler's. Operating as a spy in Africa, Muggeridge was apparently responsible for the sinking of a German submarine. He was decorated for his achievements but subsequently played them down, preferring to find his clandestine activities farcical. Such reticence would have been admirable on its own but less so was his growing habit of prating about the decline of civilization, as if the war, instead of saving it, had merely helped seal its doom. For most people of any sense, the combined effect of the Soviet Union and Nazi Germany had been to convince them of the absolute value of free institutions. But for Muggeridge it was somehow impossible to reach this conclusion.

One reason was that Muggeridge finds it either unpalatable or impolitic, or both, to express any opinion that the majority of reasonable people happen to hold. But another reason is more interesting. Muggeridge just doesn't believe that anyone in an official position, even if he has been elected to it, can be acting from any other motive except the will to power. Hence the idea of a free institution has small meaning for him, since it must inevitably express itself in the form of what he sees as manipulation, with the masses at the receiving end. Adherence to this view has always given him ample latitude to play the gadfly, but its flexibility does not make it true. It is, in fact, a lazy man's charter. Muggeridge's critique of modern society is too ill-founded to be very informative. He assumes that things have gone wrong because powerful men have willed it so. There is no suggestion that some things go wrong of their own accord, and often as a direct consequence of other things going right. Muggeridge thinks he is being sophisticated when he rejects the vulgar idea of progress, but really his idea that there is no such thing as progress is equally vulgar. Muggeridge was subject to a hail of abuse when the tabloid press misrepresented him as having attacked the Monarchy. There was a time when the same circumstances would have earned him a slit nose and cropped ears. It might not be much of an advance, but it is an advance, and one brought about by those men of all shades of moderate opinion whose labours Muggeridge finds it convenient to forget. Helping him to forget is his comprehensive lack of a historical view. He has small idea of how civilization got the way it is, beyond a vague notion that it somehow all depends on Christianity, and must necessarily collapse now that Christianity is no longer generally believed in.

Unable to believe in either the incarnation or the resurrection, Muggeridge can only loosely be described as a Christian himself, yet except in a cantankerously paradoxical mood he would probably be ready to admit that he is fairly civilized. The question of how he got that way would have given him pause long ago if he had ever been any good at self-examination, but the evidence suggests that he can contemplate his navel endlessly without drawing much enlightenment from it. He can read God's mind better than he can read his own. He knows that God regards things like contraception and legal abortion as gross interference. Muggeridge, it will be remembered, could tell which women were on the Pill by the dead look in their eyes. Those nineteenth-century women who had a baby every year until they were worn out doubtless had a dead look in their eyes too, but Muggeridge was not around to see it. Nor has he ever been able to grasp that the alternative to legal abortion is not Christian chastity or even the edifying responsibility of bringing up an illegitimate child. The alternative to legal abortion is illegal abortion. Contraception and legal abortion were brought in to help eradicate manifest injustices. They might have created other injustices on their own account, which leaves us with the not unfamiliar problem of how to stem the excesses that arise from freedom, but only a fool would have expected life to grow less complicated just because fate had been made less capricious.

Dealing in the millennium, Muggeridge never feels obliged to admit that for mankind there is no natural order to go back to, and never has been. Human beings have been interfering with nature since the cave. That's how they got out of it in the first place. Most religions of any sophistication find some way of attributing humanity's meddlesome knack of creativity to a divine impulse, but Muggeridge would rather preach hellfire than allow God the right to move in such mysterious ways. While reading Professor Hunter's book I also happened to be renewing my acquaintance with Darwin's *Voyage of the Beagle*, and was often struck by the superiority not just of Darwin's intellect but of his religious sense. Humbled but not frightened by nature's indifference to our fate, Darwin still marvels at the way purpose works itself out through chance – as if it were trying to discover itself. With due allowance for scale, if our wish is to contemplate reality while staying sane at the same time, then we probably do best to follow Darwin's example and look for harmony outside ourselves. If there is a divine purpose, then our attempts at understanding are perhaps part of it and might even be its most refined expression, but the universe cares little for us as a species and nothing for us as individuals. That much is entirely up to us. Some people will always find this an inspiring thought. Others it will reduce to despair. Muggeridge is plainly among the latter.

These things come down to personal psychology in the end, which means that they are the opposite of simple. One gains little by objecting to a man's mental condition if his mental condition is what gives him his worth. But Muggeridge's career would have been worth more had he not set his hopes on being vouchsafed an Answer. Muggeridge's real quarrel is not with the modern age but with his creator. For all the looseness of its formulation, his concept of the supreme being is painfully narrow. God is not allowed much dignity. When invoked, he seems to resemble a less tormented version of Muggeridge, whose torment arose in the first place from an incompatibility between his spiritual pretensions and the physical material they had been given to work with. 'Fornication,' Professor Hunter quotes Muggeridge, 'I love it so.' Muggeridge struggled heroically, if unsuccessfully, with his baser desires, but apparently without ever quite seeing the joke. There is no point in being shocked that God gave healthy male human beings ten times more lust than they can use. He did the same to healthy male fiddler crabs. He's a deity, not a dietitian.

Muggeridge's seriousness is incomplete. In God's name he is able to react against a popular fallacy, but he can never give the Devil his due. The result is that he is not even good at attacking a specific abuse. He is concerned but irresponsible. 'Shadows, oh shadows.' Thus Muggeridge on the subject of other people. America is full of people 'aimlessly drifting'. Most people look as if they are aimlessly drifting if you don't know what their aims are. Muggeridge rarely stops to find out. In his later phase he has been heard to contend that whereas the West leads nowhere, the Soviet Union might at least lead somewhere. 'The future is being shaped there, not in the lush pastures of the welfare state.' What does he think the Soviet Union has that the West hasn't, apart from a certain neatness? Perhaps he means belief. But what kind of belief? He can't even remember his own lessons. And if he means that the repressed learn the value of life, surely he underestimates how much they would like to be excused their schooling.

If you are talking to aimless drifting shadows you can say anything. Muggeridge canes television for its superficiality but he never seemed to mind being superficial when he appeared on it. 'Television,' opines Professor Hunter, 'a medium that inevitably takes first prize in the fantasy stakes.' On the contrary, the television personality who condescends to his audience soon unmasks himself. Despite his undoubted and much-missed willingness to say irritating things, Muggeridge stood revealed on television as someone who would rather make a splash with a bogus epigram than worry at the truth. Remorse struck only to the extent of making him blame the medium for his own histrionics. Similarly he never drew the appropriate conclusions from the fact that a good number of those old *Manchester Guardian* leading articles about moderate men and wiser counsels had been written by himself. 'Already I find leader writing infinitely wearisome,' he wrote in his diary, 'but it is easy money, and the great thing to do is just not worry about it.' Times were hard and Muggeridge had every excuse to do what paid the bills. It is even possible to imagine George Orwell doing the same – but not to imagine him not worrying about it, or regarding such an injunction as good advice. No real writer can think of his writing as something separated from his essential being. It shouldn't be necessary to state such an obvious truth, but when dealing with Muggeridge you find your values sliding: you have to spell things out for yourself. Like many people who have lost their innocence, he can make you feel stupid for wanting to be elementary. Yet without a firm grasp of the elementary there can be no real subtlety. When Muggeridge tries to make a resonant remark the facts don't fit it.

Muggeridge forgives himself for doing second-rate work in the press and television by calling them second-rate media. This self-exculpatory technique has been found to come in handy by those of his acolytes grouped around *Private Eye*. Already absolved from trying too hard by a public school ethos which exalts gentlemen above players, the *Private Eye* writers are glad to have it on Muggeridge's authority that if a thing is not worth doing then it is not worth doing well. Recently I found myself being praised by Richard Ingrams for my radio quiz performances, which evinced, he said, a properly contemptuous attitude for the job. I have no such attitude, but I have no doubt that Ingrams, despite his notoriously eager availability for such assignments, has. He burns to be on the air and yet he despises the whole business. The conflict would be hard to live with if Muggeridge had not already provided so conspicuous an example of how to become a household name while expressing the utmost contempt for the means by which one attains such a position.

Nevertheless Muggeridge deserves praise for having, while on television, been himself, even if that self is so shot through with falsity. At least he resisted the usual pressure to wheel out a mechanical persona. If he camped it up, he did so in his own manner. As a prose stylist he also deserves some praise, although not quite as much as the doting Professor Hunter thinks. Muggeridge has always overworked the trick of biblical pastiche. Hacks think him a good writer because he writes a refined version of what they write. Nor have his jokes been all that funny. There is some wit to be attained through knowingness but not as much as through self-knowledge. The human comedy begins in the soul but for Muggeridge it begins somewhere outside. In this he is like his mentors Kingsmill and Pearson, just as his *Private Eye* disciples are like him. 'Laughter belongs to the individual, not to the herd,' Professor Hunter explains, 'and is therefore repugnant to the herd and to those whose concern is the welfare of the herd.' But there is no such thing as the herd. There are only people, and until we have made some effort to prove the contrary it is usually wiser to assume that they are like us.

People who will say anything are often the victims of diminished self-esteem, but Muggeridge suffers from the opposite condition. He is stuck on himself. It isn't all that easy to see why. He is, after all, only a literary journalist. Even his obviously heartfelt admiration for Mother Teresa of Calcutta has its component of arrogance. Mother Teresa cares for those who suffer, which fits Muggeridge's idea of God's plan for the world. He would find it hard to express the same admiration for, say, Jonas Salk. Indeed he would probably regard immunization as part of the modernizing process which has led the herd astray. Yet when you think of what polio can do, to forestall such pain seems no lesser an act of mercy than to care for the dying. Preventive medicine is surely a development that the modern age has a right to be proud of, even in the light of some of its unintended consequences.

From the law of unintended consequences no human activity is exempt, not even holiness. Muggeridge has consistently belittled many original people who have brought lasting benefits to mankind. He has been helped in this by the fact that the benefits have brought liabilities in their turn. But benefits always bring liabilities. Christianity is a clear enough proof of that.

Original people do great things. Ordinary people do the world's work. Both kinds of people are apt to lose track of what their efforts add up to. The news they make needs to be made sense of as it happens. If the literary journalist thinks himself too grand to do that, he is unlikely to be much good for anything. The literary journalist keeps faith with himself by saying what is so and betrays himself by saying anything less, however powerful his reasons. Not many writers are prophets, and those who are foretell the future by the accuracy with which they report the present.

London Review of Books, 1981: previously included in
From the Land of Shadows, 1982

Postscript

Re-reading one's own work can be a bad habit if it interferes with the initial reading of someone else's. But there are two benefits that ought not to be ruled out. To keep in mind what you have already written is the best safeguard against writing it again. On top of that, it doesn't hurt to stay in touch with your winning streak: somewhere back there, you were writing the way you were meant to, and it had a lot to do with pulse and pace. Ever since I wrote it, the foregoing piece has remained my personal measure for length of sentence, balance of sentences within the paragraph, and progress from one paragraph to the next. If I can say it without sounding as conceited as Muggeridge, on the day I worked him over I was worth the money.

Muggeridge made my job simpler by his practice of expressing himself in a series of flat assertions that he must have known to be false. He thus invited a series of flat assertions that I knew to be true.

There was an element of luck, as when a duck waddles in front of one's gun and adopts the sitting position. But there was also a time element. Early in his career, a prose writer tries to get everything into a sentence, and each sentence grows subordinate clauses that have to be laboriously rooted out and recast as further sentences, because the thing as its stands is an unreadable mishmash. Later in his career, because he has so much more to say, the same thing happens again. All kinds of parentheses – between pairs of commas, semicolons, or, like this one, dashes – come crowding in to pack the sentence out. The trouble is that by this time he knows exactly what he's doing. Sentences the size of paragraphs form, with other sentences nesting inside them, like Chinese boxes or those hollow Russian wooden dolls the shape of Krushchev's wife. His readers can read them – the syntax all checks out – but can't say them. Speakability has been swamped by style.

The moment has come for the writer to go back to his middle period and find out how he used to do it, in that blessed interval between trying vainly to get too much in and trying successfully. He will find that in those days his writing was easier to read out, because the units of meaning were arranged one after the other rather than all in the one place. (The validity of this paradigm isn't absolute; there is such a thing as a perfectly good sentence that needs to be read forwards, backward and sideways; but it probably won't be one of his.) He will also find that his style sounded much less like a style. One of the things I had against Muggeridge was that everything he said and wrote was characteristic. If writing were just self-expression, a child could do it. Muggeridge's conceit was indeed monumental, but in that respect he was too modest. The conceit of the artist is to get something done that will last, even at the cost of leaving himself out of it.

2001

NIGHT, FOG AND FORGETFULNESS

PRIMO LEVI'S LAST WILL AND TESTAMENT

The Drowned and the Saved by Primo Levi, translated by Raymond Rosenthal, Michael Joseph

Primo Levi's last book, *The Drowned and the Saved* – published in Italy before he committed suicide – is the condensed, poised summation of all his written work, which includes novels, memoirs, poems, short stories, and critical articles. All his books deal more or less directly with the disastrous historical earthquake of which the great crimes of Nazi Germany constitute the epicentre, and on whose shifting ground we who are alive still stand. None of the books are less than substantial and some of them are masterpieces, but they could all, at a pinch, be replaced by this one, which compresses what they evoke into a prose argument of unprecedented cogency and force. If the unending tragedy of the Holocaust can ever be said to make sense, then it does so in these pages. The book has not been as well translated as one could wish – Levi's supreme mastery of prose is reduced to something merely impressive – but its status as an indispensable guidebook to the infernal cellars of the age we live in is beyond doubt from the first chapter.

That we need guidance is one of the things Levi was always insistent about. He insisted quietly, but on that point he never let up. In a tough joke on himself, he acknowledged his kinship with the Ancient Mariner – the epigraph of this book is from Coleridge's poem – but he didn't apologize for telling his ghastly tale. The mind will reject this kind of knowledge if it can. Such ignorance doesn't even have to be willed. It is a protective mechanism. Levi was in no doubt that this mechanism needs to be overridden. Not knowing about what didn't suit them was how people let the whole thing happen in the first place.

A powerful aid to not knowing was the scale of the horror, hard to imagine even if you were there. The SS taunted the doomed with the assurance that after it was all over, nobody left alive would be able to credit what had happened to the dead, so there would be nothing to mark their passing – not even a memory. Levi's argument, already a summary, is difficult to summarize further, but if a central tenet can be extracted it would have to do with exactly that – memory. Beyond the evidence, which is by now so mountainous that it can be challenged only by the insane, there is the interpretation of the evidence. To interpret it correctly, even we who are sane have to grasp what things were really like. Levi is trying to make us see something that didn't happen to us as if we remembered it. There are good reasons, I think, for believing that not even Levi could fully succeed in this task. We can't live with his memories, and in the long run it turned out that not even he could. But if he has failed he has done so only to the extent of having been unable to concoct a magic potion, and in the process he has written a classic essay.

In Auschwitz, most of Levi's fellow Italian Jews died quickly. If they spoke no German and were without special skills, nothing could save them from the gas chambers and the ovens. Like most of the deportees from all the other parts of Nazi-occupied Europe, they arrived with small idea of where they were, and died before they could find out. Levi's training as a chemist made him exploitable. The few German words he had picked up in his studies were just enough to convey this fact to the exploiters. In the special camp for useful workers – it is fully described in his first and richest book, *Survival in Auschwitz* – Levi was never far from death, but he survived to write his testimony, in the same way that Solzhenitsyn survived the Gulag, and for the same reason: privilege. If Solzhenitsyn had not been a mathematician, we would probably never have heard of him as a writer. But if Levi had not been a chemist we would certainly never have heard of him as a writer. In the Soviet labour camp, death, however plentiful, was a by-product. The Nazi extermination camp was dedicated exclusively to its manufacture. Luck wasn't enough to bring you through. You had to have an edge on all the others. The proposition sounds pitiless until Levi explains it: 'We, the survivors, are not the true witnesses.' The typical prisoner did not get out alive. Those at the heart of the story had no story.

Shame, according to Levi, is thus the ineluctable legacy of all who lived. Reduced to a bare ego, the victim was under remorseless pressure to ignore the fate of everyone except himself. If he had friends, he and his friends were against the others, at least to the extent of not sharing with them the extra piece of bread that could make the difference between life and death within the conspiratorial circle but if shared outside would not be even a gesture, because everyone would die. During a heatwave, Levi found a few extra mouthfuls of water in a rusty pipe. He shared the bounty only with a close friend. He might have told others about this elixir of life, but he did not. Luckily, his self-reproach, though patently bitter, helps rather than hinders his effort to re-create for us the stricken landscape in which feelings of complicity were inescapable.

One of Levi's several triumphs as a moralist – for once, the word can be used with unmixed approval – is that he has analysed these deep and complicated feelings of inexpungible shame without lapsing into the relativism that would make everyone guilty. If everyone was guilty, then everyone was innocent, and Levi is very certain that his persecutors were not innocent. The Nazis were as guilty as the Hell they built. The good citizens who decided not to know were less guilty but still guilty. There were many degrees of guilt among those who were not doing the suffering. Some of them were as innocent as you can be while still being party to a crime. But parties to a crime they all were. The victims of the crime had nothing at all in common with those who planned it or went along with it. The victims who survived, and who were ashamed because they did, were not responsible for their shame, because they were driven to it. Even if they did reprehensible things – in the area of behaviour that Levi calls the Grey Zone – they could reasonably contend that they would never have contemplated such conduct in normal circumstances, from which they had been displaced through no fault of their own.

Levi has no harsh words even for those most terribly contaminated of survivors, the *Sonderkommando* veterans. The few still alive decline to speak. Levi believes that the right to silence of these men, who chose to live at the price of co-operating with the killers, should be respected. He is able to imagine – able, momentarily, to make *us* imagine – that the chance of postponing one's own death was hard to turn down, even at the cost of having to attend closely upon the unspeakable deaths of countless others. Levi manages to sympathize even with the Kapos, not all of whom were sadists, and all of whom

wanted to live. Levi has no sympathy for the persecutors, but he is
ready to understand them, as long as he is not asked to exonerate
them. His patience runs out only when it comes to those who parade
their compassion without realizing that they are trampling on the
memory of the innocent dead. As a writer, Levi always keeps his
anger in check, the better to distribute its intensity, but occasionally
you sense that he is on the verge of an outburst. One such moment
is when he reproves the film director Liliana Cavani, who has offered
the opinion 'We are all victims or murderers, and we accept these
roles voluntarily.' Faced with this brand of self-indulgent vaporizing,
Levi expresses just enough contempt to give us an inkling of what
his fury would have been like if he had ever let rip. To confuse the
murderers with their victims, he says, 'is a moral disease or an
aesthetic affectation or a sinister sign of complicity; above all, it is
precious service rendered (intentionally or not) to the negators of
truth.'

Levi might have written like that all the time if he had wished.
But his sense of proportion never let him down. The offence was too
great for individual anger to be appropriate. Emerging from his
discussion of the Grey Zone of behaviour, in which the survivors,
pushed to the edge of the pit, were excusably reduced to base actions
that they would not have dreamed of in real life, he goes on to
discuss the inexcusably base actions of those engineers of cruelty who
made sure that even the millions of victims murdered immediately
on arrival would have an education in despair before they died. In a
chapter called 'Useless Violence', Levi reminds us that we should not
set too much store by the idea that the Nazi extermination programme was, within its demented limits, carried out rationally. Much
of the cruelty had no rational explanation whatsoever. No matter
how long it took the train to reach the camp, the boxcars were never
provided with so much as a bucket. It wasn't that the SS were saving
themselves trouble: since the boxcars had to be sent back in reasonable
shape to be used again, it would actually have been *less* trouble to
provide them with some sort of facility, however crude. There was
no reason not to do so except to cause agony. Old people who were
already dying in their homes were thrown onto the trains lest they
miss out on the death the Nazis had decided was due them, the death
with humiliation as a prelude.

You would expect Levi's voice to crack when he writes of such things, but instead it grows calmer. He doesn't profess to fully comprehend what went on in the minds of people who could relish doing such things to their fellow human beings. His tone of voice embodies his reticence. He is not reticent, however, about any commentator who *does* profess to fully understand, without having understood the most elementary facts of the matter. After the protracted and uncertain journey recorded in 'The Reawakening', Levi at last returned to Italy, and there was told that his survival must surely have been the work of Providence: fate had preserved him, a friend said, so that he might testify. In this book Levi characterizes that idea as 'monstrous': a big word for him – almost as big as any word he ever uses about the events themselves.

He is firm on the point, but this firmness is only a subdued echo of how he made the same point at the end of the 'October 1944' chapter of *Survival in Auschwitz*, where the prisoner Kuhn, after the terrifying process of selection for the gas chambers has once again passed him by, loudly and personally thanks God. In the earlier book Levi was scornful of Kuhn's selfishness in believing that the Providence that had ignored so many should be concerned to preserve him. ('If I was God, I would spit at Kuhn's prayer.') In this book, the same argument is put no less decisively, but more in sorrow than in anger, as if such folly were ineradicable, a part of being human. Though Levi was never a fatalist, at the end of his life he seems to have been readier to accept that human beings are frail and would prefer to misunderstand these things if given the opportunity. Wonderfully, however, he remained determined not to give them the opportunity. At the very time when he feared that the memory and its meaning might slip from the collective human intelligence and go back into the historic past that we only pretend concerns us, Levi's trust in human reason was at its most profound. Transparent even in its passion, level-headed at the rim of the abyss, the style of his last book is an act of faith.

From the translation, however, you can't always tell. Raymond Rosenthal has mainly done a workmanlike job where something more accomplished was called for, and sometimes he is not even workmanlike. *The Drowned and the Saved* ranks with Nadezhda Mandelstam's *Hope Against Hope* as a testament of the age, but Nadezhda Mandelstam's translator was Max Hayward, whose English was on a par with her Russian. One doesn't want to berate Mr Rosenthal, who has toiled hard, but one might be forgiven for wishing that his editors had noticed when he needed help. If they weren't aware that a paragraph by Levi always flows smoothly as a single rhythmic unit, they should at least have guessed that a sentence by Levi is never nonsense – and when it comes down to detail the translation all too often obscures what Levi took pains to make clear, dulls the impact of his most precisely calculated effects, and puts chaos back into the order he achieved at such cost.

There doesn't seem to have been much editorial control at all. Punctuation is arbitrary and spellings have been left unchecked. In the original Italian text, Levi left a handful of German words – part of the uniquely ugly vocabulary of Naziism – untranslated, so that they would stand out with suitable incongruity. In this Englished version they are treated the same way, but some of them are mis-spelled, which might mean either that Mr Rosenthal does not read German or that he does not read proofs, but certainly means that the editors were careless. A *Geheimnisträger* is a bearer of secrets. If *Geheimnisfräger* means anything, it would mean an asker of secrets, which is the opposite of what Levi intended. This kind of literal misprint can happen to anyone at any time and is especially likely to be introduced at the last moment while other errors are being cor-rected, but another piece of weird German seems to have originated with the translator himself. 'There is an unwritten but iron law, *Zurüchschlagen*: answering blows with blows is an intolerable trans-gression that can only occur to the mind of a "newcomer", and anyone who commits it must be made an example.' The word should be *zurückschlagen*, with a lower case 'z' because it is not a noun, and a 'k' instead of the first 'h'. Worse, and probably because the word has not been understood, the first comma and the colon have been transposed, thereby neatly reversing the sense. What Levi is saying is that it was against the law to strike back. The English text says that this law was called: to strike back. An important point has been rendered incomprehensible.

The translator's Italian is good enough to make sure that he usually doesn't, when construing from that language, get things backward, but he can get them sidewise with daunting ease, and on several occasions he puts far too much trust in his ear. To render *promiscuità* as 'promiscuity', as he does twice, is, in the context, a howler. Levi didn't mean that people forced to live in a ghetto were tormented by promiscuity. He meant that they were tormented by propinquity. The unintentional suggestion that they were worn out by indiscriminate lovemaking is, in the circumstances, a bad joke. Similarly, the Italian word *evidentemente*, when it means 'obviously', can't be translated as 'evidently', which always implies an element of doubt; that is, means virtually the opposite. 'Also in the certainly much vaster field of the victim one observes a drifting of memory, but here, evidently, fraud is not involved.' Thus a point about which Levi is morally certain is made tentative. Again, the word *comportamenti* is good plain Italian, but 'behaviours' is sociologese: the translator has left room for the reader to suspect that Levi was prone to jargon, when in fact he eschewed it rigorously, out of moral conviction.

Sometimes neglect attains the level of neologism. When Levi says that the daily life of the Third Reich was profoundly *compenetrato* by the Lager system, the word *compenetrato* is hard to translate; 'penetrated' isn't comprehensive enough, but you certainly can't render it as 'compentrated', which looks like a misprint anyway and, even if it had an 'e' between the 'n' and the 't', would still send you straight to the dictionary – and it would have to be a big one. Such a verbal grotesquerie, however, at least has the merit of being easy to spot. More insidious are transpositions of meaning which sound plausible. There are sentences that have, under a troubled surface, an even more troubled depth. 'But it is doubtless that this torment of body and spirit, mythical and Dantesque, was excogitated to prevent the formation of self-defence and active resistance nuclei: the Lager SS were obtuse brutes, not subtle demons.' Here *nuclei di autodifesa o di resistenza attiva*, which could have been translated in the same word order and sounded like good English, has been pointlessly inverted to sound like sociologese; and *escogitato* has been taken straight when it needed, for naturalness, to be turned into some simpler word, such as 'planned' or 'devised'. But you could make these repairs and still leave the deeper damage undisturbed. The word 'doubtless' should be 'doubtful'. Retroactively this becomes clear. The rest of the paragraph eventually tells you that its first sentence is nonsensical. There is the satisfaction of solving a brainteaser. It is an inappropriate pleasure; Levi was not writing *Alice's Adventures in Wonderland*. Having actually been through the looking-glass into the realm of perverted logic, he came back with an urgent commitment to lucidity. Watching his helpers frustrate him in this aim is not pleasant.

Most of these glitches are at the level of vocabulary and grammar. Another inadequacy, though it matters less for the purpose of initial comprehension, has the eventual effect of denying us knowledge of Levi's intimacy with the literary tradition to which he contributed and by which he was sustained. As his book of essays *Other People's Trades* explicitly reveals, Levi was cultivated in the literatures of several languages. But the literature of his own language had cultivated him. He was *compenetrato* with the poetry and prose of his national heritage. In this book he acknowledges quotations from Manzoni and Leopardi, but, like most Italian writers, he assumes that allusions to Dante need not be flagged. It was foolishly confident of the editors of this English edition to assume the same thing.

Levi often echoes Dante. All too frequently, the translator fails to alert us that this is happening. To leave the allusions unexplained is to weaken the central meaning, because they are always functional. A typical instance is in the passage about those Nazis who for ideological reasons had ended up among the prisoners: 'They were disliked by everyone.' The word *spiacenti*, which would not occur in everyday language, is a reference to 'Inferno' III, 63, where it describes those who have been rejected by both God and God's enemies. By the translator's simply rendering what is said, without explaining what is meant, a powerful use of literary allusion has been turned into patty-cake. Still, the sense survives, and there are worse faults in a translator than to be occasionally clueless. It is worse to be careless. Levi may have literally said that he was 'intimately satisfied by the symbolic, incomplete, tendentious, sacred representation in Nuremberg', but *sacra rappresentazione* means a medieval morality play and can't be used here in its literal form without making Levi sound mystical at the very moment when he is making a point of sounding hard-headed.

In Italy, the school editions of Levi's books are thoroughly anno-tated – in several cases, by Levi himself. It would have been better if his English-language publishers had waited for the school editions to come out and then had them translated, notes and all. Unfortunately, the world of publishing has its own momentum. One can't complain about there having been so much eagerness to get Levi's books translated, but a side-effect of the haste has been that his achievement, so coherent in his own language, looks fragmented in ours. He has had several translators, of varying competence. His carefully chosen titles have sometimes been mangled in translation – especially by his publishers in the United States, who have on the whole been less sensitive than his publishers in Britain to his delicate touch. *Se Questo È un Uomo*, called *If This Is a Man* in Britain, in the current United States edition is called *Survival in Auschwitz* – a journalistic come-on that no doubt has its merits as an attention-getter but can't be said to prepare the way for a narrative that dedicates itself to avoiding stock responses. In the UK, the title of *La Tregua* is trans-lated as *The Truce*, which is accurate, but in the United States it appears as *The Reawakening*, which is inaccurate, because the whole point of the book is that Levi's long voyage home was merely a pause between two periods of struggle – one to survive physically and the other to cope mentally. As for his important novel *La Chiave a Stella*, it can only be regretted that his publishers across the Atlantic tried so hard to help him. A *chiave a stella* is indeed a kind of wrench, but it is not a monkey wrench. 'The Monkey Wrench', however, would not have been as awkward a title as the one that the book was given, *The Monkey's Wrench*. To translate 'La Chiave a Stella' literally as 'The Star-Shaped Key' might have been too poetic for Levi – who is always too truly poetic to be enigmatic – but a momentary puzzle would have been better than a lasting blur. Levi's exactitude, after all, is not incidental to him. It's him.

Books have their fortunes. If the transmission of Levi's body of work into our language might have gone better, it could also have gone worse. Clearly, all concerned tried their best. It is impossible to imagine that anyone involved – whether translator, editor, designer, or executive – thought lightly of the task. Presumably, Levi's approval was sought and obtained for those clumsy titles: he could read English, and in the last years of his life he attended evening classes, so that he might learn to speak it more fluently. He was vitally interested in guarding the safe passage of his books to a wider world. Yet the results of the transference – in our language, at any rate – are less than wholly satisfactory. Thus we are given yet further evi-dence that the declension that Levi said he most feared – the way the truth 'slides fatally toward simplification and stereotype, a trend against which I would like here to erect a dike' – is very hard to stem.

How worried should we be about this tendency? Obviously, we should be very worried. But in what *way* should we be worried? The answer to that, I think, is not so readily forthcoming. Most of us choose our friends according to whether or not they understand these matters – or, at any rate, we decline to keep any friends who don't. We are already worried, and might even protest, if pushed to it, that we are worried enough – that if we were any more worried we would get nothing done, and civilization would collapse anyway. What we are really worried about is all those people who *aren't* worried, especially the young. We assume, along with Santayana, that those who cannot remember the past are condemned to repeat it. Anything written or filmed about the Holocaust – any essay, play, novel, film documentary, or television drama, from this brilliant book by Levi all the way down to the poor, stumbling, and execrated miniseries *Holocaust* itself – is informed by that assumption. Critical reaction to any such treatment of the Holocaust is governed by that same assumption. When it is argued that a rendition of the experience must be faithful to the experience, and that the effectiveness of the rendition will be proportionate to the fidelity, the argument is based on that same assumption. An assumption, however, is all it is. Hard-bitten on the face of it, on closer examination it looks like wishful thinking.

It is undoubtedly true that some people who cannot remember the past are condemned to repeat it. But some people who can't remember the past aren't. More disturbingly, many of those who can remember the past are condemned to repeat it anyway. Plenty of people who remembered the past were sent to die in the extermination camps. Their knowledge availed them nothing, because events were out of their control. One of the unfortunate side-effects of studying German culture up to 1933, and the even richer Austrian culture up to 1938, is the depression induced by the gradual discovery of just how cultivated the two main German-speaking countries were. It didn't help a bit. The idea that the widespread study of history among its intellectual elite will make a nation-state behave better is a pious wish. Whether in the household or in the school playground, ethics are transmitted at a far more basic level than that of learning, which must be pursued for its own sake: learning is not utilitarian, even when – especially when – we most fervently want it to be.

We should face the possibility that written learning, even in the unusually affecting form of an essay like *The Drowned and the Saved*, can be transmitted intact only between members of an intelligentsia already in possession of the salient facts. Clearly, the quality of written speculative discussion will influence the quality of artistic treatments of the subject, in whatever form they may be expressed. Here again, however, we should face the possibility that it might not necessarily be the artistic work of highest quality which influences the public. From Alain Resnais's breathtaking short film *Nuit et Brouillard*, of 1956, to the recent documentary *Shoah*, most of the screen treatments of the fate of the European Jews have been considered by those who know something about the subject to have spread at least a modicum of enlightenment, if only in the form of a useful myth. The exception was the aforementioned American miniseries *Holocaust*, which, although it won a few prizes, also received a worldwide pasting – especially from those critics who saw it in the United States, where it was punctuated by commercials. Even in Britain, where I saw it, any critic who found merit in it was likely to be told that he was insensitive to the subject. But whether those of us who had a good word to say for *Holocaust* were being as crass as it was crude is beside the point here. The point is that it was *Holocaust*, out of all these productions, that had the direct, verifiable historic effect. Just before the miniseries was screened in West Germany, a statute of limitations on Nazi crimes was about to come into effect. After the miniseries was screened, the statute was rescinded. Public opinion had been decisive. It could be said that this was a very late stage for the German people to get wise. It could even be said that if it took a melodrama like *Holocaust* to wake them up, then they were best left sleeping. But it couldn't be denied that a clumsy story had broken through barriers of unawareness that more sophisticated assaults had not penetrated.

Not just of Germany but of all other countries it was, of course, true that the wider public hadn't seen the more sophisticated efforts, so there was no comparison. But this merely proved that if the wider public is to be reached the message has to be popularized. Whether popularized necessarily means vulgarized is the obvious question, to which the answer, however reluctantly given, surely has to be yes. If the *mobile vulgus* is what you want to reach, then there is no virtue in constructing something too oblique for its members to be attracted by, or, if they are attracted, to understand. The more you insist that the event's implications are endless, and the more you pronounce yourself worried that the event's implications somehow haven't been taken in by the general run of humanity, the more you must be committed to some process of reduction. The trick is to popularize without traducing, to simplify without distorting – to vulgarize without violating. At its best, this process will be a distillation, but it is hard to see how dilution can be avoided for long. And, indeed, there are good reasons for supposing that any effort, even the best, to convey the importance of this subject is bound to render it less than it was. Arthur Miller's television film 'Playing for Time' was rightly praised. The performances of Jane Alexander and Vanessa Redgrave were on a par with Meryl Streep's in *Holocaust*, with the difference that Miss Alexander and Miss Redgrave were working with a screenplay that was content to evoke by suggestion what it could not show without cosmeticizing. Nothing was shirked except one thing. Though the story about the two brave lovers who escaped was a true one, it was not true that after recapture they died facing each other with one last look of love. The two recaptured runaways are given a private shared moment on the point of death, as if, though their fate was sealed, they could to some extent choose the manner of it. It is a brilliantly dramatic scene. But it is dramatic licence. In reality, there was no choice. In *The Drowned and the Saved* Levi tells what really happened to the two who fled. The Nazis did not allow them any last beautiful moment. Only a work of art can arrange that – and, of course, we want it to, we demand it. It is hard to see how, against this demand to give the meaningless meaning, the full facts, in all their dreadful emptiness, can prevail. We will always look for consolation, and will always need to be talked out of it.

Levi tried to talk us out of it. There is no reason to believe he gave up on the task, because there is no reason to believe he thought that it could ever be fully accomplished in the first place. If we think he died of disappointment, we mistake him, and underestimate the frightfulness he was telling us about. Writing about Tamburlaine, Burckhardt said there were some episodes of history so evil that they weren't even of any use in defining the good: they were simply a dead loss. For all his tough-mindedness about erstwhile horrors, Burckhardt had no inkling that there were more to come. When they came, they were worse. For Burckhardt, the slaughterhouse happened in history: he was able to look back on it with a steady gaze. For

Levi, it was life itself. The shock was never over, the suffering was never alleviated. The reason for his suicide, so bewildering at the time, is now, in retrospect, not so hard to guess. In the first chapter of this book he quotes his friend Jean Améry, who was tortured by the Gestapo and committed suicide more than thirty years later: 'Anyone who has been tortured remains tortured.' Levi's admirable sanity might have been produced in part by his dreadful memories, but it was maintained in spite of them. A fit of depression induced by some minor surgery was enough to open the way out which only a continuous act of will had enabled him to keep closed. His style to the end – and, on the evidence of this last book, even more at the end than at the beginning – had the mighty imperturbability of Tacitus, who wrote the truth as though it were worth telling even if there was nobody to listen and no prospect of liberty's being restored. But if Schopenhauer was right to call style the physiognomy of the soul, nevertheless the soul's face has a body, and in Levi's case the body had been injured. Once again, the urge for consolation can lead us astray. We would like to think that in time any pain can be absorbed, rationalized, given a place. But gratuitous violence is not like childbirth; it serves no purpose, and refuses to be forgotten.

Levi's admirers can be excused if they find it more comforting to be appalled by his demise than to admit how they had been lulled by the example of his sweet reason – lulled into believing that what he had been through helped to make him a great writer, and that the catastrophe therefore had that much to be said for it, if no more. But part of his greatness as a writer was to warn us against drawing up a phony balance sheet. The idea that it takes extreme experience to produce great literature should never be left unexamined. The great literature that arises from extreme experience covers a very narrow band, and does so at the cost of bleaching out almost the whole of life – the everyday world that enjoys, in Nadezhda Mandelstam's great phrase, 'the privilege of ordinary heartbreaks'. Catastrophes like the Holocaust – and if it is argued that there have been no catastrophes quite like the Holocaust it can't usefully be argued that there won't be – have no redeeming features. Any good that comes out of them belongs not to them but to the world they try to wreck. Our only legitimate consolation is that, although they loom large in the long perspectives of history, history would have no long perspectives if human beings were not, in the aggregate, more creative than destructive. But the mass slaughter of the innocent is not a civics lesson. It involves us all, except that some of us were lucky enough not to be there. The best reason for trying to lead a fruitful life is that we are living on borrowed time, and the best reason to admire Primo Levi's magnificent last book is that he makes this so clear.

New Yorker, 23 May, 1988: previously included in
The Dreaming Swimmer, 1992

Postscript

Why did Primo Levi kill himself? Answers abound, but the best of them still seems to me to be the counter-question I incorporated into my review: why didn't he do so earlier? Knowing what he knew, he must have found life hard to bear. Survivalism, an early form of Holocaust denial, was already in the air while he was undertaking his last great works. His reaction to Liliana Cavani's reckless bromides on the subject could have equally arisen from a hundred other stimuli. The suggestion that he was tipped over the edge by an uncomprehending book review is better than plausible, although it can't rule out the possibility that his weakened physical condition was enough to do the trick. (I was wrong, incidentally, to say that the surgery was 'minor': it was massive, and the after-effects would have been more than enough to induce terminal depression in a man who had seen nothing worse than Disneyland on a wet day.) Finally the argument about his demise is worse than useless, because it displaces the attention that should be focussed on what he achieved when he was alive: a written temple to the necessity of recollection.

As to that, I don't see why the discussion should ever stop. New forms of Holocaust denial crop up all the time. Trying to prove that Hitler never gave the order is one of them. Trying to postpone retroactively the starting date of the *Endlösung* is another. The latest, at the time of writing, is the idea that we have all heard too much on the subject. A quick answer would be that they obviously haven't heard too much in Austria. A slower answer would take in the possibility that the Nazi assault on human values was a disease of such virulence that all its antibodies are dangerous too: we will never feel well again. The best we can hope to feel is a bit more intelligent. By that measure, a sign of intelligence would be to give up looking for consolation in an area where it is not be had: whatever illuminates Virgil's *lugetes campos*, the weeping fields, it can never be the light of the sun. It was good news that in the last days of the millennium a book by a Jew, Marcel Reich-Ranicki, was at the top of the best-seller list in Germany, and that its central subject was what happened in the Warsaw ghetto. To the hungry eye, it looked like a closing of the ring, a squaring of accounts, a reassurance that the matter was in hand. But at the same moment the David Irving libel trial was getting under way in London, and the news from there could not have been worse, because whatever the outcome the innocent dead would be defiled all over again, as arguments were heard that millions of them had never died at all, and had therefore never even lived.

I was wrong about Burckhardt: he *did* guess that something awful was on the way. He just didn't realize how big it would be. Nobody did: not even the perpetrators. Just because they only gradually woke up the dizzy magnitude of what they could get away with, we should not fool ourselves that they were slow to have the intention. As Victor Klemperer's monumental diaries (*I Shall Bear Witness* and *To the Bitter End*) sadly prove, the Holocaust was under way from the moment the Nazis came to Power. The only reason we failed to spot it is that the first victims died by their own hand.

2001

HITLER'S UNWITTING EXCULPATOR

Hitler's Willing Executioners by Daniel Jonah Goldhagen, Alfred A. Knopf

There was a hair-raising catchphrase going around in Germany just before the Nazis came to power. *Besser ein Ende mit Schrecken als ein Schrecken ohne Ende.* Better an end with terror than terror without end. Along with Nazi sympathizers who had been backing Hitler's chances for years, ordinary citizens with no taste for ideological politics had reached the point of insecurity where they were ready to let the Nazis in. The Nazis had caused such havoc in the streets that it was thought that only they could put a stop to it. They did, but the order they restored was theirs. When it was over, after twelve short years of the promised thousand, the memory lingered, a long nightmare about what once was real. It lingers still, causing night sweats. A cool head is hard to keep. Proof of that is Daniel Jonah Goldhagen's new book *Hitler's Willing Executioners*, provocatively subtitled 'Ordinary Germans and the Holocaust'. Hailed in the publisher's preliminary hype by no less an authority than the redoubtable Simon Schama as 'the fruit of phenomenal scholarship and absolute integrity', it is a book to be welcomed, but hard to welcome warmly. It advances knowledge while subtracting from wisdom, and whether the one step forward is worth the two steps back is a nice question. Does pinning the Holocaust on what amounts to a German 'national character' make sense? I don't think it does, and in the light of the disturbingly favourable press endorsement that Goldhagen has already been getting, it becomes a matter of some urgency to say why.

The phenomenal scholarship can be safely conceded: Schama and comparable authorities are unlikely to be wrong about that. Tunnelling long and deep into hitherto only loosely disturbed archives,

Goldhagen has surfaced with persuasive evidence that the Holocaust, far from being, as we have been encouraged to think, characteristically the work of cold-blooded technocrats dispassionately organizing mass disappearance on an industrial basis, was on the contrary the enthusiastically pursued contact sport of otherwise ordinary citizens, drawn from all walks of life, who were united in the unflagging enjoyment with which they inflicted every possible form of suffering on their powerless victims. In a constellation of more than ten thousand camps, the typical camp was not an impersonally efficient death factory: it was a torture garden, with its administrative personnel delightedly indulging themselves in a holiday packaged by Hieronymous Bosch. Our post-Hannah Arendt imaginations are haunted by the wrong figure: for every owl-eyed, mild-mannered pen-pusher clinically shuffling the euphemistic paperwork of oblivion, there were a hundred noisily dedicated louts revelling in the bloodbath. The gas chambers, our enduring shared symbol of the catastrophe, were in fact anomalous: most of those annihilated did not die suddenly and surprised as the result of a deception, but only after protracted humiliations and torments to whose devising their persecutors devoted inexhaustible creative zeal. Far from needing to have their scruples overcome by distancing mechanisms that would alienate them from their task, the killers were happily married to the job from the first day to the last. The more grotesque the cruelty, the more they liked it. They couldn't get enough of it. Right up until the last lights went out on the Third Reich, long after the destruction made any sense at all even by their demented standards, they went on having the time of their lives through dispensing hideous deaths to the helpless.

The book concludes, in short, that there is no point making a mystery of how a few Germans were talked into it when there were so many of them who could scarcely be talked out of it. Since we have undoubtedly spent too much time wrestling with the supposedly complex metaphysics of how an industrious drone like Eichmann could be induced to despatch millions to their deaths sight unseen, and not half enough time figuring out how thousands of otherwise healthy men and women were mad keen to work extra hours hands-on just for the pleasure of hounding their fellow human beings beyond the point of despair, this conclusion, though it is nowhere

near as new and revolutionary as Goldhagen and his supporters think
it is, is undoubtedly a useful one to reach.

Unfortunately Goldhagen reaches it in a style disfigured by
rampant sociologese and with a retributive impetus that carries him
far beyond his proper objective. It would have been enough to prove
that what he calls 'eliminationist anti-Semitism' was far more widespread among the German people than it has suited their heirs, or
us, to believe. But he wants to blame the whole population, and not
just for prejudice but for their participation, actual or potential, in
mass murder. He is ready to concede that there were exceptions, but
doesn't think they count. He thinks it would be more informative,
and more just, to stop fooling ourselves by holding the Nazis responsible for the slaughter, and simply call the perpetrators 'the Germans'.
Didn't we call the soldiers who fought in Vietnam 'the Americans'?

Well, yes – but we didn't blame 'the Americans' for the atrocities
committed there, or, if we did, we knew that we were talking short-
hand, and that the reality was more complicated. No doubt many of
the soldiers involved had a ready-to-go prejudice against the Vietna-
mese, but without the ill-judged, and even criminal, initiatives of
their government it would have remained a prejudice. What needed
examining was not simply the soldiers' contempt for alien life-forms
but the government policies that had put the troops in a position
which allowed their contempt to express itself as mass murder. Much
of the examining was done by Americans at the time, sometimes
in the face of persecution by their own government, but never without
the hope of getting a hearing from the American people.
So it would make little sense, except as an *ad hoc* rhetorical device,
to say that it was the natural outcome of the American cultural
heritage to burn down peasant huts in Vietnam. Putting up Pizza
Huts would have been just as natural. And it makes no sense whatsoever to call the perpetrators of the Holocaust 'the Germans' if by that
is meant that the German victims of Nazism – including many Jews
who went on regarding themselves as Germans to the end of the line
– somehow weren't Germans at all. That's what the Nazis thought,
and to echo their hare-brained typology is to concede them their
victory. Nothing, of course, could be further from Goldhagen's intention, but his loose language has led him into it.

The Nazis didn't just allow a lethal expression of vengeful fantasy;
they rewarded it. They deprived a readily identifiable minority of

German citizens of their citizenship, declared open season on them, honoured anyone who attacked them, punished anyone who helped them, and educated a generation to believe that its long-harboured family prejudices had the status of a sacred mission. To puzzle over the extent of the cruelty that was thus unleashed is essentially naive. To marvel at it, however, is inevitable, and pity help us if we ever become blasé about the diabolical landscape whose contours not even Goldhagen's prose can obscure, for all his unintentional mastery of verbal camouflage. In a passage like the following – by no means atypical – it would be nice to think that anger had deflected him from a natural style, but all the evidence suggests that this *is* his natural style.

> Because there were other peoples who did not treat Jews as Germans did and because, as I have shown, it is clear that the actions of the German pepetrators cannot be explained by non-cognitive structural features, when investigating different (national) groups of perpetrators, it is necessary to eschew explanations that in a reductionist fashion attribute complex and highly variable actions to structural factors or allegedly universalistic social psychological processes; the task, then, is to specify what combination of cognitive and situational factors brought the perpetrators, whatever their identities were, to contribute to the Holocaust in all the ways that they did.

A sentence like that can just about be unscrambled in the context of the author's attention-losing terminology, but the context is no picnic to be caught up in for 500-plus pages, and the general effect is to make a vital dose of medicine almost impossible to swallow. This book has all the signs of having begun as a dissertation and it makes you wonder what America's brighter young historians are reading in a general way about their subject before they are issued with their miner's lamps and lowered into the archives. Clearly they aren't reading much in high school, but isn't there some spare time on campus to get acquainted with the works of, say, Lewis Namier and find out what an English sentence is supposed to do? If only jargon were Goldhagen's sole affliction, things would not be so bad, because what he must mean can quite often be arrived at by sanforizing the verbiage. A 'cognitive model of ontology' is probably your view of the world, or what you believe to be true; an 'ideational formation' is almost certainly an idea; when people 'conceptualize' we can guess he means that they think; when they 'enunciate' we can guess he means that they say; and if something 'was immanent in the structure of cognition' we can guess it was something that everybody thought.

But along with the jargon come the solecisms, and some of those leave guesswork limping. Goldhagen employs the verb 'brutalise' many times, and gets it wrong every time except once. Until recently, when the wrong meaning took over, no respectable writer employed that verb to mean anything else except to turn someone into a brute. Nobody except the semi-literate supposed that it meant to be brutal to someone. Our author does suppose that on all occasions, except when, to show that he is aware the word is being used incorrectly, he employs inverted commas on the only occasion when he uses it correctly. But a modern historian can possibly get away with inadvertently suggesting that he has never read a book written by a historian with a classical education. It is harder to get away with providing evidence that he has never read a book of history emanating from, or merely written about, the classical world. Throughout his treatise, Goldhagen copies the increasingly popular misuse of the verb 'decimate' to mean kill nearly everybody. Julius Caesar was not the only author in ancient times to make it clear that the word means kill one in ten. When Goldhagen repeatedly talks about some group of Jews being decimated, all the reader can think is: if only the death-toll had been as small as that.

Still, we know what he must mean, and no disapproval of Goldhagen's style can stave off discussion of the story he has to tell with it. In the long run he mines his own narrative for implications that are not always warranted and are sometimes tendentious, but there is no way round some of his initial propositions. From the archives he brings back three main narrative strands that will make anyone think again who ever thought that the men in the black uniforms did all the dirty work and that any culpability accruing to anyone else was through not wanting to know. The mobile police battalions who conducted so many of the mass shootings in the East were drawn from run-of-the-pavement *Ordnungspolizei* (Order Police) and many of them were not even Nazi Party members, just ordinary Joes who had been drafted into the police because they didn't meet the physical requirements for the army, let alone the SS elite formations.

So far we have tended, in the always sketchy mental pictures we make of these things, to put most of the mass shootings down to the *Einsatzgruppen*, SS outfits detailed by Himmler specifically for the task of pursuing Hitler's cherished new type of war, the war of biological extermination. Goldhagen is right to insist that this common misapprehension badly needs to be modified. (Here, as elsewhere, he could have gone further with his own case: the *Einsatzgruppen* themselves were a fairly motley crew, as Gitta Sereny, in her recent biography of Albert Speer, has incidentally pointed out while pursuing the subject of just how one of the best-informed men in Germany managed to maintain his vaunted ignorance for so long: if, indeed, he did.) The police battalions tortured and killed with an enthusiasm outstripping even the *Einsatzgruppen*, whose leaders reported many instances of nervous breakdown and alcoholism in the ranks, whereas the police seem to have thrived physically and mentally on the whole business, sometimes even bringing their wives in by train to share the sport. The few that did request to be relieved of their duties were granted a dispensation without penalty. Goldhagen draws the fair inference that all who stayed on the job were effectively volunteers. Very few among the innocent people they shot into mass graves were spared the most vile imaginable preliminary tortures. The standard scenario in a mass shooting was to assemble the victims first in the town centre, keep them there for a long time, terrorize them with beatings and arbitrarily selective individual deaths, and thus make sure the survivors were already half dead with thirst and fear before flogging them all the way to the disposal site, where they often had to dig their own pit before being shot into it. It was thought normal to kill children in front of their desperate mothers before granting the mothers the release of a bullet. The cruelty knew no limits but it didn't put new recruits off. If anything, it turned them on: granted, which the author does not grant, that they needed any turning on in the first place.

Had these operations been truly mechanical, there would have been none of this perverted creativity. If Goldhagen's limitations as a writer mercifully ensure that he can't evoke the wilful cruelty in its full vividness, he is right to emphasize it, although wrong to suppose that it has not been emphasized before. The cruelties are everywhere described in the best book yet written on the subject, Martin Gilbert's *The Holocaust*, which strangely is nowhere referred to or even mentioned in Goldhagen's effort. Raoul Hilberg's monumental *The Destruction of the European Jews* is elbowed out of the way with the assurance that though it deals well with the victims it says little about the perpetrators, but Gilbert, who says a lot about the perpetrators, doesn't get a look in even as an unacknowledged crib, as far as I can tell. (For a work of this importance, the absence of a bibliography is a truly sensational publishing development. What next: an index on request?) It is a lot to ask of a young historian who has spent a good proportion of his reading life submerged in the primary sources that he should keep up with the secondary sources too, but Gilbert's book, with its wealth of personal accounts, *is* a primary source, quite apart from doing a lot to presage Goldhagen's boldly declared intention of showing that the detached modern industrial mentality had little to do with the matter, and that most of those who died were killed in a frenzy. But Goldhagen's well backed-up insistence that a good number of the perpetrators were not Nazi ideologues but common or garden German citizens is a genuine contribution, although whether it leads to a genuine historical insight is the question that lingers.

The second main story is about the 'work' that the Jews who were not granted the mercy of a comparatively quick death were forced to do until they succumbed to its rigours. It is Goldhagen who puts the inverted commas around the word 'work' and this time he is right, because it was the wrong word. Real work produces something. 'Work' produced little except death in agony. Non-Jewish slave labourers from the occupied countries were all held in varying degrees of deprivation but at least they had some chance of survival. For the Jewish slaves, 'work' really meant murder, slow but sure. Here is further confirmation, if it were needed (he overestimates the need, because the sad fact is already well established throughout the literature of the subject), that the Nazi policy on the exploitation of Jewish labour was too irrational even to be ruthless. A ruthless policy would have employed the Jews for their talents and qualifications, concentrated their assigned tasks on the war effort, kept them healthy while they laboured, and killed them afterwards. Nazi policy was to starve, beat and torture them up to and including the point of death even in those comparatively few cases when the job they had been assigned to might have helped win the war, or anyway stave off defeat for a little longer. The Krupp armaments factories in Essen were typical in that the Jewish workers were given hell (Alfried Krupp, who might have faced the rope if he had ever admitted knowledge of the workers tortured in the basement of his own office block, lived to be measured for a new Porsche every year) but atypical in that the Jews were actually employed in doing something useful. The more usual scenario involved lifting something heavy, carrying it somewhere else, putting it down, and carrying back something just like it, with beatings all the way if you dropped it. What the something was was immaterial: a big rock would do fine. These were Sisyphean tasks, except that not even Sisyphus had to run the gauntlet. Tracing well the long-standing strain in German anti-Semitism which held that Jews were parasites and had never done any labour, Goldhagen argues persuasively that this form of punishment was meant to remind them of this supposed fact before they died: to make them die of the realization. Here is a hint of what his book might have been – he is really getting somewhere when he traces this kind of self-defeating irrationality on the Nazis' part to an ideal: perhaps their only ideal. It was a mad ideal, but its sincerity was proved by the price they paid for it. At all costs, even at the cost of their losing the war, they pursued their self-imposed 'task' of massacring people who had not only done them no harm but might well have done them some good – of wasting them.

Many of the top Nazis were opportunists. In the end, Goering would probably have forgotten all about the Jews if he could have done a deal; Himmler did try to do a deal on that very basis; and Goebbels, though he was a raving anti-Semite until the very end, was nothing like that at the beginning. During his student career he respected his Jewish professors, and seems to have taken up anti-Semitism with an eye to the main chance. He got into it the way Himmler and Goering were ready to get out of it, because even his fanatacism was a power-play. But for Hitler it was not so. According to him, Jews had never done anything useful for Germany and never could. It was a belief bound to result in his eventual military defeat, even if he had conquered all Europe and Britain with it; because in the long run he would have come up against the atomic bomb, developed in America mainly by the very scientists he had driven out of Europe. On the vital part played in German science by Jews he could never listen to reason. Max Planck protested in 1933 about what the new exclusion laws would do to the universities. In view of his

great prestige he was granted an audience with the Führer. Planck
hardly got a chance to open his mouth. Hitler regaled him with a
three-quarters-of-an-hour lecture about mathematics, which Planck
later called one of the stupidest things he had ever heard in his life.
The pure uselessness of all Jews, the expiation they owed for their
parasitism, was at the centre of Hitler's purposes until the last hour,
and the same was true of all who shared his lethal convictions.

This bleak truth is brought out sharply by the third and main
strand in Goldhagen's book, which deals with the death marches
in the closing stage of the war, when the camps in the East were
threatened with being overrun. The war was all but lost, yet the Nazis
went on diverting scarce resources into tormenting helpless civilians.
The survivors were already starving when they set out from the
Eastern camps, and as they were herded on foot towards camps in
the Third Reich their guards, who might conceivably have gained
credit after the imminent capitulation by behaving mercifully,
behaved worse than ever. They starved their charges until they could
hardly walk and then tortured them for not walking faster. This
behaviour seems beyond comprehension, and, indeed, it is – but it
does make a horrible sort of sense if we accept that for the Nazis the
war against the Jews was the one that really mattered.

Goldhagen's account of the death marches gives too much weight
to the fact that these horrors continued even after Himmler issued
instructions that the Jews should be kept alive. ('Perhaps it's time,'
he famously said to a Jewish representative in 1945, 'for us Germans
and you Jews to bury the hatchet.') Goldhagen doesn't consider that
the guards, both men and women, were facing a return to powerless-
ness and were thus unlikely to relinquish their shred of omnipotence
while they still had it. He prefers to contend that the killings went
on because the people in general were in the grip of a force more
powerful than Nazi orders: eliminationist anti-Semitism. To him,
nothing but a theory in the perpetrator's mind – in this case, the
Germans' view that the Jews were subhuman and thus beyond compassion – can explain gratuitous cruelty. But recent history has shown
that people can become addicted to torturing their fellow human
beings while feeling no sense of racial superiority to them, or even
while feeling that no particular purpose is being served by the torture.
In some of the Latin-American dictatorships, torturers who had
quickly extracted all the relevant information often went on with

the treatment, simply to see what the victim could be reduced to, especially if the victim was a woman. To construct a political theory that explains such behaviour is tempting, but finally you are faced with the possibility that the capacity to do these things has no necessary connection with politics – and the truly dreadful possibility that it might have some connection with sexual desire, in which case we had better hope that we are talking about nurture rather than nature. A genetic propensity would put us all in it: Original Sin with a vengeance.

The price for holding to the conviction about the all-pervasiveness of murderous anti-Semitism among the Germans is the obligation to account for every instance of those who showed mercy. In his discussion of *Kristallnacht*, Goldhagen quotes a Gestapo report (obviously composed by a factotum not yet fully in synch with the Führer's vision) as saying that by far the greater part of the German population 'does not understand the senseless individual acts of violence and terror'. Why shouldn't the people have understood, if their anti-Semitism was as eliminationist as Goldhagen says it was? Later, talking about one of Police Battalion 309's operations in Bialystok, he mentions a 'German army officer appalled by the licentious killing of unarmed civilians', and he dismisses a conscience-stricken Major Trapp, who, having been ordered to carry out a mass killing, was heard to exclaim, 'My God! Why must I do this?' Were these men eliminationist anti-Semites, too? We could afford to consider their cases without any danger of lapsing into the by now discredited notion that the *Wehrmacht* was not implicated. Finally, during a reflection on the Helmbrechts death march, Goldhagen mentions that some of the guards behaved with a touch of humanity. He doesn't make enough of his own observation that they were the older guards – 'Germans . . . old enough to have been bred not only on Nazi culture.'

For Goldhagen, prejudice is the sole enemy. Other scholars, such as Raul Hilberg in his *Perpetrators, Victims, Bystanders*, have tried to show how Germans overcame their inhibitions to kill Jews. Goldhagen's monolithic thesis is that there were no inhibitions in the first place. But we need to make a distinction between Germany's undeniably noxious anti-Semitic inheritance – an age-old dream of purity, prurient as all such dreams – and the way the Nazi government, using every means of bribery, propaganda, social pressure and

violent coercion in its power, turned that dream into a living nightmare. Goldhagen slides past the point, and the result is a crippling
injury to the otherwise considerable worth of his book. He could, in
fact, have gone further in establishing how early the Final Solution
got rolling. Gilbert does a better job of showing that it was, in effect,
under way after the invasion of Poland, where thousands of Jews
were murdered and the rest herded into the ghettos. Goldhagen
quotes some of Heydrich's September 21, 1939, order about forming
the ghettos but omits the most revealing clause, in which Heydrich
ordered that the ghettos be established near railheads. That can have
meant only one thing. In May of 1941, Goering sent a memo from
the Central Office of Emigration in Berlin ordering that no more
Jews be allowed to leave the occupied territories. That, too, can have
meant only one thing. Hannah Arendt was not wrong when she said
about Nazi Germany in its early stages that only a madman could
guess what would happen next. In 1936, Heinrich Mann (Thomas's
older brother) published an essay predicting the whole event, simply
on the basis of the Nuremberg laws and what had already happened
in the first concentration camps. But his was a very rare case, perhaps
made possible by artistic insight. It needed sympathy with the Devil
to take the Nazis at their word; good people rarely know that much
about evil. But well in advance of the Holocaust's official starting
date there were plenty of bad people who didn't need to be told
about mass extermination before they got the picture.

Here Goldhagen, in his unquenchable ire, provides a useful cor-
rective to those commentators who persist in extending the benefit
of the doubt to opportunists like Albert Speer. Gitta Sereny's book is
a masterpiece of wide-ranging sympathy, but she wanders too near
naivety when she worries at the non-subject of when Speer knew
about what his terrible friends had in mind and whether he had
actually read *Mein Kampf.* In 1936, a popular album about Hitler
carried an article under Speer's name which quoted *Mein Kampf*
by the chunk: of course Speer had read it, and of course he knew
about the Final Solution from the hour it got under way. The top
Nazis didn't conceal these things from one another. They did,
however, conceal these things from the German people. Why was
that? There is something to Goldhagen's contention that the people
found out anyway – that eventually everyone knew at least something.
But why, if they were so receptive to the idea, weren't the people

immediately told everything? Surely the answer is that Hitler shared the Gestapo's suspicion about the ability of the people to think 'correctly' on the subject.

He certainly had his doubts before he came to power. In the election of 1930, which won the Nazis their entrée into the political system, the Jewish issue was scarcely mentioned. And later, when the Third Reich began its expansion into other countries, in all too many cases a significant part of the local populations could be relied on to do the very thing that Goldhagen accuses the Germans of – to start translating their anti-Semitism into a roundup the moment the whistle blew. In the Baltic countries, in the Ukraine, and in Romania and Yugoslavia, the results were horrendous from the outset. A more civilized-sounding but even more sinister case was France, where the Vichy regime exceeded the SS's requirements for lists of Jewish men, and handed over lists of women and children as well – the preliminary to the mass deportations from Drancy, which proceeded with no opposition to speak of. Why weren't the Germans themselves seen by the Nazis as being thoroughly biddable from the start?

Goldhagen leaves the question untouched because he has no answer. He is so certain of the entire German population's active collaboration – or, at the very least, its approving compliance – in the Holocaust that he underplays the Nazi state's powers of coercion through violence, something that no previous authority on the subject has managed to do. He overemphasizes the idea that the German people weren't completely powerless to shape Nazi policies; he cites, for example, the widespread public condemnation of the policy that resulted in the euthanizing of physically and mentally handicapped Germans. The practice was stopped, but in that case people were protesting the treatment of their own loved ones, and the Jews were not their loved ones. There could easily have been more protests on behalf of the Jews if the penalty for protesting had not been severe and well known.

Goldhagen qualifies the bravery of the Protestant minister and Nazi opponent Martin Niemöller by pointing out – correctly, alas – that he was an anti-Semite. But he doesn't mention the case of a Swabian pastor who after *Kristallnacht* told his congregation that the Nazi assault on the Jews would bring divine punishment. The Nazis beat him to a pulp, threw him onto the roof of a shed, smashed up his vicarage, and sent him to prison. And what about the Catholic

priest Bernhard Lichtenberg, who, after the burning of the syna-
gogues, closed each of his evening services with a prayer for the Jews?
When he protested the deportations, he was put on a train himself
– to Dachau. These men were made examples of to discourage others.
They were made to pay for their crime.

Because it *was* a crime – the biggest one a non-Jewish German
could commit. In Berlin (always the city whose population Hitler
most distrusted), some non-Jewish German wives managed to secure
the release of their Jewish husbands from concentration camps, but
that scarcely proves that a mass protest would have been successful,
or even, in the long run, tolerated without reprisal. The penalties for
helping Jews got worse in direct proportion to the sanctions imposed
against them, and everyone knew what the supreme penalty was:
forms of capital punishment under the Nazis included the axe and
the guillotine. (The axe was brought back from the museum *because*
it was medieval.) Both the Protestant and the Catholic Church
knuckled under to the Nazis with a suspicious alacrity in which
rampant anti-Semitism was undoubtedly a factor, but the general
failure of rank-and-file priests and ministers to bear individual
witness has to be put down at least partly to the risks they would
have run if they had done so. (Later on, when the Germans occupied
Italy after the Badoglio government signed an armistice with the
Allies, and the extreme anti-Jewish measures that Mussolini had
stopped short of were put into effect, the roundup was a comparative
failure, partly because the priests and nuns behaved so well. But they
had not spent years with the threat of the concentration camp and
the axe hanging over them.) In Germany, everyone knew that hiding
or helping Jews was an unpardonable crime, which would be punished as severely as an attack on Hitler's life – because it *was* an
attack on Hitler's life. Why, Goldhagen asks, did the population not
rise up? The answer is obvious: because you had to be a hero to do so.

*

Eventually, of course, a small but significant segment of the German
people did rise up, because they *were* heroes. About the various
resistance groups of the pre-war years Goldhagen has little to say,
and about the participants in the attempt on Hitler's life of July 20,
1944, he concludes that they were mostly anti-Semitic and that their
rebellion against the Nazi regime was not motivated chiefly by its

treatment of the Jews. But from Joachim Fest's 1994 *Staatsstreich* (Coup d'État) we know that Axel von dem Bussche-Streithorst, who was twenty-four at the time of the plot, turned against Hitler after witnessing a mass shooting of thousands of Jews at the Dubno airfield, in the Ukraine, and that Ulrich-Wilhelm Graf Schwerin von Schwanenfeld was turned towards resistance after seeing what the *Einsatzgruppen* were up to in Poland. There are further such examples in the *Lexikon des Widerstandes 1933–1945*, an honour roll of those who rebelled, and in a 1986 collection of essays by various historians entitled *Der Widerstand Gegen den Nationalsozialismus* (The Resistance Against National Socialism). The latter volume includes a list of the twenty July plotters who, after the plot failed, told the Gestapo during their interrogation that the reason for their rebellion was the treatment of the Jews. There are several names you would expect: Julius Leber, Dietrich Bonhöffer, Adolf Reichwein, and Carl Goerdeler – men who had been scheming to get rid of Hitler even during the years of his success. But then there are names that smack of the *Almanach de Gotha*: Alexander and Berthold Graf Schenk von Stauffenberg, Hans von Dohnanyi, Heinrich Graf von Lehndorff, Helmuth James Graf von Moltke . . . There is no reason to think that these *Hochadel* sons were necessarily liberal. Some of them came from archconservative families, and no doubt a good number had grown up with anti-Semitism hanging around the house like heavy curtains. Most of them were career officers who had relished the chance to rebuild the German Army; some even nursed the hopelessly romantic idea that after Hitler was killed *Grossdeutschland* might remain intact to go on fighting beside the Western Allies against the Soviet Union. But about the sincerity of their disgust at what happened to the Jews there can be no doubt. Though it could scarcely have made things easier for them, they told the Gestapo about it, thereby testifying to the sacrificial element in an enterprise that may have failed as a plot but succeeded as a ceremony – the ceremony of innocence which the Nazis had always been so keen to drown.

The plot was already a ceremony before it was launched. The experienced Henning von Tresckow, who had been in on several attempts before, was well aware that it might fail but told his fellow conspirators that it should go ahead anyway, *coute que coute*. Claus Graf von Stauffenberg's famous last words *Es lebe das geheime Deutschland* have turned out to be not quite so romantically foolish as they sounded at the time. If there never was a secret Germany, the July plotters at least provided a sacred moment, and the Germans of today are right to cherish it. As for the aristocracy, though even the bravery of its flower could not offset the way that it helped to sabotage the Weimar Republic, at least it regained its honour, in preparation for its retirement from the political stage. Since then the aristocracy has served Germany well in all walks of life – the Gräfin Dornhoff, active proprietress of *Die Zeit*, one of the great newspapers of the world, would be an asset to any nation – but it has paid democracy the belated compliment of a decent reticence. Churchill, the instinctive opponent of Hitler and all his works, always thought that Prussia was the nerve centre of German bestiality. He was wrong about that. Hans Frank, outstanding even among Gauleiters for his epic savagery, was closer to the truth. Many of the July plotters had a background in the famously snobbish Prussian Ninth Infantry regiment, of which Frank himself was a reservist. Just before his own hanging at Nuremberg, Frank said that the Ninth's officers had never understood *Antisemitismus der spezifisches Nazi-Art* (anti-Semitism of the specific Nazi type). They had been unsound on the Jewish question.

How many of the German population were unsound on the Jewish question we can never now know. Probably there were fewer than we would like to think, but almost certainly there were more than Goldhagen allows. However many there were, there was not a lot they could do if they didn't want to get hurt. After the Nazis finally came to absolute power, the build-up to the annihilation of the Jews moved stage by stage, always with the occasional lull that allowed people to think the madness might be over. Certainly there were a lot of Jews who wanted to think that, and who can blame them? Seizing the chance to emigrate meant leaving behind everything they had. Some of them – especially the baptized and those who no longer practised their faith – never stopped thinking of themselves as Germans, believing, correctly, that the regime which criminalized them was a criminal regime. They thought Germany would get its senses back. They would scarcely have done so if they had thought that there were no non-Jewish Germans who thought the same.

From the year the Nazis took power right up until *Kristallnacht* in November 1938, the legal deprivations and persecutions looked selective, as if there might be some viable limit beyond which they would not go. After *Kristallnacht*, it became clearer that an all-inclusive, no-holds-barred pogrom was under way, but by then it was too late. It was too late for everyone, non-Jewish Germans included. But really it had always been too late, ever since the Nazis rewrote the laws so that that their full apparatus of terror could be legally directed against anyone who disagreed with them. Is it any wonder that so many of those who retained their citizenship turned their backs on the pariahs from whom it had been stripped? When one Communist shot a stormtrooper, eleven Communists were immediately decapitated in reprisal. Everyone knew things like that. Those were the first things that every German in the Nazi era ever knew – a fact worth remembering when we confidently assume that they all must have known about the last thing, the Holocaust. It can be remarkable what you don't find out when you are afraid for just yourself, let alone for your family. All you have to do is look away. And the Nazis made very sure, even when Hitler was tumultuously popular in the flush of his diplomatic and military successes, that failure to join in the exultant unanimity would not pass unnoticed. Even if you lay low, you still had to stick your right hand in the air. Max Weber defined the state as that organization holding the monopoly of legalized violence. The Nazi state overfulfilled his definition by finding new forms of violence to make legal. Probably Goldhagen realizes all that. But he doesn't say much about it, because he has a bigger, better idea that leaves the Nazis looking like last minute walk-ons in the closing scene of *Götterdammerung*: spear-carriers in Valhalla.

Here we have to turn to his account of the growth of German anti-Semitism, which means that we have to turn back to the beginning of the book. His thesis would have gone better at the end, as a speculative afterthought, but he puts it at the front because it contains the premise that for him explains everything. Since most of it is written in the brain-curdling jargon which he later partly lets drop when he gets to the Holocaust itself, this glutinous treatise would make for a slow start even if it were consistent. But the reader is continually stymied by what is left out or glossed over. An artist in the firm grip of his own brush, Goldhagen slap-happily paints a picture of anti-Semitism pervading all levels of society, without explaining how it failed to pervade the members of the political class who contrived to grant citizenship to the Jews. Beginning early in the nineteenth century, the process of emancipation moved through the German States, culminating, in 1869, with citizenship for every Jew in the North German Confederation. (The laws were carried over into the *Kaiserreich* after German unification, in 1871.) Even in the tolerant Austria-Hungary of Emperor Franz Josef, citizenship for Jews had some strings attached, whereas in Germany civil rights for Jews remained on the books until the Nazis rewrote them. Not even in the reign of Kaiser Wilhelm II, a choleric anti-Semite by the end, were people of Jewish background deprived of their rights. They undoubtedly had trouble exercising them – prejudice was indeed everywhere, in varying degrees – but that doesn't alter the fact that they were granted them.

Perhaps those nineteenth-century politicians were thorough anti-Semites, and merely stopped short of trying to put their prejudice into law. President Truman freely used the word 'nigger' among his Southern friends, but when some returning black GIs were beaten up he made the first move in the chain of legislation that eventually led (under President Johnson, who was not without prejudice, either) to voter registration by blacks in the South. There have always been people with prejudice who have nevertheless served justice, whether out of a supervening idealism, out of expediency, or out of a simple wish not to be thought provincial by more sophisticated peers. In other words, there is prejudice and there is prejudice. But Goldhagen wants all the grades of anti-Semitism, from the enthusiasm of nutty pamphleteers down to the stultifying, self-protective distaste of the *Kleinbürgertum* at their pokey dinner tables, to add up to just one thing: the eliminationist fervour that led to extermination as soon as it got its chance.

Until recent times, one of Germany's recurring troubles was that it was more integrated culturally than it was politically. A case can be made for the Jews not having been integrated at all into the political structure, although you would have to eliminate a towering figure like Walther Rathenau – which is exactly what some of the Nazi Party's forerunners did. But from the time of Goethe up until the Anschluss the Jews were, at least in part, integrated into the culture; they made a contribution whose like had not been seen in Europe since Alfonso IX founded the University of Salamanca. Though they often aroused envy and spite among non-Jewish rivals, they aroused admiration in at least equal measure. Kant said that if the Muse of Philosophy could choose an ideal language, it would choose the language of Moses Mendelssohn. Goethe said that the Jewish contribution was vital. Nietzsche ranked the Jew Heine as the most important German poet after Goethe. The novelist Theodor Fontane, who started out as an anti-Semite, gave up on the idea when he realized that the Jewish bourgeoisie was a more cultivated audience than the aristocracy, which he had tried in vain to enlighten. Even the dreadful Wagner was ambivalent on the subject: when Thomas Mann's Jewish father-in-law left Germany after the Nazis came to power, all he took with him were Wagner's letters of thanks for his having helped to build the *Festspielhaus* in Bayreuth.

Which brings us to Thomas Mann. Here one is forced to wonder if whoever gave Goldhagen high marks for his thesis ever showed it to a literary colleague. As evidence of the all-pervading nature of eliminationist anti-Semitism, Goldhagen has the audacity to rope in, without qualification or explanation, a remark by Thomas Mann. Well, there is a grain of truth in it. In 1933, when Mann had already begun his long exile, he did indeed confide to his diary that it was a pity the new regime should include him along with some of the undesirable Jewish elements it was dealing with. But against this grain of truth there is a whole silo of contrary evidence. Thomas Mann had always disliked what he saw as the rootless Jewish cosmo-politanism (shades of his beloved Wagner there) that criticized because it couldn't create, and thus gave rise to a bugbear like Alfred Kerr. Mann the Nobel Prize-winning eminence, the new Goethe, the walking cultural icon, had a bad tendency, quite normal among writers even at their most successful, to take praise as his due and anything less as sabotage. He thought, with some justification, that the annoyingly clever Kerr was on his case. But for Jews who, in his opinion, *did* create, Mann had nothing but admiration. He had it in the first years of the century, when his conservatism was still as hide-bound as the snobbery he was never to overcome: his two early encomiums for Arthur Schnitzler are models of generosity. He had scores of friendships among the Jewish cultural figures of the emi-gration and maintained them throughout the Nazi era, often at the expense of his time, effort and exchequer. For Bruno Walter, it was always open house *chez* Mann, because Mann honoured Walter as the incarnation of the Germany that mattered, just as he despised Hitler as its exterminating angel. Even to allow the possibility of our inferring that Mann might have thought otherwise is to perpetrate a truly stunning libel, and one can only hope that the excuse for it is ignorance.

Nowadays it has become fashionable to mock Mann's supposed equivocation *vis-à-vis* the Nazi regime in its first years, because of the time that passed before he publicly condemned it. At the time, his own children were angry with him for the same reason. We have to remember that his prestige, worldly goods and most appreciative reading public were all locked up in Germany; that he was deeply rooted in its complex society; and that at his age he did not fancy leading the very kind of rootless cosmopolitan life for which he had condemned men like Kerr. But his 1933–34 diaries (which one can safely recommend Goldhagen to read whole so that he will not in future run the risk of quoting a misleading fragment from a secondary source) reveal unmistakably, and over and over, that he loathed the bestiality of the new regime from its first hour. All Mann's *Tagebüche* through the Thirties and the war years – and hurry the day when the whole fascinating corpus is properly translated – show that he never wavered in his utter disgust at what the Nazis had done to his country. As for his opinion of what they were doing to the most defenceless people in it, he went public about that in his 1936 essay on anti-Semitism, in which he definitively penetrated, and devastatingly parodied, the unconscious logic of the Nazi mentality: 'I might be nothing, but at least I'm not a Jew.'

*

Historical research has by now established beyond question that the Nazi Party was principally financed not by the great capitalists of Brecht's imagination but by the *Kleinleute* – the little people. Reduced to despair by inflation and by the Depression, they assigned their hopes and their few spare pennies to the cause of the man they thought might rescue them from nothingness. He did, too – so triumphantly that they didn't suspect until the eleventh hour that he was leading them into a nothingness even more complete than the one they had come from. The Holocaust would have been unimaginable without the Nazi Party; the Nazi Party would have been unimaginable without Hitler; and Hitler's rise to power would have been unimaginable without the unique circumstances that brought the Weimar Republic to ruin. To hear Goldhagen tell it, mass murder was all set to go: a century-long buildup of eliminationist anti-Semitism simply had to express itself. But the moment when a historian says that something had to happen is the moment when he stops writing history and starts predicting the past.

After the Second World War, the British historian A. J. P. Taylor began publishing a series of books and articles which added up to the contention that Hitler's regime was the inevitable consequence of Germany's border problem, and that his depredations in the East were just a harsh version of what any German in his position would have been obliged to do anyway. Hitler's war, Taylor argued, brought Europe back to 'reality', out of its liberal illusions. Then, in 1951, the German historian Golo Mann – one of Thomas Mann's three sons – made a survey of Taylor's historical writings, and took them apart. He accused Taylor of predicting the past. The Weimar Republic, Mann pointed out, had been no liberal illusion and might have survived if extraordinary circumstances hadn't conspired to undermine it. German nationalism was not a demon that always strode armed through the land – it was in the minds of men, and could have stayed there. This confrontation between the frivolously clever Taylor and the deeply engaged Golo Mann was a portent of the intellectual conflict that blew up in Germany more than thirty years later, when the learned historian Ernst Nolte foolishly went to print with an opinion that sounded like one of Taylor's brainwaves cast in more turgid prose: he stated that Nazi Germany, by attacking Russia, had simply got into the Cold War early, and that Nazi extermination camps had been the inevitable consequence of tangling with an enemy who was up to the same sort of thing. This time there were plenty of German historians and commentators ready to oppose such views, because by now the perverse urge to marginalize the Nazis had penetrated the academic world, and had been identified as a trend that needed to be stopped. Younger historians who had looked up to Nolte hastened to distance themselves from him; the glamorous Michael Stürmer, in his virtuoso summary of modern German history *Die Grenzen der Macht* (The Limits of Power), consigned Nolte's theory to a dismissive passing reference. Stürmer also wrote a sentence about Hitler that is unfortunately likely to remain all too true: 'Even today, the history of Hitler is largely the history of how he has been underestimated.'

Why is this so? Strangely, anti-Semitism has probably played a part. We tend to think of him as an idiot because the central tenet of his ideology was idiotic – and idiotic, of course, it transparently is. Anti-Semitism is a world view through a pinhole: as scientists say about a bad theory, it is not even wrong. Nietzsche tried to tell Wagner that it was beneath contempt. Sartre was right for once when he said that through anti-Semitism any halfwit could become a member of an elite. But, as the case of Wagner proves, a man can have this poisonous bee in his bonnet and still be a creative genius. Hitler was a destructive genius, whose evil gifts not only beggar description but invite denial, because we find it more comfortable to believe that their consequences were produced by historical forces than to believe that he *was* a historical force. Or perhaps we just lack the vocabulary. Not many of us, in a secular age, are willing to concede that, in the form of Hitler, Satan visited the Earth, recruited an army of sinners, and fought and won a battle against God. We would rather talk the language of pseudoscience, which at least seems to bring such cataclysmic events to order. But all that such language can do is shift the focus of attention down to the broad mass of the German people, which is what Goldhagen has done, in a way that, at least in part, lets Hitler off the hook – and unintentionally reinforces his central belief that it was the destiny of the Jewish race to be expelled from the *Volk* as an inimical presence.

Hannah Arendt, in her long, courageous, and much misunderstood career, had her weak moments. In her popular *Eichmann in Jerusalem* (first published serially in this magazine) she undoubtedly pushed her useful notion of the detached desk worker too far. But she was resoundingly right when she refused to grant the Nazis the power of their *fait accompli*. She declined to suppose, as Hitler had supposed, that there really was some international collectivity called the Jews. Echoing the fourth count of the Nuremberg indictment, she called the Holocaust a crime against humanity.

The Jews were the overwhelming majority among Hitler's victims, but he also killed all the Gypsies and homosexuals he could find. He let two and a half million Russian POWs perish, most of them from the gradually applied technique of deprivation. The novelist Joseph Roth, drinking himself to death in Paris before the war, said that Hitler probably had the Christians in his sights, too. We can never now trace the source of Hitler's passion for revenge, but we can be reasonably certain that there would have been no satisfying it had he lived. Sooner or later, he would have got around to everybody. Hitler was the culprit who gave all the other culprits their chance. To concentrate exclusively on the prejudice called anti-Semitism – to concentrate even on *his* anti-Semitism – is another way of underestimating him.

*

At the end of this bloodstained century, which has topped by ten times Tamburlaine's wall of skulls, lime, and living men, the last thing we want to believe is that it all happened on a whim. In the Soviet Union, the liquidation of bourgeois elements began under Lenin. By the time Stalin took power, there were no bourgeois elements left. He went on finding them. He found them even within the Communist Party. They didn't exist. They never had existed. He killed them anyway. Eventually, he killed more people than Hitler, and it was all for nothing. Far from building socialism, he ensured its ruin. His onslaught had nothing to do with social analysis, about which he knew no more than he did about biology. Unless you believe in Original Sin, there is almost no meaning that can be attached to his behaviour, except to say that he was working out his personal problems.

In China, Mao Zedong went to war against the evil landlords and the imperialist spies. Neither group actually existed. The death toll of his countrymen exceeded the totals achieved by Hitler and Stalin combined. They all died for nothing. Dying innocent, they have their eternal dignity, but there are no profundities to be plumbed in their collective extinction except the adamantine fact of human evil. In Cambodia, Pol Pot encouraged the persecution, torture, and murder of everyone who wore glasses – but enough. A country, no matter how cultured, either respects the rights of all its citizens or is not civilized. The answer to the nagging conundrum of how a civilized country like Germany could produce the Holocaust is that Germany ceased to be civilized from the moment Hitler came to power. It had been before, and it has been since – a fact that might secure for Goldhagen's book, when it is published there, a considered reception, despite its contents. I look forward to reading the German critical press, especially if one of the reviewers is Marcel Reich-Ranicki. Of Jewish background (his book about his upbringing in the Warsaw ghetto is a minor masterpiece), Reich-Ranicki is one of the most brilliant critical writers in the world. I know just where I want to read his piece: in my favorite café on the Oranienburger Strasse, just along from the meticulously restored synagogue, whose golden dome is a landmark for the district. Two armed guards stand at the door, but this time in its defence – a reminder of what Germany once did not only to others but to itself, and need not have done if democracy had held together.

A shorter version first appeared in the *New Yorker*, 22 April, 1996:
also included in *Even As We Speak*, 2001

POSTSCRIPT TO GOLDHAGEN

The preceding review is reprinted in a form substantially different from the way it first appeared in the *New Yorker*. The way it looks here is much closer to the way I first wrote it. Goldhagen's book was big news at the time, so Tina Brown very properly decided that my notice should be promoted from the 'back of the book' reviews department to 'Critic at Large' status in the middle of the magazine. This unlooked-for elevation, however, proved to be a mixed blessing, because in a position of such prominence the *soi-disant* Critic at Large often finds himself not as at large as he would like. Suddenly he is held to be speaking for the magazine as much as for himself, and inevitably it is decided that his personal quirks should be suppressed, in the interests of objectivity. My animadversions on Goldhagen's prose style were held to be a potentially embarrassing irrelevance: to dispute his interpretation of factual events was going to be contentious enough, without getting into the subjective area of how he wrote his interpretation down. I didn't think that it was a subjective area; I thought the callow over-confidence of his jargon-ridden style was a clear index of how he had been simply bound to get his pretended overview of the subject out of shape from the start; but I knuckled under or we would have all been stymied.

It wasn't, after all, as if the editors wanted to change the main thrust of the piece. There is a fine line between being asked to say something differently and being required to say something different, but it is a clear one. When they do want you to say something different, of course, it's time to take the kill fee and quit. But this piece was guaranteed to give me trouble whatever the circumstances. Goldhagen's book aspires to be wide-ranging over both the political and cultural background to the Holocaust, and if you hope to show that his reach exceeds his grasp, you have to be pretty wide-ranging yourself, over a literature that it takes half a lifetime to absorb. It was probably as much a blessing as a curse that I had to write the piece against a deadline, and that I had to do much of the work on it while I was filming in Mexico City, away from my own library and any other library that held the relevant books. To a great extent I had to rely on what was in my memory. In retrospect, the restriction feels like a lucky break. Otherwise I would have ended up writing a review longer than the book, and it would have had footnotes hanging off it in festoons.

There is something to be said for being forced into ellipsis. Skimpiness, however, is inevitably part of the result. You wouldn't know, from Goldhagen's book, that the question of the Jewish contribution to German-speaking culture was far more complicated than he makes out. Unfortunately you wouldn't know from my review just how complicated it was. It was elementary work to rebut his line with a few simple examples. The editing process reduced them to even fewer, but the obvious point was made. It was also fudged. Goldhagen is clamorously wrong on that particular topic, but the evidence by which he might think himself right is stronger than I had the time, the room or – less forgivable – the inclination to make out. As my admired Marcel Reich-Ranicki explains in his *Der Doppelte Boden* (augmented edition, Fischer, 1992), some of the Jewish writers, though they enjoyed huge public acclaim, had ample motive for feeling rejected. The novelist Jakob Wasserman, for all his success as a best-seller, despaired of social acceptance. Among Jewish artists in Germany after World War I that state of mind was not rare, and in Austria it was common. Its epicentre had been registered by Arthur Schnitzler at the turn of the century, in a key passage of his great novel *Der Weg ins Freie* (The Path into the Clear), where a leading character spells out the impossibility of true assimilation with a mordant clarity not very different from the polemical Zionism of Theodor Herzl. There can be no doubt that Schnitzler was speaking from the heart.

The question abides, however, of whether he was speaking from a whole heart or only a part of it. Though insecurity was ever-present and outright abuse always a threat, the Jewish artists and thinkers, if assimilation to the German-speaking culture was what they wanted, had good reasons to think it was being achieved in those last years before 1933. Their influence, even their dominance, in the various fields of culture was widely acknowledged. On playbills, in concert programmes and on publishers' lists there were Jewish names that attracted an audience totalling millions. The career of Stefan Zweig, alone, would be enough to make Goldhagen's cultural theory look fantastic. Zweig's books were customarily translated into about thirty languages but his sales in the German-speaking countries would have been enough on their own to make him wealthy. It shouldn't need pointing out that his sales couldn't have been that big if they had been confined to an audience of Jewish background, a qualification which applied to only 300,000 people in the whole of Germany. Zweig was part of the German literary landscape, together with the liberal values he professed. Hans Scholl, the master spirit of the White Rose resistance group in Munich, had already turned against his Hitler Youth upbringing, but his trajectory towards outright subversion was accelerated after one of Zweig's books was taken away from him by a Nazi official. Scholl thought that if the Nazis were against *that*, they were against the Germany he cared about. (Goldhagen's failure to so much as mention the White Rose, incidentally, is the kind of omission that makes a mockery of his scientific vocabulary. In science, the fact that doesn't fit the theory eliminates the theory, not the other way about. Hans and Sophie Scholl were gentiles born into a household formed by liberal German culture, were well aware that Jews had helped to form that culture, and were ready to die for it rather than betray it. If Goldhagen wants to go on asking why the German population did not rise up, he might consider the manner in which those two brave young people perished. The guillotine is a big price to pay for a conviction.)

A necessary conclusion, about the large and well-informed German-speaking audience for the arts, would be that if they were all eliminationist anti-Semites, they must have been strangely ready to sideline their otherwise overmastering prejudice when it came to matters of aesthetic enjoyment. It's not a conclusion that Goldhagen feels bound to draw, because he doesn't even consider the matter. Nor does he consider that the abuse heaped on Jewish artists by the Nazi propaganda machine before the *Machtergreifung* was a measure of the success they had achieved in becoming a part of the landscape. Finally and fatally, he doesn't consider that the massive and irreversible damage done to German-speaking culture by the repression, expulsion and murder of the Jews was the full, exact and tragic measure of how they had been vital to it. Once again it is an awful thing to find oneself saying, but it has to be said: the *Reichskultur-kammer*, if it were still in business, couldn't have done a better job of treating the Jewish contributors to German culture as if they had been an irrelevance, simply begging to be swept away.

But a young historian can be forgiven for lacking the kind of cultural information that would bring such questions to the forefront. The richness of what the German-speaking Jews achieved before the Nazi era takes time to assess. Harder to understand is Goldhagen's apparent supposition that nothing much has happened in Germany *since* the Nazi era when it comes to his own field – history. You would never know, from his book, that whole teams of German historians, in the full knowledge that they are trying to make bricks from rubble, have dedicated themselves to the study of the catastrophe that distorted their intellectual inheritance. As in any other country at any time, there have been a few historians who have devoted prodigious resources to missing the point. Of the star revisionists mixed up in the *Historikerstreit*, Ernst Nolte and Andreas Hillgruber at least had the merit of being too blatant to be plausible: they pretty well blamed the Holocaust on the Soviet Union. Klaus Hildebrand and Michael Stürmer were more insidious because there was nothing wrong with their facts: after the Red Army crossed the German border, the retreating *Wehrmacht* really *was* fighting heroically for its country's heritage. Unfortunately their suggestion that post-war German patriotism might thus claim a solid base was hopelessly compromised by the consideration that part of the heritage was the Holocaust. In his various essays and open letters about the *Historikerstreit*, Jürgen Habermas (who, it is only fair to concede, admires Goldhagen's book) was marvellous on the equivocations and the delusions of the revisionists, but on the main point he didn't need to be marvellous: it was too obviously true. The revisionist historian can't reasonably hope to have a Germany that is not obsessed with the past. There can be no putting off shame to achieve maturity. The shame *is* the maturity.

Most of the German historians are well aware of this. The revisionists did not prevail, and the work entailed in rebutting them had already become part of the accumulated glory of Germany's indigenous historical studies as the terrible twentieth century neared its end. But if German culture really had been nourished at its root by eliminationist anti-Semitism, as Goldhagen argues, it is hard to see why so many of today's German historians should now be so concerned about the Holocaust. Very few of them are Jews, for sadly obvious reasons. Surely they, too, are 'the Germans', as Goldhagen would like to put it. It can only follow that their culture has other continuities apart from the one that Goldhagen picks out. Their urge to comprehend, their respect for the facts – these things could not have started up all by themselves, out of nowhere.

There are plenty of Germans, naturally enough, who would like to think that their country as they know it today *has* started up out of nowhere. For those who would like to throw off the burden of history and move on, Goldhagen's book has been a welcome gift. Purporting to bring the past home to the unsuspecting present, he has had the opposite effect. If he has not yet asked himself why his book has received such an enthusiastic reception in Germany, he might ponder why 'the Germans' should be so glad to be supplied with the argument that their parents and grandparents were all equally to blame because they inhabited a culture blameworthy in itself: we're different now. But nobody is that different now, because nobody was that different then. It will always suit the current generation of any country to blame the turpitude of their ancestors on the culture then prevailing, as if people had no choice how to act. It saves us from the anguish of asking ourselves how we might have acted had we been there, at a time when plenty of people knew there was a choice, but couldn't face the consequences of making it, and when those who did choose virtue were volunteers for torture and death.

No wonder Goldhagen is so popular. On top of leaving out the large numbers of German citizens who declined to vote for the Nazis even when there was almost no other party remaining with credible means to stop the chaos in the streets, he doesn't even mention the Germans who were so suicidally brave as to defy the Nazis after they came to power. Sacrificial witnesses to human decency, they died at the rate of about twenty-five people per day for every day that the Third Reich was in existence. They might seem to add up to a drop in the bucket, and it was terribly true that they had no real hope of having any effect, but Goldhagen is keeping questionable company when he treats a handful of powerless lives as if their deaths meant nothing in the eye of history. Some of the questionable company he is keeping is alive now. We would all find life a lot easier if we didn't have to ask ourselves how we would have measured up to the same test. Hence the temptation to suppose that nobody ever did. The challenge to one's compassion is tough enough, without compounding it by the challenge to one's conscience.

In our time and privileged surroundings there has been no such examination to pass or fail, but what makes the difference is political circumstances. The new Germany is a democracy. So was the old Germany, or it tried to be: but then the Nazis got in, and Hell broke loose. It can break loose anywhere, in any people: all peoples have hellish propensities. When Daniel Goldhagen has lived long enough to value democracy for what it prevents, he will be less ready to be astonished by what his fellow human beings are capable of when they are allowed. And the Germans really are his fellow human beings. To assert otherwise is to further the kind of argument which the Nazis, thereby achieving their sole lasting value, contrived to discredit beyond redemption.

2001

Also included in *Even As We Speak*, 2001

HOME AND AWAY

YOUR SPACE OR MINE?

The Road to Botany Bay by Paul Carter, Faber

The Oxford History of Australia. Vol. IV: 1901–1942 by Stuart Macintyre, Oxford

The Archibald Paradox: A Strange Case of Authorship by Sylvia Lawson, Penguin

The Lucky Country Revisited by Donald Horne, Dent

In its short history, Australia has weathered several storms. By world standards they were minor, but at home they loomed large. The First World War was a rude awakening; the Great Depression hit harder and lasted longer than anywhere else in the developed world; and the Second World War could have been the end of everything. Australia survived all these crises and given its usual luck should also survive the Bicentenary, although it could be touch and go.

Crocodile Dundee made Australia flavour of the month. For the Bicentenary, emulsifiers and preservatives have been added so as to make the flavour of the month last a whole year. Inevitably, the result is hard to swallow. A country is not a commodity. To treat it like one, you must submit yourself to market forces, and to the eventual discovery of just how forceful those forces can be. When publicity swamps reality, it leaves tacky deposits as it withdraws. 1989 is going to be tough. Australia, however, will still be there, perhaps even with its inborn scepticism reinforced, more worldly-wise for having just been overwhelmed.

Australian prose is at its most characteristic when ready-salted. On the whole, Australian journalists have written better history, or at any rate better-written history, than the historians, among whom Geoffrey Blainey – whose *The Tyranny of Distance* must count as the single most original historical work about Australia – is exceptional in possessing an individual style. Manning Clark, doyen of Australian historians by virtue of his five-volume *History of Australia*, in scholarship towers over all his predecessors but writes no better. Here, drawn from *A Short History of Australia*, the indispensable one-volume condensation of his *magnum opus*, is a by no means atypical sentence: 'The choir sang a Te Deum, which because of the terrible heat wafted fitfully around the arena; the flag of the new commonwealth was hoisted, and the artillery thundered and cheer after cheer ran around the great arena.'

You don't need the stylistic scrupulousness of Turgenev to see that the use of the word 'great', if it was intended to offset the repetition of the word 'arena', had the opposite effect. But it is more likely that the perpetrator simply never noticed. Let alone re-write, he doesn't even re-read. He leaves the reader to do that. Try this: 'In the mean time the Australian and New Zealand expeditionary force trained for war at their camp near Cairo, and relaxed and pursued pleasure in the cafés and low dives of Cairo . . .'

Is this, the reader hopefully asks, a rhetorical device, an obeisance towards the cool symmetry of the Gibbonian period? The reader soon gives up asking. Tolstoy didn't mind repeating a word, but knew he was doing it. Manning Clark doesn't know. But he does know his own mind. He might use the word 'bourgeois' twenty times per chapter but he knows what he means by it. He means the capitalist society which Australia has always persisted in remaining, even when presented with the opportunity to become something else. You can object to Clark's view – I do, and what's more important my mother, who elects the government, does too – but you can tell exactly what he means at all times. He means business.

What Paul Carter means in *The Road to Botany Bay* is either something more profound or else nothing at all. Unless I am a Dutchman, he means the latter, but I should say, before hacking into it, that his book comes laden with wreaths of praise, a true triumphal car of the bicentennial celebrations. 'The writing has a lyrical passion in argument that I found irresistible,' says no less a judge than David Malouf. 'I couldn't put it down.' Malouf being no fool, I am reluctant to suggest that the reason he couldn't put the book down was that it is so full of hot air it kept springing back up again. Reluctant, but compelled.

Lyrically passionate writing should always be resisted, especially by the writer. A real idea slows you down, by demanding that you make yourself as plain as possible. A big idea – the nice name for a hazy notion – speeds you up. You try to find out what you mean by examining the words in which you say it, by mixing one abstract concept into another as if two kinds of sand could make cement, by suddenly *switching to italics* as if a breakthrough into clear country had been achieved by hard sweat. Mr Carter's big idea is that most of the history written about Australia up to now has been imperial history. He has invented a better version, called spatial history. The word 'spatial' recurs in Mr Carter's prose the way 'bourgeois' does in Manning Clark's, with the difference that whereas Professor Clark's favourite word is gravid with dull significance, Mr Carter's is as brightly hollow as a Christmas bauble. Here he is, at the start of his book, announcing that Manning Clark's kind of history,

> which reduces space to a stage, that pays attention to events unfolding in time alone, might be called imperial history. The governor erects a tent here rather than there, the soldier blazes a trail in that direction rather than this: but, rather than focus on the *intentional* world of historical individuals, the world of active, spatial choices, empirical history of this kind has as its focus facts which, in a sense, come after the event. The primary object is not to understand or to interpret: it is to legitimate. This is why this history is associated with imperialism . . .

Mr Carter well knows that to call Manning Clark an imperialist historian is like saying that Bertolt Brecht had a crush on the Duchess of Windsor. But big ideas go beyond what the mind that hatches them knows: they fly into the realm where thought is pure. Mr Carter has got himself convinced that even though a historian might be a radical, the history the historian writes is imperial, because it not only sees the past in terms of what happened next, it sees a *space* in terms of how it turned into a *place*. To combat imperial history, and turn the places back into spaces, spatial history will be required. 'Such spatial history – history that discovers and explores the lacuna left by imperial history – begins and ends in language.' The reader can't say that he hasn't been warned.

Imperial history, 'the selective blandnesses of cultural discourse', has apparently been going on since the Enlightenment. If it has, then

Mr Carter is in the uncomfortable position of holding himself superior to some pretty formidable minds. He doesn't say how it came about that his own viewpoint should be so uniquely privileged, although, judging from his vocabulary, structuralism, semiotics and similar fashions must have had a good deal to do with it. The phrase 'ways of seeing' crops up, reminding us of John Berger and his allegedly penetrating double squint. The authorial assumption which remains unquestioned at the end of the book – after 350 pages in which the word 'spatial' appears rarely fewer than three times per paragraph and sometimes twice in the same sentence – is that an alternative to imperial history, namely spatial history, is not just possible but mandatory, in order to right age-old wrongs. Spatial history would, for example, have the virtue of being fair to the Aborigines.

> A spatial history of this kind would stand in a metaphorical relationship to the history the Aborigines tell themselves. It would be a comparable reflection on different historical content. And, naturally, since the medium of white history is writing, it would not simply be a book about the language of recollection. If it were to avoid the kind of passive associationism Husserl refers to, it would have to enact the language of recollection. Such a history, giving back to metaphor its ontological role and recovering its historical space, would inevitably and properly be a poetic history.

I wouldn't bet on it, unless the historian could write plain English in the first place. A few weeks ago in Sydney I had a drink with an Aboriginal actor called Ernie Dingo, who talked more poetry in five minutes than Mr Carter looks like achieving in the rest of his life, unless Husserl is forcibly withheld from him. The sad thing is that in real life Mr Carter is a literary journalist of some repute. As Robert Haupt's successor to the editorship of the *Age Monthly Review*, he inhabits a milieu, or space, in which the standards of plain speaking were set by the redoubtable Michael Davie, who really should get back there and sort out his errant protégés as soon as possible.

Good journalists should not waste time producing bad Ph.D. theses. In the academic context there is some reason for the success of pseudo-scientific guff: emptying the humanities of their true significance is a way of attaining tenure without talent. But a journalist who tries to join in is just talking his way into the madhouse. There are signs that Mr Carter might know this, deep down. It must have been some vestigial attack of sanity that led him, on page 294, to attempt a definition of the word 'bullshit'. 'Bullshit is the result of chewing the cud, the repetitive detritus of trying too hard to conjure oneself from the ground.' *Ipse dixit.*

More briefly, bullshit is empty depth. Mr Carter feels obliged to deploy his chic vocabulary not because his big idea is new but because it is a truism. Gibbon was well aware that Rome was a space before it was a place, and got the idea for writing his history when he saw the space re-emerging through the place's ruins. Those who do not think originally enough to be interesting when they write plainly will always be tempted to seek refuge in obscurantism, but a journalist, if he can do nothing else, should resist that temptation. After *The Road to Botany Bay*, Australian history might as well be left to the historians.

Stuart Macintyre, author of the fourth volume of the *Oxford History of Australia*, covers the years 1901–1942 in good plain style, with words like 'bourgeois' kept well in check and words like 'spatial' nowhere to be seen. Aiming to get at the truth, which is always more complicated than any use that can be made of it, he delivers the sort of factual account which ideologists of either wing find awkward. He mentions that the British lost three times as many soldiers killed at Gallipoli as the Australians did – a fact left out of the celebrated Australian film *Gallipoli*, in which the British appear only as cynical manipulators of Australian cannon-fodder. He mentions, on the other hand, that the Australians came out of the Dardanelles with a deep, well-founded disbelief in British military competence.

Even in his grave, Robert Gordon Menzies is regularly vilified as the Australian prime minister who would do anything for the British, including offering up his young compatriots as a blood sacrifice. Dr Macintyre is able to show that Menzies, though his bump of reverence was undoubtedly overdeveloped, was properly suspicious of Churchill and patriotically concerned that Australian troops should not be frittered away far from home. The book ends at what is seen, surely correctly, as a decisive historical moment. Succeeding Menzies as prime minister, John Curtin proclaimed the alliance with the United States to be the one that mattered militarily. At the battle of the Coral Sea the Americans stopped the Japanese from getting under

New Guinea. In the Owen Stanley ranges the Australians stopped the
Japanese from getting across it. The two events were interdependent.

The Australians can be proud of how their soldiers fought, but
without the American effort the game would have been up. British
protection was a myth that evaporated with the fall of Singapore. Dr
Macintyre faithfully repeats the hoary story about Singapore's big
guns facing the wrong way. Actually they could traverse through 360
degrees. The trouble with them was their ammunition, which was
armour-piercing for use against ships, and which therefore, when
fired against targets on the soft ground of the mainland, went off
plop among the mangroves. We had plenty of other guns, but their
ammunition was rationed, by strict order of General Percival. See, as
Dr Macintyre evidently hasn't seen, Timothy Hall's journalistic but
competent account *The Fall of Singapore, 1942.*

British military ineptitude in Malaya was almost total. Dr Macintyre is within his rights to say that the Australian general staff were
not much better, but he should have mentioned that we had some
good officers up near the fighting. Some of the greener troops
behaved badly on the Singapore docks, but on the mainland – at
Parit Sulong bridge, for example – our soldiers slowed the Japanese
down to a degree that could have been exploited if there had been
any kind of strategic grasp at command level. All of that, however,
belonged to General Yamashita, whose Imperial Guards, had they
ever got ashore in Australia, might well have turned it back from a
place into a space, as a preparation for its being transformed into
another kind of place altogether.

The last chapter of Dr Macintyre's book is disproportionate
through being only the same length as all the others. In actuality,
two years of war weighed the same as twenty years of peace, because
the war changed everything. In this way, history really *is* like space:
tumultuous events set apart from each other, and connected by
gravity. Responding to its rhythm is not easy. A metronomic beat
won't do. *Rubato* is required.

Some of the best Australian history is cultural history, not just
because better written, but because the *culturati*, eternally anxious to
place themselves in a context, try hard to evoke it. Sylvia Lawson, a
descendant of Henry Lawson, was a pioneer – *the* pioneer – Australian
woman literary journalist in the Fifties. In the editorial office of
Tom Fitzgerald's *Nation* magazine in George Street, Sydney, she would

elegantly sip the wine provided while the rest of us tried to mention a book she hadn't read. It wasn't easy, and writing as well as she did was no less of a challenge. Thirty years on, her new book *The Archibald Paradox* is disturbingly flecked throughout with words like 'text' and 'discourse', but on close examination this proves to be more of a light peppering than a full attack of the plague. Underneath, she is still a tough-minded writer, and this book springs from a real, as opposed to a big, idea.

The idea is that the famous Sydney weekly magazine the *Bulletin* was, in the twenty or so years leading up to Federation, even more interesting in the totality of its content – letters column included – than it was for its individual literary contributions. The Archibald of the title was the magazine's editor, Jules François Archibald, the embodiment of a paradox which Ms Lawson usefully defines: 'To know enough of the metropolitan world, colonials must, in limited ways at least, move and think internationally; to resist it strongly enough for the colony to cease to be colonial and become its own place, they must become nationalists.'

Archibald lived out this paradox through the pages of his magazine. Within the accepted racist limits ('Australia for the White Man', screamed the masthead at one stage, 'and China for the Chows') the *Bulletin* was a true community of voices. Every shade of white was represented. Archibald's appointee as literary editor, Alfred George Stephens, was an erudite critic who brought a full range of Europeanized refinement to the task of assessing raw native talent. The whole of the country came alive in the *Bulletin* and the whole of its history in that period comes alive in Ms Lawson's book. So solid an achievement didn't need to make the slightest gesture towards academic respectability.

When Donald Horne took over the *Bulletin* in 1961, he killed off the slogan 'Australia for the White Man'. Self-assurance was, and remains, his strong suit. Horne's writing about Australian cultural history and current affairs is a cut above journalism in a country whose journalism, at its best, has always had the virtue of being willing to get above itself. *The Lucky Country Revisited* expands on and continues the story told in his *The Lucky Country*, a book which remains essential but can only gain through being supplemented by this new volume, which includes many photographs with appropriately extended captions, along with much judicious hindsight tartly expressed.

All over again it becomes clear that Australian cultural history is the best way into Australian history, and that the best way into Australian cultural history, in modern times at any rate, is through Horne's books. His autobiographical volumes, in particular, should be high on the reading list of any foreign observer who wants to take the measure of what has been going on in Australia since World War Two. Horne's second volume of autobiography, *Confessions of a New Boy*, was on my draft list of Books of the Year for the *Observer* the year before last, but I was made to remove it because it had not been published here. Peeved at the time, I subsequently arrived at the conclusion that a good Australian book no longer needs to be legitimized by being published all over again in the UK. Horne has resolved the Archibald paradox as well as anyone can. Bringing a world view to bear on his native land, he hammers its provincialism, but always as a patriot. His kind of sceptical intelligence is exactly what the Australians fancy themselves to possess as a national characteristic, and exactly what makes them uncomfortable when they hear it propound a connected argument.

In the field of arts, letters and the *petit bonheur*, Horne is well pleased by the giant strides Australia has made away from its erstwhile diffidence and wowserism, but the vaunted energy and imagination of its entrepreneurs leave him unimpressed. In *The Lucky Country Revisited* his perennial dim view of the Australian managerial élite is brought up to date and reinforced. Horne's argument will ring a bell for those of us who have always wondered why someone who buys a brewery with money made out of lousy newspapers is called a financial genius. But Horne is not pandering to the highbrow who despises industry. Horne thinks that if the entrepreneurs are living in a dream, the intellectuals are doing too little to dispel it.

I wish Horne wasn't right about this, because Australia would be a blissful place in which to inhabit an ivory tower – you could see the beach for miles. Dreaming, however, might do for us in the end, and needs more discouragement than it is getting now. The cure is realism. Australian historians suffer from having too little history to work on. But there is plenty more coming up, and although we can't be sure what will happen, we can be sure we won't like it, unless those who take on the task of putting the past in perspective are thoughtful and disciplined enough to give us a reasonably clear account of how we got this far.

London Review of Books, 18 February, 1988: previously included in
The Dreaming Swimmer, 1992

Postscript

In France, the apparently confident onward march of post-war literary theory was readily identifiable even at the time as the tactical retreat of *gauchiste* political beliefs to an impregnable redoubt from which they could be defended for ever, whatever happened in the real world. The identifying didn't have to be done by foreigners: Jean-François Revel was merely the most articulate (and philosophically best equipped) among the local commentators who spotted what was going on right from the start. Slower to emerge was the root cause of the whole aberration. When, at long last, after more than forty years of eloquent coyness, books about what had really happened to French intellectual and creative life under the Occupation began to come out – one of the earliest remains the best, *Des écrivains et des artistes sous l'Occupation*, by Gilles Ragache and Jean-Robert Ragache, 1988 – it gradually became clear that the Nazi *Propaganda-staffel*, under the agile leadership of Otto Abetz, had worked a trick of corruption in Paris whose long-term results ran too deep for tears. Effectively, any literary figure in whatever field who had been allowed to continue publishing during the Occupation was a collaborator, right up to and including Jean-Paul Sartre himself. Sartre never said anything in support of the Nazis or the Vichy regime, but he wasn't asked to. Abetz was too smart for that: he wasn't buying approval, he was buying silence. He got it. The deportation trains left from Drancy without a hitch.

The collective bad conscience generated by this inadmissible memory gave a powerful impulse to the idea that literature might have principles of organization more interesting than its ostensible meaning. That same brainwave, nudged only a little further in the direction of absurdity, yielded the desirable bonus of removing the author from personal responsibility for anything he might have said or (even better) failed to say. From the political viewpoint, the notion of a 'text' was the self-serving product of an intellectual tradition that had been poisonously compromised, first by its passive acceptance of one totalitarian nightmare, second by its enthusiastic advocacy of another. It was an irresistibly seductive all-purpose formula: what hadn't been said about Hitler could be quietly forgotten, along with everything that *had* been said about Stalin. In France, the proliferating varieties of post-modern theoretical hocus-pocus thus added up to a get-out clause from the contract of history, which could itself – the penultimate breakthrough – be regarded as a text, a set of arbitrary interpretations imposed on reality. The ultimate breakthrough was the discovery that reality didn't even exist.

Recent political history was enough to explain why the heirs of the Enlightenment should abdicate from experience and fall prey to a galloping case of *folie raisonnante*. But for the fashionable success of literary theory on a world scale the same explanation will scarcely do. Few American-born academics had any real idea of what unlimited state power looks like close up. The younger among them thought they were seeing it in General Westmoreland's face on the cover of *Time*. For most of the Western world, totalitarianism was something you could safely accuse your government of allowing to happen elsewhere: you never had to accuse yourself of allowing it to happen here. It was generally true that the young academics who opted for literary theory and its related forms of scientism had been on the Left and were looking for a comfortable bolt-hole where they could either cherish their principles or quietly give them up, but a bad conscience was not the problem. On the contrary, many of them thought they were Noam Chomsky: an illusion on their part which depended on the mistaken idea that his structural linguistics was a form of literary theory too. But linguistics depends on scientific method, which can go wrong, as it did even for Einstein. Literary theorists are always right, like Cagliostro.

The reasons for literary theory's world-wide hit-parade status were sociological. The sociology of academia remains a largely unexplored subject which it would take a reborn Max Weber to sort out, but as a rule of thumb it can be said that in any soft option an expanding faculty, when it uses up the pool of talent, will modify the curriculum to make jobs safe for the untalented. In all its traditional forms, with the possible exception of bibliography – and even there you have to know why some books are more important than others – the study of literature requires sensitivity to literature. Literary theory requires no sensitivity to literature whatsoever. Nobody who teaches it can fail. In a country like Australia, which has a powerful egalitarian tradition, this consideration was bound to make literary theory popular, and it got a long way before a sense of the ridiculous set in. One of the nice things about Australia is that it always does, eventually: mainly because a great deal of reading gets done by ordinary citizens, who have keen antennae for the self-intoxicated flimflam of a cultural salariat.

2001

UP HERE FROM DOWN THERE

When London Calls by Stephen Alomes, Cambridge

Billed as a senior lecturer in Australian Studies at Deakin University, Stephen Alomes, with his latest book *When London Calls* – subtitled 'The Expatriation of Australian Creative Artists to Britain' – has made a timely intervention in the perennially simmering local discussion about why the Australian expatriates went away and what should be thought about them by the cognoscenti who stayed put. As its provenance and panoply suggest, this is most definitely an academic work, but the reader need not fear to be dehydrated by the post-modernist jargon that threatened, until recently, to turn humanist studies in Australia into a cemetery on the moon. Instead, the reader should fear a different kind of threat altogether.

There was a time when Australian academics could be counted on for a donnish *hauteur* when it came to treating journalistic opinions relating to their subject. Alomes goes all the other way. Without knowing much about it, he loves the world of the media. If there is ever a Chair of Cultural Journalism at Deakin University, he could fill it the way he fills his reporter's notebook. He gets out there on the interview trail himself. Most of the big names he wants to talk to, if not already dead, don't want to waste any more of their lives giving soundbite answers to the kind of questions that their work exists to answer in full, but he has the professional pest's remedy for that. He either gives them short shrift or plugs the lacunae from his clippings file, in which, it seems, any British journalist's merest mention of an Australian expatriate's activities – especially if the opinion is adverse – is preserved like holy writ, and in which anything that even the most uninspired Australian journalist makes of the British journalist's opinion is carefully appended, the whole dog-eared assemblage being regarded by its assiduous compiler as a pristine *Forschungsquelle* out of which he may construct his own opinions by an elaborate system of cross-reference. This method seems particularly Swiftian in a book which nominally devotes itself to the proposition that Australia need no longer be in thrall to how its creative efforts are perceived in the mother country. Australia is a land mass of three million square miles and geographers have long debated whether it should be called a continent or an island. The bizarre spectacle of Alomes's self-cancelling thought processes should be enough to settle the discussion. It's an island all right, and it's flying like Laputa.

No doubt seeking to legitimize his gift for inaccurate précis, Andre Malraux recommended telling the kind of lies that would become true later. In Australia it is by now widely proclaimed among the intelligentsia that the era of provincialism is over. Would that it were true, but on the evidence provided by the mere existence of a book like this it isn't yet, and later might mean never if the facts aren't faced. One of the facts is that in Australia any discussion of the arts is likely to be bedevilled with politics. Another is that the politics are likely to be infantile. As opposed to the quality of the discussion, the quality of the arts is not the problem. With a size of population which only recently overtook that of the Ivory Coast, Australia has for some time been among the most creatively productive countries on earth. In the mortal words of Sir Les Patterson, we've got the arts coming out of our arseholes. Painters, poets, novelists, actors, actresses, singers, directors: our artists are all over the world like a rash, and the days are long gone when the stars who stayed away were the only ones we had.

Nobody now would be surprised to hear that the only reason Cate Blanchett left home was to get away from her more gifted sister. In Sydney a new Baz Luhrman lurks on every block, and Brisbane bristles with *prêt-a-porter* Peter Porters. Alomes has predicated his book on the up-to-date assumption that if Australia should happen to go on producing cultural expatriates, it won't be provincialism that they flee from, because there no longer is any. The way he says so, however, would be enough in itself to make any current expatriate think twice before coming home for anything longer than a brief incognito visit, and might well recruit new expatriates by the planeload.

On a world scale, the average cultural expatriate in the twentieth century took flight because if he had stayed where he was he would have faced death by violence. His average Australian equivalent has faced nothing except death from boredom. It might sound like a privileged choice until you find out how lethal the boredom can be. Try a sample sentence.

> In this period groups and institutions were either offshore replications of Australian support organisations or precursors of official and unofficial Australian organisations.

To be fair, Alomes doesn't always succeed in being as unreadable as that. There are lingering signs that the once-excellent Australian school system has not yet fully given up on its initial aim of teaching pupils to write coherent prose. Apart from the use of 'manifest' as an intransitive verb ('Sayle's happy knack of being on the spot where things were happening manifested early') and a failure to realize that the adjectives 'new' and 'innovative' are too similar in meaning to be used as if they were different ('The film was innovative and new') he writes a plain enough English for someone whose ear for rhythm either never developed or was injured in an accident. There are whole paragraphs that don't need to be read twice to yield their sense. The question remains, however, of whether they sufficiently reward being read once, except as an unintended demonstration of the very provincialism whose obsolescence their author would like taken for granted.

The answer to the question is yes: just. Leaving his overall interpretation of them aside, the raw data are of such high interest that they inspire even the author to the occasional passage of pertinent reflection, some of it his own. He names the names of those Australians who came to London when that was still the thing to do. After World War II the tendency for the painters who went away to stay away became ingrained. Arthur Boyd, Sidney Nolan and Charles Blackman all made a life in England, even when their imaginative subject matter was drawn either from their memories of Australia or from the visits home they could make more frequently as they prospered. Alomes gives details of which painters resettled in Australia later in their careers, or else merely appeared to while maintaining their British base, and of whether their work was regarded as Australian-based or international. He occupies himself with the questions of domicile and national loyalty as if his subjects thought about these things then as hard as he does now. What seldom strikes him is the possibility that to *stop* thinking about such matters might have been one of the reasons they took off in the first place.

If Alomes had widened the scope of his book to include other destinations besides London, he would have had to deal, among the painters, with the problem posed by Jeffrey Smart, who, at the height of his long career, not only remains a resident of Tuscany but rarely paints an Australian subject even from memory. Smart had a clear and simple reason, freely admitted in his autobiography, for leaving Australia half a century ago. As an active homosexual, he had a good chance of being locked up. But his other reasons are of more lasting interest, and one of them was that he had no personal commitment to a national school of painting that depended on Australian subject matter. He knew everything about what the national painters had achieved, but he saw them in an international context. In short, he wasn't interested in nationalism.

The same can be applied to the musical luminaries here listed: Richard Bonynge, June Bronhill, Charles Mackerras, Malcolm Williamson, Yvonne Minton, Joan Sutherland and so, gloriously, on. Alomes flirts with the idea that the performing artists – the instrumentalists especially – might have hindered the development of Australian music by leaving, but he doesn't follow up on the possibility that by raising the prestige of Australian music throughout the world they might have helped more than they hindered, simply by making a musical career seem that much more exciting to a new entrant. Post-war, the arrival of Sir Eugene Goossens raised the level of Australian orchestral music, but the departure of Joan Sutherland made Australia a planetary force in grand opera – like the extra shrimp that Paul Hogan later threw on the barbie, Our Joan's impact on Covent Garden resonated throughout the world.

The resonance reached Australia itself: when the winner of the *Sun* Aria Contest set out for England, she sailed on a ship that launched a thousand sopranos. The effect that the international prestige of our expatriates had on aspiring artists in their homeland is a big subject for our author to pay so little attention to. But he pays no attention at all to an even bigger subject. He notes that the *prima donna assoluta* got a rapturous reception on her 1965 homecoming tour but neglects to mention that her every record album was received with the same enthusiasm – quietly, in thousands of middle-class households. Throughout the book, he takes it for granted that the expatriate artists ran the risk of being out of touch with an Australian audience: not even once does he consider that they might have been *in* touch with an Australian audience in the most intimate possible way – through their art. He is keener to treat the whole phenomenon of expatriation as if it had a *terminus a quo* in the old colonial feelings of inferiority and a *terminus ad quem* in the now imminent attainment of independent nationhood: because the stage at home was too small, gifted people needed to leave, and now that it isn't, they needn't. But the Sydney Opera House was already built when Joan Sutherland repatriated herself as a resident star, and although she was congratulated by music lovers for choosing to spend the last part of her career at home, she also had to cope with the patronizing opinion that her career must have been over, or she wouldn't have come back. She also faced persistent questioning – of whose impertinence Alomes seems not to be aware – about why she was not in favour of an Australian Republic. Nostalgia for Switzerland must have been hard to quell.

On the continuing problem of how a successful expatriate can make a return without being thought to have failed, Alomes could have been more searching, but at least he mentions it. The theatrical expatriates have always suffered from it most. They are all here, starting with Robert Helpmann before the war, and going on through Peter Finch, Bill Kerr, Leo McKern, Diane Cilento, Michael Blakemore, John Bluthal, Barry Humphries and Keith Michell. Michell is usefully quoted as telling a journalist 'the trouble is, when you go home, everybody says you're on the skids'. This is a handily short version of a Barry Humphries off-stage routine that he has been known to deliver to anyone *except* a journalist. Humphries relates that when he stepped off the plane on one of his early trips home, a representative of the local media asked him how long he planned to stay. When Humphries explained that he was back only for a few days, he was asked 'Why? Aren't we good enough for you?' For his next trip, he armed himself with a more diplomatic answer to the same question. When he said that this time he might be back for quite a while, he was asked 'Why? Couldn't you make it over there?'

Perhaps Alomes might like to use this parable in a later edition, although he is unlikely to get it confirmed by Humphries himself, who has already committed suicide often enough without handing the

Australian press any more ammunition. Meanwhile Alomes reports a usefully rueful comment from the distinguished theatrical producer and film director Michael Blakemore, who apparently wondered whether his film *Country Life* – a retelling of *Uncle Vanya* in an Australian setting – might not have been better received in Australia if he had launched it in America and Europe first. Blakemore was really saying that the home-based Australian journalists did him in. Alomes might have made more of that, but true to his title he is more interested in the Australian journalists who went abroad.

The list starts with Alan Moorehead, who in Europe built a justified legend as a war correspondent before moving on to write his best-selling books about the Nile. Robert Hughes has several times paid tribute to Moorehead's influence as exemplar and mentor. Moorehead was a true heavyweight, but the pick of his many successors who took the road to glory in the Street of Shame form a by no means trivial list: Paul Brickhill, Sam White, Philip Knightley, Barbara Toner, Bruce Page, John Pilger and the explosively charismatic swagman Murray Sayle, he whose happy knack of being on the spot when things were happening manifested early. They all had that happy knack, and they all shared the conviction that wherever the spot was, it wasn't in the land where they were born. You would think that at least a few of the survivors might have gone home by now, if provincialism was really over, but among the big-name byliners no instance of a permanent return is here recorded. There are less illustrious figures whose sojourns in Fleet Street and subsequent repatriation are solemnly celebrated. No doubt they brought something home with them, but what they took away with them in the first place seems, on this reckoning, no great shakes, and one would have thought that their inclusion stretched the term Creative Artist pretty far. Two women who turned out yellow drivel for the British tabloids ('You can tell a man by his underpants') have their itineraries traced in detail, in keeping with Alomes's tendency, throughout the book, to count heads without caring about the size of hat.

A conspicuous example of that same tendency is Jill Neville, enrolled among the expatriate writers. By a rough calculation she gets three times as much space as Patrick White. No doubt she had a magnetic personal attractiveness. Unduly given to the bad journalistic practice of name-checking his way through networks as if that did something to illuminate the individuals caught up in them, Alomes

makes much of Jill Neville's role in Peter Porter's life and in the circle
that formed around Charles Blackman and Al Alvarez in Hampstead.
Alvarez wasn't Australian but he liked Australians. His recent book
Where Did It All Go Right? shows how much he liked Jill Neville. If
not precisely a *femme fatale*, she certainly had the knack of making
grown male intellectuals fight like schoolboys. By the time I met her,
she had been brought low by illness and the familar cumulative
effects of a career in which literary ambitions do not fulfil themselves,
to an extent that makes the income from ordinary journalism matter
significantly less. To be trapped in Grub Street and sick too is a hard
fate. But even in the early grip of the cancer that took her away, Jill
Neville still had charm. The question was whether she had any talent.
My own assessment would be that she more or less did – her fiction,
without being incandescent, retains something better than documentary value – but Alomes doesn't say whether she did or she didn't.
He just parades her along with all the other expatriates as if she had
the same rank, and pays her more attention than almost any of them
because she happened to know so many of them personally.

The matter of talent becomes an embarrassment when Alomes
gets to what he calls the Megastars, because if he can't talk about
what they have to offer, then he can have no reason for being
interested in them apart from their celebrity. The usual four suspects
are rounded up. Robert Hughes gets fleeting treatment because he
settled in New York instead of London. Germaine Greer, Barry
Humphries and myself are worked over at length. I wish I could say I
felt flattered to be included, but flattened would be more like it. Ian
Britain started this Gang of Four caper with his book *Once an
Australian*, which at least had the merit of crediting his individual
subjects with a vestigial inner life that might yet survive somewhere
inside the airless perimeter of their fame, in the same way that the
presence of water on Mars cannot yet be ruled out. Britain was able
to contemplate that his chosen specimens might have become famous
for something – if only their way of putting things – rather than just
through wanting to be famous. But Alomes has gone beyond that.
With his innovative and new filing system, he has no need to form
a personal estimation of anything that his Megastars might have
actually done. He can just trawl through the press coverage.

Let me start by getting myself out of the road as quickly as
possible. I only wish our author had done the same, but it all goes

on for pages. A detailed case study is built up of what Alomes calls a 'professional Australian', smarming his way upwards in the capital city of imperialism by shamelessly peddling his colonial identity to con the Poms. For all I know, and in spite of its plethora of factual errors, this dossier fits the culprit: it takes a saint to be sure of his own motives. All I can say in rebuttal, if not refutation, is that I can't remember the Poms being as easy to con as all that. Even for Rolf Harris, the didgeridoo and the wobble-board weren't enough by themselves: he had to sing. And as far as I can recall after almost forty years, I had to compose a few ordinary, unaccented English sentences before I could get anybody's attention. My freckles were already fading fast, and putting zinc cream on my nose would have looked like frost-bite.

If it was conceited of me to expect some attempt at assessing the way I write – if only to demonstrate how I worked the scam – such an attempt was the least to expect when it came to the case of Germaine Greer. If you leave out her way of putting things, all you are left with is the things she puts. Her various attitudes have been shared at one time or another by many, and there might even be some who share them all. Perhaps somewhere, gathered around some dusty well, there is a group of women farsighted enough to perceive that clitoridectomy is a breakthrough for feminism. But it would be even more amazing if they could write. Germaine Greer can write, often amazingly. Her distinctiveness is in her style, where all she feels, observes and believes adds up to a passion. It might be better if it added up to a position, but it would take a fool to deny its power, and a dunce to ignore it. Alomes ignores it. Instead, he applies his method. What she said to the media, or what the media said she said, is sedulously quoted. The contradictions and anomalies that emerge are marvelled over, as if consistency had ever been among her virtues. Deep thoughts that various mediocrities have thought about what she thinks are duly shuffled into a heap, which you would have to set fire to if you hoped for any illumination. But at least obfuscation is not the aim. In the case of Barry Humphries I'm afraid it is. The stuff about him is a scandal.

A serious fellow even while he was alive, the avant-garde novelist B. S. Johnson once informed a table and the people sitting around it – I was one of them, so I can vouch for this – that he did not admire Shakespeare, because real people don't talk in verse. Showing similar powers of insight, Alomes is able to detect that Dame Edna Everage, Sir Les Patterson and others among Barry Humphries' range of stage zanies do not correspond to any actual people in our country's now advanced state of development. He further concludes that Humphries' international theatrical success is therefore damaging to Australia's image abroad. When Ian Britain favourably reviewed this book for the Melbourne *Age*, the strictures placed on Humphries were too much even for him, and he tried to point out the obvious: that Humphries' fantastic characters were found just as entertaining by an Australian audience as a foreign one. More could be said on those lines, but I doubt it would be enough to convince Alomes, who is too hipped on his idea of the 'cultural cringe' (a term he employs interminably) to let go of the possibility that large sections of the Australian audience look up to Humphries precisely because he looks down on them. Alomes wouldn't put anything past the middle class. Like many Australian soft-option academics who fancy themselves as radical political thinkers, he resolutely refuses to grasp that a middle class is the first article a liberal democracy manufactures, and the last it can do without.

Of all the people in the book, Humphries is the one to whom the term Australian Expatriate Creative Artist applies most, and of whom its author knows least. You would never guess from what is written here that Humphries, throughout his career, and in addition to commanding a mandarin prose that integrates the wild inventiveness of the Australian idiom at a level beyond the reach of even his brightest critics, has devoted tireless energy to the study, rediscovery, preservation and furtherance of Australian music, literature, painting and architecture. Humphries is learned on a world scale, but his learning began at home, and always goes back there. An expatriate he might be, but a patriot he has always been. Everyone knows that, except Alomes and the dunderheads in his filing system, prominent among whom is Dan O'Neill, described as (and this is Alomes talking, not Sir Les) 'literature scholar and radical academic at the University of Queensland'. In 1983 Radical Dan apparently asked 'How much longer can this curious ritual last, a Londoner with quick uptake, retentive memory and verbal flair coming over here on a regular basis, to tear the living fang out of us for being "Australian"?' I love that 'verbal flair': obviously a very compromising thing to be caught in possession of, like a bottle of anabolic steroids.

Not all of the names brought in to help lynch Humphries are ciphers. One of them belongs to the gifted playwright David Williamson, whose towering presence in this shambling rank of irascible homunculi is enough to prove that Alomes's book is a more serious matter than it might appear, although never in a way that its author might like to think. Williamson is quoted as calling Humphries 'a satirist who loathes Australia and everything about it'. As it happens, Humphries is a difficult customer in real life and there are things about his stage act that some of us find difficult too. I wouldn't like to be in the first three or four rows when Sir Les is propagating rancid zabaglione from the dilapidated cloaca of his mouth, and I have always sympathized with the country wife in the fifth row when Dame Edna asks her what she had to do to get the pearls. Without question there is an implacable animus boiling somewhere behind the personae. But to discern in Humphries 'almost a total hatred of Australia' (Williamson again, apparently) takes something more than a lack of humour. It takes nationalism, which is where we get down to the nitty-gritty.

For any free nation, an upsurge of nationalism is something it needs like a hole in the head. The holes are usually provided by whatever force emerges victorious from the resulting turmoil, and the heads by its innocent citizens. If the history of the previous century taught us anything, it taught us that. But one of the charms of the Australian intelligentsia is that the generality of its members aren't bound by an historical context. Unfortunately they aren't informed by one either, a deficiency which makes innocence less cute when it comes to politics. When the Australian Republican Movement gave itself a name, it was merely naive in supposing that the concept of an historically predetermined *Bewegung* would fail to arouse bad memories. But there was nothing naive, and much that was nasty, in the ARM's collective fondness for wondering whether Australians who questioned its visionary mission were quite Australian enough.

Beginning with the discovery by Paul Keating that Australia's destiny was to Stand Tall, it was suggested, with progressively increased intensity all the way to the eve of the recent referendum, that anyone who believed otherwise was guilty of standing short. Nationalist rhetoric was off and running like one of those bush fires that burn down whole states. It was too late for anyone to say, without risk of being fried to a crisp in the media, that Australia

already *was* a nation: that it had thrown off the shackles of British
imperialism even before the federation of its constituent states; and
that it was much envied in a world which had seen many other
nations with older names smashed to pieces and forced to start again
– or, like Argentina (a country directly comparable to Australia up
until the end of World War II), remaining intact only at the cost of
being consumed with grief as their natural blessings, social cohesion,
public benefits and civil rights were irrevocably frittered away in one
constitutional crisis after another.

It was too late for anyone except the Australian public, who
declined to vote for the republican proposal as it was put to them,
and might well do the same again even if the proposal is different.
It should be evident, indeed, that unless all the proposals are the
same – i.e. unless there is an agreed republican model – then
the republic will remain merely a nice idea, like a popcorn mine or the
Big Rock Candy Mountain. Personally I hope that the republicans
can agree on a model: firstly because we might need it – the Royal
Family might decide to give up – and secondly because, during the
necessary discussion, the intelligentsia will be obliged to examine
what it did wrong last time, and might reach the salutary conclusion
that its propensity for questioning the loyalty of its ideological
enemies came home to roost.

Whether a wise expatriate should come home to roost is another
question, especially if he has been tagged as a conservative. But it
probably wouldn't matter much if he stayed away. I called Alomes's
book 'timely' because in the débâcle of the lost referendum it should
teach his fellow savants, simply by its grotesque example, that the
nationalist line of thought, especially when applied to culture, is a
busted flush. But I fear it could still take many other books to teach
them that the ideal of cultural autarky has always been a pipe-
dream, in whatever country the pipe is smoked. Heine, without
whom German poetry would be cut in half, spent two-thirds of
his life in Paris. He was sheltering from repression and prejudice,
but Thomas Mann, even after Hitler's death, never came home to
Germany, because he doubted whether Germany was ready to come
home to him. Stravinsky operated on the principle that Russia went
with him wherever he went, which was everywhere except the Soviet
Union. Picasso was Spain in spite of Spain, and for James Joyce the

condition for returning eternally to Ireland in the circulating river of his work was never to set foot there again.

An artist is the incarnation of his country, wherever he might happen to hang his hat. And as for those countries that have never had direct experience of what tyranny, repression or officially imposed obscurantism are, they have always exported cultural figures as copiously as they have taken them in. Why William James stayed in the United States and his brother Henry never came home is a question open to a hundred answers, but sensibly the Americans long ago gave up on wondering which of them did their country the bigger favour, because it became evident that they both belonged to their country only in the sense that their country belonged to the world.

A nation's culture either joins it to the world or it is not a culture. Although Australians should try to be less impressed with the size of their country on the map, and remember that it contains far fewer people than Mexico City, they are right to be proud of how large their little nation looms in the world's consciousness. The expatriates have played a part in that. It might not be the biggest part, or even a necessary one – Les Murray got the whole of the modern world into his marvellous verse novel *Fredy Neptune* without ever leaving home for long – but they have certainly played a part. Which is not to say that a nation's expatriate Creative Artists need always be thought of as ambassadors, or think of themselves that way. The place they came from, even if it is the first thing in their hearts, might be the last thing on their minds, and they might remain convinced that they came away only to commit what Françoise Sagan once called the crime of solitude. But if they commit it with sufficient grace, their homeland will claim them anyway, in the course of time.

TLS, 26 January, 2000: also included in *Even As We Speak*, 2001

Postscript

I could write a book about Australian nationalism, and have recently been plagued by a nightmare in which I actually have to. In the

nightmare I occupy a cell in the old Long Bay gaol, an institution
now happily disestablished, but which in my youth was still playing
host to the most hard-to-hold recidivists in New South Wales,
including, off and on, the notoriously elusive Darcy Dugan. A small
man who could make himself smaller to wriggle between iron bars,
Dugan got himself into the language by getting himself out of any
form of incarceration the screws could devise. There was a prison
tram, a windowless steel box on wheels, which used to take criminals
back and forth from Long Bay to the court in Paddington. It once
left Long Bay with Dugan inside it and arrived in Paddington without him. He was next seen in Queensland. From the top of the hill
near my house I could look across Botany Bay to Long Bay gaol and
wonder whether Dugan was still there. He made me feel better
about school, but I was well aware even then that I lacked his talent.
In my nightmare, there is no getting out of the cell. (Scratched
into the wall about five feet from the floor is the rubric 'D. Dugan
was hear breefly.') The screws want to see a fresh thousand words at
the end of each day or they won't feed me. No outside exercise is
permitted.

On the other hand, any visitor is allowed in. Gough Whitlam
shows up. He demands to see my references to him. I show him the
one about his habit of quoting verbatim from the *Almanach de Gotha*
being somewhat anomalous for a professed Republican. He replies
with a long exposition of the Bowes-Lyon family tree. Representatives
of the Australian intelligentsia arrive. They tell me how shameful it
was that our diplomats once had difficulty explaining to President
Suharto of Indonesia why our Head of State did not live in Australia.
They do not tell me if the Indonesians had any difficulty explaining
why every occupant of their administrative structure above the level
of receptionist was called Suharto and half the economy was in
Switzerland. Paul Keating arrives to read the bits about him. He calls
me a maggot for suggesting that he lowered the tone of parliamentary
discourse by calling anyone who questioned his Republican policies
a maggot. My cell is full. So is the corridor. I will never get my book
finished, but I am not allowed to stop writing it. Stephen Alomes
arrives, wanting to know why I tried to nuke *his* book before it could
get out of the silo. I tell him *this* is why: because I didn't want to
spend the rest of my life here, compelled to make sense of a subject

with the same ontological status as the man who shagged O'Reilley's daughter.

Darcy Dugan arrives, weighed down with chains. An Australian journalist recognized him in Vancouver.

2001

ALMOST LITERATURE

THE SHERLOCKOLOGISTS

Sir Arthur Conan Doyle wrote little about Sherlock Holmes compared with what has been written by other people since. Sherlock has always been popular, on a scale never less than world-wide, but the subsidiary literature which has steadily heaped up around him can't be accounted for merely by referring to his universal appeal. Sherlock-ology – the adepts call it that, with typical whimsy – is a sort of cult, which has lately become a craze. The temptation to speculate about why this should be is one I don't propose to resist, but first there is the task of sorting the weighty from the witless in the cairn of Sherlockiana – they say that, too – currently available. What follows is a preliminary classification, done with no claims to vocational, or even avocational, expertise. Most decidedly not: this is a field in which all credentials, and especially impeccable ones, are suspect. To give your life, or any significant part of it, to the study of Sherlock Holmes is to defy reason.

*

It is also to disparage Doyle, as John Fowles pointed out in his introduction to *The Hound of the Baskervilles*, one of the four Sherlock Holmes novels handsomely reissued in Britain early last year, each as a single volume. This is an expensive way of doing things, but the books are so good-looking it is hard to quarrel, although the childhood memory of reading all the Sherlock Holmes 'long stories' in one volume (and all the short stories in another volume), well printed on thin but opaque paper, dies hard. Still, the new books look splendid all lined up, and the introductions are very interesting. Apart from Fowles, the men on the case are Hugh Greene (*A Study in Scarlet*), his brother Graham Greene (*The Sign of Four*), and Len Deighton (*The Valley of Fear*). What each man has to say is well worth hearing, even if not always strictly relevant to the novel it introduces. When you add to this four-volume set of the novels the five-volume reissue of the short story collections, it certainly provides a dazzling display.

To follow the order in which Doyle gave them to the world, the short story collections are *The Adventures of Sherlock Holmes* (introduced by Eric Ambler), *The Memoirs of Sherlock Holmes* (Kingsley Amis), *The Return of Sherlock Holmes* (Angus Wilson), *His Last Bow* (Julian Symons), and *The Case-Book of Sherlock Holmes* (C. P. Snow). The dust-wrappers of all nine volumes are carried out in black and gold, a colour combination which in Britain is supposed to put you in mind of John Player Specials, a ritzy line in cigarettes. Doing it this way, it will set you back £21.20 in English money to read the saga through.

A less crippling alternative would be to purchase the Doubleday omnibus introduced by the old-time (in fact, late) Sherlockian Christopher Morley, which reproduces the whole corpus – four novels and fifty-six short stories – on goodish paper for slightly under nine bucks, the contents being as nourishing as in the nine-volume version. The question of just how nourishing that *is* is one that begs to be shirked, but honour demands I should stretch my neck across the block and confess that Holmes doesn't seem quite so fascinating to me now as he once did. Perhaps only an adolescent can get the full thrill, and the price of wanting to go on getting it is to remain an adolescent always. This would explain a lot about the Sherlockologists.

*

The best single book on Doyle is *Sir Arthur Conan Doyle, l'homme et l'oeuvre*, a thoroughgoing monograph by Pierre Nordon which came out in its original language in 1964 and was translated into English as *Conan Doyle* a couple of years later. By no coincidence, it is also the best thing on Sherlock. In his chapter on 'Sherlock Holmes and the Reading Public' Nordon says most of what requires to be said about the basis of Sherlock's contemporary appeal. On the sociological side our nine introducers can't do much more than amplify Nordon's points, but since all of them are working writers of fiction (with the exception of Hugh Greene, who has, however, a profound knowledge of the period's genre literature) they usually have something of technical moment to add – and disinterested technical analysis is exactly what the Sherlock saga has for so long lacked. The Sherlockologists can't supply it, partly because most of them are nuts, but mainly because the deficiencies of Doyle's stories are what they thrive on: lacunae are what they are in business to fill, and they see Doyle's every awkwardness as a fruitful ambiguity, an irrevocable licence for speculation. The professional scribes, even when they think highly of Doyle, aren't like that. They haven't the time.

Hugh Greene reminds us that the Sherlock stories were head and shoulders above the yellow-back norm. This is still an essential point to put: Doyle was the man who made cheap fiction a field for creative work. Greene also says that *A Study in Scarlet* is broken-backed, which it is. Graham Greene calls one of Doyle's (brief, as always) descriptive scenes 'real writing from which we can all draw a lesson' but doesn't forget to insist that the subplot of *The Sign of Four* is far too like *The Moonstone* for comfort. (He also calls the meeting of Holmes and Watson in *A Study in Scarlet* unmemorable, an accurate perception denied to the Sherlockians who gravely installed a plaque in St Bartholomew's hospital to commemorate it.)

Of *The Hound of the Baskervilles*, the only successful Sherlock novel, John Fowles gives an unsparing critical analysis, on the sound assumption that anything less would be patronizing. He sees that Doyle's great technical feat was to resolve 'the natural incompatibility of dialogue and narration' but isn't afraid to call Doyle's inaccuracy inaccuracy. (He is surely wrong, however, to say that if Doyle had really wanted to kill Holmes he would have thrown *Watson* off the Reichenbach Falls. It is true that Sherlock couldn't exist without Watson, but there is no possible question that Doyle was keen to rub Holmes out.)

Len Deighton, a dedicated amateur of technology, assures us that Doyle really *did* forecast many of the police methods to come – the business with the typewriter in 'A Case of Identity', for example, was years ahead of its time. Since Nordon, eager as always to demystify Sherlock, rather downrates him on this point, it is useful to have the balance redressed. Unfortunately Deighton says almost nothing pertaining to *The Valley of Fear*, the novel which he is introducing. It seems likely that there was no editor to ask him to.

*

So it goes with the introductions to the short story collections. All of them are informative, but some of them tell you the same things, and only one or two illuminate the actual book. Kingsley Amis, as he did with Jane Austen and Thomas Love Peacock, gets down to fundamentals and admits that the Sherlock stories, for all their innovations in space and compression, are seldom 'classical' in the sense of playing fair with the reader. Eric Ambler talks charmingly about Doyle's erudition; Angus Wilson pertinently about the plush Nineties (1895–1898, the years of *The Return*, were Sherlock's times of triumph); Julian Symons penetratingly about how Doyle shared out his own personality between Holmes and Watson; and C. P. Snow – well, he, of all the nine, it seems to me, is the one who cracks the case.

His personality helps. Lord Snow not only sees but admits the attractions of the high position in society to which Sherlock's qualities eventually brought him, with Watson striding alongside. It might have been Sherlock's bohemianism that pulled in the crowds, but it was his conservatism that glued them to the bleachers. This was Pierre Nordon's salient observation on the sleuth's original appeal, but Lord Snow has outsoared Nordon by realizing that the same come-on is still operating with undiminished force. Sherlock was an eccentrically toothed but essential cog in a society which actually functioned.

The life led by Holmes and Watson in their rooms at 221B Baker Street is a dream of unconventionality, like Act 1 of *La Bohème*. (A Sherlockologist would step in here to point out that Henri Murger's *Scènes de la Vie de Bohème*, the book on which the opera was later based, is perused by Watson in *A Study in Scarlet*.) Although Len Deighton is quite right to say that the busy Sherlock is really running the kind of successful medical consultancy which Doyle never enjoyed, it is equally true to say that Holmes and Watson are living as a pair of Oxbridge undergraduates were popularly thought to – and indeed did – live. Holmes is a maverick scientist who treats science as an art, thereby conflating the glamour of both fields while avoiding the drudgery of either. He is free of all ties; he does what he wants; he is afraid of nothing. He is above the law and dispenses his own justice. As with Baudelaire, boredom is his only enemy. If he can't escape it through an intellectual challenge, he takes refuge in drugs.

Sherlock in *The Sign of Four* was fixing cocaine three times a day for three months: if he'd tried to snort it in those quantities, his aquiline septum would have been in considerable danger of dropping off. Morphine gets a mention somewhere too – perhaps he was also shooting speedballs. Certainly he was a natural dope fiend: witness how he makes a cocktail of yesterday's cigarette roaches in 'The Speckled Band'. In *The Valley of Fear* he is 'callous from over-stimulation.' All the signs of an oil-burning habit. Did he quit cold turkey, or did Watson ease him down? Rich pickings for the ex-Woodstock Sherlockologists of the future. All of this must have been heady wine for the contemporary reader endowed by the Education Act of 1870 with just enough literacy to read the *Strand* Magazine, helped out by a Sidney Paget illustration on every page.

*

George Orwell thought Britain needed a boys' weekly which questioned society, but Sherlock, for all his nonconformity, set no precedent. He fitted in far more than he dropped out. Sherlock was the house hippie. His latter-day chummings-up with crowned heads (including the private sessions with Queen Victoria which drive card-carrying Sherlockologists to paroxysms of conjecture) were merely the confirmation of a love for royalty which was manifest as early as 'A Scandal in Bohemia'. 'Your Majesty had not spoken,' announces Holmes, 'before I was aware that I was addressing Wilhelm Gottsreich Sigismond von Ormstein, Grand Duke of Cassel-Felstein, and Hereditary King of Bohemia.' The language, as so often in the Holmes stories, is part-way a put-on, but the relationship is genuine: Sherlock is as eager to serve as any of his cultural descendants. From Sanders of the River and Bulldog Drummond down to Pimpernel Smith and James Bond, all those gifted amateur soldiers can trace their ancestry to Sherlock's bump of reverence. Physically a virgin, spiritually he spawned children numberless as the dust.

At least 30 per cent of London's population lived below the poverty line in Sherlock's heyday, but not very many of them found their way into the stories. Doyle's criminals come almost exclusively from the income-earning classes. They are clinically, not socially, motivated. There is seldom any suggestion that crime could be a symptom of anything more general than a personal disorder. Doyle's mind was original but politically blinkered, a condition which his hero reflects. When Watson says (in 'A Scandal in Bohemia') that Holmes loathes 'every form of society with his whole Bohemian soul', it turns out that Watson means socializing. Society itself Holmes never queries. Even when he acts above the law, it is in the law's spirit that he acts. Nordon is quite right to insist that Sherlock's London, for all its wide social panorama and multiplicity of nooks and crannies, shouldn't be allowed to get mixed up with the real London. (He is quite wrong, though, to suppose that Orwell – of all people – mixed them up. Orwell said that Doyle did, but Nordon has taken Orwell's paraphrase of Doyle's view for Orwell's own opinion. He was helped to the error by a misleading French translation. Pan-culturalism has its dangers.)

*

Holmes was a nonconformist in a conformist age, yet still won all the conformist rewards. It was a double whammy, and for many people probably works the same magic today. I suspect that such reassurance is at the centre of the cosy satisfaction still to be obtained from reading about Sherlock, but of course there are several things it doesn't explain. The first of these is the incessant activity of the hard-core Sherlockologists, the freaks who are on the Baker Street beat pretty well full time. Most of them seem to be less interested in getting things out of the Sherlock canon than in putting things in. Archness is the keynote: coyly pedantic about imponderables, they write the frolicsome prose of the incorrigibly humourless. The opportunity for recondite tedium knows no limit. This playful racket has been going on without let-up since well before Doyle died. The output of just the last few months is depressing enough to glance through. Multiply it by decades and the mind quails.

Here is *Sherlock Holmes Detected*, by Ian McQueen. It is composed of hundreds of such pseudo-scholarly points as the contention that 'A Case of Identity' might very well be set in September, even though Holmes and Watson are described as sitting on either side of the fire – because their landlady Mrs Hudson is known to have been conscientious, and would have laid the fire ready for use even before winter. And anyway, Mr McQueen postulates cunningly, Holmes and Watson would probably sit on either side of the fire *even if it were not lit*. Apparently this subtle argument puts paid to other Sherlockologists who hold the view that 'A Case of Identity' can't possibly be set in September. Where that view originated is lost in the mists of fatuity: these drainingly inconsequential debates were originally got up by Ronald Knox and Sydney Roberts and formalized as an Oxford *vs.* Cambridge contest in dead-pan whimsy, which has gradually come to include the less calculated ponderosity of interloping enthusiasts who don't even realize they are supposed to be joking. Mr McQueen's book sounds to me exactly the same as Vincent Starrett's *The Private Life of Sherlock Holmes*, which came out in 1933 and seems to have set the pace in this particular branch of the industry.

Two other volumes in the same Snark-hunting vein are *The London of Sherlock Holmes* and *In the Footsteps of Sherlock Holmes*: both written by Michael Harrison, both published recently, and both consisting of roughly the same information and photographs. Both bear the imprint of the same publishing house, which must have an editor whose blindness matches the blurb-writer's illiteracy. Mr Harrison goes in for the same brand of bogus precision as Mr McQueen. We hear a lot about what 'must have' happened. We are shown a photograph of the steps which Sherlock's brother Mycroft 'must have used' when going to his job at the Foreign Office. This music hall 'must have been visited' by Sherlock. There is the usual interminable speculation about the whereabouts of 221B, coupled with the usual reluctance to consider that Doyle himself obviously didn't give a damn for the plausibility of its location. The only authentic problem Mr Harrison raises is the question of which of his two books is the sillier.

*

Messrs McQueen and Harrison are toddling in the giant footsteps of W. S. Baring-Gould, who compiled *The Annotated Sherlock Holmes*, which went into such scholastic minutiae with the determination of mania. Baring-Gould was also the father of yet another branch of the business – fake biographies. In his *Sherlock Holmes: A Biography of the World's First Consulting Detective* (1962) Baring-Gould sent Sherlock to Oxford. In her contribution to H. W. Bell's *Baker Street Studies* thirty years earlier, Dorothy Sayers sent him to Cambridge. Doyle sent him to neither.

Current biographical efforts are in the same footling tradition. Here is an untiringly industrious novel by John Gardner called *The Return of Moriarty*, in which the Greatest Schemer of All Time returns alive from the Reichenbach. It doesn't daunt Mr Gardner that he is transparently ten times more interested in Moriarty than Doyle ever was. In 'The Final Problem' Sherlock tells Watson that the silent struggle to get the goods on Moriarty could be the greatest story of all, but Doyle never wrote it. The reason, as Angus Wilson divines, is that Moriarty was a less employable villain than his side-kick, Moran. Moriarty was merely the Napoleon of Crime, whereas Moran was the 'best heavy game shot that our Eastern Empire has ever produced' – which at least *sounded* less vague.

But the vagueness in Doyle is what the speculators like. And here is *The Seven-Per-Cent Solution*, pretending to be 'a reprint from the reminiscences of John H. Watson, M.D., as edited by Nicholas Meyer.' This time Sherlock and Mycroft turn out to be repressing a shameful, nameless secret. In books like this, speculation is supposed to be veering towards the humorous. The transgression would be funny, if only it made you laugh. Mr Meyer's comic invention, however, is thin. But at least he is *trying* to be silly.

*

The most foolish book of the bunch, and quite frankly the loopiest stretch of exegesis since John Allegro dug up the sacred mushroom, is *Naked is the Best Disguise*, by Samuel Rosenberg, which has been welcomed in the United States with reviews I find inexplicable. Mr Rosenberg's thesis, briefly, is that Moriarty is Nietzsche and that Doyle is acting out a psycho-drama in which Sherlock is his superego suppressing his polymorphous perversity. Even if it had been reached by a convincing show of reasoning, this conclusion would still be far-fetched: fetched, in fact, from halfway across the galaxy. But it has been reached by no kind of reasoning except casuistry. Mr Rosenberg argues in one place that if a Sherlock Holmes adventure is set in a house with two storeys, that means there are two *stories* – i.e., two levels of meaning. His arguing is of the same standard in every other place.

It seems that Mr Rosenberg used to work as a legal eagle for a film studio, protecting it from plagiarism suits by finding a common literary ancestor who might have influenced both the plaintiff's script and the script the studio had in the works. He must have been well worth his salary, because he can see similarities in anything. (His standards of accuracy spring from the same gift: he spells A. J. Ayer's name wrongly on seven occasions.) It would be overpraising the book to call it negligible, yet both *Time* and *The New York Times,* among others, seem to have found it a meaty effort.

Though *Naked is the Best Disguise* considers itself to be high scholarship, it reveals itself instantly as Sherlockology by worrying over the importance of minor detail in stories whose major action their author could scarcely be bothered to keep believable. The chronology of the Holmes saga is indefinitely debatable because Doyle didn't care about establishing it. Early on, Sherlock was ignorant of the arts and didn't know the earth went around the sun: later, he quoted poetry in several languages and had wide scientific knowledge. Sherlock was a minor occupation for Doyle and he was either content to leave such inconsistencies as they were or else he plain forgot about them. Mysteries arising from them are consequently unresolvable, which is doubtless their attraction. Programmes for explicating Sherlock are like Casaubon's Key to All Mythologies, which George Eliot said was as endless as a scheme for joining the stars.

*

Uniquely among recent Sherlockiana, *The Sherlock Holmes Scrapbook,* edited by Peter Haining, is actually enjoyable. It reproduces playbills, cartoons, production stills, and – most important – some of the magazine and newspaper articles which set Sherlockology rolling. (One of them is a piece of joky speculation by Doyle himself – a bad mistake. If he wanted to trivialize his incubus, he couldn't have chosen a worse tactic.) Basil Rathbone easily emerges as the most likely looking movie incarnation of Holmes. Sidney Paget's drawings are better than anything else then or since. (What we need is a good two-volume complete *Sherlock Holmes* with all of Paget and none of Baring-Gould.) The whole scrapbook is a great help in seeing how the legend grew, not least because it shows us that legends are of circumscribed interest: too many supernumeraries – belletrist hacks and doodling amateurs with time to burn – contribute to them. As you leaf through these chronologically ordered pages you can see the dingbats swarming aboard the bandwagon.

Doyle's brainchild could scarcely survive this kind of admiration if it did not possess archetypal attributes. Sherlockology is bastardized academicism, but academicism is one of the forces which Doyle instinctively set out to fight, and Sherlock, his Sunday punch, is not yet drained of strength. Sherlock was the first example of the art

Dürrenmatt later dreamed of – the art which would weigh nothing in the scales of respectability. Doyle knew that Sherlock was cheap. What he didn't guess before it was too late to change his mind was that the cheapness would last. The only coherence in the Holmes saga is a coherence of intensity. The language is disproportionate and therefore vivid. 'He was, I take it, the most perfect reasoning and observing machine that the world has seen.' The images are unshaded and therefore flagrant. 'I took a step forward: in an instant his strange headgear began to move, and there reared itself from among his hair the squat diamond-shaped head and puffed neck of a loathsome serpent.'

*

But Sherlock's world was all fragments, and no real world could or can be inferred from it. In *The Valley of Fear* the Scourers work mischief to no conceivable political purpose. Moriarty machinates to no ascertainable end. The Sherlockologists would like to believe that this abstract universe is concrete, and that large questions of good and evil are being worked out. But the concreteness is only in the detail; beyond the detail there is nothing; and the large questions must always lack answers.

Doyle asked and tried to answer the large questions elsewhere, in the spiritualist faith which occupied his full mental effort. Eventually his seriousness went out of date, while his frivolity established itself as an institution. But since his mind at play could scarcely have played so well if it had not been so earnest a mind, there is no joke.

New York Review of Books, 20 February, 1975: previously included in
At the Pillars of Hercules, 1979

Postscript

Genre fiction presents the critic with an insoluble problem, because he is the last person it was written for. Writers of science fiction and crime novels, though they have always craved respectability, could once count on being smothered with learned commentary only in the fanzines. In the post-modern era, respectability for the genre writers has arrived with a rush: *Hannibal* got as much attention in the culture pages on one weekend as Kafka did in a lifetime. Things were probably better the way they were. In the genres, inventiveness counts most and writing counts least, which is lucky, because hardly anyone who can invent can write. The few who can do both (with Simenon as the outstanding example) are worthy of celebration, but those literary critics who celebrate too hard betray themselves as finding literature dull. When young I read and re-read almost everything by Arthur Conan Doyle except the historical romances. I can still remember the excitement of trekking back up to Kogarah's house-sized public library to renew my take-out of *The Complete Professor Challenger Stories*, a chubby volume whose heft is imprinted so exactly in my brain that fifty years later I am reminded of it when I pick up something of the same weight. I was born in a small private hospital just around the corner, and in retrospect my trips to the library seem part of the same process.

Youthful passion is the right kind of attention to give genre fiction. Mature consideration, especially if it has never been preceded by the youthful passion, is the wrong kind. I still think Doyle was some kind of great man. But to place him among the literary artists is bound to shrink the vocabulary we should have available for acknowledging those who really are. If we have to go back to the radiant books of our youth, it is better to go back as a comedian than a critic. What we will rediscover is the way we used to daydream, and our superseded daydreams of glamour, sex, bravery and deductive brilliance are always funny when they are not shameful. The best-ever traveller *à la recherche du trash perdu* was S. J. Perelman in *Listen to the Mockingbird*. Paying his belated respects to *The Sheik, Graustark, Black Oxen and Three Weeks*, he hit a rich seam of comic stimuli. But not even he could mine it for long, because he soon ran out of bad books that he had once truly loved. Bad books that you merely liked won't do. The present equipoise doesn't work without the past madness.

2001

RAYMOND CHANDLER

'In the long run,' Raymond Chandler writes in *Raymond Chandler Speaking*, 'however little you talk or even think about it, the most durable thing in writing is style, and style is the most valuable investment a writer can make with his time.' At a time when literary values inflate and dissipate almost as fast as the currency, it still looks as if Chandler invested wisely. His style has lasted. A case could be made for saying that nothing else about his books has, but even the most irascible critic or most disillusioned fan (they are often the same person) would have to admit that Chandler at his most characteristic is just that – characteristic and not just quirky. Auden was right in wanting him to be regarded as an artist. In fact Auden's tribute might well have been that of one poet to another. If style is the only thing about Chandler's novels that can't be forgotten, it could be because his style was poetic, rather than prosaic. Even at its most explicit, what he wrote was full of implication. He used to say that he wanted to give a feeling of the country behind the hill.

Since Chandler was already well into middle age when he began publishing, it isn't surprising that he found his style quickly. Most of the effects that were to mark *The Big Sleep* in 1939 were already present, if only fleetingly, in an early story like 'Killer in the Rain', published in *Black Mask* magazine in 1935. In fact some of the very same sentences are already there. This from 'Killer in the Rain':

> The rain splashed knee-high off the sidewalks, filled the gutters, and big cops in slickers that shone like gun barrels had a lot of fun carrying little girls in silk stockings and cute little rubber boots across the bad places, with a lot of squeezing.

Compare this from *The Big Sleep*:

> Rain filled the gutters and splashed knee-high off the pavement.

Big cops in slickers that shone like gun barrels had a lot of fun carrying giggling girls across the bad places. The rain drummed hard on the roof of the car and the burbank top began to leak. A pool of water formed on the floorboards for me to keep my feet in.

So there is not much point in talking about how Chandler's style developed. As soon as he was free of the short-paragraph restrictions imposed by the cheaper pulps, his way of writing quickly found its outer limits: all he needed to do was refine it. The main refining instrument was Marlowe's personality. The difference between the two cited passages is really the difference between John Dalmas and Philip Marlowe. Marlowe's name was not all that more convincing than Dalmas's, but he was a more probable, or at any rate less improbable, visionary. In *The Big Sleep* and all the novels that followed, the secret of plausibility lies in the style, and the secret of the style lies in Marlowe's personality. Chandler once said that he thought of Marlowe as the American mind. As revealed in Chandler's *Notebooks* (edited by Frank McShane and published by the Ecco Press, New York), one of Chandler's many projected titles was *The Man Who Loved the Rain*. Marlowe loved the rain.

Flaubert liked tinsel better than silver because tinsel possessed all silver's attributes plus one in addition – pathos. For whatever reason, Chandler was fascinated by the cheapness of LA. When he said that it had as much personality as a paper cup, he was saying what he liked about it. When he said that he could leave it without a pang, he was saying why he felt at home there. In a city where the rich were as vulgar as the poor, all the streets were mean. In a democracy of trash, Marlowe was the only aristocrat. Working for 25 dollars a day plus expenses (Jim Rockford in the TV series *The Rockford Files* now works for ten times that and has to live in a trailer), Marlowe was as free from materialistic constraint as any hermit. He saw essences. Chandler's particular triumph was to find a style for matching Marlowe to the world. Vivid language was the decisive element, which meant that how not to make Marlowe sound like too good a *writer* was the continuing problem. The solution was a kind of undercutting wit, a style in which Marlowe mocked his own fine phrases. A comic style, always on the edge of self-parody – and, of

306 Almost Literature

course, sometimes over the edge – but at its best combining the exultant and the sad in an inseparable mixture.

For a writer who is not trying all that hard to be funny, it is remarkable how often Chandler can make you smile. His conciseness can strike you as a kind of wit in itself. The scene with General Sternwood in the hot-house, the set-piece forming Chapter Two of *The Big Sleep*, is done with more economy than you can remember: there are remarkably few words on the page to generate such a lasting impression of warm fog in the reader's brain. 'The air was thick, wet, steamy and larded with the cloying smell of tropical orchids in bloom.' It's the rogue word 'larded' which transmits most of the force. Elsewhere, a single simile gives you the idea of General Sternwood's aridity. 'A few locks of dry white hair clung to his scalp, like wild flowers fighting for life on a bare rock.' The fact that he stays dry in the wet air is the measure of General Sternwood's nearness to death. The bare rock is the measure of his dryness. At their best, Chandler's similes click into place with this perfect appositeness. He can make you laugh, he gets it so right – which perhaps means that he gets it too right. What we recognize as wit is always a self-conscious performance.

But since wit that works at all is rare enough, Chandler should be respected for it. And anyway, he didn't always fall into the trap of making his characters too eloquent. Most of Marlowe's best one-liners are internal. In the film of *The Big Sleep*, when Marlowe tells General Sternwood that he has already met Carmen in the hall, he says: 'She tried to sit in my lap while I was standing up.' Bogart gets a big laugh with that line, but only half of the line is Chandler's. All that Chandler's Marlowe says is: 'Then she tried to sit in my lap.' The film version of Marlowe got the rest of the gag from somewhere else – either from William Faulkner, who wrote the movie, or from Howard Hawks, who directed it, or perhaps from both. On the page, Marlowe's gags are private and subdued. About Carmen, he concludes that 'thinking was always going to be a bother to her.' He notices – as no camera could notice, unless the casting director flung his net very wide – that her thumb is like a finger, with no curve in its first joint. He compares the shocking whiteness of her teeth to fresh orange pith. He gets you scared stiff of her in a few sentences.

Carmen is the first in a long line of little witches that runs right through the novels, just as her big sister, Vivian, is the first in a long line of rich bitches who find that Marlowe is the only thing money can't buy. The little witches are among the most haunting of Chandler's obsessions and the rich bitches are among the least. Whether little witch or rich bitch, both kinds of woman signal their availability to Marlowe by crossing their legs shortly after sitting down and regaling him with tongue-in-the-lung French kisses a few seconds after making physical contact.

All the standard Chandler character ingredients were there in the first novel, locked in a pattern of action so complicated that not even the author was subsequently able to puzzle it out. *The Big Sleep* was merely the first serving of the mixture as before. But the language was fresh and remains so. When Chandler wrote casually of 'a service station glaring with wasted light' he was striking a note that Dashiell Hammett had never dreamed of. Even the book's title rang a bell. Chandler thought that there were only two types of slang which were any good: slang that had established itself in the language, and slang that you made up yourself. As a term for death, 'the big sleep' was such a successful creation that Eugene O'Neill must have thought it had been around for years, since he used it in *The Iceman Cometh* (1946) as an established piece of low-life tough talk. But there is no reason for disbelieving Chandler's claim to have invented it.

Chandler's knack for slang would have been just as commendable even if he had never thought of a thing. As the *Notebooks* reveal, he made lists of slang terms that he had read or heard. The few he kept and used were distinguished from the many he threw away by their metaphorical exactness. He had an ear for depth – he could detect incipient permanence in what sounded superficially like ephemera. A term like 'under glass', meaning to be in prison, attracted him by its semantic compression. In a letter collected in *Raymond Chandler Speaking*, he regards it as self-evident that an American term like 'milk run' is superior to the equivalent British term 'piece of cake'. The superiority being in the range of evocation. As it happened, Chandler *was* inventive, not only in slang but in more ambitiously suggestive figures of speech. He was spontaneous as well as accurate. His second novel, *Farewell, My Lovely* (1940) – which he was always to regard as his finest – teems with show-stopping metaphors, many of them dedicated to conjuring up the gargantuan figure of Moose Malloy.

In fact some of them stop the show too thoroughly. When

Chandler describes Malloy as standing out from his surroundings like 'a tarantula on a slice of angel food' he is getting things backwards, since the surroundings have already been established as very sordid indeed. Malloy ought to be standing out from them like a slice of angel food on a tarantula. Chandler at one time confessed to Alfred A. Knopf that in *The Big Sleep* he had run his metaphors into the ground, the implication being that he cured himself of the habit later on. But the truth is that he was always prone to overcooking a simile. As Perelman demonstrated in *Farewell, My Lovely Appetizer* (a spoof which Chandler admired), this is one of the areas in which Chandler is most easily parodied, although it should be remembered that it takes a Perelman to do the parodying.

'It was a blonde,' says Marlowe, looking at Helen Grayle's photograph. 'A blonde to make a bishop kick a hole in a stained-glass window.' I still laugh when I read that, but you can imagine Chandler jotting down such brain-waves *à propos* of nothing and storing them up against a rainy day. They leap off the page so high that they never again settle back into place, thereby adding to the permanent difficulty of remembering what happens to whom where in which novel. The true wit, in *Farewell, My Lovely* as in all the other books, lies in effects which marry themselves less obtrusively to character, action and setting. Jessie Florian's bathrobe, for example. 'It was just something around her body.' A sentence like that seems hardly to be trying, but it tells you all you need to know. Marlowe's realization that Jessie has been killed – 'The corner post of the bed was smeared darkly with something the flies liked' – is trying harder for understatement, but in those circumstances Marlowe *would* understate the case, so the sentence fits. Poor Jessie Florian. 'She was as cute as a washtub.'

And some of the lines simply have the humour of information conveyed at a blow, like the one about the butler at the Grayle house. As always when Chandler is dealing with Millionaires' Row, the place is described with a cataloguing eye for ritzy detail, as if F. Scott Fitzgerald had written a contribution to *Architectural Digest*. (The Murdock house in *The High Window* bears a particularly close resemblance to Gatsby's mansion: *vide* the lawn flowing 'like a cool green tide around a rock'.) Chandler enjoyed conjuring up the grand houses into which Marlowe came as an interloper and out of which he always went with a sigh of relief, having hauled the family skeletons out of the walk-in cupboards and left the beautiful, wild elder daughter sick with longing for his uncorruptible countenance. But in several telling pages about the Grayle residence, the sentence that really counts is the one about the butler. 'A man in a striped vest and gilt buttons opened the door, bowed, took my hat and was through for the day.'

In the early books and novels, before he moved to Laurel Canyon, when he still lived at 615 Cahuenga Building on Hollywood Boulevard, near Ivar, telephone Glenview 7537, Marlowe was fond of Los Angeles. All the bad things happened in Bay City. In Bay City there were crooked cops, prostitution, drugs, but after you came to (Marlowe was always coming to in Bay City, usually a long time after he had been sapped, because in Bay City they always hit him very hard) you could drive home. Later on the evil had spread everywhere and Marlowe learned to hate what LA had become. The set-piece descriptions of his stamping-ground got more and more sour. But the descriptions were always there – one of the strongest threads running through the novels from first to last. And even at their most acridly poisonous they still kept something of the wide-eyed lyricism of that beautiful line in *Farewell, My Lovely* about a dark night in the canyons – the night Marlowe drove Lindsay Marriott to meet his death. 'A yellow window hung here and there by itself, like the last orange.'

There is the usual ration of overcooked metaphors in *The High Window* (1942). Lois Morny gives forth with 'a silvery ripple of laughter that held the unspoiled naturalness of a bubble dance'. (By the time you have worked out that this means her silvery ripple of laughter held no unspoiled naturalness, the notion has gone dead.) We learn that Morny's club in Idle Valley looks like a high-budget musical. 'A lot of light and glitter, a lot of scenery, a lot of clothes, a lot of sound, an all-star cast, and a plot with all the originality and drive of a split fingernail.' Tracing the club through the musical down to the fingernail, your attention loses focus. It's a better sentence than any of Chandler's imitators ever managed, but it was the kind of sentence they felt able to imitate – lying loose and begging to be picked up.

As always, the quiet effects worked better. The back yard of the Morny house is an instant Hockney. 'Beyond was a walled-in garden containing flower-beds crammed with showy annuals, a badminton court, a nice stretch of greensward, and a small tiled pool glittering angrily in the sun.' The rogue adverb 'angrily' is the word that registers the sun's brightness. It's a long step, taken in a few words, to night-time in Idle Valley. 'The wind was quiet out here and the valley moonlight was so sharp that the black shadows looked as if they had been cut with an engraving tool.' Saying how unreal the real looks makes it realer.

'Bunker Hill is old town, lost town, shabby town, crook town.' *The High Window* has many such examples of Chandler widening his rhythmic scope. Yet the best and the worst sentences are unusually far apart. On several occasions Chandler is extraordinarily clumsy. 'He was a tall man with glasses and a high-domed bald head that made his ears look as if they had slipped down his head.' This sentence is literally effortless: the clumsy repetition of 'head' is made possible only because he isn't trying. Here is a useful reminder of the kind of concentration required to achieve a seeming ease. And here is another: 'From the lay of the land a light in the living room . . .' Even a writer who doesn't, as Chandler usually did, clean as he goes, would normally liquidate so languorous an alliterative lullaby long before the final draft.

But in between the high points and the low, the general tone of *The High Window* had an assured touch. The narrator's interior monologue is full of the sort of poetry Laforgue liked – *comme ils sont beaux, les trains manqués*. Marlowe's office hasn't changed, nor will it ever. 'The same stuff I had had last year, and the year before that. Not beautiful, not gay, but better than a tent on the beach.' Marlowe accuses the two cops, Breeze and Spangler, of talking dialogue in which every line is a punch-line. Criticism is not disarmed: in Chandler, everybody talks that kind of dialogue most of the time. But the talk that matters most is the talk going on inside Marlowe's head, and Chandler was making it more subtle with each book.

Chandler's descriptive powers are at their highest in *The Lady in the Lake* (1943). It takes Marlowe a page and a half of thoroughly catalogued natural detail to drive from San Bernardino to Little Fawn Lake, but when he gets there he sees the whole thing in a sentence. 'Beyond the gate the road wound for a couple of hundred yards through trees and then suddenly below me was a small oval lake deep in trees and rocks and wild grass, like a drop of dew caught in a curled leaf.' Hemingway could do bigger things, but small moments like those were Chandler's own. (Nevertheless Hemingway got on Chandler's nerves: Dolores Gonzales in *The Little Sister* is to be heard saying 'I was pretty good in there, no?' and the nameless girl who vamps Marlowe at Roger Wade's party in *The Long Goodbye* spoofs the same line. It should be remembered, however, that Chandler admired Hemingway to the end, forbearing to pour scorn even on *Across the River and into the Trees.* The digs at Papa in Chandler's novels can mainly be put down to self-defence.)

The Little Sister (1949), Chandler's first post-war novel, opens with Marlowe stalking a bluebottle fly around his office. 'He didn't want to sit down. He just wanted to do wing-overs and sing the prologue to *Pagliacci.*' Ten years before, in *Trouble Is My Business,* John Dalmas felt like singing the same thing after being sapped in Harriet Huntress's apartment. Chandler was always ready to bring an idea back for a second airing. A Ph.D. thesis could be written about the interest John Dalmas and Philip Marlow take in bugs and flies. There is another thesis in the tendency of Chandler's classier dames to show a startling line of white scalp in the parting of their hair: Dolores Gonzales, who throughout *The Little Sister* propels herself at Marlowe like Lupe Velez seducing Errol Flynn, is only one of the several high-toned vamps possessing this tonsorial feature. 'She made a couple of drinks in a couple of glasses you could almost have stood umbrellas in.' A pity about that 'almost' – it ruins a good hyperbole. Moss Spink's extravagance is better conveyed: 'He waved a generous hand on which a canary-yellow diamond looked like an amber traffic light.'

But as usual the would-be startling images are more often unsuccessful than successful. The better work is done lower down the scale of excitability. Joseph P. Toad, for example. 'The neck of his canary-yellow shirt was open wide, which it had to be if his neck was going to get out.' Wit like that lasts longer than hyped-up similes. And some of the dialogue, though as stylized as ever, would be a gift to actors: less supercharged than usual, it shows some of the natural balance which marked the lines Chandler has been writing for the movies. Here is Marlowe sparring with Sheridan Ballou.

> 'Did she suggest how to go about shutting my mouth?'
> 'I got the impression she was in favour of doing it with some kind of heavy blunt instrument.'

Such an exchange is as playable as anything in *Double Indemnity* or *The Blue Dahlia.* And imagine what Laird Cregar would have done with Toad's line 'You could call me a guy what wants to help out a

guy that don't want to make trouble for a guy.' Much as he would
have hated the imputation, Chandler's toil in the salt-mines under
the Paramount mountain had done things for him. On the other
hand, the best material in *The Little Sister* is inextricably bound up
with the style of Marlowe's perception, which in turn depends on
Chandler's conception of himself. There could be no complete screen
rendition of the scene with Jules Oppenheimer in the studio patio.
With peeing dogs instead of hot-house steam, it's exactly the same
lay-out as Marlowe's encounter with General Sternwood in *The Big
Sleep*, but then there was no filming *that* either. The mood of neurotic
intensity – Marlowe as the soldier-son, Sternwood/Oppenheimer as
the father-figure at death's door – would be otiose in a film script,
which requires that all action be relevant. In the novels, such passages
are less about Marlowe than about Chandler working out his
obsessions through Marlowe, and nobody ever wanted to make a
film about Chandler.

In *The Long Goodbye* (1953) Marlowe moves to a house on Yucca
Avenue in Laurel Canyon and witnesses the disintegration of Terry
Lennox. Lennox can't control his drinking. Marlowe, master of his
own thirst, looks sadly on. As we now know, Chandler in real life
was more Lennox than Marlowe. In the long dialogues between these
two characters he is really talking to himself. There is no need to be
afraid of the biographical fallacy: even if we knew nothing about
Chandler's life, it would still be evident that a fantasy is being worked
out. Worked out but not admitted – as so often happens in good-
bad books, the author's obsessions are being catered to, not examined.
Chandler, who at least worked for a living, had reason for thinking
himself more like Marlowe than like Lennox. (Roger Wade, the other
of the book's big drinkers, is, being a writer, a bit closer to home.)
Nevertheless Marlowe is a daydream – more and more of a daydream
as Chandler gets better and better at making him believable. By this
time it's Marlowe *vs.* the Rest of the World. Of all Chandler's nasty
cops, Captain Gregorius is the nastiest. 'His big nose was a network
of burst capillaries.' But even in the face of the ultimate nightmare
Marlowe keeps his nerve. Nor is he taken in by Eileen Wade, superficially the dreamiest of all Chandler's dream girls.

It was a near-run thing, however. Chandler mocked romantic
writers who always used three adjectives but Marlowe fell into the
same habit when contemplating Eileen Wade. 'She looked exhausted

now, and frail, and very beautiful.' Perhaps he was tipped off when Eileen suddenly caught the same disease and started referring to 'the wild, mysterious, improbable kind of love that never comes but once'. In the end she turns out to be a killer, a dream-girl gone sour like Helen Grayle in *Farewell, My Lovely*, whose motherly clutch ('smooth and soft and warm and comforting') was that of a strangler. *The Long Goodbye* is the book of Marlowe's irretrievable disillusion.

> I was as hollow and empty as the spaces between the stars. When I got home I mixed a stiff one and stood by the open window in the living-room and sipped it and listened to the ground swell of the traffic on Laurel Canyon Boulevard and looked at the glare of the big, angry city hanging over the shoulder of the hills through which the boulevard had been cut. Far off the banshee wail of police or fire sirens rose and fell, never for very long completely silent. Twenty-four hours a day somebody is running, somebody else is trying to catch him.

Even Marlowe got caught. Linda Loring nailed him. 'The tip of her tongue touched mine.' His vestal virginity was at long last ravished away. But naturally there was no Love, at least not yet.

Having broken the ice, Marlowe was to be laid again, most notably by the *chic*, leg-crossing Miss Vermilyea in Chandler's next novel, *Playback* (1958). It is only towards the end of that novel that we realize how thoroughly Marlowe is being haunted by Linda Loring's memory. Presumably this is the reason why Marlowe's affair with Miss Vermilyea is allowed to last only one night. (' "I hate you," she said with her mouth against mine. "Not for this, but because perfection never comes twice and with us it came too soon. And I'll never see you again and I don't want to. It would have to be for ever or not at all." ') We presume that Miss Vermilyea wasn't just being tactful.

Anyway, Linda Loring takes the prize, but not before Marlowe has raced through all his usual situations, albeit in compressed form. Once again, for example, he gets hit on the head. 'I went zooming out over a dark sea and exploded in a sheet of flame.' For terseness this compares favourably with an equivalent moment in *Bay City Blues*, written twenty years before.

> Then a naval gun went off in my ear and my head was a large

pink firework exploding into the vault of the sky and scattering and falling slow and pale, and then dark, into the waves. Blackness ate me up.

Chandler's prose had attained respectability, but by now he had less to say with it – perhaps because time had exposed his daydreams to the extent that even he could see them for what they were. The belief was gone. In *The Poodle Springs Story*, his last, unfinished novel, Marlowe has only one fight left to fight, the war against the rich. Married now to Linda, he slugs it out with her toe to toe. It is hard to see why he bothers to keep up the struggle. Even heroes get tired and not even the immortal stay young forever. Defeat was bound to come some time and although it is undoubtedly true that the rich are corrupt at least Linda knows how corruption ought to be done: the classiest of Chandler's classy dames, the richest bitch of all, she will bring Marlowe to a noble downfall. There is nothing vulgar about Linda. (If that Hammond organ-*cum*-cocktail bar in their honeymoon house disturbs you, don't forget that the place is only rented.)

So Marlowe comes to an absurd end, and indeed it could be said that he was always absurd. Chandler was always dreaming. He dreamed of being more attractive than he was, taller than he was, less trammelled than he was, braver than he was. But so do most men. We dream about our ideal selves, and it is at least arguable that we would be even less ideal if we didn't. Marlowe's standards of conduct would be our standards if we had his courage. We can rationalize the discrepancy by convincing ourselves that if we haven't got his courage he hasn't got our mortgage, but the fact remains that his principles are real.

Marlowe can be hired, but he can't be bought. As a consequence, he is alone. Hence his lasting appeal. Not that he is without his repellent aspects. His race prejudice would amount to outright fascism if it were not so evident that he would never be able to bring himself to join a movement. His sexual imagination is deeply suspect and he gets hit on the skull far too often for someone who works largely with his head. His taste in socks is oddly vile for one who quotes so easily from Browning ('the poet, not the automatic'). But finally you recognize his tone of voice.

It is your own, daydreaming of being tough, of giving the rich bitch the kiss-off, of saying smart things, of defending the innocent, of being the hero. It is a silly daydream because anyone who could really do such splendid things would probably not share it, but without it the rest of us would be even more lost than we are. Chandler incarnated this necessary fantasy by finding a style for it. His novels are exactly as good as they should be. In worse books, the heroes are too little like us: in better books, too much.

1977: previously included in *At the Pillars of Hercules*, 1979

Postscript

The most terrible thing that ever happened to Raymond Chandler was not his failed suicide attempt but what was said by one of the cops who were called to the scene. The cop said that Chandler dramatized himself. One is sure he did, although he never admitted it in print. He wanted to appear hard-bitten; the turmoil in his own soul was off limits; and his determination to keep it that way was the chief reason why he remained a writer of genre fiction despite the talent which always promised something else. Whether something else would necessarily have been something better is another question. Examining his own thought processes would have given him more to take in, but by temperament he was not particularly exploratory even when it came to the outside world, a less dangerous place: he was essentially one of those house-bound writers who take their ivory tower with them wherever they go, even into the underworld. A few months on the fringes of the low life gave him the atmospheric details for a whole career, as we can tell by the way they steadily go out of date when we read him through. In Hollywood he barely left the bungalow: he was right in the middle of the richest single subject America could present, but the thought of writing about it either never occurred to him or posed too great a challenge to his protective self-regard. Instead, sadly for both him and us, he wrote *for* Hollywood, fulfilling the requirements.

He did the same for his genre, except that he over-fulfilled them.

The thrill of his books was that they were so much better written than they needed to be. The thrill remains. I still go back to him: not for his stories, which despite their wilful complexity seem thinner all the time, but for the rightness of the metaphor, the balance of the sentence, the drive of the paragraph. If I had not already grown out of genre fiction when I started to read him, he would have helped me to. He was right about style – which is, after all, the only thing we take away from that warehouse of expendable fables we absorbed when we were young. The style *was* the substance. From all those hundreds of jobbing writers who give us their candy-flavoured fantasies, we synthesize an ideal of resonant narrative, and look for it again in the artists who give us reality. There could be a worse way in. Think what it would be like to be brought up on literature: neat gin through a rubber teat, and rump steak for pabulum.

2001

PRACTICALLY ART

SOULS ON ICE:
TORVILL AND DEAN

Tomorrow in Ottawa the World Championships commence in which Jayne Torvill and Christopher Dean will defend their ice-dance title for the last time, so this might not be the only article on the subject in today's newspapers. But it will be the only article on the subject written by someone whose own talent for ice-dancing is beyond question.

It was at Peterborough last year that I invented the difficult ice-dancing manoeuvre now generally known in the sport as 'landing on the money'. The rink was crowded and I was attempting to astonish my small daughter with sheer speed. Twenty-five years had gone by since I had last skated, but all the old style was still there – ankles touching the ice, nose level with the knees, arms flailing. Tripping over some young fool's trailing skate, I took off, sailed high, and fell with my body so perfectly arched that my upper thighs were the first part of it to hit the ice. The small change in my trouser pocket was driven through the flesh almost to the bone. The purple bruise could not only be seen for weeks afterwards, it could be read: ELIZABETH D. G. REG F. D. · 1976.

So what follows is essentially a tribute from a fellow-skater. But by now, however distinguished one's qualifications, there is no hope of attaining piercing new insights into the art of Torvill and Dean. A whole literature already exists. In addition to John Hennessy's excellent book *Torvill and Dean* (David and Charles, 1984) there are deeply researched magazine articles without number, down to and including *Family Circle*'s indispensable analysis of how Jayne cossets her dry skin, 'cleaning with RoC gentle milk and tonic and moisturising with Clinique'. All one can do, while quietly cosseting the embossed bruise on one's thigh, is to attempt a synthesis.

A big help in this department is a newly rush-released video called *Torvill and Dean: Path to Perfection* (Thames), which features all the glittering routines in which they have given us so much, plus several prime examples of the interviews in which they have very sensibly given us so little. Jayne's definition of the difference in character between Chris and herself is obviously the longest sentence she can, or at any rate wants to, utter. 'He panics and I don't.' The video thus reminds us directly of what the book and articles admit only by default: that these two speak a language beyond words.

Ice-dancing, until recent years, was barely respectable. Pairs skating, its snootier elder sister, was not only athletically more taxing but had an apparent monopoly of aesthetic clout. Indeed ice-dancing wasn't even an Olympic sport until 1976, by which time pairs skating was a full decade into the era pioneered by the Protopopovs, the Russian couple whose name sounded like a moped misfiring, but whose skating was so lyrical that you couldn't wait to see them again.

There was no problem about seeing them again because they won everything for years on end, but in fact the epoch they inaugurated had them as its apex. Ten years or so onward, another pair of Russians, Rodnina and Zaitsev, similarly creamed all opposition, but their awe-inspiring athleticism was no more lyrical than two mastiffs fighting on a flat-bed truck moving at 60 mph. Zaitsev was Rodnina's second partner and it was easy to believe rumours that she had eaten the first.

If anyone was going to top the Protopopovs it would have been two young Americans wonderfully called Tai Babilonia and Randy Gardner, but injury cut short their career. Even had it continued, they would have been obliged to expend much of their energy on aerobatics. That was and is, in too many senses of the word, the catch: in pairs skating the man lifts the woman up, drops her and catches her. Or he throws her away and she does three turns in the air before landing on one blade. Or three and a quarter turns before landing in the audience. In pairs skating the stunts are there for the doing and time spent on just looking beautiful costs points.

But while waiting in vain for the spirit of the Protopopovs to be reincarnated in the pairs skating, the dedicated voyeur gradually noticed that ice-dancing had outgrown its original jokey status. British couples had always been prominent in this branch of the sport but their approach, to the art-hungry eye, looked strictly *Come*

Dancing, with lots of hand-posing from both lady and gentleman, the catsuit-clad buttocks of the latter tending to be flagrantly salient. The Russians, once they put their collectivized minds to it, rapidly took over the rink, principally by fielding some sensational-looking women with long legs joined to short waists. The man's job was to show the woman off. Called something like Bustina Outalova, she was exuberance personified, obviously having been raised in a luxury one-room flat full of bootleg Beatles records.

Jazz and rock, still forbidden fruit for the Russian ballet dancers, were allowed for the ice-dancers, who, like the gymnasts, were judged to inhabit an idea-free realm in which Western influence was tolerable. Besides which, no Russian ice-dance couple ever dreamed of uncorking a hep-cat sequence of steps without following it up by a homage to the Soviet folk-dance tradition involving a lot of heel down, toe up, and arms folded. Anyone who has sat through an all-Soviet folk-dancing display in the Kremlin's Palace of Congresses knows how a single evening can seem like an entire five-year plan, but when the jollification took place on ice it was redeemed by bounce. Also the heel-kicking fervour of the quick bits favoured languor in the slow bits by way of contrast, with the world champions Moiseyeva and Minenkov looking particularly classy. Among their awed admirers in the late 1970s were the new young British couple from Nottingham, Torvill and Dean – he a policeman, she an insurance clerk, but they, in their double heart, already a single conduit of artistry.

Artistry was what they were after even in their first endeavours, although for a while it took a keen eye to spot it. They did well from the start, but with a lot of pace-changing razzle-dazzle like the Russians, while their costumes were still in the fine old British tradition of crotch-catcher catsuit for him and bumfreezer frilled frock for her. Their new trainer, Betty Callaway, was eventually to make all the difference, because she had the international connections which could secure for them what all artists demand by right – ideal conditions. But at the beginning the Callaway Connection manifested itself mainly in a comprehensive neatening up of what they could do already.

As research now shows, however, the two-person revolution was already under way. In 1981 Torvill and Dean became European and World Champions with what looked like a refined version of the conventional fast-slow-fast free dance programme, but with hindsight it wasn't a finished product so much as a whole new heap of raw material. Sandwiched between the usual bravura displays of quick footwork there was a smouldering rumba to 'Red Sails in the Sunset'. Here could already be seen some of the pay-off for the investment they had put in by taking instruction from Gideon Avrahami, a Ballet Rambert teacher who helped them make their arms and bodies part of the total picture.

The moment the pace dropped, Torvill and Dean looked different from any other couple. It was the same in the days of be-bop: playing flat out, the great names all sounded equally bewildering, but in the slow numbers Charlie Parker emerged as the unmistakable genius. You can dazzle people with technique, but you can't move them. Torvill and Dean's first all-conquering free dance programme was stunning in the fast bits, but in the slow bits it was better than that. The idea of making the whole thing slow, however, was still too daring, or too obvious, to be seriously entertained.

Torvill and Dean's big idea snuck up on them, and on the world, through the OSP – the Original Set Pattern. As the experienced watcher of television ice-dance competitions has long been aware, this necessary preliminary to the free dance not only counts for a high proportion of the total marks, it absorbs a high proportion of the total inventiveness. Torvill and Dean made this more true than ever, to the point where their OSP began regularly transmitting a unified aesthetic charge which their free dance couldn't match until the following year, if at all.

From 1981 onwards they were competing mainly against themselves, winning everything except the 1983 European Championships, from which they were forced to withdraw after a training accident in which Jayne fell flat on her back from shoulder height, with results even more painful than those engendered by the present writer's famous thigh-dive on to the bunched coins. But they competed with themselves the way artists do, growing impatient with the merely spectacular, pushing the original to extremes, joining the intensities together.

Their first fully-thought-through free dance was the 'Mack and Mabel' routine, using undoctored music from the show of the same name. Here was the embodiment of their new prosperity. The

Callaway Connection had by now won them a home-away-from-home in Oberstdorf, southern Bavaria, where they could get six hours' unhindered ice-time a day on three different rinks, one of them with mirrors. The Labour-controlled Nottingham City Council had imaginatively granted them four years' sustenance up to the 1984 Olympics. A few demented voices protested that they should therefore be training in Nottingham instead of Oberstdorf, but nobody sane wanted to see them condemned to the old, punishing, late-night sessions at the local rink. It wouldn't have been enough.

Their gold costumes, on the other hand, were too much. Poised to begin, they looked like two packets of Benson & Hedges cigarettes in a refrigerator. But if the colour was garish, the cut was a distinct improvement on days of old. Erstwhile champion ice-dancer Courtney Jones had taken command of their general appearance. Jayne's hem-lines were lower; contrariwise, her knickers were cut higher at the sides; the combined effect being a greater length of leg more decorously revealed.

Jayne is ten inches shorter than Chris and must stretch to match him on the long edges. She looks good doing so and never looked better than in the slow sections of 'Mack and Mabel'. There was a central, essentially T&D moment when she, after describing a wide circle using him as pivot, pulled him towards her as if her strength was temporarily in the ascendant. The fast sections featured comparably witty moments – there was a celebrated passage where she lay across his back doing little weightless steps sideways – but your attention was not allowed to linger. The emphasis was on breathtaking, not heart-touching.

In their slow blues OSP to 'Summertime', however, the pace was cut back to the limit the rules allowed. This wasn't dancing on ice – it was ice-dancing, a different thing. The tempo never varied but everything else did, with the movements forming an unbroken sequence which made you grateful that the rules said it must be repeated twice. Torvill and Dean, who admire Astaire and Rogers, with this routine achieved something comparable to the great Fred and Ginger dance duets in the RKO musicals of the 1930s. Dean, as Astaire was, is the innovator, and Torvill, as Rogers was, is the ideal partner, but a more instructive element of comparison is in the drive towards unity, a linking of highlights. Astaire simplified the photography until the whole routine could be filmed in one shot. Dean controlled the tempo so that there was no break in the emotional tension. Seeing the results, Fleet Street couldn't believe that Jayne and Chris were not in love. Even more unbelievable was that this miracle of compressed visual eloquence was being accompanied by the mouth organ of Larry Adler, regarded by many experts as the most verbose man in England.

Their free dance for 1982 was 'Barnum on Ice'. It was rabble-rousing stuff but struck at least one fan as several hundred intricate steps backwards. The tempo was mixed but that was only to be expected: an all-slow free dance was still inconceivable at that stage. What grated was the mime. Michael Crawford was brought in to advise on how to imitate jugglers, wire-walkers, etc. They did all this very well, but for those of us in the audience who had been brought up in film societies it aroused terrible memories of Marcel Marceau. Also it transferred the source of the action to the upper body, instead of leaving it where it belonged, in that mysterious space between the boots and the blades, the inch of air through which you can see the speeding ice. The speed is transformed upwards into beauty, which the hands can do a lot to express, but not when they are pretending to juggle.

The white and ice-blue costumes, though, were an improvement on the gold fag packets, and there was an increased use of rubato, with no fixed intervals between the two skaters – they were always catching each other up and passing, sinking only to rise, rising only to sink again. They made the stiff-backed Russian couples look like sentries. The face-freezing moment, once again in a slow section, was when she, stationary on the toe of one skate, leaned on him while he drew a circle of maximum radius around her. Wanting a whole routine of beauty-spots like that was probably like wanting a whole meal of desserts, but it was hard not to be wistful.

They granted the unspoken wish in double measure, with the *paso doble* OSP and the free dance to Ravel's *Boléro*. Each routine, in my opinion, is better than the other. The *paso doble* has a theme but it is not obtrusive. The 'Mack and Mabel' theme was a bit obtrusive because you had to know she was a comedienne; the 'Barnum' theme was very obtrusive because you had to know they were in a circus; but in the *paso doble* all you have to know is that she is not the matador's girlfriend, she is his cape. It is not hard to guess this because she is dressed in a cape, a crêpe creation carefully weighted so as to drape properly at all angles. In the properly draped crêpe cape, she is flung about by the strutting matador. The moment of truth comes when he, trailing her behind him, takes three enormous strides down the long axis of the rink, stops on one skate and goes backwards.

But the *paso doble* OSP was the same thing three times. The *Boléro* free dance is just the one thing, steadily developing all the way through, the tempo constant but the variations manifold, the full organic wow. Once again there is a theme – something about two lovers chucking themselves into a volcano – but you don't need to know the details. The opening sequence is enough to tell you that this is a story about two kids in trouble. They are running away from something. Perhaps it is their costume designer, who has gone mad with the blue paint. But no: the silk drapes lovingly, a big advance on the days when their outfits cost them every penny they didn't have.

If the camera is in the right spot – and it is, in the version recorded on the *Path to Perfection* tape – you see a delicious moment not long after the start, when they come towards you with his arms folded around her from behind. She is wrapped up in him, head bowed. Then she seems to wake, slowly spreading her arms wide, which opens his arms too, because they have been holding hands. While this is going on they are picking up speed. At such a moment, which turns out to be the precursor of an unbroken sequence of moments equally expressive, Torvill and Dean look like figments of a love-sick imagination.

But they would be the first to admit that it is all an illusion. Jayne has a nice face but it is Princess Anne's drawn by Charles Schulz. Chris, apart from his watchful eyes, has an indeterminate set of features betraying nothing of the immense physical strength with which he can wrap Jayne around his little finger while balancing on a metal edge not much bigger than the one he shaves with in the morning. Off the ice, they are beaten hollow by the average Russian couple: a rink-minx from Minsk toting a white mink muff, backed up by a tank commander built like Lenin's mausoleum. On the ice they are transfigured from within.

And appreciated from within. Everyone gets the point. The international judges showed little resistance to this new British monopoly – not even the Russian judge, whose marking had been a point of interest ever since the night he or she gave six for technical merit after Zaitsev dropped Rodnina on her bottom with a thump that cracked the rink. More interestingly, ordinary people everywhere spontaneously decided that these two were the straight goods. While I was preparing this article, two men cleaning my office window knocked on the glass and indicated that they would like me to screen the 'Summertime' routine all over again. It was evident that their head-shaking appreciation had no element of ogling. Only Fleet Street feels cheated at being left out of the secret of whether Torvill and Dean go to bed together. ('On St Valentine's morning,' wrote *The Times* correspondent from Sarajevo, 'Dean gave his partner an orchid. We cannot know of what it spoke.') Ordinary mortals, from the Queen to the window-cleaners, are responding to a deeper secret than that. Not many artists in any field can unite a nation.

And not even Torvill and Dean can do that for more than a few minutes. After the World Championships they will presumably turn professional; a move which has so far meant, for the great skaters, the loss of their grip on the public imagination. John Curry and Robin Cousins have mounted imaginative professional ice shows, but you have to go to see them – apart from the occasional television special, they don't come to you. Also it is hard to believe, despite frequent protestations from the newly wealthy ex-champions, that to be freed from the artificial restrictions of the sport is to be released into the untrammelled possibilities of art. More likely it is the sport's strict rules which provide the obstacles inspiration needs.

Torvill and Dean have level heads and will survive their success. Whether the sport will survive their success is another question. Women's figure skating never fully recovered after the reign of Peggy Fleming, who set a standard of expression which left everyone who came later straining for effect. The same applies to John Curry's impact on the men's figure skating, which Robin Cousins could reproduce but not exceed. As for what the Protopopovs did to the pairs skating, it was all summed up in one moment, when she floated towards him in an arabesque and he, with a flick of the fingers, sent her, her stately pace unchanging, all the way around in a slow wide circle and back to his extended hand. That, without leaving the ice, was as high as pairs skating ever went, although in the years to come every lady competitor learned to balance her pelvic girdle on the gentleman's upstretched finger and pretend to be an aeroplane, usually a MiG 21.

Which was why Torvill and Dean chose ice-dancing instead of pairs – because you didn't have to spend half the routine just gathering speed for a lift or a jump. But even in ice-dancing there might be a limit to expression. It is the fate of all the art-sports that the period in which they are more art than sport is restricted to a few years.

Only the innovator makes art, and the great innovator tends to exhaust the opportunities he creates. As Torvill and Dean rest in Oberstdorf before their final challenge, the rest of us are doomed to follow in their footsteps, of which the most memorable, surely, were those three long *paso doble* strides down the ice to stop on one skate. At Peterborough next Saturday afternoon I might try that myself, if my thigh is better.

Observer, 18 March, 1984

Postscript (i)

Scarcely was this piece irrevocably published before Bestemianova and Bukhin revealed themselves as Torvill and Dean's worthy successors, not just for technical merit but for artistic impression as well. I was, moreover, unwarrantedly deterministic about what happens to ice-skating after it turns professional. The following year, the World Professional Figure-Skating Championships were shown on television in Britain for the first, and so far only, time. It immediately became clear that the Protopopovs, to take only the most salient example, had in no way lessened their lifetime commitment to an art writ in water. If one is to age with dignity, on ice is no doubt the place to do it, but to do that and to create new beauty at the same time merits applause.

Snakecharmers in Texas, 1988

Postscript (ii)

To take the art-sports seriously was probably the most serious thing I ever did as a journalist, because it looked the most frivolous, and so, in those pre-post-modern times, could not be done without risk to the reputation. A cannier operator would have kept such enthusiasms for the pub. But I had always been impressed and con-soled by how the aesthetic thrill could turn up in unexpected places. All too often it hadn't turned up in the expected places – in almost the entirety of Schoenberg after *Verklärte Nacht*, for example – and although I tried to be confident about blaming the desert for being arid, there was always the chance that I should have been blaming myself for being stupid. From the art-sports I took heart. They proved that creativity is indivisible. The skaters, the divers and the gymnasts reminded me that what I read in books, saw in pictures and heard in music had all started in a fundamental human compulsion to give dynamism shape. If I had been blessed with a better gift for what I do, I would never have needed reminding. I would have seen the evidence every day, in that snow-boarding lout who nearly took my head off at Aspen, or a girl I knew in primary school who could skip salt-and-pepper backwards with her arms crossed. There are moments in Shakespeare when he sets three or four ideas all travelling at once through each other's trajectories. He couldn't have been thinking of Bach, who wasn't born yet. But he might well have been thinking of a juggler he stopped to watch on the way to work.

None of this means that the idea of a hierarchy of artistic achieve-ment is meaningless. It really is more important to listen to Beethoven's late quartets than to re-run your tape of Greg Louganis finding the most intricately beautiful way down from the tower to the water. But the two events are products of the same urge. There is no hierarchy of impulse, and although it is all too true that very few people can make art, they make it over a much wider range of activities than the doctrinaire aesthete would like to allow. Not to accept this awkward fact can be a killing restriction to criticism, which depends on discrimination in the second instance, but is lost without receptivity in the first. The bad critic is almost always the one who has no real aesthetic enthusiasms outside his field, and who has convinced himself that the artists inside his field felt the same way. But they didn't. They were interested in everything, even when they didn't appear to be.

2001

PICTURES IN SILVER

Camera Lucida: Reflections on Photography by Roland Barthes, translated by
Richard Howard, Jonathan Cape

The flow of photographic images from the past suggests that what
we are already experiencing as a deepening flood in the present
will seem, in the near future, like a terminal inundation. Most of
the theoretical works purporting to find some sort of pattern in the
cataract of pictures only increase the likelihood that we will lose our
grip. But occasionally a book makes sense of the uproar. Appearing
in the author's native language just before his death, Roland Barthes's
Camera Lucida, now published posthumously in English, will make
the reader sorrier than ever that this effervescent critic is no longer
among the living. Barthes was the inspiration of many a giftless tract
by his disciples but he himself was debarred by genuine critical talent
from finding any lasting value in mechanized schemes. By the end
of his life he seemed very keen to re-establish the personal, the
playful, and even the quirky at the centre of his intellectual effort,
perhaps because he had seen, among some of those who took his
earlier work as an example, how easily method can become madness.

Whatever the truth of that, here is a small but seductively argued
book which the grateful reader can place on the short shelf of truly
useful commentaries on photography, along with Walter Benjamin's
Das Kunstwerk im Zeitalter seiner technischen Reproduzierbarkeit,
Susan Sontag's *On Photography*, John Szarkowski's promotional
essays, and the critical articles of Janet Malcolm. Also asking for a
home on the same shelf is the recently published *Photography in
Print*, edited by Vicki Goldberg and including many of the best
shorter writings about photography from its first days to now. As
well as the expected, essential opinions of everyone from Fox Talbot

to Sontag, there are such out-of-the-way but closely relevant pieces as a reminiscence by Nadar which suggests that Balzac pre-empted Benjamin's idea about photographs robbing an object of its aura; a stunningly dull critique written by one Cuthbert Bode in 1855 which shows that photography has always generated, as well as a special enthusiasm, a special intensity of patronizing scorn; and a brilliantly turned *Hiawatha*-metre poem by that fervent shutterbug Lewis Carroll.

> From his shoulder Hiawatha
> Took the camera of rosewood
> Made of sliding, folding rosewood;
> Neatly put it all together.
> In its case it lay compactly,
> Folded into nearly nothing;
> But he opened out the hinges,
> Pushed and pulled the joints and hinges,
> Till it looked all squares and oblongs,
> Like a complicated figure
> In the second book of Euclid.

There is, of course, a much longer shelf, indeed a whole wall of long shelves, packed with commentaries which are not particularly wrong-headed. But they are platitudinous, and in the very short run it is the weight of unobjectionable but unremarkable accompanying prose which threatens to make a minor art boring. The major arts can stand the pressure.

Barthes at his best had a knack for timing the soufflé. The texture of *Camera Lucida* is light, making it suitable for a heavy message. The message is heavy enough to be called subversive. Barthes finds photography interesting, but not as art. An awful lot of would-be artists are going to be disappointed to hear this. But before they smash up their Nikons in frustration they should hear the argument through, because if Barthes is disinclined to treat photographers as artists he is uncommonly inclined to examine what they do with an intelligently selective eye. 'A photograph is always invisible,' he writes, 'it's not it that we see.' Barthes says that what we see is the subject matter: 'the referent adheres'. Barthes airily dismisses all talk of composition. Indeed he goes a long way towards saying that a photograph hasn't got any formal element worth bothering about. He claims for himself, where photography is concerned, 'a desperate resistance to any reductive system' – pretty cool, when you consider the number and aridity of reductive systems his example has given rise to.

Barthes says that what he brings to the average photograph is *studium* – general curiosity. What leaps out of the exceptional photograph is a *punctum* – a point of interest. In Kertész's 1926 portrait of Tristan Tzara (unfortunately not reproduced in this book), the *studium*, says Barthes, might have to do with a Dadaist having his picture taken but the *punctum* is his dirty fingernails. In William Klein's photograph, 'Near the Bowery' (1954), you and I might have our attention drawn by the toy gun held to the smiling boy's head, especially if the scene arouses an echo of the Viet Cong prisoner being summarily executed in one of the most famous pieces of news film footage to have come out of Vietnam. But Barthes can't help noticing the little boy's bad teeth. Barthes is not always startled by what the photographer finds startling and is never startled by what the photographer rigs to be startling – abstract and surrealist concoctions leave him cold.

A photograph, says Barthes, does not nostalgically call up the past. Instead it shows the past was real, like now. Photography proves the past to be a reality we can no longer touch. Instead of the solace of nostalgia, the bitterness of separation. Photography is powerless as art but potent as magic. Thus his little book concludes as it began, with a confident emphasis on subject matter.

When John Szarkowski, in his 1966 critical anthology *The Photographer's Eye*, showed that for every master photographer's laboriously created definitive statement there was at least one amateur snapshot equally interesting, the photographic world had the choice of inferring either that the artists weren't artistic or else that the amateurs were artistic too. On the whole the latter course was taken, mainly because Szarkowski so persuasively extended the range of what it was possible to discuss about a photograph, so that the mere business of selecting what to shoot stood revealed for what it is – an artistic choice at some level, however diffident.

Similarly Barthes's potentially devastating re-emphasis is mollified by his willingness to concede that the selectivity involved is not just his own unusually receptive eye for the *punctum*. The photographer is allowed the faculty of selectivity too. Barthes does not seem to allow even the best photographer much more, but perhaps he just never got around to developing his argument, which nevertheless is an attractive one as it stands. If one famous American classical photographer's photograph of trees has ever worried you by looking indistinguishable from another famous American classical photographer's photograph of trees, here is a way out of your dilemma. The identity of subject matter tends to render the alleged compositional and tonal subtleties nugatory in each case. There is no reason to feel guilty just because we have got one of the Westons mixed up with one of the others.

The composition of a photograph can be analysed usefully, but not as long as it can be analysed uselessly. As with a literary work, there is a line to be drawn between the critical remark that yields meaning and the analytical rigmarole which tells you little beyond the fact that some ambitious young academic has time on his hands. Barthes's thesis is a refreshing simplification. But a fresh look doesn't always simplify. In *Before Photography: Painting and the Invention of Photography*, the catalogue for the Museum of Modern Art exhibition which will next be seen in Los Angeles and Chicago, Peter Galassi cunningly advances the deceptively simple thesis that some paintings prepared the way for the invention of photography by manifesting 'a new and fundamentally modern pictorial syntax of immediate, synoptic perceptions and discontinuous, unexpected forms'.

Galassi's argument has already been examined at some length by Charles Rosen and Henri Zerner. I will not rehearse their analysis beyond saying that they find Mr Galassi's achievement as impressive as I do. They argue that Mr Galassi gives an incomplete account of perspective. Galassi says that over the centuries the original pictorial strategy, to make a three-dimensional world out of a flat medium, gradually reversed itself, and became the new pictorial strategy of making a flat picture out of a three-dimensional world – at which point photography, which might have been invented much earlier if anyone had really wanted it, finally showed up in order to answer the new need. Rosen and Zerner recommend that Galassi should take into account the implications of the empirical representation developed by the fifteenth-century Flemish painters. No doubt they are right, but I can think of someone else who might fit Galassi's theory even more instructively – Velázquez.

As Ortega explains in *The Dehumanisation of Art*, Velázquez was the first to look into the distance with a dilated pupil and so blur the focus of things near. That is why foreground figures in some of his pictures – one thinks particularly of 'Las Meninas' – look so strange. They are strange because they are the unexamined familiar. They look the way things look when we are looking past them, as if they were floating, *converdidas en gases cromáticos, en flámulas informes, en puros reflejos.* Converted into chromatic gases, into formless flames, into pure reflections. (Ortega's writings on aesthetics are so poetic that they constitute an aesthetic problem in themselves.)

Unless I have got it hopelessly wrong, Ortega uncovered in Velázquez a concern with focus and depth of field which presages just those aspects of the photographic vision. No doubt Velázquez developed these perceptions out of a desire to mimic how the eye actually sees, but Galassi seems to be saying that the photographic pictorial strategy developed out of just that impulse, away from conceptual ordering and towards the randomly inclusive. Ortega, who said that you could see a Velázquez in one gulp, even has a vocabulary that seems ready-made for Galassi's thesis. Ortega says that the closely focused analytic vision is feudal and that the distantly focused, synthetic vision is democratic.

Doubtless other readers of Galassi's essay will have their own ideas, not just because his argument is the kind that makes us recognize something we already suspected, but because so many of us have a head full of references. By now Malraux's *musée imaginaire,* the Museum Without Walls, has transferred itself from books of reproductions into our own skulls. But a brain which already has a few hundred of the world's great paintings arranged inside it is likely to panic when asked to take in several thousand of the world's putatively great photographs as well. Yet we can retain the notion of the photographer as artist without feeling obliged to accept his every creation as a work of art.

By and large that is what John Szarkowski does in his excellent introductory essay to *The Work of Atget,* Vol. 1: *Old France,* the magnificently produced and highly desirable catalogue volume for the first of what will be four Museum of Modern Art exhibitions devoted to Atget's work, the cycle being due to complete itself in 1984. The material will take a long time to show and took even longer to get ready. Berenice Abbott gave the museum her collection of about 5,000 Atget prints in 1968. Maria Morris Hambourg, Szarkowski's co-scholar on the project, has been occupied with nothing else since

1976. Together they have performed prodigies of research, but one expects no less. Less predictable was the way Szarkowski, while diving around among all this visual wealth like Scrooge McDuck in Money Barn No. 64, has managed to keep his critical balance, something that a man with his capacity for enthusiasm does not always find easy.

Echoing the useful distinction he established in 1966 between documentary and self-expression, Szarkowski is able to divide Atget's work up into the large number of photographs which are of historical interest and the smaller number in which the historical interest is somehow ignited into an aesthetic moment – in which, that is to say, the *studium* acquires a *punctum*. But the viewer who finds his attention not only attracted but delighted by some of these pictures will be hard pressed to decide where the *punctum* is. Is it in the plough or the well, the overhanging tree or the doorway in the wall?

It soon becomes clear that the best of Atget's photographs, while they are unlikely to hold your interest as long as paintings might do that are nominally of the same subject, nevertheless owe their aesthetic authority to much more than an isolated piquancy. They really do imply some kind of controlling artistic personality, however attenuated. The notion of *punctum*, while necessary and welcome, is too limited a critical criterion to be sufficient. On the other hand, Barthes's other and larger notion, the one about the thereness of the past and the lost reality which rules out nostalgia, is underlined with full force. Leaving aside the soft tones of the albumen process, here is Old France looking close enough to touch and as irrecoverable as the Garden of Eden – an effect only increased by Atget's reluctance to include human beings even when the exposure time would have allowed it.

On a smaller scale but still good to have, *The Autochromes of J. H. Lartigue* shows us an unfamiliar side of another indisputable artist – his work in colour. The autochrome process has the effect, when the prints are reproduced today, of making everything look like a pointilliste painting. Since Lartigue's sensibility was so like Seurat's anyway, the echo effect is often uncanny, but in fact Lartigue was no more likely than his predecessor Atget to ape painting. In his late teens when he started shooting autochromes, he kept it up from 1912 to 1927. The best surviving results are given here, prefaced by a typically charming interview with the master himself.

It is a small book but makes a substantial supplement to his indispensable *Diary of a Century*, which chronicles his work in black and white and proves him to have been the first great lyrical celebrator of human beings at play. In black and white the relatively short exposure time enabled him to capture movement. In autochrome he couldn't do that, but his joyous personality still comes bubbling through. He had an inexhaustible supply of pretty girl acquaintances trying out new scooters, dashing brothers who built flying machines, etc. Perhaps other photographers were similarly blessed, but Lartigue knew exactly what to include in the frame and when to press the button or squeeze the bulb. Highly endowed with a knack for what Cartier-Bresson was later to call the guess, Lartigue could see a *punctum* a mile off. He could see *puncta* in clusters. In other words, he had a self to express.

As time increases the total number of photographers and it becomes increasingly obvious that there is no room for all of them to express themselves, it may become permissible to suggest that documentary interest is a sufficiently respectable interest for a photographer's work to have, and that if a photographer can go on getting good documentary results for a long time then he is artist enough. To have such a point conceded would make it easier to save some of the masterly but less than outstanding photographers of the past from an otherwise inevitable public revulsion against the indigestibly strident claims made for their seriousness.

The Photography of Max Yavno, for example, is a book well worth having. Yavno has been taking thoughtful photographs since the 1930s. Not all of them are as striking as his famous 1947 picture of the San Francisco cable car being swung on the turntable by its balletically swaying attendants. The picture adorns the jacket of this book, is superbly reproduced in a plate within, and features in just about every anthology of photographs published in the last thirty years. It should be possible to allow a man a few such happily sought-out and taken chances without trying to find the same significance in the rest of his work, which the law of averages dictates will be more *studium* than *punctum*. Luckily, the mandatory prose-poem captions (once again it is hard to suppress a blasphemous twinge of regret that James Agee and Walker Evans ever got together) are largely offset by an appended interview with Yavno in which he reveals himself to be admirably, indeed monosyllabically, unpretentious.

Except when generously reminiscing about his fellow veteran prac-
titioners, he keeps things on the yep-nope level, Gary Cooper style.

Much the same applies to *Feininger's Chicago 1941*, in which
Andreas Feininger, in a lively introduction written forty years later,
keeps his ego perhaps excessively within bounds. Forgetting to inform
us that he was a Bauhaus-trained intellectual who personally invented
the super-telephoto camera, Feininger gives humble thanks that he
was obliged to view Chicago with the fresh eye of the displaced
European. Here are parking elevators at a time when cars were just
about to lose their running-boards, Union and Dearborn stations
when the silver trains still ran, Lake Shore Drive before Mies van der
Rohe built his apartments, and the kind of skyscraper that Stalin
copied and that now exists nowhere except in the Soviet Union.
Feininger presents his lost city without any accompanying verbal
elegies.

The Weston family tends to be less taciturn. *Cole Weston: Eighteen
Photographs* enshrines the colour work of one of Edward Weston's
sons. Like Brett Weston, another son, Cole seems to have inherited
from his father a deep sense of mission. As is recounted in Charis
Wilson's introduction to this volume, Edward Weston had Parkinson's
disease and young Cole had to help him work the camera. It's like
reading about Renoir *père et fils* – an apostolic succession. On the
other hand it is not like that, since the painter and the film-maker
each had a separate, fully developed artistic vision which makes their
blood kinship remarkable, whereas one suspects that for photography
to run in the family is no more startling than for carpentry to run
in the family, as a craft to be learned rather than an inner impulse
to be bodied forth. Nonetheless, here are sumptuous colour prints
of California surf, Nova Scotia fishing coves, Utah aspens, and similar
Americana. A close-up of rust on a water tank looks like abstract
expressionism, showing that painting still has its pull despite all the
disclaimers. Also a nude lady seen from the same angle as the Rokeby
Venus reclines on an old stone staircase in Arizona. She looks exactly
like a confession that the staircase would not be very interesting
without her.

Cole and Brett Weston take you back to Edward Weston, to
Paul Strand, to Minor White, to Ansel Adams – to every master
photographer, in fact, who has ever gone out into the American
landscape and tried to isolate a clean piece of nature within his metal

frame. Some of the results are collected in *American Photographers and the National Parks*, edited by Robert Cahn and Robert Glenn Ketchum. The pictures are arranged chronologically, starting with a William Henry Jackson study of Yosemite Falls in 1898. Jackson got a terrific action shot, in colour, of the Yellowstone Great Geyser in 1902. Edward Weston's Zabriskie Point picture of 1938 reminds you of just how good the old man was at waiting for the right shadows. The Ansel Adams pictures will be familiar to most readers but still stand out. They don't stand out so far, though, as to convince you that subject matter is anything less than very important. Even for Adams, to pursue too closely the light patterns on a cactus was to court inanity. In Barthes's terms, the referent adheres. If it doesn't, you've got nothing.

Adams deserves our lasting respect for the reverent skill with which he photographed a mountain, even though a modern amateur with up-to-date equipment might fluke a picture not entirely risible by comparison. After all, Adams knew what he was doing, and could do it again. So could Paul Strand when taking pictures of clapboard houses. Nevertheless *New England Reflections, 1882–1907* features, among other things, enough clapboard houses, photographed with more than enough verve, to set you wondering whether that particular form of architecture ever needed Paul Strand to bring out its full beauty. All the pictures were taken by the three Howes brothers, who formed themselves into a commercial outfit and toted their tripods around New England persuading people, obviously with profitable results, that great moments in life should be permanently recorded. The glass-plate negatives having miraculously survived to our own day, here is the permanent record. It is a fascinating little book which Richard Wilbur honours with a foreword that you might wish were longer, since Wilbur's distinguished, visually fastidious sensibility is exactly what such material requires to give it a proper context. But Gerald McFarland provides a useful historical introduction and anyway the pictures are so rich themselves that you would be drowning in *puncta* even if you didn't know where and when they came from.

All seems in order, even the home for the handicapped, whose inmates have formed up for a serene group shot as if Diane Arbus did not exist – which, of course, she as yet didn't. Here is the irrecoverable past only a few inches away. Some of the buildings are still intact, so that inhabitants of New England who buy this book will be able to stand in the right spot and look through time. Paradoxically, the Howes brothers were just going about their everyday business, with not much thought of preserving a threatened heritage, whereas Atget, who had a Balzacian urge to register his epoch, saw much of what he photographed destroyed within his lifetime, and if he were to come back now would find almost nothing left.

If a photographer wants to express himself but fears that his personal view might be short on originality, originality of subject matter is one way out of the trap. The only drawback to this escape route is that the number of subjects, if not finite, is certainly coterminous with the known universe. Already most topics are starting to look used up. In *Man as Art: New Guinea*, Malcolm Kirk has persuaded an impressive number of New Guinea natives to pose in full warlike and/or ceremonial make-up and drag. Thus we are able to observe, in plate 74, that a Western Highlands warrior male called Nigel resembles, when fully attired for battle, Allen Ginsberg in blackface with a Las Vegas hotel sign on his head.

Some of the pictures are stunning, or at least startling, but there is no denying that the natives have shown at least as much invention as the photographer, whose skill in lighting them and pressing the button can scarcely be compared to theirs in caking their skins with clay, inserting bones in their noses, and pulling on their grass skirts. Nor, more damagingly, is there any denying that we have already seen most of this in the *National Geographic*, albeit on a smaller scale. Much of the justification for these big picture books is that they give you big pictures, but there is also the consideration that what looks appropriately dramatic when bled to the edges of a full page in a magazine starts looking emptily pretentious when pumped up to folio size. Not only is it bigger than the negative, it's bigger than the reality. In real life you would learn all you need to know about Nigel without going quite so close.

Still on the *National Geographic* beat, *Rajasthan: India's Enchanted Land* comprises pictures by Raghubir Singh which suggest that its title might not be a complete misnomer, although for at least this viewer the *puncta* which are obviously meant to be bursting out of such a picture as 'A Gujar Villager, Pushkar' remain defiantly quiescent. Far from being amazed that a man with a turban is wearing a watch and smoking a cigarette, I'd be amazed if he were not. More exciting, or less unexciting, is another shot in which all the village males, after a hard day's work supervising the women, are rewarding themselves by sucking popsicles. There is a foreword by Satyajit Ray to remind us that for Indian artists of all kinds Rajasthan is a fairly resonant part of the subcontinent, but you can see how a foreign photographer with a reputation to make might want a more jazzy angle.

In *Falkland Road, Prostitutes of Bombay,* Mary Ellen Mark shows how this can be done. She moved in with the eponymous hookers, became part of the scenery, and ended up by reaching such a level of acceptance that the girls and their clients allowed her to photograph them *in flagrante.* The results are unlikely to put you off sex, with which the activities in Falkland Road seem to have only a parodic connection, but they might well put you off India. The girls work in cubicles the size of packing crates and perform their ablutions in a bucket. Hepatitis hangs in the air like aerosol spray. For the alert customer the whole deal would be a bit of a downer even if Ms Mark were not poised in the rafters busily snapping the action. The intrepid photographer contributes her own introduction, in which she spends a lot of time conveying her deep affection for the girls without ever raising the topic of whether she, too, might not be said to be drawing sustenance from the sad traffic, and in a much safer way. Still, Cartier-Bresson photographed whores in Mexico in 1934.

Already responsible for nine books, Ms Mark was born in 1940 and graduated from the University of Pennsylvania. Susan Meiselas, author of *Nicaragua,* is a Sarah Lawrence graduate who does not give her age but can safely be adjudged even younger than Ms Mark. Both women are getting well known fast, not because either of them is Giselle Freund or Lotte Jacobi reborn but because they both know how to get in and get the story. Ms Meiselas's story is the Nicaraguan version of with-Fidel-in-the-Sierra, down to and including the berets, Che moustaches, and .45 automatics triumphantly raised in adolescent fists. 'Yet unlike most photographs of such material,' says an accompanying note from John Berger, 'these refuse all the rhetoric normally associated with such pictures.' Not for the first time one wonders how Berger, inventor of the purportedly illuminating concept 'ways of seeing', actually does see. His eyes certainly work differently from mine, which find Ms Meiselas's every second picture laden with rhetoric. But despite more recent reports from Nicaragua, one concedes that the rhetoric might be, in this case, on the side of the angels. Nor can it be gainsaid that people calling on themselves to be courageous often behave rhetorically. Who looks natural when nerving himself for battle?

Photographs, according to Barthes, never entirely leave the world of words. In *Visions of China* Marc Riboud's photographs taken between 1957 and 1980 constitute, even more than Eve Arnold's recent volume on the same subject, a reminder that if we know nothing about the background we might well make a hash of interpreting the foreground. Orville Schell's introduction makes much of Riboud's supposed ability to see past the rhetoric to the reality beneath. Certainly Riboud got off the beaten track and managed to hint that not all was harmony, but it should not need saying – and yet it does – that he got nowhere near recording the full impact of the Cultural Revolution, which we were allowed to see nothing of in the form of pictures and have since had to hear about in the form of words. Most of these words were emitted between sobs, since those victims who survived are often unable to recall their sufferings with equanimity.

This fact should lend additional significance to such a photograph as plate 89, 'Student Dancer, Shanghai, 1971'. It shows a radiantly happy girl being inspired by the mere presence of Mao's little red book. But in this case the *punctum*, instead of crossing from the photograph to the viewer's mind, travels in the other direction. Today's viewer will have heard that the Chinese ballerinas were sent by Mrs Mao to have their muscles ruined in the fields. The dancers were already suffering at the time when Shirley MacLaine, a dancer herself, was wondering, in her television documentary about China, why the Chinese looked so happy. The viewer haunted by these considerations is unlikely to look on Riboud's photograph of a Chinese dancer as being anything more edifying than a pretty picture.

But where any pictures are hard to get, all pictures have some value, even if they seem to point in the wrong direction until interpreted. So it is with China and so it will probably always be with the Soviet Union. Vladimir Sichov's *The Russians* deserves immediate notice, since the standard of photography in the Soviet Union is so blandly low that any attempt at realism looks like a sunburst. Sichov was born in 1945 and in 1979 was permitted to leave for the West. He brought 5,000 rolls of film out safely – his whole archive. The full effect is of a dowdiness so comprehensive that it becomes almost enthralling. Unfortunately Sichov seems to have concentrated on the routine dowdiness of old women in shapeless coats rather than the more interesting dowdiness of young ones in the latest fashions from GUM. The true visual squalor in the Soviet Union resides in what is thought to be chic, a fact which Sichov has subsequently had ample opportunity to realize, because he is nowadays an ace catwalk photographer for the Paris fashion shows, a task to which he brings the hungry eye of a man raised during a famine. Photographers brought up on a visual diet in which swimsuits look as if they have been cut out of motel shower curtains tend to be especially grateful for what Yves Saint-Laurent hangs on Jerry Hall.

William Klein makes America look almost as scruffy as Russia but in the case of his collection *William Klein* much of the flakiness is due to inky printing. Klein has issued a protest about how his publishers have treated him and if later copies look like my early copy then he is right. Some of the pictures look like action shots of a black cat in a coal bunker. In the ones you can see, however, *puncta* proliferate. The snap Barthes liked of the little boy with the toy gun to his head is here spread over two pages, making the bad teeth more attention-getting than ever. But most viewers will probably still take the gun, rather than the teeth, to be the main point. Mainly because he runs forward to involve himself instead of hanging back to be objective, Klein is very good at catching the vivid moment. There are also pictures taken in Italy, Russia, and elsewhere, but really Manhattan, where he was born, is Klein's precinct. He can see the casual calligraphic symmetry of window signs offering breaded veal cutlets for $1.05. So could every American urban photographer back to Weegee and beyond, but the thereness never fails to grip.

More involved even than Klein, more involved even than Hemingway, almost as involved as the soldiers themselves, Don McCullin gets his camera into the war. An Englishman, McCullin started by photographing his own country's dark underside, but he was not alone. Covering Cyprus in 1964 he discovered his own bailiwick, up where the bullets were flying. Since then he has been in all the wars, most notably Vietnam, where his work was on a par with that of Philip Jones Griffiths. But his eye is not so spoiled by the adrenalin of action that it refrains from dwelling on the aftermath. Dead soldiers in every variety of contortion and civilians in every stage of starvation are duly recorded.

Scanning the worst of McCullin's horrors, you find yourself wishing that Barthes were less right about the past really having been there. But anyone not capable of realizing that these things happen will not be much struck by the photographs anyway, so John Le Carré's introductory exhortations about McCullin's mission to 'appall the comfortable' are themselves somewhat cosy. It is a characteristic of the English intellectual middle class to believe that the mass of the public is uninstructed in the world's grim realities and needs waking up. McCullin is too bravely independent to share so smug an attitude but it has helped make him famous – the most dazzling current example of the photographer singled out by subject.

Not many photographers would have the nerve to follow reality as far as McCullin does in search of their own territory, even supposing that there were any territory left. The alternative has always been to take the reality nearby and fiddle with it. By now I think it is becoming clear that for photographers abstraction and surrealism are a dry well, partly because, *pace* Galassi, painting always seems to exert at least as strong a pull on photography as photography does on painting. The moment the photographer starts treating the objects of experience symbolically, the referent ceases to adhere, and what he composes gravitates seemingly inexorably towards something already made familiar by the painters.

Herbert List: Photographs 1930–1970 collects the best work of a photographer with an impressive intellectual background. Trained by Andreas Feininger, List consorted with the visiting English writers in the Germany of the early 1930s and after leaving Germany in 1936 he became the leading purveyor of surrealist-tinged photographs to the slick magazines. But in this collection it is precisely the portrait photography which looks permanent and the surrealist compositions which seem to have been overtaken by time. Barthes should give us the courage to confess our difficulties about getting interested in the artificially arranged *punctum*.

Most of List's cleanly lit and composed surrealist confections flare to life only when they include a couple of strapping young men standing around in G-strings. Immediately you get interested in the life going on off camera. Stephen Spender evokes some of it in the introduction, which like everything he writes about the Germany of the time makes you sorry not to have been there. He is much better than Isherwood at giving you some idea of the mental excitement. Isherwood, even today, concentrates on the physical excitement.

Drawing on their memories, writers can pursue their own tastes into old age. For photographers it is not so easy. List gave up after the war, feeling that once he had explored the limits of his own technique he was through as an artist, always supposing he had ever been one. Some of the portraits are good enough to make you think he judged himself too harshly, but there is no getting away from the fact that even with them the interest resides at least partly in the identity of the sitter. It is Morandi, Cocteau, Bérard, Chirico, Picasso, Montherlant, Auden, and Somerset Maugham who lend List renown, and not vice versa.

Anyone who finds it hard wholly to admire List is going to make heavy weather of admiring Robert Rauschenberg. *Robert Rauschenberg Photographs* shows what he has been up to in a medium to which he is not new, since he started off as a photographer. Having achieved fame, and presumably fulfilment, as a painter, he has recently revisited his first passion.

Rauschenberg's chief trick in any medium is to juxtapose ready-made images. I can remember wondering, when I saw his exhibition of paintings at the Whitechapel Gallery in the East End of London in the early 1960s, why he didn't juxtapose them more tightly, suggestively – in a word, wittily. I liked what he was doing but didn't think he took it any distance, and resented the suggestion, made on his behalf by eager commentators, that the grubby white space left in each of his large canvases was meant to give my own imagination room to work. My own imagination was already *at* work, wondering how much of Rauschenberg's allegedly selective creativity was doodling.

All the same doubts go double here, where there are not even a few swipes of paint to indicate personal intervention. In plate 45 a Mona Lisa tea-towel hangs over the back of a canvas chair which is also variously draped and decorated with discarded clothes and a folded newspaper. If you buy the theory that a pure response to the Mona Lisa is no longer possible, here is food for thought. But for anyone to whom the Mona Lisa is still the Mona Lisa whatever happens, the inevitable reaction is a fervent wish that Rauschenberg would paint his own pictures and leave Leonardo's alone.

'So what?' is not necessarily a philistine reaction. Sometimes it is required for the preservation of sanity, especially when one is presented with the intentionally meaningless and told to find it meaningful. John Pfahl's *Altered Landscapes* shows us how a competent photographer can beautifully photograph landscapes in the same way as any other equally competent photographer can beautifully photograph landscapes, but pick up extra, reputation-making acclaim by 'altering' them, hence the title. A picture taken in Monument Valley includes a piece of red string squiggling along the ground, which enables it to be called 'Monument Valley with Red String'. Some of the pictures generate a sufficient frisson to make record album covers. Rock groups with metaphysical proclivities often favour the sort of album covers in which a line of large coloured spheres marches across the Sahara: altered landscapes for altered states.

Sam Haskins, it hardly needs saying, is better than competent, especially when photographing pretty young girls, for whom he has a hawk eye. But *Sam Haskins/Photo graphics* reveals a desire to be something more than the kind of craftsman whose output the uninitiated might mistake for soft porn. The term 'photo graphics' calls up Moholy-Nagy's photograms. Think of a Moholy photogram, add colour, focus the composition on the exquisitely lit, plumply swelling pantie-cupped crotch of a young girl lying back thinking pure thoughts about a sky full of roses, and you've got a Haskins photo graphic. You have to take it on trust that the picture bears no relation to a hot paragraph by Terry Southern. This is a meticulously produced book by whose technical accomplishment Haskins's fellow-photographers will no doubt be suitably cowed, but the sceptical viewer could be excused for wondering whether a picture of a rainbow shining out of a pretty girl's behind might not be a more direct indication of the artist's state of mind than the circumambient surrealist trappings.

With *Bill Brandt: Nudes 1945–1980* we are in another, less ambiguous, part of the forest. The model and inspiration for the young British photographers of the 1960s, the one home-grown loner they could admire without reserve, Brandt dedicated his career to photographing Woman in a way that would resolve her sensual appeal into a formal design. Hiding the lady's face and applying every device of elongation, distortion, and convolution, he pushed the formal design towards the abstract. But it approached the abstract

asymptotically, as if Brandt were aware that when the referent ceased
to adhere the result would be not just no woman but no anything.

Brandt's hermetic commitment cost him a great deal and won
him deserved admiration. Looking at these pictures, even the most
clueless viewer will sense himself in the presence of a rare concentration of thought and feeling. But it is still possible to say, I think,
that in treating the human body as a sculptural form Brandt was
unable to avoid the gravitational pull of sculpture itself. Warm
bottoms become cold Brancusis. Hips turn into Arps. Finally, in his
most recent phase, Brandt unexpectedly and shockingly starts to load
his nudes down with ropes and chains, as if it were his new ambition
to take a studio on Forty-second Street or set up in partnership with
Helmut Newton. It looks like a despairing confession that whereas a
painter can significantly change the woman in front of him and
make her part of something more significant, a photographer can't
significantly change her without destroying her significance altogether. But with all that said, nobody should mistake this book for
anything less than the work of a unique isolated master photographer.

In the long run the photographers who glorified women individually, rather than rendering them all symbolically impersonal, stood a
better chance of being called artists. The Hollywood portrait photographers rarely thought of themselves as much more than craftsmen,
but John Kobal's essential book *The Art of the Great Hollywood
Portrait Photographers* has no doubt given the survivors a higher, and
well-merited, estimation of themselves. Likewise assembled by Kobal
from his unrivalled archive, *Hollywood Color Portraits* is the colour
supplement to the black-and-white standard work. Less weighty than
its predecessor, it is still well worth having. Not only was colour less
adaptable than black and white to subtle lighting; it was also much
harder to retouch, so in this book you see some of the stars as they
really looked, right down to the enlarged pores and – in Burt Lancaster's case – the five o'clock shadow of Nixonite tenacity.

Theories of the hunger towards realism suffer a setback when
faced with this order of evidence. Black and white was the ideal,
colour was the real, and the ideal looked realer. Bob Coburn's colour
picture of Rita Hayworth in 1948 is just a pretty girl. 'Whitey'
Schaefer's 1941 black-and-white portrait of her is an angelic visitation. Yet surely the black and white is the more true to the way she
was. Not many of us who are grateful for her talent can look at such

a photograph without feeling the bitterness of the irrecoverable reality that Barthes talks about. There was a day when supreme personal beauty was impossible to capture fully and so could fade without its possessor being too forcibly reminded of its loss. That time is past – one certain way, among all the conjectural ones, in which photography has changed the world.

For reasons of space and self-preservation I have had to leave many current books out of this survey. Nor are all the books I have included likely to prove essential in the long run. But *A Century of Japanese Photography* I can confidently recommend to any institution concerned with photography and to any person who can afford the price. Compiled in Japan and presented for Western consumption by John W. Dower, the book is a treasure city, a Kyoto of the printed image. Barthes would have been so shot through with *puncta* that he would have felt like Saint Sebastian, or Toshiro Mifune in the climactic scene of *Throne of Blood*. Peter Galassi will find his theory simultaneously borne out and borne away, since so much of Japanese painting led up to photography (what else did Hiroshige and Hokusai do with their winter landscapes but bleach out the inessential?) and so many of the Japanese master photographers are drawn back into the established pictorial tradition.

Since the Meiji restoration the Japanese have been photographing one another and the inhabitants of every country they have invaded. They seem rarely to have decapitated anyone without getting some carefully framed before-and-after shots. The level of violence in the book is made even more terrifying by the degree of delicacy. You feel that you are at a tea ceremony with Mishima and that he might behead you and disembowel himself at any moment and in either order.

The photographs of war put McCullin's work in its proper perspective. McCullin might be trying to awaken our dormant psyches but for the Japanese the gap between everyday tranquillity and stark horror seems always to have been only a step wide. And just as readily as they photographed the violence they inflicted, they photographed the violence inflicted on them. Elegantly judged, Pompeii-like photographs of the charred bodies after the Tokyo fire raids may be edifyingly compared with similar studies obtained in Nagasaki and Hiroshima. Proudly saluting from the cockpit, a kamikaze pilot taxis past a class of schoolgirls waving cherry branches in farewell. Words are needed to tell us where he is flying to, but once we know that, the picture tells us that he was there. Probably some of the schoolgirls are still alive and can pick themselves out in the picture. They were there too. Reality is the *donnée* of photography and sets the limit for how much the photographer can transform what he sees into a personal creation. For the artist photographer the limit is high but it still exists. To think it can be transcended is to be like Kant's dove, which, upon being told about air resistance, thought it could fly faster by abolishing the air.

New York Review of Books, 17 December, 1981: previously included in
Snakecharmers in Texas, 1988

Postscript

Like writing about television, writing about photography was a chance to talk about everything. If someone had taken a photograph in China, I could talk about China. Doing a roundup of all the world's books about photography in the past and present, I could go on for pages about time, space and the history of the world. But I couldn't go on for long about photography itself, because apart from the technicalities there isn't much to discuss, and criticism based solely on technicalities is doomed to famine. It can sound impressive, but so can an actor pretending to be a doctor. The specialist photography magazines are full of articles specifying shutter speed, focal length and what have you. No doubt it all means a lot to the adept, but it leaves the layman facing the same void as he always does when an aesthetic event is discussed in mechanical terms. A solo by Darcey Bussell, for example, can be registered on the page as a set of steps and poses with French names. Unfortunately every member of the *corps de ballet* can do them too. So the writer has evoked precisely nothing. In the case of photography the problem is exacerbated by the remorseless industrial effort to get all the relevant expertise into the camera itself, and out of the fallible hands of the goof holding it. There is indeed a miracle of creativity involved, but it is all inside the mechanism: more than a hundred and fifty years of intense technical development, none of which, if it were all forgotten tomorrow, even the most gifted photographer could begin to recapitulate.

Making a television programme about a safari in Kenya, I was supplied by my producers with the very latest Nikon. All I had to do was point it and twist the bit that stuck out until something I could see through the little window was in focus – anything. I can't even remember if I had to press a button. Perhaps it pressed its own button and told me afterwards. Anyway, I got a close-up of an angry lion's face. The lion was angry because the car I was in woke it up, and some idiot human sticking out of the top of the car was pointing a sinister-looking box of tricks at it. When the photograph came back from the chemist's, I was as open-mouthed as the lion. Cartier-Bresson would have swallowed his hyphen with envy. The photograph was as sharp as a tack, impressive as the crack of doom, frightening to chill the mind. It could have gone straight into a glossy magazine, full page, bled to the edges. There is a lot I could say concerning that photograph. I could talk about my fear and the lion's nobility, Africa's tragedy and the pathos of civilization. But there is almost nothing illuminating to say about the technique with which I secured it. With a camera like that, the lion could have taken a photograph of me.

Art is safe from such developments. We aren't, but it is. At once primitive and infinitely protean, art wasn't born of consciousness: consciousness was born of it. As long as human life lasts, art will go on being the one activity for which no amount of calculation can provide a substitute, and the job of the critic will be to explain why this is so. The ability to realize that he can never attain to an exhaustive analysis of the thing he loves best is the indispensable qualification for signing on. What he has to offer is his life, of which his learning can only be a part: the more he knows the better, but if he thinks that nothing else counts then he will count for nothing. *Primum vivere, deinde philosophari* is a rap that nobody can beat.

2001